W9-CDD-628

www.wadsworth.com

wadsworth.com is the World Wide Web site for Wadsworth and is your direct source to dozens of online resources.

At *wadsworth.com* you can find out about supplements, demonstration software, and student resources. You can also send email to many of our authors and preview new publications and exciting new technologies.

wadsworth.com
Changing the way the world learns®

FROM THE WADSWORTH SERIES IN SPEECH COMMUNICATION

Adams/Clarke, *The Internet: Effective Online Communication*

Adler/Towne, *Looking Out/Looking In Media Edition,* Tenth Edition

Albrecht/Bach, *Communication in Complex Organizations: A Relational Perspective*

Babbie, *The Basics of Social Research,* Second Edition

Babbie, *The Practice of Social Research,* Tenth Edition

Benjamin, *Principles, Elements, and Types of Persuasion*

Berko/Samovar/Rosenfeld, *Connecting: A Culture Sensitive Approach to Interpersonal Communication Competency,* Second Edition

Bettinghaus/Cody, *Persuasive Communication,* Fifth Edition

Braithwaite/Wood, *Case Studies in Interpersonal Communication: Processes and Problems*

Brummett, *Reading Rhetorical Theory*

Campbell/Huxman, *The Rhetorical Act,* Third Edition

Campbell/Burkholder, *Critiques of Contemporary Rhetoric,* Second Edition

Conrad/Poole, *Strategic Organizational Communication,* Fifth Edition

Cragan/Wright/Kasch, *Communication in Small Groups: Theory, Process, Skills,* Sixth Edition

Crannell, *Voice and Articulation,* Third Edition

Dwyer, *Conquer Your Speechfright: Learn How to Overcome the Nervousness of Public Speaking*

Freeley/Steinberg, *Argumentation and Debate: Critical Thinking for Reasoned Decision Making,* Tenth Edition

Geist Martin/Ray/Sharf, *Communicating Health: Personal, Cultural and Political Complexities*

Goodall/Goodall, *Communicating in Professional Contexts: Skills, Ethics, and Technologies*

Govier, *A Practical Study of Argument,* Fifth Edition

Griffin, *Invitation to Public Speaking,* Preview Edition

Hall, *Among Cultures: Communication and Challenges*

Hamilton, *Essentials of Public Speaking,* Second Edition

Hamilton/Parker, *Communicating for Results: A Guide for Business and the Professions,* Sixth Edition

Hoover, *Effective Small Group and Team Communication*

Jaffe, *Public Speaking: Concepts and Skills for a Diverse Society,* Third Edition

Kahane/Cavender, *Logic and Contemporary Rhetoric: The Use of Reason in Everyday Life,* Eighth Edition

Knapp/Hall, *Nonverbal Communication in Human Interaction,* Fifth Edition

Larson, *Persuasion: Reception and Responsibility,* Ninth Edition

Liska/Cronkhite, *An Ecological Perspective on Human Communication Theory*

Littlejohn, *Theories of Human Communication,* Seventh Edition

Lumsden/Lumsden, *Communicating with Credibility and Confidence: Diverse Peoples, Diverse Settings,* Second Edition

Lumsden/Lumsden, *Communicating in Groups and Teams: Sharing Leadership,* Third Edition

Metcalfe, *Building a Speech,* Fourth Edition

Miller, *Organizational Communication: Approaches and Processes,* Third Edition

Morreale/Bovee, *Excellence in Public Speaking*

Morreale/Spitzberg/Barge, *Human Communication: Motivation, Knowledge, and Skills*

Orbe/Harris, *Interracial Communication: Theory Into Practice*

Peterson/Stephan/White, *The Complete Speaker: An Introduction to Public Speaking,* Third Edition

Rothwell, *In Mixed Company,* Fourth Edition

Rubin/Rubin/Piele, *Communication Research: Strategies and Sources,* Fifth Edition

Samovar/Porter, *Intercultural Communication: A Reader,* Tenth Edition

Samovar/Porter, *Communication Between Cultures,* Fourth Edition

Sellnow, *Public Speaking: A Process Approach,* Media Edition

Sprague/Stuart, *The Speaker's Handbook,* Sixth Edition

Thomas, *Public Speaking Anxiety: Conquering the Fear of Public Speaking*

Ulloth/Alderfer, *Public Speaking: An Experiential Approach*

Verderber/Verderber, *The Challenge of Effective Speaking,* Twelfth Edition

Verderber/Verderber, *Communicate!,* Tenth Edition

Westra, *Active Communication*

Williams/Monge, *Reasoning with Statistics: How to Read Quantitative Research*

Wood, *Communication Mosaics: An Introduction to the Field of Communication,* Second Edition

Wood, *Communication in Our Lives,* Third Edition

Wood, *Communication Theories in Action: An Introduction,* Second Edition

Wood, *Gendered Lives: Communication, Gender, and Culture,* Fifth Edition

Wood, *Interpersonal Communication: Everyday Encounters,* Third Edition

Wood, *Relational Communication: Continuity and Change in Personal Relationships,* Second Edition

The Rhetorical Act

Thinking, Speaking, and Writing Critically

Third Edition

Karlyn Kohrs Campbell
University of Minnesota

Susan Schultz Huxman
Wichita State University

THOMSON
WADSWORTH

Australia • Canada • Mexico • Singapore • Spain • United Kingdom • United States

THOMSON

WADSWORTH

Executive Editor: *Deirdre Anderson*
Publisher: *Holly J. Allen*
Editorial Assistant: *Mele Alusa*
Technology Project Manager: *Jeanette Wiseman*
Marketing Manager: *Kimberly Russell*
Marketing Assistant: *Neena Chandra*
Project Manager, Editorial Production: *Katy German*

Print/Media Buyer: *Rebecca Cross*
Permissions Editor: *Robert Kauser*
Photo Researcher: *Laura Molmud*
Copy Editor: *Patterson Lamb*
Cover Designer: *Andrew Ogus*
Text and Cover Printer: *Phoenix Color Corp.*
Compositor: *Scratchgravel Publishing Services*

COPYRIGHT © 2003 Wadsworth, a division of Thomson Learning, Inc. Thomson Learning™ is a trademark used herein under license.

ALL RIGHTS RESERVED. No part of this work covered by the copyright hereon may be reproduced or used in any form or by any means—graphic, electronic, or mechanical, including but not limited to photocopying, recording, taping, Web distribution, information networks, or information storage and retrieval systems—without the written permission of the publisher.

Printed in the United States of America

1 2 3 4 5 6 7 06 05 04 03 02

For more information about our products, contact us at:
Thomson Learning Academic Resource Center
1-800-423-0563

For permission to use material from this text,
contact us by:
Phone: 1-800-730-2214
Fax: 1-800-730-2215
Web: http://www.thomsonrights.com

Library of Congress Control Number: 2002110933

ISBN 0-534-56097-0

Wadsworth/Thomson Learning
10 Davis Drive
Belmont, CA 94002-3098
USA

Asia
Thomson Learning
5 Shenton Way #01-01
UIC Building
Singapore 068808

Australia
Nelson Thomson Learning
102 Dodds Street
South Melbourne, Victoria 3205
Australia

Canada
Nelson Thomson Learning
1120 Birchmount Road
Toronto, Ontario M1K 5G4
Canada

Europe/Middle East/Africa
Thomson Learning
High Holborn House
50/51 Bedford Row
London WC1R 4LR
United Kingdom

Latin America
Thomson Learning
Seneca, 53
Colonia Polanco
11560 Mexico D.F.
Mexico

Spain
Paraninfo Thomson Learning
Calle/Magallanes, 25
28015 Madrid, Spain

Photo Credits
Page 253: LBJ Library Video by DNC. **Page 261:**
(a) NASA/NSSDC; (b) Getty Images; (c) NASA;
(d) © 2002 America's Dairy Farmers and Milk Processors;
(e) AP/Wide World Photos; (f) AP/Wide World Photos;
(g) Getty Images; (h) TIMEPIX; (i) © Charles H. Porter/
Corbis Sygma; (j) AP/Wide World Photos; (k) Los Angeles
Times, photo by David Bohrer; (l) AP/Wide World Photos

To all those who have struggled
for the right to speak,
in the hope that what this book contains
will help to give them voice

About the Authors

Karlyn Kohrs Campbell (PhD, University of Minnesota) is a Professor and Chair of the Department of Communication Studies at the University of Minnesota. She is author of *Man Cannot Speak for Her: A Critical Study of Early Feminist Rhetoric*, 2 volumes (1989); co-author with Kathleen Hall Jamieson of *Deeds Done in Words: Presidential Rhetoric and the Genres of Governance* (1990) and *The Interplay of Influence: News, Advertising, Politics, and the Mass Media* (5th ed., 2001); co-author with Thomas Burkholder of *Critiques of Contemporary Rhetoric* (1997); and editor of *Women Public Speakers in the United States, 1800–1925* (1993) and *Women Public Speakers in the United States, 1925–Present* (1994) as well as many journal articles. She is currently the editor of the *Quarterly Journal of Speech*. She has received a number of awards, including a fellowship at the Joan Shorenstein Center in the Kennedy School of Government of Harvard University, the National Communication Association Distinguished Scholar Award, and the National Communication Association Woolbert Award for scholarship of exceptional originality and influence. Recently she was selected as the 2002 Distinguished Woman Scholar in the Humanities and Social Sciences by the Office of the Vice President for Research at the University of Minnesota. She has taught at the University of Kansas, City College of C.U.N.Y, S.U.N.Y. at Binghamton and at Brockport, the British College in Palermo, Sicily, and California State University at Los Angeles.

Susan Schultz Huxman (PhD, University of Kansas) is an Associate Professor at the Elliott School of Communication at Wichita State University. She received her undergraduate degree from Bethel College in Kansas and her master's and doctoral degrees in communication studies with an emphasis on rhetoric from the University of Kansas. She has won numerous teaching awards and regularly teaches public speaking, rhetorical criticism, media literacy, and strategic communication in organizations. An active scholar, she has published in the field of rhetorical criticism and U.S. public address. She engages in a range of professional speaking opportunities each year to showcase scholarship in action.

Brief Contents

Contents

PART THREE
Problems of Rhetorical Action

Chapter 8
Obstacles Arising from the Audience   184

Chapter 9
Obstacles Arising from the Subject and Purpose   206

Chapter 10
Obstacles Arising from the Rhetor   224

PART FOUR
Special Constraints on Rhetorical Action

Chapter 11
Understanding Evaluation   248

Preface

The third edition of *The Rhetorical Act* preserves the conceptual core of the first two editions while extending the book's scope and relevance. In a nutshell, it aims to teach students of the liberal arts how to craft and critique messages that influence. The new edition combines *rhetorical criticism, media literacy,* and *strategic public speaking* into one important skills-set package. Its expanded title—*Thinking, Speaking, and Writing Critically*—bears testament to that confluence.

The new text is committed to the *integration* of rhetorical theory and practice; critical thinking, speaking, and writing; traditional (speeches) and nontraditional (media) rhetorical forms; rhetorical history (e.g., Lincoln, Douglass, Grimké, Stanton, Wells, Martin Luther King, Jr.); and provocative pop culture (e.g., Web sites, newspaper and magazine feature editorials, and news stories and photography).

This edition remains firmly committed to the ancient idea of the relationship between art and practice, the belief that you cannot improve a skill such as speaking or writing unless you understand the theory, the concepts, and the ideas on which it is based. Conversely, you cannot understand the theory unless you use it and test it in practice. In our view, this ancient relationship demands that those who would learn about rhetoric must take the posture of a *rhetor-critic*. The rhetor is an initiator of rhetorical action who tries to make the choices that will make her or him the most effective moral agent. The critic describes, analyzes, and evaluates rhetorical acts to understand what they are, and how and for whom they work. As a *rhetor-critic*, you learn to critique your own rhetoric in order to improve it, and as a *critic-consumer*, you learn to analyze others' rhetoric in order to make decisions as intelligently as possible.

Consistent with the first two editions, the third edition of *The Rhetorical Act* is different from traditional textbooks of criticism and public speaking in several ways. First, the book treats rhetorical action as the joint effort of rhetor and audience, emphasizing the audience's active, collaborative role. In Aristotelian terms, it treats enthymemes, arguments produced cooperatively by rhetor and audience, as "the substance of persuasion." Second, *The Rhetorical Act* approaches rhetoric in all its varieties as a "strategy to encompass a situation" (Kenneth Burke) and as "that art or talent by which discourse is adapted to its end" (George Campbell). Third, *The Rhetorical Act* treats all forms of rhetoric as points on a single continuum of influence. There is no separate treatment of speaking or writing to inform or entertain. Finally, *The Rhetorical Act* does not emphasize "schools of criticism"; rather, it concentrates on the descriptive, analytical, and evaluative tools that compose the critical process. It introduces students to a comprehensive critical "grammar" and "vocabulary." A *critical model* for helping students discern the meaning of messages is introduced early and threads its way throughout each chapter.

Specifically, what has changed? For starters, there are now two authors, although we speak with one voice, the authorial "I," to maintain a more intimate relationship with the reader. (The second author, a colleague and former student of the first author, teaches the kinds of hybrid rhetorical criticism/media literacy and strategic public speaking courses for which this third edition is targeted.) The expanded title—*Thinking, Speaking, and Writing Critically*—captures the integrated, humanistic skills set that is the foundation of the book.

Of special note, the third edition has four sections instead of three. The new Part Four, entitled "Special Constraints on Rhetorical Action," examines "Understanding Evaluation," "Understanding Visual Rhetoric," "Understanding the Medium of Transmission," and "Understanding Occasion." Chapters 12 and 13 are both new and capture the fundamentals of *media literacy*. Chapters 11 and 14 are considerable expansions from the second edition on the special challenges of judging rhetorical acts and understanding the persistent influences of the *Aristotelian genres* in crafting and critiquing contemporary messages.

Other important changes include:

- *All new illustrations* (over 50 charts, graphs, photos, and diagrams) are included to appeal to visual learners and recall the valuable tradition of the ancients and the elocutionists in learning a repertoire of "topoi" and "tropes."
- *New "Material for Analysis"* in every one of the 14 chapters acquaints students with the "classics" from U.S. rhetorical history or "newsworthy" examples from popular culture.
- *Updated exercises* in each chapter test students' critical thinking, writing, and speaking in innovative ways; encourage collaborative critiques and presentations; and serve as "test banks." A semester-long "Portfolio Project" threads through each chapter's exercise section, inviting students to showcase their critical writing abilities around self-selected rhetorical acts. In addition, each chapter has a critical exercise tied to InfoTrac College Edition® to encourage students to use the Internet in researching and problem solving.
- Greater prominence is given to *strategic public speaking*, beginning with Chapter 3. Students are instructed in how to assess audience resistance, evaluate Internet sources, and troubleshoot for preparation, message, and delivery expectations. Specific speech assignments are related to the six rhetorical purposes outlined in Chapter 1, and they range from *storytelling, defining, explaining, performing public service*, and *initiating policy* to *celebrating special occasions*. Full texts of student speeches are used for illustration.
- An all new *Appendix* contains six speaking *evaluation forms* and a *Web site critique* template.
- Finally, Parts Two and Three from the old editions have been reversed—"Resources for Rhetorical Action" (evidence, argument, organization, and language) are introduced before "Obstacles to Rhetorical Action" (obstacles arising from audience, subject, and rhetor)—in order to maintain the trajectory of conceptual complexity.

We wrote this new edition of *The Rhetorical Act* because we have a passion to educate students on how to become discerning consumers and articulate practitioners of all varieties of rhetorical acts. We are committed to the humanistic approach to rhetoric—

that the understanding of who we are as symbol users will foster greater appreciation of, and heighten the moral sensibilities of our students toward, our rhetorical universe. It is our fervent hope that this edition of *The Rhetorical Act* expands the relevance and scope of the previous editions and that it will continue to stimulate the kind of critical discussion so essential to developing analytical thinking, speaking, and writing skills. In Ciceronian terms, we wish to mold "citizen-orators" for our times.

We thank all those whose comments and criticisms have made this a better book, including the reviewers: Cathy Gillotti, Purdue University at Calumet; John Jackson, University of Colorado at Boulder; E. Anne Laffoon, University of Colorado at Boulder; and Leah White, University of Northern Iowa. In particular, we thank research assistants Zornitsa Keremidchieva and Mariko Izumi in the Communication Studies department at the University of Minnesota and the many bright students in rhetoric courses at Wichita State University who provided valuable criticism on early drafts. Susan also thanks Jesse, her North Star, who maintains her perspective, and Julia, Emily, and Connor, her Muses, who create "perspective by incongruity."

chapter 1

A Rhetorical Perspective

Through its title, *The Rhetorical Act*, this book boldly announces that it is about rhetoric. Because mass media commentators often use *rhetoric* to mean "hot air" or "lies," you may well ask why you should study rhetoric in a class or read a book about rhetorical action. One way to answer this question is to define *rhetoric* properly and to show the possible value of a rhetorical perspective on human action.

A "perspective," literally, is a way of looking through (*per* = through; *specere* = to look), an angle of vision, a way of seeing. All perspectives are partial and, in that sense, distorted or biased: Each looks at this rather than that; each has its particular emphasis. Because someone is always doing the looking and seeing, it is impossible to avoid taking some point of view.

Just what is a rhetorical (as opposed to a philosophical or scientific) perspective? Whereas scientists would say the most important concern is the discovery and testing of certain kinds of truths, rhetoricians (who study rhetoric and take a rhetorical perspective) would say, "Truths cannot walk on their own legs. They must be carried by people to other people. They must be explained, defended, and spread through language, argument, and appeal." Philosophers and scientists respond, rightly, that whenever possible, assumptions should be tested through logic and experiment. In fact, they

1

would argue that you and I should pay more attention to how conclusions are reached and tested. Rhetoricians reply that unacknowledged and unaccepted truths are of no use at all. Thus, the bias of a rhetorical perspective is its emphasis on and its concern with the resources available in language and in people to make ideas clear and cogent, to bring concepts to life, to make them salient for people. A rhetorical perspective is interested in what influences or persuades people.

Those strongly committed to a rhetorical perspective argue that some scientists and philosophers delude themselves, claiming that they are not persuaders and do not use rhetorical strategies in their writings. In a review of two books reporting research on Neanderthals, for example, Stephen Jay Gould, who taught biology, geology, and the history of science at Harvard, said that humans are storytelling creatures and comments on "the centrality of narrative style in any human discourse (though scientists like to deny the importance of such rhetorical devices—while using them all the time—and prefer to believe that persuasion depends upon fact and logic alone)."[1] When objectivity is highly valued, some feel that any hint of subjectivity must be denied. Similarly, feminist challenges to traditional philosophy call attention to possible sources of bias in modes of philosophizing, pointing to rhetorical impulses in the works of great philosophers.[2] In other words, rhetoricians can identify persuasive elements in all discourse, including scientific and philosophical communication.

A rhetorical perspective, then, focuses on social truths, that is, on the kinds of truths that are created and tested by people in groups and that influence social and political decisions. These truths represent what a group of people agrees to believe or accept; such truths become what the group takes to be "common sense." Among the important social truths a rhetorical perspective might teach you to examine are the processes by which taxpayers, parents, congressional committees, school boards, and citizens respond to issues that cannot be resolved solely through logical analysis and experimental testing. Should affirmative action programs, for example, be used to rectify past discrimination against minorities and women? Early acceptance of affirmative action as an appropriate remedy for past discrimination has shifted as doubts arise about "quotas" or "reverse discrimination." What constitutes discrimination? What remedies for past discrimination are fair to all those who compete for jobs and admission to educational programs? As another example, should air quality standards be set high enough that cars must be redesigned to use alternative energy sources, gasoline reformulated, and industries converted to use less polluting fuels? How can we balance our concern for healthy industries that create good jobs with the impact of pollution on the environment and on human health? Still another example: Will harsh penalties for convicted rapists provide better protection for women, or will such penalties increase the reluctance of juries to convict? For social questions such as these, philosophers can point out contradictions in our thinking and spell out the implications of a given position. Social scientists can give us the best available data about the lack of women and minorities in categories of employment, about available pools of minority applicants for jobs, about causes and effects of pollution, and about the low conviction rates of accused rapists. When we have looked at the data and examined the logic of the conclusions drawn from them, we still must make decisions that go beyond the facts and make commitments that go beyond sheer logic.

From its beginnings, this emphasis on social truths has been the distinctive quality of a rhetorical perspective. What fragmentary historical records exist seem to indicate that rhetoric was first studied and taught early in the fifth century B.C.E. by sophists or

Why Has Rhetoric Become a Dirty Word?

Not so long ago, the predominant meaning was "the art of expressive speech" or "the science of persuasion"; now the much-abused word, with a root related to "oratory," is laden with artificiality: empty talk is "mere" rhetoric. . . .

But rhetoric, in its positive sense, fills a linguistic need: "The technique of articulate argument" is too much of a mouthful. If we mean "empty talk," or wish to deride the fulsome fulminations of a blowhard, we already have a large selection of sneering synonyms available: from the euphemism "bushwa" to the acronym "bomfog." ([The word] "bomfog," an acronym for "brotherhood of man, fatherhood of God," is not written in caps—because it relies on its similarity to two small words.)

The most effective way to rehabilitate "rhetoric," I think, is to offer a colorful, yet suitably pedantic term to cover its pejorative meaning. The word I have in mind is *bloviation*, a noun backformed from the verb *bloviate*. (A verb is useful, too—you can't say "rhetoricize," and "orate" does not have the specifically spurious connotation.)

Bloviation is most often associated with the statements of Warren Gamaliel Harding— "Gamalielese," H. L. Mencken called it—but the word has deep roots as an authentic Americanism. In their *Dictionary of Slang, Jargon, and Cant*, Albert Barrete and Charles Leland placed *bloviate*'s origin before 1850, and defined it as "verbosity, wandering from the subject, and idle or inflated oratory or blowing, but which word it was probably suggested, being partially influenced by 'deviate.'"

So, if you mean "bloviating," get off "rhetoric's" back: We need "rhetoric" to do a job that no other word does as well.

Source: William Safire, *Safire's New Political Dictionary* (New York: Random House, 1993).

wise men in Greek city-states around the Mediterranean. These city-states began to become more democratic, and as citizens met together to decide the laws under which they would live, as they brought suits and defended themselves against charges of wrongdoing, and as they celebrated the values that gave them a sense of identity, the need to speak cogently and clearly became increasingly important. Accordingly, men such as Gorgias of Leontini, Protagoras, Isocrates, and others began to teach male citizens (only males were allowed to speak and vote) how to present their ideas more effectively and to write about what made some speeches more persuasive and some speakers more appealing than others.

WHAT IS RHETORIC?

The first major treatise on the art of rhetoric that still exists was written by Aristotle in fourth-century-B.C.E. Athens. The Greek word for rhetoric comes from *rhêtorikê, -ikê* meaning "art or skill of," and *rhêtor*, meaning an experienced political/public speaker. Both in *On Rhetoric* and in his other works, Aristotle distinguished among kinds of truth. He believed that there were certain immutable truths of nature, which he designated as the province of metaphysics or science (*theoria*). He recognized a different sort of wisdom or social knowledge (*phronêsis*) as needed to make choices about matters affecting communities or a whole society. These truths, not discoverable through science or analytic logic, he described as contingent, that is, as dependent on cultural values, the situation or immediate context, and the nature of the issue. They were the special concerns of the area of study he called "rhetoric."

Figure 1–1
What Is Rhetoric?

- Rhetoric is the study of what is persuasive.
- Rhetoric is the purposive use of messages to invite assent.
- Rhetoric is the craft of producing reason-giving discourse that is grounded in social truths.

The contingent qualities of social truths can best be illustrated by looking at what it means to say that something is "a problem." Put simply, a problem is the gap that exists between what you think ought to be (value) and what is; it is the discrepancy between the ideal and the real, between goals and achievements. As you will realize, what is a problem for one person may not be a problem for another person. Some students, for example, are satisfied with C's in most courses. Their goal is to get the "ticket" represented by a college degree with a minimum of inconvenience. They plan to exert their energies after they begin work at an occupation or position of their choice. Other students are devastated by anything less than an A in any class. Their goal is graduate school or highly specialized study and work. They need very high averages and the best possible preparation and achievement now. For these different students, the same fact—a grade of C—can be a big problem or no problem at all. In other words, a problem can literally be defined out of existence!

For you as students and for society as a whole, defining problems depends on goals and values, and these can change. In this same sense social truths—and thus rhetoric—are "subjective" and "evaluative"; rhetoric addresses issues that arise because of people's values, and these will change through time in the face of altered conditions.

Rhetoric is, of course, also concerned with data that establish what exists and with logical processes for drawing conclusions from facts and implications from principles and assumptions. Indeed, Aristotle considered rhetoric an offshoot of logic, and a rhetorical perspective is characterized not only by an emphasis on social truths but also by an emphasis on reason-giving or justification in place of coercion or violence. This distinction can be subtle. In general, rhetorical efforts seek to affect the free choices of groups or individuals, whereas coercion creates situations in which only one choice seems possible—the costs of any other option are too high, the pressure too great, the threat too terrible. Violence coerces by threatening bodily harm or death if any choice but that desired is made. Reason-giving assumes that by presenting the implications of the available options, one can persuade an audience to choose from among them freely, based on the reasons and evidence offered. Rhetoric presumes that audiences have some real freedom of choice.[3]

Of course, not all of the reasons used by rhetors (those who initiate symbolic acts seeking to influence others) will make sense to logicians or scientists. Some rhetorical reasons are grounded in facts and logic, but many others are grounded in religious beliefs, history, or cultural values, in associations and metaphors, in hunger, resentments, or dreams. A rhetorical perspective is eclectic and inclusive in its search for what is influential and why. In fact, rhetoric's concern with justification grows out of its focus on social truths tested by people in their roles as voters, property owners, consumers, workers, parents, and the like. In other words, reasons are presented to the decision makers and evaluators to whom the rhetoric is addressed, the audience.

Obviously, in some situations you can say, "Do this and don't ask any questions—just trust me," but such situations are rare. Reasons can be omitted only when your relationship to those addressed is so close and strong that the relationship itself is the reason for action or belief.

In most cases, then, even those involving your nearest and dearest, you must give reasons, justify your views, explain your position. And you must do so in terms that will make sense to others. Rhetors must "socialize" or adapt their reasons to reflect shared values. It is more acceptable, for example, to explain that you run several miles every day to maintain your weight and protect your health than to say that you run for the joy of it, for the sheer physical pleasure it gives you. "Socialized" reasons are widely accepted, meaning they are agreed to by most people. U.S. culture is strongly pragmatic; therefore, "good" reasons tend to show that an act is useful and practical. U.S. culture is strongly capitalistic; therefore, good reasons tend to show that an act is profitable, or assume that an action should be judged by its impact on "the bottom line." Other societies and some U.S. subcultures place greater emphasis on the sensual and aesthetic; for them, good reasons affirm behavior that is pleasurable and expressive, such as precision iceskating, acrobatic skateboarding, skillful hang gliding, dancing the tango really well, losing oneself in musical sound, singing in close harmony, rapping, or savoring and preparing unusual foods.

Because rhetoric is addressed to others, it is reason-giving; and because it is social and public, it uses as reasons the values accepted and affirmed by a subculture or culture. In this way, rhetoric is tied to social values, and rhetors' statements will reflect the social norms of particular groups, times, and places.

Because it is addressed to others, providing justifications that they will understand and feel, rhetoric is a humanistic study, and, as such, it examines all kinds of human symbol use, even the bizarre and perverse. From the beginnings of rhetoric in classical antiquity, rhetoricians have understood that persuasion occurs through both argument and association, through the cold light of logic and the white heat of passion, through explicit values and subconscious needs and associations. Accordingly, the field of rhetoric examines all of the available means by which we are influenced and by which we can influence others.

In summary, rhetoric is the study of what is persuasive. The issues with which it is concerned are social truths, addressed to others, justified by reasons that reflect cultural values. Rhetoric is a humanistic study that examines all the symbolic means by which influence occurs.

The defining characteristics of rhetoric are represented by seven words beginning with the letter *p* (see Figure 1–2). First and foremost, rhetoric is *public*, that is, it is addressed to others. It is public because it deals with issues and problems that one person, by herself, cannot answer or solve; the issues are communal; the solutions require

Figure 1-2
The Seven p's of Rhetoric

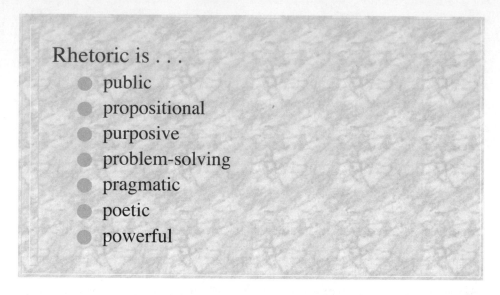

Rhetoric is . . .

- public
- propositional
- purposive
- problem-solving
- pragmatic
- poetic
- powerful

cooperative effort. As a result, rhetoric is *propositional*; it is developed through complete thoughts. That's the case because one person's ideas must be made intelligible and salient for others whose cooperation is needed; that's also the case because much rhetoric is argumentative, making claims and offering reasons in their support. In that sense, rhetoric is not random thoughts but some kind of coherent, structured statement about an issue or concern. As you will immediately recognize, rhetoric is *purposive*, aimed at achieving a particular goal, such as selling a product or obtaining some kind of support or action. Even the most apparently expressive discourse can have some kind of instrumental or purposive goal; for example, cheering for a team expresses the feelings of fans, but it raises the morale of players and may improve their performance, helping them to win. That's closely related to rhetoric's emphasis on *problem-solving*. Most rhetorical discourse arises in situations in which we as audience and rhetors experience a felt need: a desire for closure (farewell address), a desire to mark beginnings and initiate a process (inaugural address), a desire to acknowledge death and to memorialize (eulogy). In some cases, of course, the problem is more concrete: How can a fair and accurate resolution be reached about the 2000 presidential election? What are the possible options? Which alternative would be most satisfactory to those involved?

Closely related to rhetoric's purposive, problem-solving qualities is an emphasis on the *pragmatic*. The Greek word *praxis* or action is the root for practical, meaning that it can be put into effect or enacted. Pragmatic is a synonym of practical, but it also stresses facts and actual occurrences but with an emphasis on practical outcomes. In this sense, rhetoric is material; it produces actions that affect us materially; it is active, not just contemplative.

And, in what may seem to be a contradiction, rhetoric is *poetic*; that is, rhetoric frequently displays ritualistic, aesthetic, dramatic, and emotive qualities. The rhetoric of the mass, of communion, and of other religious rituals reinforces belief; what is pleasing and appealing to our senses, such as metaphor and vivid description, invites our participation and assent. What is dramatic narrative captures our attention and involves us with characters, dialogue, and conflict and excites us emotionally so that we care about what happens and identify with the people we encounter. Those rhetorical works we call eloquent are good examples of these qualities, illustrated here and in subsequent chapters by speeches by Abraham Lincoln and Martin Luther King, Jr., and by essays that involve us in the lives of people whose stories teach us lessons.

Finally, because it is all of these—public, propositional, purposive, problem-solving, pragmatic, and poetic—it is *powerful*, with the potential to prompt our participation, invite identification, alter our perceptions, and persuade us. Accordingly, it has the potential to help or harm us, elevate or debase ideas, and make or break careers.

RHETORICAL ACTS

As I have described it, a rhetorical perspective takes note of the rhetorical or persuasive dimension in all human behavior. Although all human actions can be considered implicitly persuasive, I do not wish to define "the rhetorical act" so broadly. The lines separating rhetorical acts from other acts are difficult to draw, however, and in this book I shall treat the concept of rhetoric in both its broad and its narrow senses.

The broadest view of rhetoric is expressed in the statement, "You can never not communicate," meaning that whatever you do or say (or don't do or say) can be observed and interpreted. For example, an unsmiling expression can be interpreted as evidence of sadness (rather than thoughtfulness), a young African American man walking home from work is perceived by some as menacing, or a woman walking home late from work is sometimes assumed to be extending a sexual invitation. Any behavior can become rhetorical when someone interprets or misinterprets it and is influenced by that interpretation, whatever the actors' intentions may have been.

Of course, many acts are intentionally rhetorical—advertisements, music videos, editorials, book and movie reviews, and films, essays, sermons, and speeches that declare a position and seek to defend it or make it attractive to others. When I address you as speakers or writers, I am speaking of rhetorical acts as intentional, deliberate attempts to influence others. When I act as critic or analyst and address you as critics and analysts, however, I comment on all possible persuasive effects, both intentional and unintentional. To understand rhetoric, you must fathom all the processes of influence, and, as a rhetor, you must come to terms with unintended and accidental effects—especially because some of them may work against your purpose.

In other words, defined most broadly, *rhetoric* is the study of all the processes by which people influence each other through symbols, regardless of the intent of the source. A *rhetorical act,* however, is an intentional, created, polished attempt to overcome the obstacles in a given situation with a specific audience on a given issue to achieve a particular end. A rhetorical act creates a message whose shape and form, beginning and end, are stamped on it by one or more human authors with goals for an audience. If you study all forms of influence, you will become aware of all the available resources for persuasion. Similarly, when you analyze your rhetoric and that of others, you must consider persuasive effects that may not have been fully under the control of or consciously intended by the source.

RHETORICAL PURPOSES

Because intention and impact are so important to a rhetorical perspective, I want to consider the range of meanings included in the words *persuasion* and *influence*. From the persuader's point of view, these meanings describe a range of purposes or intentions, not simply agreement or opposition. From the point of view of a reader, listener, or viewer, they reflect processes that constantly engage us as we experience the world, try to understand it, and decide what actions, if any, would be appropriate as responses. In other words, rhetorical purposes are conscious attempts to influence processes that are occurring in us all of the time as we come in contact with the world and the people in it.

Creating Virtual Experience

Through their use of symbols, rhetors call up ideas, pictures, and experiences in those they address. If I write, "The burning sun beat down on the stubble in the oat field, and seen through a haze of sweat, the stalks suddenly seemed to be hair sprouting in a crew cut from the scalp of a red-haired giant," you can draw on past sensations and experiences to re-create your own mental picture. Although each reader's picture will be different, and each will reflect the reader's unique past, most will concern summer in a rural area. Fundamentally, to act rhetorically is to communicate or to initiate an act—to express something in symbols—that someone else can translate into virtual experience. When something is virtual, it does not exist in fact; it is *as if* it existed. There is no sun, no stubble, no sweat, no scalp, no red hair, no giant on this page. But if I write about them vividly enough, you can imagine them; it is as if you saw and heard and felt them here and now. That re-creation in your mind is virtual experience. In response to my words, you imagine a scene, create a mental picture, and what you experience is virtual experience, experience called forth and shaped by your response to the symbols produced by someone else. Effective communication creates an image or idea in your mind that approximates the image or idea that the speaker or author wished to convey.

In other words, the fundamental rhetorical purpose, the most basic kind of influence—communicating—requires you to initiate a rhetorical act that can be translated into virtual experience by others. The most basic question in rhetoric is how to do that.

One kind of rhetorical action is intended primarily to produce virtual experience. Most works of literature, for example, are written to expand and shape our experience. In them, one sees, hears, smells, tastes, and touches vividly and concretely and feels intensely, and these sensations are shaped and formed into a satisfying and complete experience. When such works are transformed into dramas presented on stage or in film or television, the words become lived experience incarnated in actors' dialogue, movements, and feelings. In such processes, producers, directors, and actors do what all of us do each day as we translate the symbols we encounter into units of meaning based on our own experiences; the greater the range of our experiences, the greater our potential for imagining these dramas on the stages of our minds, of comprehending and identifying with the messages of others.

Altering Perception

Literary works can also have political effects. Charles Dickens's *Oliver Twist*[4] re-created the experiences of orphans in English poorhouses so movingly that readers demanded reform. Harriet Beecher Stowe's *Uncle Tom's Cabin*[5] depicted scenes of slavery so vividly that the book became a major force for its abolition. The same sensory or aesthetic stimuli that enliven good literature are a major means of persuasion. In other words, by creating virtual experience—the more vivid the better—literature can contribute to the second rhetorical purpose I want to discuss: altering perception.

George Washington wrote, "The truth is the people must *feel* before they will *see*." Whether or not you must experience something before you can comprehend it, it is surely true that vivid experience improves our capacity to understand.

For an example of how an author can change the meaning of an experience for an audience—that is, alter perception of that experience—consider what Corlann Gee Bush does to one's experience of a series of paintings by the famous Western artist and sculptor, Charles M. Russell. In her essay "The Way We Weren't: Images of Women and Men in Cowboy Art" she writes about how cowboy art has influenced viewers to believe in "the romantic West, the West of myth and legend."[6] She is particularly concerned with how women were depicted and uses five portraits of a Keeoma woman by Russell as illustrations. In these paintings, an American Indian woman is shown in either a reclining or hip-slung pose as a highly sensual and spirited person. As ordinary viewers, we are likely to assume that these are portraits of a real person and take them as indications of the character of Keeoma women in the nineteenth century. To alter such a perception, Corlann Bush tells us:

> The truth is that Russell's wife, Nancy, was the model for the paintings. To pose, she dressed in buckskin and surrounded herself with artifacts. Russell painted the objects realistically; he painted her as an Indian. In this way he was able to paint his wife as the sensual woman he knew her to be while preserving her place within the moral code of white society. . . . This repressed sexuality was transposed onto an Indian woman who did not exist but who lived, nonetheless, deep in the subconscious of white American males. (27)

Once we have this information, we see the paintings differently; they become a visual record not of a Keeoma woman of the past but of the stereotypes of white and American Indian women in the nineteenth century that persist in the paintings.

Our impressions of the U.S. West have also been influenced by popular culture, including the novels of Louis L'Amour, John Wayne Westerns, television series such as *Bonanza* and *Gunsmoke*, and by miniseries based on Larry McMurtry's novels. If your images of the West come from such sources, your perceptions may be altered by information provided by historians. For example, although African Americans rarely have appeared in the West of popular culture, I was surprised to learn that "George W. Saunders of the Trail Drivers Association, as valid an authority as there is, estimated that about 25 percent of all cowhands were black."[7] Although they constituted only a small percentage of Western settlers, Robert Haywood explains why such a large percentage of cowhands were African Americans:

> In an age when blacks were stereotyped as either foolish or primitive and where their opportunities to advance, either socially or economically, were limited, ranch-related jobs offered more dignity and more opportunity for self-expression than any other employment available. Whites in the ranching business realized the importance of the contributions of all cowboys—black, white, or Mexican—and adjusted their prejudices accordingly. . . . The mutual interdependence left little room for arrogant displays of racial superiority or overt discrimination, no matter how ingrained. (169)

If we accept it as true, Haywood's information may alter our perceptions of the popular culture portrait of the West, and he makes his rather surprising data more plausible by explaining why African Americans tended to congregate in this somewhat unlikely occupation.

To recapitulate, the most minimal rhetorical purpose, the smallest effect produced, is to add to the sum of your audience's experiences. If you can frame such experiences, you may be able to influence how those virtual experiences are interpreted.

Explaining

If we evaluated rhetorical acts by how much they altered beliefs, nearly all would be failures. Normal, healthy human beings whose physical environments are under their own control do not change their beliefs in response to a single message—whether the message lasts five minutes or five hours. If people are influenced to alter their beliefs, they do so over weeks, months, or even years, and in response to many different messages.

The need for explanation is most strongly felt when we encounter an intense, apparently irrational experience. Let us suppose, for example, that you read or hear news reports about an investment banker jogging in Central Park in New York City who is attacked by a gang of youths who rape and beat her and leave her for dead. Or you read of an African American youth from the Bronx going to look at a used car in Brooklyn who is attacked and shot by a gang of local Euro-American youths. In response to these events, many editorials appeared trying to explain why these events happened and what they meant, often accompanied by statements about how we should respond to them. Like these editorial writers, rhetors often provide explanations for events that have disturbed those they address. Note, however, that an encounter with a disturbing event precedes the felt need for explanation. As a result, rhetors sometimes begin by creating that kind of experience through vivid language and disturbing information and then offer and justify what they believe is the most plausible explanation.

Linda A. Fairstein, director of the Sex Crimes Prosecution Unit in the Manhattan District Attorney's Office, began prosecuting rape cases in the mid-1970s and is the author of a book called *Sexual Violence: Our War Against Rape*.[8] Much of the book describes the changes that have occurred in rape laws, which no longer require corroboration of an alleged victim's testimony, for example. Because it is partly a memoir of her career and partly a series of real-life crime stories, the book's vivid virtual experience of how the criminal justice system treats rape victims describes the experiences of individuals with whom we can identify. This evidence is obviously intended to alter perception. However, Fairstein goes beyond the data to explain and to argue that rape is different from other violent crimes because it is so much more intimate, which emphasizes the significance of the sexual element in this crime. Her views will find a ready audience because women, particularly the millions of rape victims, have found rape to be a special kind of outrage whose impact often persists for years in nightmares and sleeplessness. Fairstein's book provides much evidence about rape and about its treatment in the criminal justice system; it documents the horrors that occur but gives hope that legal changes have made the system better able to understand the crime and to punish those who commit it.[9]

Formulating Belief

By this time it should be apparent that rhetorical action is not a one-shot event but a process. Although there is a somewhat orderly progression from enlarging audience experience to altering perceptions, which, in turn, leads to a search for explanations, followed by efforts to determine which interpretation is most satisfactory, these are not discrete, separable processes for coming to terms with experience nor are they discrete rhetorical purposes. Virtual experience occurs within some kind of framework; new experience can alter a framework to change perception. When perceptions change, we seek explanations; sometimes we demand explanations before we consider altering our perceptual framework, perhaps even before participating in the creation of virtual experience. As these other processes overlap and intersect, so, too, do the processes by which we formulate a belief or discard one belief for another. Similarly, the processes by which a rhetor urges us to believe arise out of prior experience and conceptualization.

As an illustration, let us return to the nineteenth-century U.S. West. Virtual experience might be created by the autobiography of Nat Love, the "Deadwood Kid," one of the West's most notorious African American cowboys,[10] or by reading the memoir of Charlie Siringo, the "cowboy detective" who wrote of experiences on the trail with African American trail riders,[11] or from the biography of Print Olive, one of Dodge City's toughest ranchers, whose life was saved by James Kelly during a shootout in a saloon.[12] The experiences they provide would challenge those in most popular culture. Before prior perceptions were abandoned, however, you might seek out historical works, such as *The Negro on the American Frontier* by Kenneth W. Porter or *The Black West* by Loren Katz (both cited earlier), testing whether the experiences depicted were accurate and typical and seeking explanations of why African Americans were disproportionately represented among cowhands in the West.

Once that was completed, new questions might arise. Why haven't Western novels, films, and television programs reflected this reality? At this point, you are an audience member prepared to consider the claims of a rhetor who attempts to convince you that these omissions were no accident but a result of the racism that is a legacy of the history of slavery in the United States. Such a rhetor might have gone through the process I've described to reach a point at which everything seemed to fall together and a belief emerged. Many rhetorical acts attempt to produce such a "precipitating moment" in which the audience agrees, "That's it. That's the way it is." Few rhetorical acts succeed, however, in taking members of an audience through all these stages to transform their attitudes. At best, most confirm a position already being considered (somewhere between the search for explanation and the choice of one interpretation) or reinforce an explanation the audience has pondered and considers plausible. Indeed, those who achieve such modest goals have been resounding successes as persuaders.

Initiating Action

Let us suppose, however, that you are present at a rhetorical event that formulates the beliefs of a group about the misrepresentation of African American cowhands in the West. The pleased rhetor now urges action—but finds that most audience members are not ready to do anything about it. Those who share this belief may not write novels or produce films or television programs; indeed, they may not have the resources to do any of those things. Even if they share this attitude, they may not believe that action is needed; concern about misrepresentation may be a low priority.

As this example suggests, shared belief is not necessarily linked to a willingness or an ability to act. At such a moment, doubts arise about whether beliefs have really been formulated, and such doubts have merit. But an examination of rhetorical processes suggests that the situation is normal. Even when beliefs are formulated, action will not follow unless that belief is reinforced, rendered salient, and then channeled so that action seems appropriate, possible, and necessary. Note that these processes are the primary function of most religious discourse, which is designed to urge people to act on their faith, to put their beliefs into practice.

Although the audience in this case might not include writers or television or film producers, it may well include parents, perhaps even members of school boards. A skillful rhetor might want to urge the inclusion of more material about African American history in elementary and secondary schools and suggest that this misrepresentation is just one example of the lack of such material, an example that is particularly telling because it reflects a distortion that reduces the African American past to slavery, ignoring the diverse, positive images that all students need to encounter in order to form a more accurate picture of the nation's past.

The chances of success in initiating action would increase if other messages reinforced such proposals. The 1993 film *Posse*, which was about African American cowboys and was directed by Mario Van Peebles, an African American, attempted to correct the distorted impressions created by past Westerns.[13] The killings of African Americans in Howard Beach and Brooklyn, New York, call attention to contemporary evidence of racism among young whites, suggesting the importance of teaching more African American history. Television specials on racism, produced in response to these killings, included studies demonstrating that many African American children still have negative self-images, first identified in earlier studies by Kenneth Clark that formed part of the basis for the 1954 Supreme Court desegregation decision in *Brown v. Board of Education* [347 U.S. 483 (1954)].[14] Buttressed by such reinforcing messages, a rhetor who proposed action to change curriculum and textbooks would have a better chance of succeeding.

If messages and events support each other and are publicized, beliefs will be strengthened, and concerned individuals will form or join groups to formulate plans for influencing the school board and textbook publishers. Rhetorical acts aimed at initiating action will appear. An editorial will urge that units on African American history be developed and included in the curriculum; a parents' group will press the school administration to act and formulate a committee to coordinate efforts to modify textbooks.

Maintaining Action

Then, when the intense interest generated by dramatic events lessens, rhetorical acts will be needed to ensure that the new units remain in the curriculum, that as history texts are revised they continue to include such materials, that teachers continue to use them in classes, that African American teachers and principals are hired, retained, and supported. Such rhetorical action perpetuates what has been institutionalized, as illustrated by the yearly report to the PTA on test scores and dropout rates that reaffirms the school's successes with its varied pupils; the Sunday sermon to the regular churchgoer, which urges continued support and attendance; the monthly ritual of prayer and reports of activities at the Phyllis Wheatley women's club that reinforces their motto of "lifting as we climb";[15] the singing of the national anthem before baseball games, which proclaims the patriotism of sport.

This progression reflects the rhetorical dimensions in all human behavior and links them to the purposes that emerge in rhetorical acts (see Figure 1–3). It should suggest

Figure 1-3
Range of Rhetorical Purposes

Creating virtual experience	Altering perception	Explaining	Formulating belief	Initiating action	Maintaining action
Use sensory cues to re-create an experience	Give a fresh angle on an old topic	Develop the who, what, where, why when, and how	Prepare a one-sided case	Urge behavioral change	Rally the troops
Creates identifi- cation	Combats inattention	Satisfies the search for knowledge	Refines issues	Transforms convictions into deeds	Reinforces commitment to causes
Film: IMAX theater experience	Bumper Sticker: Trust in God, She will provide	Book: *Kids &Guns*	Editorial: "The Problem with School Vouchers"	Website: N.O.R.M.L.	Advertising: Pre-sale savings for preferred customers

to you as a prospective persuader that your choice of a purpose should reflect the prior experiences of your audience and should be attuned to the events taking place in your environment.

THE DISCIPLINE OF RHETORIC

A discipline is a field of study, an area of expertise, a branch of knowledge. A discipline provides theory, application, and experimentation, and criticism to test them all. *Theories* are explanations that seek to account for processes and data. Rhetorical theories seek to account for the processes in language and people that influence belief and action. *Applications* are rules for action that are developed from theory. Rhetorical applications suggest how you can use rhetorical principles to be an effective moral agent and to protect yourself as you participate in rhetorical action initiated by others. *Experimentation* seeks to isolate variables or elements in the persuasive process and to test theoretical explanations as carefully as possible. *Critical analysis* examines rhetorical acts in order to describe processes of influence and explain how they occur. Both experimentation and criticism (of theories, applications, experimental research, and rhetorical action) contribute to the modification and application of theory.[16] In the chapters that follow, I develop theory about the nature and application of rhetorical processes, which is supported by experimental research and critical analysis that qualify, refine, and illustrate these theoretical concepts.

In its theory, the discipline of rhetoric examines the symbolic dimensions of human behavior in order to provide the most complete explanations of human influence. This broad view is tested by critical analysis. Rhetorical application focuses more narrowly on rhetorical acts—written and spoken messages designed to achieve predetermined effects in an audience. Experimental studies of persuasion focus more narrowly on rhetorical acts and test the adequacy of prior explanations of them and the appropriateness of rules for application.

As a discipline, rhetoric is the study of the art of using symbols. This understanding is reflected in many well-known definitions of rhetoric: "That art or talent by which discourse is adapted to its end" (George Campbell);[17] "the use of language as a symbolic means of inducing cooperation in beings that by nature respond to symbols" (Kenneth Burke);[18] "Let rhetoric be [defined as] an ability, in each [particular] case, to see the available means of persuasion" (Aristotle).[19] Rhetoric provides theory, application, experimentation, and critical analysis. It studies the social use of words by people in groups, the political use of words to decide who shall make what kinds of decisions, and the ethical use of words to justify belief and action through cultural values. Rhetoric is related to logic and empirical validation because it uses these materials. It is different from philosophy and science because it studies all the available processes for influencing people, and it defines influence broadly. Accordingly, it considers how people use language to alter perception, to explain, to change, reinforce, and channel belief, and to initiate and maintain actions. Put in more traditional terms, it studies all the ways in which symbols can be used to teach, to delight, and to move.

This book is based on the ancient idea of the relationship between art and practice—the belief that you cannot improve a skill such as speaking or writing unless you understand the theory, the concepts, and the ideas on which it is based. Conversely, you cannot understand the theory unless you use it and test it in practice. In my view, this ancient relationship demands that those who would learn about rhetoric must take the posture of a rhetor-critic. The rhetor is an initiator of rhetorical action who tries to make the choices that will make her or him the most effective moral agent. As a rhetor, you come to understand all the forces at work in persuasion, some of which are outside your control. The critic analyzes, describes, interprets, and evaluates rhetorical acts to understand what they are, and how and for whom they work. As a critic, you learn to criticize your own rhetoric to improve it, and as a critic-consumer you learn to analyze others' rhetoric in order to make decisions as intelligently as possible.

CRITICISM IS FEEDBACK

Every book addressed to students of communication begins with a model of the process that looks something like Figure 1–4. Most of you already know that the name for the receiver's response is "feedback," the kind of information used in guidance systems to keep a projectile on the correct path. When you speak or write, the immediate audience gives you useful but limited feedback. If you speak, they look at you intently, smile in amusement, frown in puzzlement, look away in annoyance or boredom, read the paper, sleep, take a note to check out a statistic, and the like. If you write a letter to the editor or an op-ed, your piece may be rejected or printed in an altered, edited form and provoke rejoinders. If you are in a class and your instructor has other students discuss your speech or essay, you will discover that most reactions were not evident from facial reactions or movements. You will discover that the messages you could not see or misinterpreted or were only implied by editing are very important—perhaps the most important. Similarly, when your instructors discuss your speech or essay in class or write comments, you will discover that their observations are different—less superficial, more helpful, linked to concepts you have studied and discussed in class. Such feedback is criticism—the careful analysis and evaluation by an experienced student of rhetoric who has heard and read many rhetorical acts, pondered many critical analyses, studied

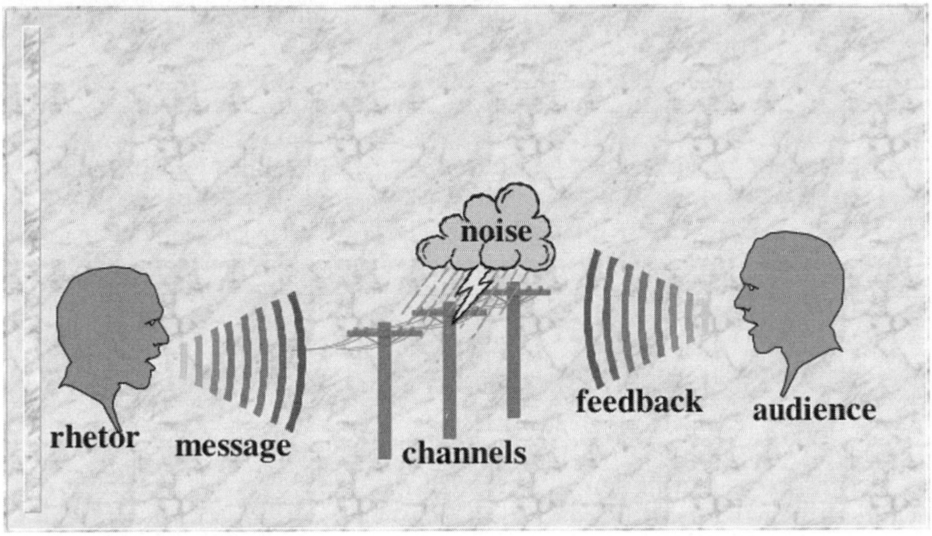

Figure 1-4
The Rhetorical Process

available theories, and read many experimental studies. Ideally, you should aspire to be such a critic, and the aim of this book is to teach you to be one. If you understand rhetorical processes, you have the best chance of steadily improving your performance and of succeeding consistently. You will know how to evaluate your own work, and you will be prepared to consider carefully and learn from the rhetoric of others.

No one can teach you rules that will apply in all cases or even predict the occasions for rhetorical action that each of you will encounter. If you are to be an effective persuader, able to communicate your experiences, to place them in interpretive frameworks, to justify your interpretation as most plausible, and to initiate and maintain action consistent with your interpretation, you will need skills that enable you to find the words that will create virtual experience in your audience, to discover a framework that is intelligible in that particular time and place, to select justifications with salience on that specific issue, and so on. As a result, this book does not try to teach you universal rules (there are none!) but instead tries to teach you to be a critic. In each case, theory and application are related to critical analysis of rhetorical acts, with the goal of teaching you how to analyze your own and others' rhetoric. To the degree that I succeed in doing that, the process of learning that begins here can continue outside the classroom and throughout your life.

MATERIAL FOR ANALYSIS

Excerpt from "Madness Visible: Kosovo Diary"
by Janine DiGiovanni[20]

1   Mehije has the deadest eyes. She sits on a pile of old blankets in the corner of a converted factory and silently watches me across the room. Except for her eyes, her face is still. When I kneel next to her, she stares wordlessly, oblivious to the whimpering two-year-old at her feet—her daughter Duka.

2   It is cold in the factory, but Mehije wears only a sweater, muddy bedroom slippers, and thin cotton socks, pink ones. She has a long messy plait running down her back. She does not return my tentative smile; instead, she reaches behind her back and hands me a package of loose rags tied with a blue ribbon. She motions me to open it, and when I do, I see that the bundle of rags is alive, a tiny baby with gaping bird mouth. It makes no sound. It is Mehije's seventh child, a boy born four days before in the woods while she was fleeing the Serbs.

3   Mehije registers my shock. Then she begins to talk about her flight from Kosovo. She is an ethnic Albanian from the village of Mojstir, and she has to think to calculate her age: 38. Married to Abdullah, a farmer. When she left Mojstir, it was burning. It is now a place that will cease to have any history, like the more than 800,000 people who have trudged over the mountain passes out of Kosovo, leaving behind a gutted country.

4   Before March 1998, when the war escalated in Kosovo, Mehije had a simple life that she did not question: pigs, cows, the children in school, Abdullah earning a meager living. But in the past few years, as Serb forces grew more prevalent in the area and Serb civilians more antagonistic, it became harder for Albanians to find employment, and there was an increase in tension. Throughout this last pregnancy, she had a nagging, ominous feeling.

5   "We felt something different, something strange in the air" is how her sister-in-law, Senia, who is sitting on a blanket next to Mehije, describes it.

6   Mehije does not understand military strategy, NATO maneuvers, political insurrection. She doesn't know that 4,000 people an hour are pouring over the Kosovan borders and will probably never return to their villages. She does not remember Yugoslav president and Serb leader Slobodan Milosevic's rabid speech to the Serb minority in Kosovo on April 24, 1987. It was a speech that played to the Serbs' many resentments, recent as well as ancient. It was a speech that set in motion a hideous cycle of nationalism and ethnic hatred, first in Slovenia and Croatia, then Bosnia, and now spiraling wildly out of control in Kosovo.

7   She doesn't care about any of that. The only things Mehije ever knew were how to be a wife and a mother, how to bake bread, milk cows.

8   This is what happened: Sunday, March 28, was the fifth day of the NATO bombing, a campaign that does not make sense to her and her neighbors ("Our lives were easier before NATO got involved"). It was also Bajram, an important Muslim holiday, traditionally a day when children are scrubbed and dressed in their best clothes and families gather to eat special food, like roast lamb. Mehije was in her kitchen when the door burst open and her Serb neighbors— people she had known all of her life—pointed guns in her face and ordered her family out of their house. Her neighbors were not masked. She saw their faces, saw the anger and the determination.

9   "Take nothing. Just go quickly," they said, waving their guns. Mehije and Abdullah rounded up the children, put some bread in their pockets, and ran. "I had the birth pains when I was running," she told me. But despite the warning of an imminent labor, "I ran anyway."

10   The family did not have a car, but found neighbors who were fleeing on a farm tractor. They stopped in a sheltered forest near Mojstir and tried to build temporary huts from branches. Other villagers—Mehije thinks around 200—were there, too, foraging in the snow for wood to make a fire, for small animals to eat, for water. Families were separated; there was the sound of wailing children. People kept asking: Have you seen my father? Have you seen my sister? Most of them were lacking papers: the Serbs had liberated them out of their documents, making sure they would never return to Mojstir, in the same generous way that Serbs are charging refugees to cross the border out of Kosovo.

11   In the forest, Mehije's group heard reports of what was happening in the village. Their houses were on fire. Everything they owned had either been destroyed or loaded onto trucks and driven away.

12   Mehije stayed in the forest for three days. Her labor began. The temperature dropped to freezing. Then the same Serbs who had ordered them out of their village came back and ordered them to march up the mountain and over the border to Albania, a walk which would take three days. "Go back to your country!" they jeered. "Your village is burned! You have nothing left."

13   "I had never been to Albania before," Mehije says. "My family has always lived in Kosovo." But she did not argue. She gathered her six children and began to walk. She started to time her contractions, which were coming closer together.

14   The baby, whom she called Leotrim, came while they were wading through waist-deep snow. Mehije walked until she could not walk anymore and then she dropped to her knees. The men cleared a space for her in the snow, and she lay on twigs. Senia, who has an eighth-grade education and no nursing experience, acted as midwife. There was no water, no blankets, no food, no privacy. Mehije says the baby came quickly, within three hours. Senia cut the cord with a knife. Afterward, when her sister-in-law handed her the baby, Mehije remembers thinking that this last child came into a world of confusion, of terror, born under a strange, foreign sky. He will never know his home.

15   "He won't remember this," Mehije says, holding Leotrim. She is still in shock: she has the look of a raw, bleeding animal that someone has kicked and beaten. She repeats herself, as if by saying it, she can make it a reality: "He won't remember any of this."

16   She says the baby has nothing, not even diapers. She says she has not seen Abdullah since the family arrived in Rozaj, a town on the Montenegrin-Kosovan border about 50 kilometers from her home. She is worried for his safety.

17   "We heard they were taking away men and boys," another one of the women sitting near her on a mattress says in a frightened voice. It is a chilling thought, because everyone in the room remembers what happened in Bosnia, at Srebrenica, when the supposed U.N. safe haven finally fell in July 1995: the men were rounded up and sent to the forest and never returned.

18   I stand and say I will go to the village to try to find Abdullah (who, it will turn out, is fine; they had been inadvertently separated in the chaos of the march) and to get some things for the baby at the apothecary. On the way out of the factory, I pass an old man with a bloody stump instead of an arm. He wears a beret and is sitting upright in a wheelbarrow, smoking. He is talking to himself, muttering the same thing over and over in Albanian. No one is listening to him.

19   This is what it is like: no matter how many times you listen and record someone's story, no matter how many refugees you see crossing over mountaintops wearing plastic bags on their heads to protect themselves from freezing rain—you don't ever really get used to it. And yet, when there are so many, it is easy to dehumanize them. They have the same faces, the same stories; they come down

the road with their lives in two carrier bags. And by the time they get herded into abandoned schools or warehouses, you forget that once they had lives and read books, that they have birthdays, wedding anniversaries, love affairs. You forget they had a favorite television show, a dog or a cat that they loved.

20   This is what ethnic cleansing means for them: they lose their history, their identities, their sense of belonging. Nothing feels safe anymore. Anything can happen.

Questions for Analysis

1. What rhetorical purpose(s) does the title suggest?
2. What rhetorical purposes are evident in this article? Which ones are most pronounced?
3. In what ways does the author function as a rhetor? As a critic?
4. In what ways does this rhetorical act underscore the 7 p's of rhetoric?

EXERCISES

1. Consider how some widely publicized events illustrate the range of rhetorical purposes described in this chapter. For example, how did the impeachment hearings of President Bill Clinton affect attitudes toward privacy and the press, the meaning of sexual relations, the value of an independent counsel? How did the mass shootings at Columbine High school in Littleton, Colorado, influence attitudes on gun control? Media violence? Parental responsibilities? How did the events of 9/11/01 change attitudes about civil liberties? About intelligence agencies? About Arab Americans? About the threat of terrorism? About the Israeli–Palestine conflict? Do these examples illustrate the movement from one rhetorical purpose to another? How?

2. The history of rhetoric and communication is embedded in and revealed by the meanings, usage, and origins of these terms. Both the history and the varied meanings of these words can be discovered this way: Ask each student or assign groups of students to look up rhetoric and communication (or communications) in one of the following: *Encyclopedia of Rhetoric*, *Encyclopedia of Rhetoric and Composition*, *The Oxford English Dictionary*, *Roget's Thesaurus*, *Encyclopedia of Philosophy*, *A Dictionary of Word Origins*, *The Dictionary of the Social Sciences*, M. H. Abrams's *A Glossary of Literary Terms*, William Safire's *Safire's New Political Dictionary*, *Encyclopedia Britannica* (compare essays in different editions), or other similar references. Then, in class, compare and contrast the definitions, meanings, and information about word origins that were found. How old is the study of rhetoric? Of

communication? What is the difference between *communication* and *communications*? Edward Schiappa has made a strong case in *The Beginnings of Rhetorical Theory in Classical Greece* (Yale, 1999) that Plato is the person who coined the word *rhetoric*. Given Plato's hostility to rhetoric, how might that have affected its meaning?

3. Consider the following scenarios. Which rhetorical purpose is most evident? Explain your choice:
   a. When students in a college sociology class must use a wheelchair for a full day to go anywhere and record their observations of how people interact with them, what rhetorical purpose is achieved?
   b. When food critics write such descriptions as: "Taste the melt-in-your-mouth tender cuts of beef sautéed in a succulent garlic butter sauce and topped with braised scallions, spicy peppercorn, and lightly cooked whole mushrooms," they are engaged in what rhetorical purpose?
   c. When it's Girl Scout Cookie time, Girl Scouts will knock at doors asking individuals to sign their pledge cards and order. What rhetorical purpose do they hope to fulfill?
   d. When an advertisement reads: "As a Sears valued customer, we will offer you a 'sneak preview' of our Fall Sale. We appreciate your continued support and hope to see you Saturday," it is hoping to achieve what rhetorical purpose?
   e. When President Clinton was called before Independent Counsel Kenneth Starr to testify about his relationship with Monica Lewinsky, what rhetorical purpose was expected to be fulfilled?

4. A rhetorical perspective recognizes that social truths are shaped by scientific and philosophical discourses as much as by religious beliefs, history, cultural values, collective aspirations, common metaphors and associations. Using InfoTrac® College Edition, locate the article "Healing Before Birth: An Ethical Dilemma" by John C. Fletcher, which appeared in the *Technology Review* (January 1984), p. 26. Conduct a simulation game in which you attempt to resolve the ethical controversy surrounding fetal surgery. As a first step, produce a list of the various interest groups who would be involved or affected. How many interested parties can you identify in the fetal surgery debate, besides the fetus and the mother? As a second step, identify the kinds of knowledge (science, religion, politics, philosophy, etc.) on which each interest group relies in building their case. Drawing from these sources of knowledge, what might their perspective on this issue be? Whose perspective do you think is most likely to be privileged or ignored? Why? Step three asks you to make some critical decisions. If you were a member of a Senate committee addressing the issue of fetal surgery and you had to come up with a statement defining the government's policy on this issue, how would you negotiate among these various social truths? What criteria would you use to sort out these various interests?

Portfolio Project: An Overview

One of the best ways to make criticism a practical, marketable activity is to showcase your critical thinking and writing abilities in accessible project form to potential employers. Increasingly, portfolios are a popular way to do that. A portfolio is a collection of your best coursework assignments, arranged artfully and presented in a slick binder, three-ring notebook, or bound book. Sometimes, portfolio samples represent sustained work, like a campaign or research project. The portfolio project suggested here is of that sort. In each chapter, you will be given a specific entry to work on. The first, careful decision you must make is to choose an issue that is important to you. Find three interesting and sufficiently complex rhetorical selections about this issue drawing from different forms of expression (newspapers, magazines, books, speeches, films, Web sites, TV and radio programming) created by different rhetors and fulfilling different rhetorical purposes. Selections must be cleared by your instructor. Craft an opening paragraph that explains why you are interested in this particular social issue and why you have selected these three rhetorical artifacts to represent that issue. Be sure to give full source citations for your rhetorical selections. Then proceed to the various portfolio entries. You may want to consult the three components of a good introduction outlined in Chapter 3 for more specific help.

5. **Portfolio Entry 1: Purpose**
   Explain the ways in which each artifact fulfills different purposes on the range of rhetorical purposes. What do you learn about this issue from identifying how rhetors use rhetoric for different ends?

NOTES

1. Stephen Jay Gould, "So Near and Yet So Far," *New York Review of Books*, October 20, 1994, p. 26.

2. In "Feminists and Philosophy," *New York Review of Books*, October 20, 1994, pp. 59–63, Martha Nussbaum, a professor of philosophy, classics, and comparative literature at Brown University and a visiting professor of law at the University of Chicago, reviews a collection of essays by feminist philosophers who write in defense of reason, yet she comments: "feminists note that males who wish to justify the oppression of women have frequently made a pretense of objectivity and of freedom from bias in sifting evidence, and have used the claim of objectivity to protect their biased judgments from rational scrutiny" (pp. 60–61).

3. Some behaviorists argue that all choice is an illusion; if so, all efforts at influence are pointless. Consider whether media coverage of "terrorist rhetoric" is misnamed. Is it, rather, "terrorist coercion"?

4. *Or, The Parish Boy's Progress* (London: R. Bentley, 1838).

5. (London: J. Cassell, 1852).

6. *The Women's West*, ed. Susan Armitage and Elizabeth Jameson (Norman: University of Oklahoma Press, 1987), pp. 19–33. Cited material is on p. 27.

7. J. Marvin Hunter, ed., *The Trail Drivers of Texas: Interesting Sketches of Early Cowboys* (Austin: University of Texas Press, 1985, p. 453), cited in C. Robert Haywood, " 'No Less a Man': Blacks in Cow Town Dodge City, 1876–1886," *The Western Historical Quarterly*, May 1988, pp. 161–82, cited material on p. 169. See also Kenneth W. Porter, *The Negro on the American Frontier* (New York: Arno Press, 1971),

pp. 521–22; William Loren Katz, *The Black West* (Garden City, NY: Doubleday, 1971), p. xi.

8. New York: William Morrow & Company, 1993. For additional analysis of rape laws and the difficulties of prosecution, see Stephen J. Schulhofer, *Unwanted Sex: The Culture of Intimidation and the Failure of Law* (Cambridge, MA: Harvard University Press, 1998).

9. Another example of rhetorical explanation is *Reproducing Rape: Domination Through Talk in the Courtroom* (Chicago: University of Chicago Press, 1993), in which Gregory Matoesian analyzes transcripts of rape trials to show how courtroom talk by lawyers can shape or socially construct the victim's testimony to fit male standards of legitimate sexual practice, transforming the experience of rape into routine consensual sex.

10. *The Life and Adventures of Nat Love . . .* (1907; Baltimore: Black Classic Press, 1988).

11. Charles A. Siringo, *Riata and Spurs* (Boston: Houghton Mifflin, 1927), pp. 17–18, 28.

12. Harry E. Chrisman, *The Ladder of Rivers: The Story of I. P. (Print) Olive* (Denver: Sage, 1962), p. 122.

13. See William Loren Katz, author of *Black People Who Made the Old West* (Trenton, NJ: Africa World Press, 1992) and of *The Black West*, letter to the editor, *New York Times*, June 2, 1993, p. A10.

14. Kenneth B. Clark, *Dark Ghetto: Dilemmas of Social Power* (New York: Harper & Row, 1965).

15. Phyllis Wheatley (1753–1784), a West African slave from Boston, was bought by Quakers who opposed slavery and educated her and promoted her writing talent. A collection of her poetry, *Poems on Various Subjects*, was published in 1773. She was free but penniless after her mistress died. She married, but her husband first abused, then deserted her. Impoverished, she and her three children died in an epidemic. "Lifting as we climb" is the motto of the National Association of Colored Women's and Girls' Clubs.

16. Karlyn Kohrs Campbell, "The Nature of Criticism in Rhetorical and Communicative Studies," *Central States Speech Journal* 30 (1979): 4–13.

17. *The Philosophy of Rhetoric*, ed. Lloyd F. Bitzer (Carbondale: Southern Illinois University Press, 1963), p. 1.

18. *A Rhetoric of Motives* (1950; Berkeley: University of California Press, 1969), p. 43.

19. *On Rhetoric: A Theory of Civic Discourse*, trans. George Kennedy (New York: Oxford University Press, 1991), 1.2.1355b.26.

20. *Vanity Fair*, 1999, pp. 81–82. Reprinted by permission of the author.

chapter 2

The Rhetorical Act

In the first chapter, I discussed rhetoric, the rhetorical dimension in all human action, and rhetorical acts in general. In this chapter, I examine two rhetorical acts in some detail. Here I play the role of critic. In Chapter 1, you were introduced to the idea that criticism is specialized feedback—careful analysis and evaluation of rhetorical acts. Here the term is examined more fully. Criticism is an acquired thinking, speaking, and writing *skill* that occurs in stages: description, interpretation, and evaluation. As a craft, it requires *specialized tools*—in this case a handy lexicon for clear and meaningful explication. Criticism also demands a certain *attitude*—a passion to decipher symbols born out of appreciation and suspicion of the many ways rhetoric influences us. Whether or not you aim toward a career in which writing or speaking plays a central role, you must function as a critic in order to cope in an age of information explosion that will require you to sift and evaluate massive amounts of discourse—in news reports, advertising, and entertainment programming as well as political debates and speeches at various levels of government. Think of learning to be a critic as a form of consumer protection, protecting you as a consumer of persuasion. The four visuals on the following pages capture the skill sets, attitude, and lexicon you will need to perform criticism (Figures 2–1, 2–2, 2–3, and 2–4).

Figure 2–1
What Is Criticism?

- An acquired thinking, speaking, and writing skill
- A process of description, interpretation, and evaluation
- A certain attitude: a passion to uncover the many ways in which rhetoric influences us

Figure 2–2
The Five Characteristics of the Critic

The critic is . . .

- knowledgeable/has expertise
- able to communicate clearly and efficiently
- passionate about what he/she critiques
- able to tell us the nonobvious
- able to educate and edify listeners about a message

ELEMENTS OF RHETORICAL ACTION

I have developed a lexicon or set of terms that allows critics to talk about the elements or parts of a rhetorical act. The terms name seven general categories of descriptive analysis as follows:

1. **Purpose:** the conclusion argued (thesis) and the response desired by the rhetor. Some purposes are *instrumental*; they seek overt action from the audience. Some purposes are *consummatory*; they seek appreciation, contemplation, conferring honor or blame.

Figure 2–3
*The Critic vs.
the Reporter*

Critic

- How was it said?
- Why?
- Motive
- Implicit
- Analysis
- Depth
- Detective
- Color commentator
- Persuasive
- Moral

Reporter

- What was said?
- Where/Who/When?
- Facts
- Explicit
- Paraphrase
- Surface
- Police officer
- Play-by-play
- Informative
- Amoral

Figure 2–4
*Reporting vs.
Criticism:
An Example*

- Bill Clinton delivered a short, 1500-word Inaugural Address today. He stressed themes of sacrifice, responsibility, cultural diversity and global interdependence. He was interrupted 15 times for applause. International issues did not emerge from the address; rather, Clinton stated that domestic and foreign policy issues were intertwined, but then went on to discuss mostly domestic issues like healthcare, influence peddling on capitol hill and crime.

- In his first act as President, Bill Clinton shook off the labels he acquired during the campaign as being a rather long-winded speaker. In a speech lasting only 14 minutes, half as short as Reagan's or Bush's inaugural addresses, Clinton managed, nonetheless, to invoke the memories of Washington, Jefferson, Lincoln, JFK, MLK, and the Bible in artistically fulfilling the expectations for inaugural addresses while legitimizing his principles on the domestic front. To no one's surprise, words like "change," "global competitiveness," and "investment in America" dotted the speech, but other words such as "sacrifice"—often a code word for taxes—were a surprise.

2. **Audience**: the receiver of a rhetorical act. This includes an immediate audience, a target audience, a role created by the rhetor for the audience, or specialized audiences (VIPs) with social or political power to effect change.
3. **Persona**: the role(s) adopted by the persuader in making the argument (e.g., teacher, preacher, reporter, prophet, mediator, and the like).
4. **Tone**: the rhetor's attitude toward the subject (detached, emotional, satirical, and so forth) and toward the audience (personal/impersonal, authoritative/egalitarian/supplicant, and so on).
5. **Evidence**: the different kinds of support material for the argument.

6. **Structure**: the way the materials are organized to gain attention, develop a case, and provide emphasis.
7. **Strategies**: the adaptation of all of the above, including language, appeals, and argument, to shape the materials to overcome the obstacles the rhetor faces (the rhetorical problem).

These categories (and their subcategories) of descriptive analysis provide a set of labels or terms that permit critics and rhetors to talk about a rhetorical act in order to possess, understand, and analyze it (divide it into its parts) and describe it as fully and carefully as possible. Some of these categories are basic and are essential starting points. For instance, as a rhetor, you must decide your purpose and determine just whom you are addressing very early in the process. You must select a method of organization and the supporting materials you will use, although as these acts indicate, there are many options. The simplest role would be to speak or write as a peer to your classmates (but there are always the problems of the teacher, who is not a peer, and of a subject on which you are more expert than your classmates). You may also try to treat tone very simply, by saying, "Oh, I'll be objective," but in most cases, you will find that you have beliefs and commitments and personal involvements, and you must decide how to handle these. The category of strategy is the most difficult, and it requires the most experience. You will need to read and hear many rhetorical acts to see the possibilities, and you will also need to use your instructor as a resource to get suggestions about approaches you might use to overcome special elements of the rhetorical problem.

As you will discover, these elements are always present and almost always important in understanding how and why a rhetorical act succeeded or failed in its purpose. If you are to talk to yourself and to others about anything, you must share a common language. This chapter offers some crucial terms in the lexicon or vocabulary needed to talk about rhetorical acts.

Descriptive analysis provides you with a vocabulary for discussing rhetorical action and with a method of identifying what is distinctive about a particular persuasive effort (Figure 2–5). Both a vocabulary and a method are needed if you are to become sophisticated consumers of contemporary persuasion. Skillful rhetors understand both their

Figure 2-5
Seven Elements of Descriptive Analysis

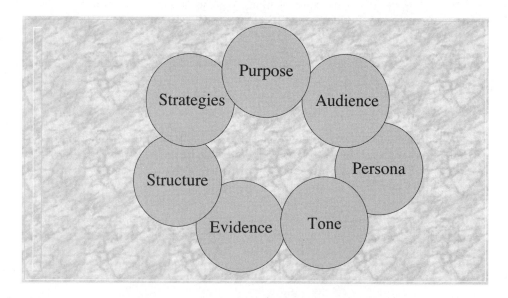

own acts and those of others. Your ability to initiate rhetorical action and to control how others influence you depends in part on your accuracy in describing discourse.

The first rhetorical act to be analyzed is one of the most famous in U.S. history, the speech that President Abraham Lincoln made on November 19, 1863, at the battle-field at Gettysburg where the Union won an important but costly battle in July of that year. As the address makes clear, the war was not yet over.

MATERIAL FOR ANALYSIS I

Lincoln's Gettysburg Address

Four score and seven years ago our fathers brought forth on this continent, a new nation, conceived in liberty, and dedicated to the proposition that all men are created equal. Now we are engaged in a great civil war, testing whether that nation, or any nation so conceived and so dedicated, can long endure. We are met on a great battlefield of that war. We have come to dedicate a portion of that field, as a final resting place for those who here gave their lives that this nation might live. It is altogether fitting and proper that we should do this.

But, in a larger sense, we cannot dedicate—we cannot consecrate—we cannot hallow—this ground. The brave men, living and dead, who struggled here, have consecrated it, far above our poor power to add or detract. The world will little note nor long remember what we say here, but it can never forget what they did here. It is for us the living, rather, to be dedicated here to the unfinished work which they who fought here have thus far so nobly advanced. It is rather for us to be here dedicated to the great task remaining before us—that from these honored dead we take increased devotion to that cause for which they gave the last full measure of devotion—that we here highly resolve that these dead shall not have died in vain—that this nation, under God, shall have a new birth of freedom—and that government of the people, by the people, for the people, shall not perish from the earth.

Rhetorical Analysis of Lincoln's Gettysburg Address

To the question why do criticism? comes this analysis of Lincoln's Gettysburg Address. In using the seven elements of descriptive analysis, the critique addresses: (1) why this speech has "lived" on as a rhetorical force, (2) how the speech reveals Lincoln's rhetorical artistry, (3) how the speech helps us appreciate the symbolic virtuosity of humans, (4) and how words contribute to the making of history? (See Figure 2–6.)

Elements of Descriptive Analysis Applied

Purpose

Instrumental (what action is expected?): To dedicate ourselves to complete the unfinished work to preserve the Union ("It is for us the living, rather, to be here dedicated to the unfinished work . . .")

Consummatory (what feelings are prompted?): To memorialize those who fought and died here; to honor the slain soldiers ("We have come to dedicate a portion of that field, as a final resting place for those who here gave their lives . . .")

Figure 2-6
*Seven Elements
of Descriptive
Analysis*

Purpose (aim)
ends vs. means

Audience (public)
immediate, target, created,
VIPs

Persona (character assumed)
rhetor–audience relationship
role

Tone
attitude toward subject
attitude toward audience

Structure (pattern)
parts of act
forms of organization

Evidence (support)
visuals, analogies, stories,
experts, statistics

Strategies (tactics)
language
appeals
arguments

Range of rhetorical purposes: Formulate belief/initiate action

Response desired: The Union must be preserved and be constituted as a nation of free people (belief to be formulated). We must commit ourselves to advancing the cause of liberty and to preserving a unified nation (action to be initiated)

Thesis: We must be "dedicated to the unfinished work which they who fought here have thus far so nobly advanced" and that this nation, "dedicated to the proposition that all men are created equal . . . shall not perish from the earth."

Persona
Relationship to audience: Peer (repetition of "we" and "our")

Relationship to subject: Inferior ("The brave men, living and dead, who struggled here, have consecrated it, far about our poor power to add or detract. The world will little note, nor long remember, what we say here . . .")

Role: Camouflaged presence (no "I" statements; no references to himself as president or commander-in-chief). If anything, Lincoln emerges as an apolitical figure, a moral voice, the conscience of the nation: "In a larger sense, we cannot dedicate— we cannot consecrate—we cannot hallow this ground."

Tone
Formal, solemn: "Four score and seven years ago . . ."

Plain, simple: Ordinary language ("We are met on a great battlefield of that war. We have come to dedicate a portion of the field, as a final resting place . . .")

Moral: "this nation, under God, shall have a new birth of freedom—and . . . shall not perish from the earth."

Structure
Chronology: Starts with "Four score and seven years ago . . ." and ends with the future, "the great task remaining before us . . ."

Evidence
No statistics, no authorities, no stories
One comparison: Past nation and future nation

Strategies
Language: Birth imagery ("brought forth," "conceived," "new birth," "perish")
Repetition: "dedicate" is repeated six times; "here" recurs seven times
Policy language: "proposition," "testing," "cause," "highly resolve"
Parallel structure: " we cannot dedicate—we cannot consecrate—we cannot hallow . . ."
Personification: Nation conceived in liberty

Appeals:
Patriotism: "liberty," "freedom," "our fathers"
Sacrifice, service, duty: "those who here gave their lives that that nation might live"
Equality: "all men are created equal"
Religious: "that this nation, under God, . . . shall not perish from the earth"

Arguments:
Deductive: "the proposition that all men are created equal"
Enthymeme: We should support the Union because it is most consistent with the principles underlying the nation
Analogy: Our nation was conceived in liberty 87 years ago and must continue to be committed to that same noble cause

Note that in each instance, a Claim (or conclusion) is followed by Proof (evidence from the speech). The third step is Analysis: Why is this element present? What insights about the rhetoric emerge from recognizing this claim in the discourse? The Questions for Analysis section at the end of this chapter encourage you to wrestle with these critical "why" questions.

Questions for Analysis: Gettysburg Address

1. How do language strategies help Lincoln accomplish two purposes: formulating belief and initiating action?
2. Why is Lincoln's persona so understated?
3. What is the tone of this address? Is it fitting for the occasion?
4. Who is his target audience? Why is this tricky given the occasion?
5. Considering Lincoln's daunting rhetorical challenge, why do you think this speech is still considered a masterpiece of rhetorical action?

MATERIAL FOR ANALYSIS II

The rhetorical act I analyze below is the conclusion to the last speech of the Reverend Martin Luther King, Jr., delivered in Memphis, Tennessee, on April 4, 1968. A strike by sanitation workers had begun on February 12, 1968, but little progress had been made toward resolving their grievances. A protest march led earlier by King on March 28, 1968, was poorly planned and organized and ended in violent encounters between marchers and police. The momentum of the civil rights movement as a whole had lessened, and King was struggling to be an effective leader. The need to encourage his audience of striking sanitation workers, to raise their morale, was great, but the past events were hardly cause for optimism. In the face of these obstacles, King spoke, ending with a memorable peroration or conclusion.

Conclusion of the Reverend Martin Luther King, Jr.'s, Speech, April 4, 1968[1]

1 And I want to thank God once more for allowing me to be here with you. You know several years ago I was in New York City autographing the first book that I had written. And while sitting there autographing books, a demented black woman came up. The only question I heard from her was, "Are you Martin Luther King?" And I was looking down writing, and I said yes. The next minute I felt something beating on my chest. Before I knew it, I had been stabbed by this demented woman. I was rushed to Harlem hospital. It was a dark Saturday afternoon. That blade had gone through and the x-rays revealed that the tip of the blade was on the edge of my aorta, the main artery. And once that's punctured, you drown in your own blood; that's the end of you. It came out in the *New York Times* the next morning that if I had merely sneezed, I would have died.

2 Well, about 4 days later, they allowed me, after the operation, after my chest had been opened and the blade had been taken out, to move around in a wheel chair in the hospital. They allowed me to read some of the mail that came in, and from all over the states and the world, kind letters came in. I read a few but there's one of them I will never forget. I had received one from the president and the vice president. I've forgotten what those telegrams said. I'd received a visit and a letter from the governor of New York, but I've forgotten what that letter said. But there was another letter that came from a little girl, a young girl who was a student at the White Plains high school, and I looked at that letter, and I'll never forget it. It said simply, "Dear Dr. King, I am a ninth grade student at the White Plains high school." She said, "While it should not matter, I would like to mention that I'm a white girl. I read in the paper of your misfortunes and of your sufferings. And I read that if you had sneezed, you would have died. I'm simply writing you to say that I am so happy that you didn't sneeze."

3 Because if I had sneezed, I wouldn't have been around here in 1960 when students all over the South started sitting in at lunch counters. And I knew that as they were sitting in, they were really standing up for the best in the American dream and taking the whole nation back to those great wells of democracy which were dug deep by the founding fathers in the Declaration of Independence and the Constitution.

4 If I had sneezed, I wouldn't have been around here in 1961 when we decided to take a ride for freedom and ended segregation in interstate travel.

5 If I had sneezed, I wouldn't have been around here in 1962 when Negroes in Albany, Georgia, decided to straighten their backs up. And whenever men and women straighten their backs up, they're going somewhere, because the man can't ride your back unless it is bent.

6 If I had sneezed, I wouldn't have been here in 1963 when black people of Birmingham, Alabama, aroused the conscience of this nation and brought into being the civil rights field.

7 If I had sneezed, I wouldn't have had a chance later that year in August to try to tell America about a dream that I had had.

8   If I had sneezed, I wouldn't have been down in Selma, Alabama, to see the great movement there.

9   If I had sneezed, I wouldn't have been in Memphis, to see a community rally around those brothers and sisters who are suffering. I'm so happy that I didn't sneeze. And they were telling me, now, it doesn't matter now, it really doesn't matter what happens now.

10   I left Atlanta this morning, and as we got started on the plane, there were six of us. The pilot said over the public address system, we're sorry for the delay. But we have Dr. Martin Luther King on the plane, and to be sure that all of the bags were checked, and to be sure that nothing would be wrong on the plane, we had to check out everything carefully. And we've had the plane protected and guarded all night. And then I got into Memphis. And some began to say the threats or talk about the threats that were out, what would happen to me from some of our sick white brothers. Well, I don't know what will happen now.

11   We've got some difficult days ahead but it really doesn't matter with me now, because I have been to the mountain top. And I don't mind. Like anybody, I would like to live a long life; longevity has its place. But I am not concerned about that now. I just want to do God's will. And He's allowed me to go up to the mountain, and I've looked over and I've seen the promised land. I may not get there with you, but I want you to know tonight that we as a people will get to the promised land. So I am happy tonight. I am not worried about anything. I'm not fearing any man.

12   Mine eyes have seen the glory of the coming of the Lord.

Sample Critique: "I've Been to the Mountain Top"

Concepts illustrated:
a. How to apply the seven elements of descriptive analysis
b. How to use "the critical equation" (Figure 2–7)

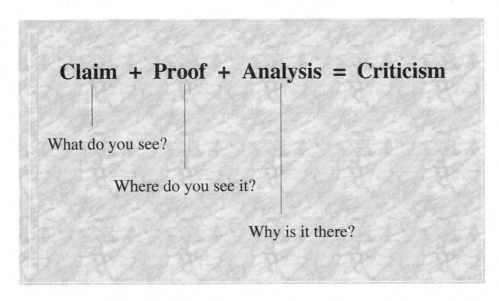

Figure 2–7
The Critical Equation "CPA"

1. Purpose

Instrumental: King rallies the troops to action

Consummatory: King eulogizes himself

Continuum of rhetorical purposes: Maintaining action

Responses desired: To inspire civil rights activists to continue the campaign for racial equality

Thesis: Like the former Jewish slaves wandering in the wilderness, the former black slaves in the United States will reach the promised land.

The Critical Equation: CPA (Claim + Proof + Analysis)

King's speech aims to maintain action by inspiring civil rights activists to continue the campaign for racial equality. That is most evident in paragraphs 3–9 in which he catalogs the many past successes of the movement. Such a tactic is important at this stage in the movement when disillusionment might overwhelm idealism. King's primary argument is an enthymematic one, that is, King relies on his audience to use comparison to draw this conclusion: Like the Jewish slaves in Egypt who were freed and reached the promised land, the former black slaves in the United States will achieve their goals. This central claim is most apparent when he says, "I want you to know tonight that we as a people will get to the promised land." Assuming that the audience sees the connection, that thesis is strategic because it invests the effort for civil rights with righteousness and associates it with a biblical success story. King's purpose, thus, is primarily instrumental because he wants to rally the troops to rededicate themselves to the cause. King also expresses some satisfaction about what the movement has accomplished, however, and his speech commemorates the movement and his work.

The expressive dimensions of what he says can be seen in such lines as these: "[I]t doesn't really matter with me now, because I have been to the mountain top. And I don't mind. Like anybody, I would like to live a long life; longevity has its place. But I am not concerned about that now. . . . I am not worried about anything. I am not fearing any man." Because King was assassinated shortly after he made this speech, the expressive value of the speech is greater now. The speech reads in places as if he had a premonition of his own death and delivered a eulogy for himself.

2. Audience

Immediate: Striking sanitation workers and their supporters

Target: Civil rights sympathizers, particularly African Americans

Created: You are part of a great and noble cause; rededicate yourselves to it

Agents of change: Not addressed directly

The Critical Equation: CPA (Claim + Proof + Analysis)

King spoke directly to striking sanitation workers in Memphis. Although this group was his immediate audience, his target audience was broader. He is trying to reach African Americans who support the movement to achieve their civil rights. Passages to support this claim include all the abbreviated references to civil rights successes, from the sit-ins in North Carolina to the freedom rides all over the South, to the activism of "Negroes in Albany, Georgia" and the activism of "black people in Alabama" and supporters who came to the nation's capital in 1963 to take part in the demonstration at which King delivered his well-known "I have a dream" speech, to those fighting against injustices in Selma, Alabama, and Memphis (see paragraphs 3–9). King creates a role of activist for his target audience to play as he retells stories of heroism in the rank and file and prophesizes that the movement will succeed eventually, even if he is no longer around (see paragraph 11). Those who have the power to bring about the changes are legislators and judges. The effort to obtain full civil rights required both political and legal reform, yet in this speech excerpt, King does not address these agents of change or explain how his target audience can attract the attention of the political elite. King recognizes that the movement is in the doldrums and that his speech will be transmitted to other audiences through print and electronic media, King uses the occasion of speaking to Memphis sanitation workers to address a larger constituency and to urge them to rededicate themselves to the cause.

3. Persona
Relationship with the audience: Superior
Role adopted: Prophet

The Critical Equation: CPA (Claim + Proof + Analysis)
King adopts a superior relationship with his audience. There are many self-references ("I" statements), 45 to be exact. Further, that King uses only personal examples to support his claims lets the listener/reader know that he is a powerful authority on this subject. More important, however, King cultivates the role of prophet. Prophets are people who are "called out" from the larger society by God. They stand alone. They are fearless and courageous. They are tested for their strength of character. They bring a divine message. They are visionaries. From the outset, King develops this important biblical role. He says, "I want to thank God once more for allowing me to be here with you" (paragraph 1). He then tells the story of his near death experience (paragraphs 1–2), which like a true prophet allows us to see that he had been tested and chosen. He is a visionary because, like Moses who is allowed to glimpse the promised land from Mount Nebo, he has "been to the mountain top" and done "God's will" and has "seen the promised land." This prophet persona is strategic for giving the cause an aura of invincibility and for giving it a biblical mandate because if King is a modern Moses, his cause will surely succeed.

4. Tone
Attitude toward subject: (1) Reflective, intuitive, serene; (2) confident, hopeful, inspirational, visionary
Attitude toward audience: Respect, commendation

The Critical Equation: CPA (Claim + Proof + Analysis)
King's tone varies. He is reflective (past tense dominates the progression of his speech), intuitive ("I may not get there with you"), and serene ("I am not fearing any man"). This attitudinal cluster reinforces the consummatory purposes of the speech and is consistent with his prophetic persona. King is also hopeful and inspirational ("We as a people will get to the promised land." . . . "Mine eyes have seen the glory of the coming of the Lord.") This attitudinal cluster reinforces his prophetic persona and effectively meets the rhetorical challenge of buoying the hopes of disheartened people.

5. Evidence
Example: Two extended personal examples; several brief references to historical instances
Statistics: None

Authority: None other than the speaker
Analogy: Enthymematic comparison of Israelite slaves and U.S. slaves

The Critical Equation: CPA (Claim + Proof + Analysis)
King uses little evidence. Two detailed personal examples, one of his near-death experience in New York City (paragraphs 1–2), the other of his security difficulties in Atlanta (paragraph 10), compose the bulk of the supporting material. Other abbreviated examples of civil rights successes cluster in paragraphs 3–9. That King uses no other direct evidence except the example works well for his purposes. Prophets are authority figures; they do not need corroborating evidence for claims they make. Further, the example appeals to us on an emotional level. The story of the little girl's heart-felt get-well letter is memorable and inspirational. Remember, too, that he is speaking to the committed, not to detractors, so the need for other forms of proof (statistics, authorities) is minimal. The analogy King develops is implicit. He does not say that U.S. blacks and Israelite slaves are similarly situated, but that is clearly the connection he wants the audience to make if they know their Bible. Hence, the analogy is enthymematic; it relies on audience participation.

6. Structure
Macro structure (Intro/body/conclusion): Conclusion is evident
Micro structure: Chronology

The Critical Equation: CPA (Claim + Proof + Analysis)
The speech excerpt analyzed here is the conclusion to a much longer speech. It is recognizable as a conclusion because of its foreshadowing of the end of the speech: "And I want to thank God once more for allowing me to be here with you." It also rises in intensity; hence, it is a *peroration*. It ends with a dramatic flair: "Mine eyes have seen the glory of the coming of the Lord." For the purposes of this speech, that kind of rousing ending is important. Strategically embedded in the context of that conclusion is chronological structure. King goes back to the earliest success of the movement in 1960, systematically works his way up to the present ('61, '62, '63, . . . '68), then ends with a visionary look into the future. Chronology is an especially good structure for showcasing the scope of a subject and gaining perspective on it. By using chronology, King is able to rekindle enthusiasm by reminding his audience of its scope and asking them to keep current troubles in perspective; the larger cause still looks good. Prophets, of course, have this ability to see the "big picture," the panoramic view.

7. Strategies
Language: Repetition, allusion, simple sentences
Appeals: Emotional, democracy, righteousness, patriotism
Arguments: Enthymeme

The Critical Equation: CPA (Claim + Proof + Analysis)
King uses repetition ("If I had sneezed" is repeated seven times) to invite audience participation, contribute to his inspirational tone, reinforce his "tested" status as a prophet of the movement, and structure his message. He uses two allusions, the death of Moses after climbing Mount Nebo ("I've seen the promised land. I may not get there with you") and the words of the "Battle Hymn of the Republic" ("Mine eyes

have seen the glory of the coming of the Lord") to associate the cause with righteousness and patriotism. The biblical connection makes the cause righteous. The line from the "Battle Hymn of the Republic" links the cause to patriotism and foreshadows success; Julia Ward Howe wrote that poem during the Civil War for the Union armies. King uses simple words throughout the conclusion, which reinforces his belief in the simplicity of his message and is an adaptation to his audience, many of whom have been deprived of advanced education.

The psychological appeals in the speech are many. An emotional appeal is made when King retells the story of the little white girl at the White Plains High School. An emotional appeal is made in the retelling of the stabbing incident, and the "if I had sneezed" refrain is a haunting reminder of the precarious circumstances of his life. King appeals to democracy and patriotism when he speaks of "those great wells of democracy which were dug deep by the founding fathers in the Declaration of Independence and the Constitution" and "the American Dream" and the reference to the "Battle Hymn of the Republic." There are Christian/moral appeals in such lines as "I just want to do God's will," and "I want to thank God once more for allowing me to be here with you."

The arguments in this speech are enthymematic. This is not a logical, deductive presentation in which claims and proof and warrants are spelled out for the audience. In other words, it is not a logical speech; rather, the arguments are supplied by the audience from fragmentary clues that King provides. King claims that the civil rights movement will succeed. His proof for that claim is the sharing of his vision. The warrant for this argument is that his premonition is adequate proof for such a claim when the speaker is a prophetic figure. Another argument is that the civil rights message is a simple plea for equality; it is not a "black" demand or a "white" fear. Proof comes from the contrasting examples of the demented black woman who almost kills him and of the little white girl who admires him.

Given the length of time King had been active in the movement and that he is targeting those already committed to civil rights for all, it is appropriate that his arguments be exclusively enthymematic.

EXERCISES

1. Practice your critical abilities by using "the critical equation" (Claim + Proof + Analysis) for the following excerpts from "Madness Visible," the material for analysis from Chapter 1.

   a. Excerpt 1—Category Persona: What is the rhetor's (reporter's) relationship to her audience based on this passage?

   "Mehije does not understand military strategy, NATO maneuvers, political insurrection. She doesn't know that 4,000 people an hour are pouring over the Kosovan borders and will probably never return to their villages. She does not remember Yugoslav president and Serb leader Slobodan Milosevic's rabid speech to the Serb minority in Kosovo on April 24, 1987. It was a speech that played to the Serbs' many resentments, recent as well as ancient. It was a speech that set in motion a hideous cycle of nationalism and ethnic hatred, first in Slovenia and Croatia, then Bosnia, and now spiraling wildly out of control in Kosovo."

   b. Excerpt 2—Category Tone: What is the attitude conveyed in this passage?

   "It is cold in the factory, but Mehije wears only a sweater, muddy bedroom slippers, and thin cotton socks, pink ones. She has a long messy plait running down her back. She does not return my tentative smile; instead she reaches behind her back and hands me a package of loose rags tied with a blue ribbon. She motions for me to open it, and when I do, I see that the bundle of rags is alive, a tiny baby with gaping bird mouth. It makes no sound. It is Mehije's seventh child, a boy, born four days before in the woods while she was fleeing the Serbs."

   c. Excerpt 3—Category Audience: Who is the target audience in this passage?

"This is what it is like: no matter how many times you listen and record someone's story, no matter how many refugees you see crossing over mountaintops wearing plastic bags on their heads to protect themselves from the freezing rain—you don't ever really get used to it. And yet, when there are so many, it is easy to dehumanize them. They have the same faces, the same stories; they come down the road with their lives in two carrier bags. And by the time they get herded into abandoned schools or warehouses, you forget that once they had lives and read books, that they have birthdays, wedding anniversaries, love affairs. You forget they had a favorite television show, a dog or a cat that they loved."

2. Arrange for the class to attend a speech together, perhaps a chapel or convocation speaker or a lecturer brought to campus for a special event. Spend the next class period describing that event analytically. What does such an analysis reveal that wasn't immediately apparent while you were listening to the speech?

3. Select an editorial from your local or school newspaper. Be prepared to present your analysis of it using one or more of the elements of descriptive analysis that your instructor has assigned. Practice using the critical equation seamlessly.

4. Using InfoTrac College Edition, locate two contrasting articles (advocating opposite positions) on one of the following topics: global warming, genetic cloning, or security in a post "9-11" world. Conduct a descriptive analysis of each. How is using the seven elements of descriptive analysis useful in discerning the rhetorical choices in each piece of scholarship? Which article is most compelling? Why? Which element of descriptive analysis is easiest to apply? Hardest? Why? Using selected elements of descriptive analysis, what suggestions can you make for how each article might be more successful in advancing its purpose?

5. **Portfolio Entry 2: Persona/Tone**
Compare and contrast how your three rhetorical selections use persona and tone to advance their purposes. This will require that you construct critical equations for each artifact—two to three pages.

NOTE

1. This is a transcription by the author of the conclusion as delivered. From "I've Been to the Mountaintop," by Martin Luther King, Jr. Reprinted by arrangement with the Estate of Martin Luther King, Jr., c/o Writers House as agent for the proprietor, New York, NY. © 1968 Dr. Martin Luther King, Jr., copyright renewed 1991 Coretta Scott King.

chapter 3

Your Rhetorical Act

The prospect of initiating rhetorical action is frightening, even for the most skilled practitioners. In fact, one survey reported that Americans fear speaking before a group more than they fear snakes, heights, disease, or even death.[1] Those of us who speak regularly never overcome the fear of seeming boring, saying something foolish, or forgetting important material. Anyone can misread a situation, presenting material the audience already knows and, hence, produce a humdrum act. Anyone can forget something important, be ill prepared, or make a silly or foolish statement. Anyone can be rattled by unexpected noise or by a restless or a very large audience. The important point is that nervousness is normal, and the sooner you accept that (and join all the rest of us who feel as you do), the more enjoyable and relaxed your presentations will be.

In one sense feeling apprehensive about speaking is normal because speakers are the very enactment of their ideas. We sometimes feel more ownership and, thus, more vulnerability about ideas we speak than those we write. Think about this for a minute. If you were to turn in a sloppy essay on capital punishment to your teacher, only you and she would know it. On the other hand, if you were to give an unrehearsed speech on capital punishment, the whole class would witness it. Another reason speech anxiety plagues so many students is because they have so little opportunity to practice speaking in public to peers before arriving at the university. With the exception of show-and-tell in the early grades, oral presentations are not the primary ways in which students are expected to show their mastery of information. No wonder students sometimes dread oral performances. The unfamiliar is scary.

Recognize, however, that nervousness can be beneficial. Like the "game day" athlete who performs better under pressure, you too can use an adrenaline surge to enliven your presentation. In fact, I worry more about the student who says, "I'm not the least bit nervous." Such speakers tend to be lethargic and underestimate the challenges of public speaking.

Although nervousness is normal and even beneficial, high levels of speech anxiety can be counterproductive. What follows are a series of tips for how to manage anxiety productively:

- *Speak on subjects you know well.* Anxiety decreases if you have a strong attachment to your subject and feel comfortable with the material. If you can focus on the content of your presentation, you will be less self-conscious, and focusing on content is much easier when you speak on subjects on which you have built-in knowledge and enthusiasm.
- *Know your audience.* Gathering plenty of information about the audience will help you control for the unexpected and craft a more interesting presentation. Find out about its size, its demographic makeup, and the room configuration. If you can discover audience attitudes toward your subject, that's even better. It is startling to think you are speaking to 12–15 college students in a lounge only to arrive and see 200 students with parents in an auditorium!
- *Practice, practice, practice.* If you have practiced the speech standing up and out loud to a sympathetic friend, even a mirror, and timed it carefully, the speech will show it. If you haven't practiced (rehearsing in your head does not count), and you are "winging" it, you deserve to feel petrified!
- *Don't memorize.* Why raise the stakes any more than you have to? Memorization can lead to mental blocks and embarrassing silences if you forget what comes next. Speaking with minimal notes is preferable. Note cards are a fine "security blanket."
- *Use physical activity.* There's no need for aerobics before speaking, but if you can take slow deep breaths, clench and unclench fists, flex your arms and shoulders, roll your neck, or even yawn repeatedly, you are working off excess levels of adrenaline to stay flexible and relaxed.
- *Check out the speaking location.* It's easier to visualize yourself giving a strong performance if you know in advance where you will be standing, what kind of sound system, if any, you will be using, what sort of podium, lighting, space, and technology you can use for visual aids, and what the room looks like. Try to arrive early and arrange to meet a technician. If that's not possible, ask the program planners about these matters.
- *Be very familiar with your opening remarks.* This may appear to contradict the "don't memorize" advice, but it shouldn't. Getting off on the right foot is critical to a smooth speech. Your confidence will carry over to the rest of your speech if your introduction (usually not more than one minute) is delivered with minimal to no notes because you know it so well.
- *Stay positive.* Immediately before speaking, think positively about the audience and reassure yourself that what you have to say is interesting. Mentally review your introduction and check to see that you have all of your notes and visual aids.

The material in the rest of this chapter is designed to provide you with more detailed insurance against nervousness when you speak or write for an audience. I divide my suggestions into four areas: picking a topic, researching a subject, organizing your material, and preparing for the final presentation.

PICKING A TOPIC

Much of the fear you feel in a rhetorical situation arises from a sense that the situation is not under your control. Admittedly, unforeseen things can happen, but they are much less likely if you choose an appropriate topic. The most basic advice to the rhetor is: Speak and write from your own knowledge and experience! If you do, you will prepare with greater ease and confidence because you are working from familiarity. You will have general knowledge against which you can test information from other sources. Your experiences will provide a stock of examples that will make the subject more personal and vivid for the audience. If you share values and experiences with audience members, your relationship to the topic will make it easier to connect them to the topic. In addition, research will be easier because you will have access to firsthand information from people who work with or experience the topic directly every day. Here are some general questions to help you find suitable topics for speeches or essays:

1. *Where did you grow up?* Each of you has special knowledge from growing up on a farm, in the inner city, on army bases, in a mining town, in the mountains, or in the desert. These experiences can be the starting point for a speech or essay. In the past, students who have grown up on farms have spoken on support prices, insecticides, fertilizers, beef imports; students from cities have written about red-lining, street repair, and variations in police protection in areas of the city. In no case was the personal experience of the student sufficient, but in each case, the research was easier, and familiarity with the subject increased the rhetor's confidence.

2. *What are your parents' occupations?* As the child of a plumber, a lawyer, an assembly line worker, or the owner of a hardware, you have access to a source of firsthand information. For example, in the past, students have used this background to explain how plumbers are licensed and why they command such high pay, the feasibility of converting factories from oil to coal (a parent sold such machinery), medical malpractice, carpal tunnel syndrome, awards from juries and the high cost of credit card debt (the child of a bankruptcy lawyer). Once again, your experience can be the starting point for your rhetorical act, and you will write and speak with familiarity.

3. *What jobs have you done?* Even temporary or part-time work teaches you a lot. For instance, a grocery clerk discussed the arguments for and against automated checkout equipment; a student who had worked as a building inspector wrote about city laws governing apartments and how to make complaints to compel landlords to meet the requirements of the building code; a student who had worked as the manager of a fast-food restaurant discussed the pros and cons of franchises.

4. *What are your hobbies and interests?* In past classes, a member of the track team talked about why some shoes increase your speed and last longer; a collector of stamps argued for their value as an investment; a student who had raced cars claimed that

55 mph is the safest maximum speed limit; an auto buff spoke about why changing the oil regularly is the single most important maintenance task a car owner can perform.

5. *Have you family or friends with special problems, distinctions, or unusual characteristics?* Many rhetorical acts spring from tragedy. An alcoholic father prompted a speech on organizations that help the families of alcoholics; a schizophrenic sister prompted a speech on megavitamin therapy—what it is and how it works; the suicide of a friend's brother prompted an essay on suicide among college students; an epileptic brother occasioned a speech on misconceptions about epilepsy; a father's death from a shot of penicillin inspired an essay on the perils of allergies.

Success and honor can also be the source of topics: the daughter of a mother who patented a new chemical process talked about how patents are acquired; a basketball player used the career of Jackie Stiles, a star of women's basketball at Southwest Missouri State University, the first NCAA Division I woman player to score more than 1,000 points in a season, to write about the limited opportunities for extraordinary women athletes; a scholarship student in ballet demonstrated and explained the basic movements of ballet as part of a speech to increase appreciation of ballet performances.

6. *Have you had unusual experiences?* The survivor of a severe automobile accident wrote vividly of seat belt safety; a girl who was threatened by a drunken boy with a loaded gun argued for gun control; a foreign exchange student spoke about currency problems.

Speaking or writing from your own experience has additional benefits. In most cases, you will be deeply involved in your topic and your sincerity will be catching—the audience will care too. When you draw on personal experience, your audience will find you knowledgeable and credible, worthy of being believed. Your rhetorical act will not seem to be an exercise for a class; rather, the audience experiences your telling them something you know about firsthand, that you care about, and they will consider what you write or say seriously and with respect. You will be on the way to a successful presentation.

If you have considered these questions carefully, you will recognize some weak approaches. Don't write from research you did for last semester's term paper unless you can personalize the topic for yourself and your audience. A similar warning goes for a rhetorical act drawn from articles in newspapers, magazines, or on the Internet. Don't pick a topic just because you read about it in a magazine in the dentist's waiting room. Again, do pick a subject that is close to you, one you know about personally.

Firsthand experience and personal knowledge alone, however, are not sufficient. You must test your experience and broaden your knowledge with information drawn from other sources.

RESEARCHING A SUBJECT

If you want to be an effective speaker or writer, you must make the library, the Internet, and area professionals your helpful friends. They are primary resources for testing personal experience, refining understanding of the subject, and collecting concrete material that will explain and prove your claims and make your subject vivid.

Begin with a general survey of libraries at your school and at other schools nearby along with convenient public libraries. Find out where things are and what procedures you must follow to take out materials. Locate the computerized card catalog in each, and learn how to use it; locate the reference room and write down the hours when reference librarians are there to help you. Find out what computerized resources exist in your library and how to use them. Find the periodicals room and the reserve room. Find out where there is a government documents depository, and learn where microfilms are kept. Find out how to request materials through interlibrary loan. Does a computer printout show which periodicals the library holds and where they are? Does the computerized card catalog indicate if someone has the book you want? If it is on reserve? Are there special libraries for certain kinds of materials, such as artistic works or archives? Many libraries provide tours; most have brochures identifying materials and listing hours. In other words, "case the joint" carefully before mounting an assault to find specific materials.

What do you need to know and how can you find it? Obviously, your needs and problems will differ (for each effort), but there are some general procedures you can follow. First, because personal experiences ordinarily are limited, you will need general background on a particular subject and an understanding of terms and concepts. Begin in the reference room. Here you will find general sources of information and indexes that will lead you to more detailed information.

General Sources

There are three basic general sources to help you: encyclopedias, dictionaries, and almanacs and statistical yearbooks. The least specialized and most general sources are large encyclopedias such as the *Encyclopedia Britannica,* now available on-line, or the *Encyclopedia Americana.* These will give you general and historical information on people, places, concepts, and events. The articles are written by experts, and each ends with a list of books and articles that will provide additional information. You may also find it helpful to look up your topic or related subjects in slightly more specialized but still encyclopedic references, such as the *Encyclopedia of Philosophy,* the *Encyclopedia of Social Work,* or the *American Negro Reference Book.* Once again, these will give you background plus a list of more detailed sources.

You are familiar with general dictionaries such as *Webster's International Dictionary* and the *Oxford English Dictionary* and their more compact and abridged versions. You can check the meanings of terms in them, the history of changes in meanings, and the etymology or the linguistic origin of meanings. As with encyclopedias, specialized dictionaries may be helpful. For example, the *Dictionary of the Social Sciences* explains terms peculiar to or with special meanings in the social sciences, *the Oxford Classical Dictionary* focuses on figures from ancient Greece and Rome and on concepts needed to study classical literature and philosophy. There are similar dictionaries for medicine, law, sociology, psychiatry, and the like. Some of these may be available on CD-ROM, described below.

If you need more recent information, particularly quantitative information, turn to almanacs and statistical yearbooks. These contain information, usually covering one year, compiled by agencies usually named in the titles—the *CBS News Almanac,* the *New York Times Almanac,* the *Reader's Digest Almanac, World Almanac, Information Please Almanac,* among others. These sources are usually current within a few months of the events you may be researching. Similarly, the *Statistical Abstract of the United States* provides quantitative information of all sorts for a single year (often with comparisons to other, recent years).

The Internet is a research tool full of promise and peril. Its special strengths and weaknesses are discussed in Chapter 13. Without some basic guidance, excursions into cyberspace can be daunting. The Web is cluttered with over 800 million sites, which means you need navigational tools. Search engines, the most familiar being Yahoo!, are specialized computer programs that catalog Web content. Beware, however. They are not all created equal. According to a recent study by the Research Institute in Princeton, New Jersey, not one of the top 11 major Internet search engines indexed more than 16 percent of the Web. Northern Light ranked first in the sheer number of Web pages cataloged for a specific query, followed by Snap, AltaVista, HotBot, Microsoft, Infoseek, Google, Yahoo, Excite, and Lycos. Because none of the search engines is keeping up with Web growth, multiple searches with several engines are necessary, say the researchers. Further, most Web content is commercial, such as company home pages, which make up a whopping 82 percent! Trailing far behind are other noncommercial sites (often with .org, .net, or .edu URL addresses).[2]

In addition to the library and Internet, don't overlook the relevance and practicality of interviewing professionals in your area and even your peers on campus. Quoting experts or peers from an interview that you conduct gives you enhanced credibility. It showcases your investigative prowess and your creativity. If you want an area professional, begin with the phonebook. If you want a faculty member, consult a campus directory and your university's media guide or Web site, and, of course, use faculty from your own classes. Keep in mind the following tips for successful interviewing in person, over the phone, or by e-mail:

• Identify yourself and your intention clearly.
• Have prepared a focused, short set of open-ended questions.
• Check the credentials of your source.
• Thank the people you interview for their time.

Remember to be respectful in your requests for information from area experts and recognize that they are busy people who may not be able to assist you at your convenience. Following up with a note or call of appreciation shows your professionalism in the research transaction. One of the best ways to involve classmates in the research process is to formulate a brief survey for in-class distribution. This does two things: (1) it is a great way to tailor your rhetorical act to the needs of your specific audience; and (2) it adds relevance to the evidence gathering process because it is highly personalized. Students are curious about what others like them think and believe.

Specific Sources

When you have gathered material from general sources, you will need more detailed information and specialized analyses. Material in books is likely to be more comprehensive, based on more research, and drawing on a variety of sources. Because book publication takes time, such material is not as contemporary as that found in current newspapers and periodicals and on-line sources. Reading books on your subject will give you general background and a familiarity with research already done; on the other hand, if you have a "hot" or emerging topic, there may be no books on it, or such material may be out of date.

One efficient way to search for contemporary material is through computerized databases. In exploring the library, you may have learned something about the available and useful sources for doing research via computers and some basic information about gaining access to those databases. Remember that every filing system, including computerized library catalogs and indexes, reflects a way of looking at reality. Because your perceptions and those of the catalogers may differ, prepare a list of subjects related to your topic so you search under a variety of headings.

Each computerized library has an on-line system, which includes a catalog of most of the books and periodicals in the library's collections, as well as many indexes of periodicals and newspapers. Through your personal computer you can gain access to the on-line system of the library you intend to use before you actually go there. Most universities make available telephone numbers that you dial in order to connect your computer to the on-line system.

Another useful computer system is CD-ROM (Compact Disc, Read-Only Memory), which is a technology that uses optical discs produced and read by means of a laser. CD-ROMs are a powerful research tool in retrieving information relevant to your speech topic. Periodical Abstracts Ondisc and Newspaper Abstracts Ondisc, for example, are two CD-ROM products. The Periodical Abstracts Ondisc includes indexing and brief abstracts of articles, published from 1986 to 1994, in over 1,300 general-interest, scholarly, and trade periodicals covering current events, as well as the arts, science, health, business, and consumer-related topics. The Newspaper Abstracts Ondisc includes indexing and brief abstracts to eight major national newspapers, including the *New York Times*, *Wall Street Journal*, *Chicago Tribune*, and *Los Angeles Times*.

The *Readers' Guide to Periodical Literature* is an index to general subscription magazines from 1900 to the present. (The first page lists the periodicals that are included.) You will need to go to this source if you are looking for information prior to the 1980s.

Another large and helpful index is that of the *Congressional Record*, a record of debates in Congress, which contains articles and items that are inserted in it by members of Congress. As a result, it covers many topics and contains much useful information.

Some newspapers, including the *New York Times*, the *Wall Street Journal*, and the *Washington Post*, also have print indexes. Check to see which newspaper indexes your library holds, keeping in mind that if you seek information from an unindexed newspaper, you will need to have a rough idea of the dates on which material appears or face a long search.

In addition to the computerized indexes discussed above, you might go to the *Humanities Index* and the *Social Sciences Index*, which list articles published in scholarly journals.

There are also print indexes to special kinds of information. For example, the *Book Review Digest* and the *Index to Book Reviews in the Humanities* will guide you to what reviewers have said about books you may be using as sources, and the *Dramatic Criticism Index* cites reviews of plays. Again, check to see which are available via computer, and which can be searched only in the reference room.

Most students have a greater comfort level with finding specific Internet resources. Remember, as discussed earlier in the chapter, not to overestimate the amount and relevance of information on the Web. At the risk of listing Web sites that may no longer be available once this book is in print (the dynamic feature of the Web allows for timely postings that may last only a short time), you may find the following sites useful for preparing rhetorical acts of interest to college students and, in particular, students with an interest in communication issues.

General Sources:	www.refdesk.com
	www.britannica.com
Government Sources:	www.access.gpo.gov
	www.firstgov.gov
	www.thomas.loc.gov
Media Literacy and	www.medialit.org
Consumer Advocacy:	www.mediachannel.org
	www.publiccitizen.org
	www.adcritic.com
	www.filmcritic.com
News and Information:	www.c-span.org
	www.totalnews.com
	www.tvnews.vanderbilt.edu
	www.vote-smart.org
	www.allcampus.com
	www.assignmenteditor.com
	www.powerreporting.com
	www.ire.org
	www.drudgereport.com
History:	www.historyplace.com
	www.greatwomen.org
	www.historychannel.com
	www.biography.com

Once you have decided to use a Web site for evidence, you must carefully evaluate it, much more so than traditional library sources, because there is no gatekeeper, no editor of the World Wide Web. Everything from science to scams, from fact to fiction competes for your attention, often with no ratings, citations, authorship, or seals of approval. If you're not vigilant, it's highly likely you'll be duped into thinking a study is valid when on closer scrutiny it turns out to be the ranting of a nonexpert. You may remember that in 1996 when TWA Flight 800 crashed mysteriously off the Long Island coast, one veteran ABC newsman and former press secretary for President Kennedy, Pierre Salinger, claimed on national television that he had evidence that a U.S. Navy missile shot down the plane. That information was erroneous. Salinger later apologized for getting his information from the Internet and thinking it was true![3]

The check sheet in Figure 3–1, courtesy of Michigan State University Libraries (http://www.lib.msu.edu),[4] itemizes what is necessary to confirm the value of your Web site.

In Chapter 11, you will be exposed to four general standards of evaluation for all rhetorical acts (effects, truth, ethics, and aesthetics); here the evaluative tips are more focused. You must ascertain what expertise (*authority*) the author of your Web site has. Sometimes this is tricky and requires e-mailing the Webmaster for credentials. You must try to corroborate (*verify*) the information on your site by using "links" to other sites that claim much the same thing. You must discover when the site was last updated (*timeliness*) to know whether data, especially statistical data are still valid. You must articulate how your Web site is appropriate (*relevant*) for the topic under investigation. Is it one that scholars or enthusiasts visit with some frequency? You must keep an eye out

Figure 3–1
*Assessing Internet
Sources*

- AUTHORITY
- VERIFIABLITY
- TIMELINESS
- RELEVANCE
- BIAS
- ORDERLINESS
- CLARITY
- VALIDITY

for hidden agendas (*bias*). Although the site may have an authoritative name, such as "government action," the domain name may be purchased by an advocacy group with interests that slant the content presented. You must make some judgment on navigational ability (*orderliness*) and ease of digesting material (*clarity*). Some sites are maddeningly frustrating to browse. This lack of artistry is more than a cosmetic distraction. It should make you suspicious about the authenticity (*validity*) of its content and the sophistication of its authors.

As a credible rhetor, you will also need to know the qualifications and experience of persons you quote as authorities from printed library sources. Among the special references that can help you are the *Directory of American Scholars, American Men and Women of Science,* and *Who's Who in America*. Sources such as these will help you judge the authority and credibility of a source and indicate to the audience how much weight should be given to a person's statement.

As you expand your knowledge of library and Internet resources, you will find that you are expanding your abilities as a rhetor.

ORGANIZING YOUR MATERIAL

Chapter 6 discusses organization in detail. You may wish to consult that chapter when you have finished reading this material. What follows are some preliminary and general considerations to use in limiting your topic and in planning the structure of your rhetorical act.

Narrowing or Limiting Your Topic

Most rhetorical acts are relatively brief, a five- to seven-minute speech or a 1,500-word essay. Our culture is fastpaced; even most presidential addresses can be fitted into a half-hour for transmission by television or radio. Because of school schedules, speeches and essays for classes have to be fairly short. Your first concern, then, is to narrow your topic. Three questions will help you do this:

focuses attention 1. What parts of this topic are most significant and interesting for this audience?

circumstances 2. What parts of this topic are most important, serious, or have the broadest implications?

clarity & simplification 3. What aspect of the topic is most easily explained or what aspect can be discussed most fully in the time or space allotted?

The first question focuses your attention on the audience. What aspects of the topic will be new to them? What parts of the topic touch their lives or are directly related to their immediate circumstances? As an example, imagine that you want to talk about energy problems. Most college students do not pay utility bills directly, and some do not own cars, so the price of gas may not be salient. Few live in houses heated by solar energy; in most cases, few will have the necessary expertise to compare coal and gas as sources of energy. If there is no nuclear plant in the area and none proposed, even the dangers of nuclear power may not be particularly relevant.

Assume, however, that student activity fees have been raised because of the increased costs of heating and cooling the student union, and that fees for board and room in dormitories have been raised for the same reason. Some research leads to the discovery that these buildings waste energy because of the way they were built. Perhaps your topic should be narrowed to the relationship between architecture and construction and energy consumption. Recognize that you are trying to alter the perceptions of this particular audience, and that your first concern should be to approach the topic so that its significance for them is apparent.

The second question is designed to fit your subject to the particular circumstances of the audience. Consider here what any audience should know about this subject. On the basis of your research, you may decide that the problems of nuclear energy are the most pressing despite their remoteness from the immediate concerns of the audience. If so, you need to think carefully about how you can make this facet of the energy question significant for the audience. You might decide to begin with the nuclear plants built more than 20 years ago, which are now obsolete, but no one knows how to protect, make safe, or dismantle them. Such dangers can be made concrete and personal for a community and for individuals. Members of the audience can identify with dangers to people like themselves and to communities similar to their own.

Whatever facet of the subject you choose, this second question will help you explain to the audience why you have chosen it. If you decide to discuss the relationship between building construction and fossil fuel consumption, you may need to explain briefly why you are not discussing nuclear power but instead have selected what may appear to be a less important part of the subject of energy. (Obviously, the need for energy in general and for nuclear energy in particular would be lessened if consumption dropped. You might argue that that makes the question of construction an important one.)

The third question, what aspect of the topic can be treated fully in the time or space allotted, is designed to call the rhetor's attention to clarity and intelligibility. In Chapters 8 through 10, which examine the rhetorical problem, I discuss the problems created by the complexity of some topics and purposes. The decision you make on this question is intended to simplify appropriately so the audience will understand what you are discussing.

For example, the problems of energy are many, and each is complex. The problems of nuclear power alone cannot be discussed in five minutes or in 1,500 words. In order to make sense of the subject, you might decide to limit your discussion entirely to the problem of what to do with existing nuclear plants that are out of date. This choice ignores a great deal—whether there is sufficient uranium, whether nuclear wastes can be disposed of, whether the products of breeder reactors can be kept from terrorists, whether alternative energy sources exist, and on and on. But it focuses on a concrete problem that already exists: At the year 2000, there were more than 100 inactive atomic plants, and hundreds of smaller nuclear installations, such as nuclear medicine facilities and navy ship reactors, have ceased to operate. All of them will stay radioactive for hundreds or even thousands of years, and they remain a serious threat.

A rhetorical act on this subject may be a case study of the problems of nuclear power, as a concrete way for you to explore the kinds of problems that exist in the use of atomic energy. It's important, it's concrete, and it's sufficiently limited to be explained and explored in a relatively short rhetorical act. In other words, the third question should bend your energies toward finding a facet of the subject that you can cover thoroughly and clearly in the time or space allotted.

In sum, narrowing the topic should take into consideration the ways in which the subject is significant for the audience, the most important facets of the topic, and which aspects of the subject can be treated fully and carefully in a limited time or space.

Choosing a Thesis

Narrowing your topic leads naturally into the most important decision you make about organization: the selection of a thesis. Ordinarily, the general purpose of a rhetorical act is determined by the occasion or assignment. For example, editorials, feature stories, and general news stories have rather clearly defined general purposes, but writers must choose how they will translate the general purpose into a specific purpose. Occasions for speeches also usually define a general purpose—commencement speakers are expected to praise the new graduating class and talk about their future; sermons are intended to reinforce belief; reports are expected to provide information and create understanding. In each case, the rhetor must decide just how he or she will translate the general purpose into a specific thesis.

Deciding on a thesis or central idea is difficult, and you should expect to find it troublesome. First, it represents a commitment that is hard to make—"I want the audience to know and understand precisely this: 'Storage facilities for nuclear wastes cannot be guaranteed safe for longer than 20 years.'" When you choose such a thesis, you make a claim to knowledge; in effect you say, "I have researched this topic, and I stake my credibility and authority on the accuracy of my research." In addition, you eliminate material and limit yourself drastically. In this case, all research that does not bear directly on storage of nuclear wastes must be discarded, so the choice of a thesis is a decision that specifies the precise claim you want to make and represents a drastic limitation of the topic. The thesis should be a simple declarative sentence that answers the question, "Just what do I want the audience to know or understand (or believe or do) when I finish?"

Here are some examples of good theses:

Building a solar home or converting a home to solar energy are practical solutions to the energy crunch for individuals.

Note that the topic is narrowed in two ways: to solving the energy problem for individuals (not industry, for example) and to solar energy. It is a good thesis because it focuses on practicality. As the audience for this rhetorical act, we would expect to hear about costs of building and conversion, availability of materials, ease of construction, availability of materials and knowledge for maintenance, climatic conditions needed, and so forth. It is also good because the claim of the rhetor is explicit and clear, and we know how to judge whether or not the claim is adequately supported.

Nuclear breeder reactors are unsafe.

This is a larger and more difficult claim that is aimed at a speech to formulate belief. It is good, however, because it narrows the topic to breeder reactors and because it narrows the perspective to questions of safety. As an audience, we would expect such a rhetorical act to focus on the problems of disposing of plutonium wastes and of preventing nuclear material suitable for explosive devices from falling into unauthorized hands.

The maximum safe speed limit is 55 mph.

This is a good thesis because the claim is specific—the fastest safe speed limit is 55 mph. Note that it ignores questions of energy altogether and focuses only on questions of safety. We would, as an audience, expect to hear about reaction times, stopping distances at various speeds, statistics on auto deaths, and the relation of auto deaths to speed. Note again that the thesis is clear, explicit, and limiting.

Here are some poor thesis statements:

The deregulation of natural gas.

This is poor because it isn't a sentence and doesn't make a claim. It isn't clear what we are to know or understand about deregulation. That makes it a poor thesis, although it narrows the subject to natural gas and to questions about the relationship between price, availability, and government controls. Contrast this statement with a more explicit version:

The deregulation of natural gas will increase both the supply and the price.

Here is a poor statement that reflects a common error:

How a nuclear plant runs.

It is not a sentence and does not state a purpose or a goal. One may rightly ask, why should I know or care about how a nuclear plant runs? The thesis ought to give an answer. Contrast this statement with a more explicit one:

A nuclear power plant has a major impact on the environment.

This claim cannot be substantiated without explaining how a plant runs, but it also says, Here's why you should know how it runs.

Recall that you, as rhetor, must always concern yourself with relevance and significance. Just as you may ask about classes and lecture materials, Why should I learn that? Your audience always asks, Why should I know? Why should I care? What difference does it make to me? Your thesis should be a statement that gives an answer.

People should drive more carefully.

This statement is a sentence, and it has a purpose, but it's hard to imagine how anyone could disagree. It's also hard to see how it could be developed or argued. No matter how careful drivers are, they could still drive more carefully. This seems to put the statement beyond argument. Just what is meant by "more carefully"? That general phrase, open to many interpretations, ought to be translated into more concrete terms: not driving while on medication, while ill, while drunk, or in a car with poor brakes. A speech or essay on a particular kind of carelessness would come to grips with an issue that should challenge you and the audience.

People drive too fast.

This statement is a sentence, and it has a purpose. Its problems arise from its generality. The rhetor who uses this thesis will be all right if she or he narrows and specifies in the speech or essay just what benefits are to be derived from slower driving, although "too fast" is vague. Contrast it with a more specific statement:

You can save lives and money by obeying the 55 mph speed limit.

The following sentence is a problem because it contains two theses and implies two different rhetorical acts:

We must build nuclear power plants and convert industries to coal.

Each claim is adequate separately, but the rhetorical act that combines them will be at odds with itself. Each claim could be stated more clearly. "There is no economically feasible alternative to nuclear power," for example, is a clearer statement of the first claim. It is still general, and it implies that the speaker will prove that natural gas, oil, solar energy, geothermal energy, and coal will all be proved inadequate. Actually, the only economically feasible alternative to nuclear energy that has been proposed, at least in the short run, is coal, so the best statement would be:

Our supplies of coal are inadequate to meet our energy needs.

That statement explains why the two theses were combined. If coal is not adequate to our needs, then nuclear plants will have to be built (unless we reduce consumption greatly). In this case, however, the rhetor should consider whether both of these claims can be treated in a single rhetorical act, given constraints of space or time.

A good thesis statement should

- State a specific claim
- Express a single unified purpose
- Indicate significance and relevance

You will have conquered many of the problems of organizing your material when you have decided on a thesis and stated it clearly. As will be evident from the examples I have given, clearly stated theses imply the internal organization of the speech or essay. The structure of your rhetorical act is the development of your thesis. The main points of the rhetorical act should be statements (sentences making claims) that prove and explain the thesis. These main points should answer the questions: Why? or How do I know? For example, the thesis "The deregulation of natural gas will increase both the supply and the price" implies a two-part development:

A. It will increase the supplies available across state lines.
B. It will raise the interstate price to the level of the intrastate price.

The statement "Nuclear breeder reactors are unsafe" implies that the main points will give reasons why such power plants are unsafe.

A. There are no safe methods for storing plutonium wastes.
B. There is no way to prevent the theft of plutonium.

Note that these reasons will need to be developed, in turn, by statements that show how the rhetor knows these things to be true or highly probable.

The specific purpose, making people believe that "The maximum safe speed limit is 55 mph," suggests a development with main points like these:

A. Under ideal conditions, a car traveling at 55 mph requires a distance of more than seven car lengths to stop.
B. Road and weather conditions limit visibility and maneuverability.
C. Reaction times of drivers are increased by age, medications, and the consumption of alcohol.
D. The substantial decline in deaths in auto accidents since the speed limit has been lowered demonstrates the greater safety of lower speeds.

For your initial exercise, you should do only two additional things to organize your material: indicate how you will develop these main points, and plan an introduction and conclusion. For example, if you were to take as a thesis the statement "The 55 mph speed limit on our highways saves lives and money," your outline might look like this:

A. The 55 mph speed limit is better suited to actual driving conditions.
   1. Under ideal conditions, an alert, healthy driver needs about seven car lengths to stop a car going 55 mph.
      a. This distance includes reaction time (thinking distance) and braking distance.
      b. Small increases in speed make a difference because the distance needed to stop and the force of impact increase geometrically.
   2. Many drivers aren't in ideal condition.
      a. We have an aging population that will see and hear less well and react less quickly.
      b. Medicines and alcohol are even bigger problems.
         (1) Over-the-counter remedies affect driving ability.
         (2) Many commonly used prescription drugs are a serious threat to safe driving.
         (3) Even relatively small amounts of alcohol impair driving ability.
   3. Road and weather conditions are often less than ideal.
      a. Many sections of our best highways are in poor condition.
      b. More limited visibility at night has always required lower speed limits.
      c. Rain, as well as ice and sleet, is a serious driving hazard, especially on limited access roads.
   4. Many cars are poorly maintained.
B. The 55 mph speed limit also saves lives.

1. Since its enactment, for the first time in our history, there has been a dramatic drop in the number of highway fatalities.
2. This drop is caused by lower speeds as well as less travel.
C. The 55 mph speed limit also saves money and energy.
   1. Most cars burn fuel with maximum efficiency at about 50 mph.
   2. Efficient gas use by all Americans saves energy.

Now two things need to be added, an introduction and a conclusion. The introduction should get the attention of the audience and indicate the significance of the topic. If you chose this topic because of a tragic or near-tragic personal experience, that story might be the ideal way to begin. A student who made a speech on this topic came to class scratched and bruised. He told of his and his companions' miraculous survival in an accident in which the driver had avoided a head-on collision only by taking to the ditch and hitting a tree. He told the story of the accident, reported that they had been traveling between 60 and 65 mph, and said that he, personally, was now convinced that speed kills. He talked about his attitude and the attitudes of other people he knew about the 55 mph limit. He said his purpose was to defend that limit, not just because it saved energy, but because it also saved lives. That was a superb introduction. It was vivid, personal, attention-getting. It located accurately the attitudes of the audience. It showed his personal commitment to the topic and purpose. It prepared us for what followed; we knew what to expect. In other words, a good introduction:

- Gets attention
- Shows relevance
- Previews main points

> Good intro

In this case, the introduction also showed the relationship between the rhetor and the subject, a highly desirable characteristic of introductions.

The conclusion of a rhetorical act is good if it is such that the act ends rather than stops. Ideally, a conclusion should do two things:

- Summarize the major ideas
- Fix the specific purpose in the audience's mind

> good conclusion

You need to plan carefully just how you will end. In the case of the student who had the near-tragic accident, the speaker said something like this: "I've shown you that if you are healthy and alert, if your car is in good mechanical condition, and if you're driving 55 mph, it will take you 218 feet from the time you see a problem until you can stop. If you're tired, if you've had a drink or have taken an antihistamine, if your tires are worn or your brake fluid is down, if it is dusk or raining, it will take you longer. When you drive over 55, you are not only breaking the law and wasting gas, you also may be driving too fast to avoid an accident. And I've got the cuts and bruises to prove it."

That conclusion is simple and effective. It recalls most of the major ideas of the speech so it summarizes, but it does so in concrete terms that will be relevant and intelligible to each member of the audience. That helps to make each idea memorable. In addition, the speaker uses himself as a vivid visual reminder of the dangers of fast driving. The conclusion illustrates another useful technique for concluding—the explicit reference to an anecdote or example that was used in the introduction. This creates the effect of "completing a circle" and hence creates a strong impression of completeness.

> Refer back to intro in conclusion

PREPARING YOUR PRESENTATION

The quality of your final presentation depends on your skills as a critic and on your willingness to practice or rewrite. You can develop and refine your critical skills through preparing the strategy report described at the end of the chapter. A strategy report is a written analysis of the choices you made in preparing your rhetorical act, in light of the obstacles you faced and your purpose. In addition, if the act is oral, you must practice it aloud, standing, and, at the same time, try to imagine yourself as a member of the audience. If your act is written, you must learn to polish and refine your efforts through rewriting, a process made much easier if you use a wordprocessor.

At this point, you have an outline that states the specific purpose, lists the main points, and cites the evidence you will use to explain and prove your assertions. You have made some rough notes for what you will say in the introduction and conclusion. You now need to move from the outline toward the composition of a complete and finished rhetorical act. Your first concern should be clarity. Focus your attention on two areas: the clarity of the relationships among ideas and the clarity of each piece of evidence you will present.

The clarity of the relationships among the main ideas depends on the soundness of the argument's structure and on the kinds of transitions or bridges made between ideas. If you have done your outline carefully and have made certain that your main points answer the questions Why? and How do I know? the relationships among the main points should be clear. There is a relatively simple test you can apply to determine the adequacy of your argument. If your main points are A, B, C, and D, then, if the argument is sound, the following should apply:

If A is true, if B is true, if C is true, and if D is true, then it should follow that the claim you make in your specific purpose is true.

If you apply this test to the outline about 55 mph speed limits, you will notice the "fit" between the main points and the specific purpose. The material under A.1, however, will need some explanation to show how these figures were arrived at. In main point A.3, the rhetor is saying that ideal driving conditions rarely exist. After you eliminate stretches of limited access superhighways, the places with the best visibility, fewest traffic problems, and best surface, driving hazards are likely to increase. That needs to be clear as the argument is presented. Point A.2 is saying that even young and healthy persons can have slowed reactions from cold medicine or a couple of beers, and this needs to be emphasized. Also, the audience may wonder about enforcement—are people really driving more slowly? If you think about the whole argument, you will realize that the rhetor is admitting that there may be places and persons and times that it's safe to drive faster than 55 mph; but he or she is saying that 55 mph is the maximum realistic speed limit, and a speed limit should not be set for ideal but for real and normal driving conditions. The rhetorical act should emphasize that point if it is to be effective. Note that such a survey of the outline helps to clarify for the rhetor just what the purpose is, what should be emphasized, and what qualifications may need to be made, as for example, the recognition that it might be safe to drive faster under some conditions. In spite of such qualifications, you can make a strong and forceful argument, and by qualifying your claim you may avoid resistance from members of the audience who recognize exceptions.

Transitions are statements made to ensure that the audience understands and recognizes the relationships among ideas. Although some members of your audience will listen or read actively, testing your arguments and trying to understand, others will listen or read more passively and will not see relationships unless you make them explicit. Here are some examples of transitions that might be used in the rhetorical act on 55 mph speed limits:

> A good speed limit is geared to averages—normal reaction time, normal mechanical conditions, normal conditions of visibility and road surfaces. As a result, I'll begin by talking about optimums—ideal reaction time, ideal mechanical conditions, ideal visibility and road conditions. But I'll also talk about the use of common medications and alcohol and about the conditions of roads and the problems of weather.

That statement creates connections and also previews what will happen in the speech. It is the sort of transition that usually connects the attention-getting introduction to the body of the rhetorical act (the section that develops the specific purpose). It clarifies by creating expectations: Here is what I shall do and here is the general relationship among all these ideas.

The next transition explains two parts of one subpoint: the distance it takes to stop a car at a particular speed.

> Two elements are involved in stopping a car: thinking distance and braking distance. The first refers to the distance you will travel during your reaction time. The second refers to the distance you travel after you've stepped on the brakes. It is a measure of the distance it takes for your car to stop mechanically. Let's consider reaction times first.

This transition clarifies by reminding the audience that there are two parts and allows the speaker to talk about each separately while creating in the audience an awareness of their relationship.

The next transition is really an explanation of how you and the highway department arrived at certain conclusions:

> To understand how far you travel at different speeds, the State Highway Department talks in feet per second. The math works like this: there are 5,280 feet in a mile. At speed 60, you travel one mile per minute or 5,280 divided by 60 or 88 feet per second.

The transition clarifies by explaining, but it also shows the relationships among speed, reaction time, and the distance it takes to stop.

Here's another kind of transition and explanation, one on the deregulation of natural gas:

> I've shown you how and why federal deregulation will increase the supplies of natural gas across state lines. What I've told you should make it pretty obvious that increased supplies depend on and are a result of higher prices for interstate gas shipments. In fact, deregulation will raise interstate prices to the intrastate level and will probably raise the prices for both in a few years.

This is a transition between two main points to indicate their relationship to each other. In addition, the transition is a preview of what the rhetor intends to do under the second main point. It clarifies by showing the relationship between these two parts of the argument.

Practicing aloud and editing/rewriting are the processes by which rhetors prepare oral and written rhetorical acts, respectively. Both are essential to produce a good final product. Practicing aloud serves two purposes: First, it creates a physical memory of what you intend to say that will help you speak smoothly. It prevents your oral presentation before the audience from being especially frightening because it is the first time you make your speech. Part of the fear associated with speaking is the fear each of us has about doing things that are new and different and in which we feel unskilled. You can diminish that by oral practice. Stand up as if you were before the audience, hold your notes as you intend to, and speak your speech as you plan to on the actual occasion. If there are tongue twisters, you'll find them and be able to overcome them or make changes. If there's complicated material that's hard to explain, you'll discover it and have time to make some changes. Moreover, by the time you give your speech, it won't be the first time—it will be the ninth or tenth—and the material will feel familiar when you begin your speech. Second, it is the means for refining and reorganizing. For example, you practice your 5-minute speech aloud, and it runs 15 minutes or what was supposed to run 1,500 words actually runs 3,000. Clearly, you haven't narrowed the topic enough, and you need to do some cutting. Or, as you listen to yourself or read what you've written, you realize that to be clear you have to add something—and you figure out how to add it and how to make the idea clearer. Please note, however, that none of these benefits occurs unless you read your work with the critical eye of a stranger or practice aloud exactly as if you were presenting the speech to your audience and listen to yourself critically. You must pretend to be your own audience, listening to the speech or reading the essay as someone unfamiliar with the subject. It is such listening and reading that enables you to catch problems and make needed changes. (Of course, you can also snag a cooperative roommate or friend and ask that person to respond candidly about questions and problems that arise in reading or listening to what you say. But such a person is only a poor substitute for developing your abilities as your own best listener and editor.)

Your speech should be presented from notes, not from a manuscript on which you have written out, word by word, what you intend to say. Presenting a speech from a manuscript is a difficult skill, as illustrated by the varying skills of presidents in reading from a TelePrompter. Do not add to your problems by attempting this in the initial exercise. Tailor your notes to your personal needs. You might decide to memorize the introduction and write only one or two words from it on a card. You may need a chain of terms to create associations to help you remember all the elements of the story you want to tell and the order you want to follow.

After these terms, write a phrase or word that will suggest the transition into the thesis or specific purpose, and then write out the purpose in full. Next write a word or phrase suggesting the transition into the first main point and write this main point out in full. You should depart from outline or key term form only for evidence that should be written out in full so you can cite it accurately and completely, along with its source. Here is an example of the notes for the speech on the 55 mph speed limit:

(*intro.*) alive today bec lucky
Friday nite, returning from KC, hwy 10, 60–65 mph, car passing, head-on collision

	couldn't stop, into ditch, hit tree, injuries—minor bec of seat belts
	I now believe speed kills
(trans.)	attitudes of others; possible change in national policy
(thesis)	The 55 mph speed limit saves lives and money.
(trans.)	ideal vs. real: reaction time, mechanical condition of car, road, and weather conditions

A. 55 mph better for actual driving conditions
  1. Under ideal conditions, ideal driver needs 7 car lengths to stop going 55 mph.
     a. Combines reaction time (thinking distance) and braking distance

(evidence)   At 55 mph, travel 80.66 ft. per second, so takes 218 ft. to stop from time see problem
Ks. Driving Handbook, p. 42

(trans.)   what difference if lower only 5–15 mph?
     b. Small increases in speed make big difference.

(evidence)   Distance needed to stop and force of impact increase geometrically; if double speed, 4 times distance to stop. Ks. Driving Handbook, p. 42.

(trans.)   but drivers, roads, and cars aren't in ideal condition
  2. Many drivers aren't in ideal shape.
     a. aging population
(evidence)   b. over-the-counter remedies, e.g., Dristan or Sinutabs.
        Ks. Driving Handbook, p. 46.
     c. warnings about drowsiness on prescription drugs, e.g., tranquilizers, pain remedies, antihistamines
     d. alcohol

(evidence)   Driving is impaired by as little as 1 drink of whiskey or 2 beers.
Ks. Driving Handbook, p. 46.

(trans.)   boast of our fine roads, but many problems, and these compounded by weather

(evidence)   3. Many sections of best highways in poor condition, e.g., Interstate 80. NYTimes, 6/18/94
     4. Weather conditions: ice and sleet obvious; also rain esp. on limited-access highways.

(evidence)   hydroplaning: when so much water on highway tires can't "wipe" the road so car starts to run on film of water. Starts at 35 mph, by 55 car traveling entirely on water and out of control. Ks. Driving Handbook, p. 45.

(trans.)   can be more realistic and save money and energy and lives
B. 55 mph saves lives
  1. For first time in history, sudden and dramatic drop in number of highway fatalities.
(evidence)   Motor Trend, August 1994, p. 37.
  2. Drop came from a combination of less travel and less speed.

<table>
<tr><td>*(evidence)*</td><td>Study of 31 turnpikes showed that traffic was down 18% but fatalities were down 60%. *Motor T,* p. 38.
C. 55 mph also saves $ and energy.</td></tr>
</table>

                     1. Most cars burn fuel with maximum efficiency at about 50 mph, so get most for gas $.

                     2. Efficient gas use by all Americans would save energy—travel farther on energy $

(concl.)   if healthy and alert
if car well maintained
if drive 55, need 7 car lengths to stop
    BUT
if tired, had a drink, or taken an antihistamine
if tires worn or brake fluid down
if dusk, night, raining
—takes longer
when drive over 55, breaking law, wasting gas
may also be driving too fast to prevent accident
I have cuts and bruises to prove it.

As you practice, add whatever notes you need for changes or additions. Be sure that what you have written on the cards is easily legible. Hold your notes slightly above waist level and use them every time you practice. Do not try to avoid looking at them (you will lose your place, fail to shift the cards as you progress, and have to search desperately if you need to consult them). Practice looking at them regularly, and plan to consult each card, moving the top card to the bottom as you finish the ideas it covers. Stand up firmly, speak aloud, try to imagine the audience in front of you. Practice until you can present the whole speech smoothly and easily. When your moment arrives, you will be well prepared to make a competent presentation.

The suggestions in Figure 3–2 include tips designed to help you remember that effective rhetorical acts must be poetic and pragmatic.

Figure 3–2
Message Tips

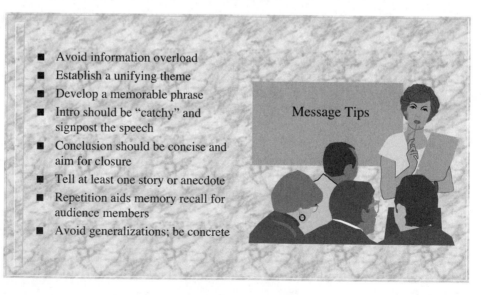

- Avoid information overload
- Establish a unifying theme
- Develop a memorable phrase
- Intro should be "catchy" and signpost the speech
- Conclusion should be concise and aim for closure
- Tell at least one story or anecdote
- Repetition aids memory recall for audience members
- Avoid generalizations; be concrete

Message Tips

DELIVERING A SPEECH

Concerns about delivery are closely related to communication apprehension or stage fright. As discussed at the outset of this chapter, fears about speaking are normal and appropriate. Speaking involves a social risk, and we fear isolation from and rejection by others. In most speaking situations, the audience clusters together in comfortable anonymity while the speaker stands alone. Nonverbally, it feels as if it's you against them. Because rhetorical action asks for and requires the participation of others, every speaker risks rejection. In face-to-face situations, the evidence is immediate and unavoidable. Audience members send hundreds of nonverbal messages registering their responses. All good speakers, even those with much experience, feel some apprehension. On every occasion, a speaker takes responsibility for a commitment, is partially isolated from the audience, and chances a rebuff. Apprehension is recognition of what is involved in acting as a rhetor.

Such fears diminish greatly with practice, however. If you have prepared carefully and practiced aloud so that you are in command of your material, your fears will be manageable after a few sentences. Human beings are symbol-using creatures, and despite our fears, we take pleasure in communicating with others, in expressing our ideas and feelings. You will enjoy the experience even more if you consider the following bits of advice.

Preparing the Scene

Insofar as possible, take control of the scene. If you are speaking, arrive early and case the joint. If possible, move chairs so you lessen your distance from the audience. This will make you more comfortable and create an environment in which participation by the audience is easier. If the audience is scattered over a large area, ask them to move forward so that they are closer together. Unless the occasion is extremely formal, be sure that lights are arranged so that you can see the audience. Stage lighting separates you from the audience and turns you into a performer or entertainer, a role that can limit your rhetorical efforts.

In general, avoid the use of a lectern and stand in front of tables or desks. A lectern shuts off much of your nonverbal communication and reduces your immediacy. Both lessen ease of audience participation. Use a lectern or table if you will feel more comfortable behind one or if you are in a situation in which you must use a manuscript, but do everything you can to minimize the barrier between you and the audience. Try standing next to the lectern. In this way you will be able to rest one hand on the lectern, and yet you won't be as "fenced off" from the audience.

Check to ensure that all materials you need are present and working. Test the microphone and look for a blackboard or a place to put visual aids. If any machines are to be used, be sure that they are there and working. Nothing destroys your efforts more quickly than a tape recorder that won't work or a beautiful visual aid that keeps collapsing.

If there are problems that can't be solved, acknowledge them to the audience in good humor. Try to make them your confederates in struggling to cope with a cold room, a noisy radiator, a defective mike, or whatever. Your role as rhetor requires you to take charge of the scene and to be responsive to what goes on in it (Figure 3–3).

Figure 3–3
Preparation Tips

- Check out speaking location, sound system, platform
- Know where you are in the program and who introduces you
- Time your speech carefully to meet program restrictions
- Use large notecards; write large
- Don't memorize
- Be most familiar with opening and closing remarks
- Nervousness is normal
- Know your audience (composition, disposition, size)

Using Visual Aids

Audiovisual aids such as PowerPoint, charts, maps, pictures, posters, actual objects, demonstration assistants, handouts, and taped or filmed materials create special problems. Use them only when they contribute something essential to your presentation, and prepare them carefully. Visual aids are essential when presenting large amounts of statistical material or when ideas and relationships are difficult to explain verbally—for example, locations on maps.

Obviously, visual aids are a useful persuasive tool. As you prepare such aids, follow the general guidelines in Figure 3–4.

Figure 3–4
Visual Aid Tips

- Visuals must be a sidelight, not spotlight
- Limit visuals if you want them to be memorable
- Practice with visuals so delivery is seamless
- Do not talk to your visual aids!
- Position visuals so all audience members can see
- Don't clutter words on visuals
- Point specifically to key features of your visual aids
- Use visual aids when you need them, then remove them promptly
- Be prepared to give speech without visuals in the event of technological malfunction
- Avoid using a chalk or marker board or passing out items while you are speaking

Visual Aid Tips

Presenting Yourself

Dress with due consideration for the occasion, the role you will play, your purpose, and the expectations of the audience. Clothing is a major source of messages for the audience, and it can detract and distract. Follow these simple rules:

- Dress for comfort and ease of movement. Avoid tight, stiff clothing, high heels that wobble, or climbing shoes that squeak.
- Dress to avoid distraction. Avoid bright, busy, loud patterns that attract attention away from your message. Eliminate any item that can rattle, such as coins, keys, or bracelets.
- Dress in an outfit that is harmonious. Minimize the time the audience will spend remarking on your clothes.

Posture and Gesture. Before you begin to speak, walk slowly to the front of the room and position yourself comfortably. Do not begin to speak until you are standing firmly on both feet. You will create anticipation for what follows, and you will take charge of the scene. Avoid standing on one foot, rocking back and forth, and slouching. Arrange your hair so that it does not fall into your face, and avoid repetitive motions flicking it back. All of these distract from your message and suggest discomfort and lack of involvement. Feel free to move about, but move with purpose and for emphasis.

Hold your notes at chest level in one hand for easy reading and gesturing. Do not clasp your hands in front of you or behind you, fold your arms, or play with your notes. Avoid pointless or repetitious gestures. Aim for movement that will in no way distract from what you are saying. Never take a pen or pencil with you; it's easy to play with such an item without thinking, making it a major distraction, especially if you click it open and shut!

Your eyes are a major source of contact with the audience. To establish your involvement and to hold attention, you will be most effective with most U.S. audiences if you look at them directly. Be sure to include everyone. For the audience, your gaze is a primary indicator of immediacy, and, of course, you can't respond to messages from the audience unless you are looking at them.

Voice. The ideal speaking voice is easy to hear and pleasing to listen to. Good delivery involves vocal variety and patterns of pause and emphasis that increase our understanding of what is said. The most common vocal problem among novice speakers is speaking too fast for clear articulation or comprehension. Writing "slow down" on each note card is a useful reminder, and practicing at slower rates helps to change habits. Audiences may respond to rapid speech as dynamic, however, and most native speakers will be able to decode all but the most hurried speech.

These suggestions for delivery are grounded in the principles of nonverbal communication. As a rhetor, your goal is participation by the audience. Initiating joint action requires dynamism on your part. Your eyes, face, arms, and body should communicate your interest and involvement. Participation is made easier by indicators of immediacy such as lessening the distance between you and the audience and maintaining eye contact. As the initiator, you must establish your authority and competence. Gestures, posture, and physical relaxation all bespeak your competence. If rhetorical action is

Figure 3–5
Delivery Tips

- Take a slow, deep breath to begin on a strong note
- Aim for vocal variety
- Enthusiasm is contagious
- Don't abandon a conversational style
- To be articulate, lots of teeth must show
- Stand on balls of feet, knees slightly bent, thrust shoulders back to project confidence
- Locate friendly faces in you audience from various sections of the room and make sustained eye contact
- Allow sufficient pause time for audience response
- Are you having fun yet?

your goal, you must seek it both verbally and nonverbally. And remember that, while these hints may be helpful, preparing your speech carefully and practicing it aloud are probably the best ways to improve oral presentation (Figure 3–5).

STRATEGY REPORT

At this point you, the rhetor, have the preliminaries to produce your first rhetorical act and to do it with some competence. In the next chapters we explore the resources that are available to you as a speaker or writer.

For each rhetorical act, prepare a written strategy report to be turned in at the time of your presentation (Figure 3–6). The report makes explicit at least part of the process

Figure 3–6
Strategy Report

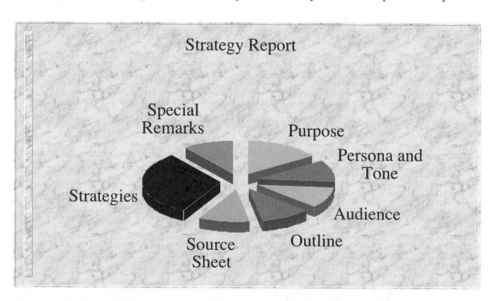

Strategy Report

Special Remarks · Purpose · Persona and Tone · Strategies · Audience · Source Sheet · Outline

you go through in preparing for rhetorical action. As such, it is not an end in itself but a tool for learning. It should help make you aware of the choices that you make in initiating rhetorical action.

The strategy report has seven parts, some of which can be quite short:

1. Purpose
2. Persona (role) and tone
3. Audience
4. Outline
5. Source sheet
6. Strategies
7. Special remarks

1. *Purpose*: First, try to define the rhetorical purpose of your speech in terms of the general response you seek from the audience: to alter perception, to explain, to formulate belief, to initiate action, to maintain belief or action. Recall that each of these purposes is related to assumptions you are making about what your audience knows, feels, and believes.

Second, state as briefly and precisely as you can what you would like the audience to know, feel, believe, or do when you are finished. In other words, indicate what you would consider ideal responses from your audience.

2. *Persona (role) and tone*: A speaker or writer assumes a persona or role in relation to the audience, and the tone of the language reflects her or his attitude toward the subject and relationship to the audience. Indicate whether you will speak as a peer or as an expert, and if you will shift roles during the act. Similarly, indicate whether your tone will be relatively impersonal and objective (appropriate for an expert, for instance) or personal and conversational (appropriate for a peer) or ironic (appropriate for a skeptic).

3. *Audience*: Discuss whether the exposed audience is your target audience and whether it includes agents of change. If there are discrepancies between those exposed and those you seek to reach or who can act (and if there are not, why rhetoric?), discuss some specific obstacles you face from this audience in transforming them into an ideal audience. Consider how you might appeal to them to play a real role that would lead them to respond as you desire.

4. *Outline*: With some practice, most students have little difficulty in making outlines. Look at the examples in Chapter 6 and be sure that your outline is in complete sentences, particularly as it expresses your thesis and your main points. Leave a wide margin on the left in order to label what you are doing at each point, such as kinds of evidence, transitions, organizational patterns, and strategies. Use the margin for an abbreviated descriptive analysis of your own rhetoric.

5. *Source sheet*: In preparing for a speech or essay, your personal experience and your imagination are important sources from which to draw material and shape it for your audience. But almost no one's personal experience is so broad or insight so penetrating that she or he cannot benefit from the knowledge in secondary sources or the challenge of responding to the ideas of others.

For each rhetorical act, provide a list of annotated sources—that is, sources with a short paragraph for each describing the nature of the source and what you used it for.

Sources may be of four types. Use all these types in rhetorical acts throughout this course so you become familiar with different kinds of resources.

a. Popular sources. Mass circulation newspapers and magazines are popular sources. Articles in *TV Guide* or *Newsweek* or your local newspaper are intended for general audiences. They provide useful evidence and often stimulate thinking. Most Internet material falls into this category.

b. Specialized sources. Periodicals intended for limited audiences of specialists are specialized sources. They present articles by experts for specialists, and they analyze more thoroughly topics that are discussed generally or superficially in popular sources. In the *Quarterly Journal of Speech, Signs, Foreign Affairs*, or the *Monthly Labor Review*, for example, you can gain greater understanding, gather data, and verify claims made in popular sources. You should learn to do research that takes you beyond the *Readers' Guide to Periodical Literature*.

   Note: A distinction between popular and specialized sources can be made, in many cases, between books written for the mass market and those written by specialists for a specialized audience.

c. Interviews. The world is full of all kinds of experts, and you should take the opportunity to talk to those available in your area on your subject. Such interviews, including the person's credentials, should be listed as part of your source materials.

d. Personal experience. You may have direct knowledge of your subject that goes beyond the ordinary. If you have such experience, and it is relevant to your subject, cite your own expertise and describe its nature. Be reminded, however, of the importance of testing your experience against data gathered by others and the opinions of experts.

Cite your sources in proper bibliographic form. Here are examples for a periodical and a book:

Lang, Susan S. "Sick Building Syndrome Linked to Fibers." *Human Ecology Forum* 22, no. 1 (Winter 1994): 4.

Clotfelter, Charles T., and Philip J. Cook. *Selling Hope: State Lotteries in America*. Cambridge, MA: Harvard University Press, 1989.

Here is an example from a URL address on the internet:

<http://www.c-span.org.html> 24 Nov. 2001.

If your source is an interview with an expert or personal experience, simply make a note of the nature of the interview or the experience. For example:

On October 20, 1992, I interviewed Diana Lisak, an assistant professor of psychology at the University of Massachusetts, Boston. She discussed research on the motivational factors underlying male sexual aggression, including examples from studies of 15 unreported rapists and 15 control subjects, that she believes suggest the importance of child-rearing practices in understanding the motivations of rapists.

From September 1987 to September 1989, I was a volunteer for the Sexual Violence Program at the University of Minnesota. As a result of my training and of my experience, I have detailed knowledge of the incidence of rape on a large urban Midwestern university campus and personal experience of the impact of rape, including acquaintance rape, on undergraduate women students' lives.

6. *Strategies:* It may take you only a sentence or two to describe your purpose, your persona and tone, and your audience, but it will take you several paragraphs to describe your strategies adequately. In this section, you must discuss the means you will use to achieve your purpose and the choices you will make to overcome the obstacles you face. Your statement should have two parts.

First, given your subject and purpose, how is your audience likely to respond? Here you should explore the rhetorical obstacles of complexity, cultural history, cost, control, and reasons that the audience might be hostile or indifferent to your subject or to what you propose (see Chapter 9).

Second, discuss specific choices you made to create your audience, to transform the exposed audience into the target audience and agents of change. Specifically, discuss your choice of perspective, evidence, organizational patterns, introductory and concluding remarks, appeals to needs or values, and statements made to indicate your relationship to the subject. Strategies should reflect the ways that you have adapted materials to your audience in order to achieve your purpose.

7. *Special remarks:* Use this section to discuss anything you believe significant that does not fit into the other sections. It may be that you have no special remarks, but many rhetorical acts are unusual, and you may need this section to talk about elements you believe are unique or out of the ordinary.

MATERIAL FOR ANALYSIS

Speaking to Explain
Student Speech 1: Schizophrenia
Jarrod Acquistapace[5]

Introduction:

I. Adam "was a wonderfully, sweet young man," his mother said. He was a high school athlete and captain of his soccer team, active in his college fraternity, a good student. He had graduated from college and started working while studying for a professional certification exam when something inside him changed. . . . Adam stopped being careful about his personal appearance. He told his parents he suspected them of communicating with each other in secret ways, such as in sign language, which he couldn't understand. He began to hear his mother's voice in his head and he asked her why she was sending him messages. . . . Adam was diagnosed with schizophrenia.

II. According to Dr. E. Fuller Torrey's book: *Surviving Schizophrenia*, 1 out of every 100 people will be directly affected by schizophrenia in their lifetime; and yet far too often this disease goes undiagnosed and unnoticed.

III. I for one never thought I would ever have any kind of mental illness, let alone something like schizophrenia; I was in the gifted program since the 6th grade, wrote music and played guitar, and was well liked in school. Certainly, I was exempt from this "bizarre" illness. Yet this is far from the truth. No one is invulnerable to this illness, as I have learned the hard way.

IV. Today, I want to explain to you what schizophrenia is, how it affects those afflicted, and what treatments are available.

Body:

I. So, what exactly is schizophrenia?

    A. First, we must know what schizophrenia is not.

        1. Those afflicted are not homicidal (January 2001 "Schizophrenia Update")

        2. Those afflicted are not retarded; hopefully, I am evidence of this.

    B. Now that we know what schizophrenia is not, we can effectively state what it is.

        1. (www.psychlaws.org; General Resources) Schizophrenia is a neurological brain disorder that affects 2.2 million Americans today, or approximately 1 percent of the population.

        2. Schizophrenia can affect anyone at any age, but most cases develop between ages 16 and 30.

        3. (www.psychlaws.org; Briefing Papers; Schizophrenia) Since the early 1980s, with the availability of brain imaging techniques and other developments in neuroscience, the evidence has become overwhelming that schizophrenia is a disease of the brain, just as multiple sclerosis, Parkinson's disease, and Alzheimer's disease are diseases of the brain.

          a. The brains of individuals with these diseases are measurably different from individuals who do not have these diseases, both structurally and functionally.

          b. Look at these brain images to see the differences (show visuals on Elmo). Notice

            • the enlarged ventricles of the brain

            • a reduced volume of gray matter in the brain

            • an enlarged part of the brain known as the amygdala

            • increased amounts of white matter

II. Now we know what schizophrenia is on a clinical level, how does it affect those afflicted?

    A. (www.psychlaws.org; General Resources) Schizophrenia interferes with a person's ability to think clearly, manage emotions, make decisions and relate to others.

    B. Specific abnormalities with schizophrenia include

        1. delusions and hallucinations (sometimes I think people are plotting against me)

        2. alterations of the senses (sometimes I experience what can best be described as "emotional flatness"—a kind of numbness to pain or joy)

        3. an inability to respond appropriately (you've seen me in class have trouble sitting still or staying engaged for long on a topic; some have erroneously concluded that I suffer from attention deficit disorder)

III. Now that we know how people are affected by schizophrenia, how can schizophrenia be treated?

    A. Hospitalization is often necessary in cases of acute schizophrenia.

        1. This is not the *One Flew Over the Cuckoo's Nest* experience. Rather, such treatment ensures the safety of the affected person and allows for observation by trained mental health professionals to determine whether schizophrenia is the appropriate diagnosis.

2. According to a friend of mine, who requested to remain anonymous, the structure of mental hospitals is usually tailored specifically to the individual, and allows for a little or a lot of social interaction depending on his or her current mental state.

B. Medication is also a common and effective treatment for schizophrenia.

1. (www.schizophrenia.com; An introduction to Schizophrenia) Antipsychotic drugs (also called neuroleptics), available since the 1950s, can dramatically improve the functioning of people with schizophrenia.

2. Once the most troubling symptoms are controlled by medication, the person often does not require hospitalization.

3. Medication also prevents harsh relapses by regulating symptoms that could otherwise get out of hand. I know this firsthand!

Conclusion:

I. I want you all to remember what Josh Lyman, Adult Compeer Coordinator, Mental Health Association of Central Kansas, told me: "While there is no cure for schizophrenia, it is a highly treatable disorder." In fact, he says, the treatment success rate for schizophrenia is comparable to the treatment success rate for heart disease!

II. I hope I have helped everyone understand what schizophrenia is, how it affects people, and how it can be treated.

III. If anyone has any questions about this illness or is worried about him or herself or loved ones, or would like more information on Schizophrenics Anonymous (I have brochures), don't hesitate to ask me in private, and I'll be happy to address your concerns.

Questions for Analysis

1. How well does this speech fulfill the rhetorical purpose of explaining? Does it adequately address the who, what, where, when, and why questions that such a purpose demands? Is this topic one that needs explaining? For whom? Is it frequently misunderstood? Mysterious? Complex? In other words, what subject-related rhetorical obstacles (see Chapter 9) are evident with this topic? What is the thesis? How does it involve another rhetorical purpose: to alter perception?

2. How does this speech illustrate suggestions made in this chapter for (1) how to pick a topic, (2) researching a subject, and (3) preparing your presentation? Analyze content carefully for strengths and weaknesses.

3. Do the introduction and conclusion meet all the criteria outlined in this chapter for what these parts of speech should accomplish? How?

4. What specific "Message Tips" do you see in this speech? Is the speech a strong example of how rhetoric should be poetic and pragmatic?

Speaking to Initiate Action
Student Speech 2: The Unfair Treatment of Arabs in U.S. Media
Saideh Eftekhari[6]

Introduction:

I. Last September, a twelve-year old Palestinian boy, Muhammad Al-Durrah and his father Jamal spent the afternoon in Gaza, Palestine, searching for a used car. They never found a car; rather, they found themselves crouching behind a concrete wall in an attempt to avoid Israeli troops' bullets. Four of those bullets found their way to Muhammad's abdomen and eventually caused this innocent boy's death. (Here is the picture of the incident—Show enlarged news photo on Elmo). Even the driver of the ambulance carrying Muhammad was shot and killed. This entire scene was captured by video. As a result, the whole world witnessed Muhammad's death. Months later, an image from the footage was entered into MSNBC's "Year in Pictures 2000" contest, where visitors to the Web site could vote for their favorite picture. According to a March 2, 2001, article in the *New York Times*, the "photo of the boy was the clear leader; but after a widespread e-mail campaign by supporters of Israel urging votes for any other photo. . . the photo of the boy dropped to sixth place" (Murphy). (Remove picture) This is just one example of the way in which Arabs are treated unfairly in the United States' media.

II. If we hope to improve our ties with the peoples of the Middle East, and if we hope for lasting peace in that region, we must strive for a more just and unbiased treatment of Arabs in our media.

III. In the next few minutes, I will explain the various problems of the media, provide some solutions to the problems, and show the benefits of those solutions to you.

Body:

I. The first things we should all be aware of are the various problems of the U.S. media in portraying Arabs.

    A. Many of these problems relate to the latest Palestinian uprising.

        1. When referring to the uprising, much of the U.S. media portray Arabs inaccurately and communicate a pro-Israeli bias.

            a. For example, Ali Abunimah, a media activist, states, "because the media talk about violence in Israel, the public is not made aware that the Israeli army is in Palestinian cities in violation of international law, or that all but two Israeli deaths occurred in occupied territory" (Adas 63).

            b. Also, Abunimah cites "a study by the Fairness and Accuracy in Reporting which found that only 4 of 99 U.S. network reports on the Middle East from September 28 to November 2, 2000 mentioned occupation," especially when referring to the West Bank and Gaza (Adas 63).

            c. Finally, Abunimah says that "the American media present the conflict as though it were between equally matched opponents, with the Israeli army defending itself from Palestinian gunmen," although "armed Israeli settlers are not called 'gunmen' and most of the Palestinians killed were civilians who were not carrying guns" (Adas 63).

    B. But even before the current uprising, the U.S. media portrayed Arabs inaccurately and communicated a pro-Israeli bias.

        1. For example, when on May 8, 1997, Amnesty International released a report on the Israeli government's use of torture, Peter Jennings of World News Tonight reported on this story with two sentences on the Amnesty International report, which was used only to introduce a

lengthy story on the way the Palestinian government treated prisoners (Digiovanna).

    2. Similarly, Edward Said, a Palestinian activist and Columbia University professor, was vilified as "abhorrent and primitive" in an October 2000 *New York Times* article simply because he threw a small stone from newly liberated Southern Lebanon over the border to Israel where nobody was hurt by the stone (Arenson). When the festive Germans destroyed the Berlin Wall, we celebrated their actions. When Edward Said celebrated the end of Israeli occupation of Lebanon by flinging stones to the other side, his action was deemed unacceptable.

II. The second thing we should be aware of is that there are solutions to this problem.

   A. One solution requires that U.S. journalists actually go to the occupied territories, rather than operate through Tel Aviv in Israel.

    1. I recently interviewed Dr. Debra Gordon, a Women's Studies professor at WSU, who spent her sabbatical doing research in Gaza. She said that news programs in Palestine were much more news oriented than programs in the U.S. and that Arab and even British journalists went straight to places of conflict in the Middle East to gather their information rather than simply phoning representatives of governments for information. She also added that even the Israeli media had a far more Palestinian perspective than the U.S. media!

   B. Another solution requires that U.S. journalists be fluent in the languages of the areas they cover, which in this case would be Arabic.

    1. Edward Said, in his eye-opening book, *Covering Islam*, states: "Not knowing the language is only part of a much greater ignorance for often the reporter is sent to a country with no preparation or experience . . . so instead of trying to find out more about the country, the reporter takes hold of what is nearest at hand, usually a cliché" (ii).

III. The third thing we should all be aware of is that the solutions I proposed do have real benefits.

   A. One benefit is that you will be able to draw your own informed conclusions about the Middle East conflict after receiving less biased coverage.

    1. When you receive less biased, more accurate information about the situation, you can decide objectively whether or not more Jewish settlers should occupy lands, or whether or not Arab stone throwers are dangerous.

   B. Another benefit concerns achieving an understanding between the United States and the Middle East.

    1. If we treat Arabs more fairly in our media, it is more likely that they would do the same to the United States. When I lived in Iran, there was much pro-Palestine, anti-Israel, anti-American hysteria. Now that I live in the U.S., I find anti-Palestine, anti-Iran hysteria, but pro-Israeli hysteria. There is no need for hysteria, only a need for understanding both sides of the issue, so we may prevent such conflicts.

Conclusion:

  I. In the end, we must reverse the unfair treatment of Arabs in the U.S. media. I have explained how before and during the current Palestinian uprising, the

U.S. media wrongly portrayed Arabs while communicating a pro-Israeli bias. I have explained that there are solutions to this problem. And, I have explained the benefits of these solutions.

II. Today, I urge all of you to think twice every time you see or hear news stories about Arabs. I urge you to consider the source of the information, and to actively seek articles written by Arabs. I also urge you to read Edward Said's book, *Covering Islam*, for an in-depth analysis of U.S. media coverage of the Middle East.

III. Perhaps in some small, but important, way we may eventually prevent deaths like Muhammad al-Durrah's from occurring again.

Works Cited:

Adas, Jane. "At Princeton, Activist Ali Abunimah Critiques U.S. Media Coverage." *Washington Post on Middle East Affairs*, Jan. (2001): 63.

Arenson, Karen W. "Columbia Debates a Professor's 'Gesture.'" *New York Times* 19 Oct. 2000, natl. ed.: B3.

DiGiovanna, James. 22 April 2001. http://www.tucsonweekly.com/tw/05-15-97/book1.htm.

Gordon, Deborah. Personal interview, April 2001.

Murphy, Dean E. "Mideast Strife Spills over into Photo Contest." *New York Times* 2 Mar. 2001, natl. ed.

Said, Edward W. *Covering Islam*. New York: Vintage Books, 1997.

Questions for Analysis

1. How well does this speech fulfill the rhetorical purpose of initiating action? What is the thesis? Does it adequately support a need for action that such a purpose demands? Is this topic one that creates adequate dissonance (psychological discomfort) for audiences to contemplate action (see Chapter 6)? For whom? What audience-related rhetorical obstacles (see Chapter 8) are evident with this topic? What Persona/Tone is best suited for such a purpose?

2. How well does this speech follow the Motivated Sequence, the organizational pattern tailored specifically for speeches to initiate action (see Chapter 6)?

3. How does this speech illustrate suggestions made in this chapter for (1) how to pick a topic, (2) researching a subject, and (3) preparing your presentation? Analyze content carefully for strengths and weaknesses.

4. Do the introduction and conclusion meet all the criteria outlined in this chapter for what these parts of speech should accomplish? How?

5. Which of these two speeches is the most memorable? Why? Which has the strongest ethos appeal (credibility of the speaker)? Logos appeal (soundness of argument and evidence)? Pathos appeal (emotional impact)? How is your judgment affected by subsequent events (Chapter 11) related to these topics, especially the Academy Award–winning film *A Beautiful Mind* and the political fallout from 9/11, respectively?

EXERCISES

1. One of the best ways to reduce high levels of speech anxiety is to speak in front of your classmates often in 30-second to 1-minute impromptu performances. These are low-key, low-risk speaking exercises that

help you practice critical thinking and delivery skills. Your instructor may want to prepare an envelope full of topics ranging from "Famous Proverbs" to "Current Events" to "Reading Checks." Each day three to five students can practice public speaking skills. The keys to an effective impromptu speech, one that does not wander, or turn into a comic routine, are (1) State your point clearly; (2) Illustrate your point with a brief explanation and a few examples; and (3) Re-state your point. The more "unadorned" the better for these 1-minute speaking exercises.

2. Prepare a four- to five-minute speech to alter perception that includes a visual aid or an excerpt from a novel, short story, or poem as a major piece of evidence. You will be evaluated based on preparation, message, presentation, and visual aid tips presented in this chapter. See Appendix form "Speech to Alter Perception" for assignment specifics.

3. Prepare a five- to seven-minute speech or 2,000-word essay to explain some concept, event, or process that includes detailed personal experience and research from secondary sources. See Appendix form "Speech to Explain" for assignment specifics.

4. Prepare a 1,500-word essay that applies a fable, tale, myth, or story to a current problem in order to formulate belief. Use such stories as Aesop's fables, Greek and Roman mythology, the fairy tales of Hans Christian Anderson or the Grimm brothers, or a biblical parable. See Appendix form "Speech to Formulate Belief" for assignment specifics.

5. The choice of a thesis is a decision that specifies the precise claim you want to make, and it represents a drastic limitation of the topic. In choosing a thesis, speakers take into consideration not only their own interests and goals, but also the potential benefits for their audience.

Here is an exercise to walk you through the process of selecting a topic and deciding on your position and purpose. Select a controversial topic that is currently being discussed in the media but for which you can say, "I am unable to take a stand on the issue of . . ." Consider drafting a proposal for a new course that will educate students on this controversial topic. Start by answering these three questions: What is the topic you wish to explore? Why are you interested in it? Why do you think other students should be paying attention to it (i.e., what do you think is at stake in the debate)? and Why can't you make up your mind at this time? Go to InfoTrac College Edition and gather information about the different concerns and interests involved in the controversy. Identify the major point of disagreement. Draft a syllabus that reflects the anatomy or history of the debate—who is involved, what are their concerns, what are the origins of the controversy? What is the central idea you would like students to retain upon completing your course? Considering all the points and counterpoints that you have collected, can you now take a stand on the controversy? What arguments and evidence turned out to be most persuasive in helping you make your stand? Why?

Go to InfoTrac College Edition and look up topics such as nuclear disarmament, welfare reform, or globalization. Imagine that you were a member of an academic committee on campus that is in possession of limited funds for peer education. The program will involve offering a series of free workshops to students and inviting prominent guest lecturers. Your funds will be sufficient for coverage of only one of the above topics. Based on your InfoTrac College Edition research, which topic should be considered the most significant, urgent, or beneficial to students? Draft a short speech in which you address the committee and make your recommendation for allocating the money. You need to provide clear arguments and to demonstrate that you have in mind the best interests of the student body.

NOTES

1. "The Only Thing We Have to Fear Is Speaking Before a Group," 1988, *Psychology Today*. Reprinted, [Minneapolis] *Star Tribune*, 19 March 1991.

2. "Wanted: Search Engines with Uncommon Sense." *Kansas City Star*, Aug. 10, 1999, p. D16.

3. James Coates, "Internet Is Awash in Unsubstantiated 'News.' " *Wichita Eagle*, November 10, 1996, pp. 1, 12A.

4. See also Esther Grassian, Thinking Critically About World Wide Web Resources, UCLA College Library; Evaluating Information found on the Internet from Johns Hopkins University Library.

5. Reprinted with permission of Jarrod Acquistapace, Honors Public Speaking class, Wichita State University, 2001.

6. Reprinted with permission of Saideh Eftekhari, Honors Public Speaking class, Wichita State University, 2001.

chapter 4

The Resources of Evidence

No public speaking class or any textbook can prepare you for the occasions on which you will be expected to present materials, make a case, defend a conclusion, or memorialize a beloved friend. What both can do is prepare you to think about how to respond to the circumstances in which you find yourself. Accordingly, the chapters that follow explore the resources that you have to cope with different kinds of situations and the kinds of obstacles that you are likely to face because of the subject or purpose of your rhetoric, because of the attitudes and characteristics of audiences, and because of your personal history. In the next three chapters I explore three important resources you have as a rhetor—the evidence or supporting materials you can use, the arguments you can develop, and the organization or structure of your discourse. This chapter explores the resources of evidence, the most basic building blocks of rhetorical action. The next chapter explores the kinds of arguments you can marshall, units that include the kinds of supporting materials described in this chapter. Then I turn to the largest building blocks, the ways in which you can structure your material in order to make the ideas as compelling as possible.

Writing long ago in his *Rhetoric*, Aristotle said: "A speech has two parts. You must state your case, and you must prove it" (1.414a.30-1).[1] Those statements emphasize the role of a central claim or thesis, arguments in its support, and data in persuasion.

As Aristotle also noted in the *Rhetoric*, however, proof comes in different forms. He wrote about three sources of persuasion arising out of the discursive (definitional or logical) qualities of language (*logos*), out of the feelings, attitudes, or states of mind of the audience (*pathos*), and out of the audience's perceptions of the rhetor (*ethos*). Aristotle was also concerned with the resources in language, particularly the resources of figurative language or metaphor.

Aristotle's ideas are still valid. We cannot discuss evidence solely in logical or empirical terms. We must also consider its psychological impact on the audience—whether evidence makes ideas vivid and clear or affects attitudes toward the rhetor.

In practical terms, every piece of evidence must be judged by two criteria:

1. What are its logical or empirical strengths and limitations?
2. What are its psychological powers?

Ideally, good supporting materials show the truth of a claim; they are clear, vivid, and concrete; and they present the rhetor as competent and trustworthy.

In order to illustrate the resources of evidence, I shall use selections from an evidence-rich essay by Bill McKibben entitled "A Special Moment in History."[2] It's a good source to explore the resources of evidence because it deals with an important but difficult subject—global warming—and it argues that we Americans have to change our ways now if we are to avert a worldwide catastrophe. In other words, it is targeted at us, and it asks us to do things we don't particularly enjoy doing, such as cutting back drastically on the burning of fossil fuels. I will use excerpts from the essay to talk about how the author attempts to use supporting materials—all kinds of evidence—in an effort to persuade us to take this issue seriously, to recognize the threat that it poses, and to take action despite our cultural attachment to gas-guzzling cars, for instance.

There are five categories of evidence that are resources for rhetors: *stories* or examples, *statistics* or numerical data, interpretive statements from *experts* (sometimes referred to as authority evidence), *analogies* or comparisons and *visuals* or pictorial representations (see Figure 4–1). These different types of evidence rarely occur in isolation,

Types of Evidence (VASES)	Visuals	Analogies	Statistics	Experts	Stories
Psychological Appeal	✓	✓			✓
Rational Appeal		✓	✓	✓	
Primary Strength	Package ideas holistically	Alter perception	Amplify scope	Enhance credibility	Invite empathy
Primary Weakness	Over-simplified	Irrelevant	Incomprehensible	Distorting	Un-representative

Figure 4–1
Types of Evidence (VASES)

as the examples used below will show, because each has weaknesses that can be offset by combining it with other kinds of evidence. In the sections below the strengths and weaknesses of each type will be explored and illustrated.

STORIES

In "A Special Moment in History," Bill McKibben argues that we now face a special kind of pollution problem:

> It's not that we're running out of stuff. What we're running out of is what the scientists call "sinks"—places to put the by-products of our large appetites. Not garbage dumps (we could go on using Pampers till the end of time and still have empty space left to toss them away) but the atmospheric equivalent of garbage dumps. . . . New kinds of pollution come . . . from normal human life—but there are so many of us living these normal lives that something abnormal is happening. And that something is so different from the old forms of pollution that it confuses the issue even to use the word.
>
> Consider nitrogen, for instance. Almost 80 percent of the atmosphere is nitrogen gas. But before plants can absorb it, it must become "fixed"—bonded with carbon, hydrogen, or oxygen. Nature does this trick with certain kinds of algae and soil bacteria, and with lightning. Before human beings began to alter the nitrogen cycle, these mechanisms provided 90–150 million metric tons of nitrogen a year. Now human activity adds 130–150 million more tons. Nitrogen isn't pollution—it's essential. And we are using more of it all the time. Half the industrial nitrogen fertilizer used in human history has been applied since 1984. As a result, coastal waters and estuaries bloom with toxic algae while oxygen concentrations dwindle, killing fish; as a result, nitrous oxide traps solar heat. And once the gas is in the air, it stays there for a century or more. (64)

The general problem or claim is that we now face new kinds of pollution and the example used to illustrate that claim is nitrogen, a naturally occurring, harmless gas and element. In order to make that example more powerful, however, the author provides a statistical comparison of the amount of nitrogen bonded or "fixed" through natural processes with the additional amount that is now being produced. The example of the increased use of nitrogen fertilizer is a way to make this problem more concrete—this is a kind of bonded nitrogen we use in our gardens. At the end of the second paragraph, there are undetailed examples of the kinds of problems created by increasing amounts of nitrogen—toxic algae blooms that we probably have read about and a reference to the ability of nitrogen to trap solar heat. Because these are specific, they help us to understand the kinds of effects that increased uses of nitrogen can produce.

Although the nitrogen example is detailed and although statistical data is provided to indicate the extent of the change in amount of nitrogen produced, it still has the weaknesses that are typical of examples: It is just one case. So, you say, there are problems with nitrogen, but that's just one thing and with experimentation, we probably can find substitutes that will enable us to reduce our use of nitrogen fertilizer without making major changes in our overall use of fossil fuels.

There is another example in this material, the reference to Pampers, a brand of disposable diapers. The author is drawing a sharp contrast between finding space for such waste and the special problems posed by the special forms of pollution he describes. The contrast helps us to understand the difference between the pollution he is talking about and the kinds of wastes with which we are more familiar. Note, too, that there is a figurative analogy in the opening of this material, a reference to the need for "sinks" in which to dispose of these special kinds of pollution. That familiar term makes it easier for us to understand the kind of disposal systems that are needed.

As this excerpt illustrates, an example is a *story* of a case or an instance, real or hypothetical, detailed or undetailed, used to illustrate an idea or to prove that a particular kind of event has happened or could happen. Such an example is a weak form of evidence when judged logically or empirically. It merely shows that something happened once or is true in one case, and if the example is hypothetical or imaginary, it does not even do that.

In order to illustrate the weakness of the example as proof, I tell my students the true story of a woman who was killed instantly while asleep in her bed by the fall of a large meteor. No matter how dramatically I tell the story or how detailed I make it, they are never frightened. From their personal experience, from the experience of others, and from news reports and astronomical data, they know that meteors rarely fall all the way to the ground on our planet, especially in sizes that would be harmful, and that they rarely strike people or animals. The students' reaction is, "Okay, it happened once. The odds are that it won't ever happen again, and the chances of its happening to me are infinitesimal."

The rhetorical force of an example lies in its capacity to make us imagine a scene, imagine ourselves in it, and identify with the people and events. The more detailed the story—and the more skillfully the details are chosen—the more we identify with the problem or situation and participate in it. It is this capacity for stimulating identification that makes examples such extremely powerful pieces of evidence psychologically. They clarify through detail; they engage us by creating the bases for identification or by making a problem concrete and real.

Stories can be more or less effective. In most cases, a real example of an actual event or person is better than a hypothetical or imaginary case, but real examples are not always available. No terrorist as yet has acquired a nuclear device. If a rhetor is to describe such an event, it will be necessary to develop a hypothetical example, and events of this kind already have become the subjects of works of fiction. As proof, both logically and psychologically, a hypothetical example is strongest when it seems most plausible to the audience, when it has, in literary terms, the greatest verisimilitude, the appearance of truth or likelihood, when it creates virtual experience. In other words, the details of the example should conform to what is known—imaginary presidents must behave like their real-life counterparts; imaginary nuclear accidents must account of all the levels of protection in real-life nuclear plants, and so forth. Television films based on real-life events, such as the capture by terrorists of the *Achille Lauro* cruise ship and the murder of Leon Klinghoffer, the rescue of "Everybody's Baby" Jessica McClure from a well, or the wedding of Prince Charles and Lady Diana, capitalize on (exploit?) the feelings and excitement the original event aroused in order to attract a large audiences. Real examples too—indeed all examples—are judged by their plausibility and verisimilitude. Although no example by itself can demonstrate its own representativeness, it should conform to common knowledge of what is plausible and likely. In addition, our willingness to accept examples is heightened by the amount of detail that is provided or that we can provide from our experience. Plausibility is not just a function of the example itself, it is a function of the similarity between what happens in the example and the experiences of the audience.

If an example is to create identification and induce participation by the audience, it must fit their experience; otherwise you, as rhetor, must be prepared to show through other evidence that the case you provide is representative or relatively common.

In addition, you should note that a number of examples will strengthen an individual instance so that, as a series, they suggest that each is typical or representative of a larger number of instances. After the material that I cited above about nitrogen, for instance, the author immediately presents another example, that of carbon dioxide, in order to strengthen the point he is making.

Examples also contribute to the ethos of the rhetor. They suggest that the rhetor is concerned with real people and events and imply that she or he has had firsthand experience with the situation. Very often, examples demonstrate the goodwill of the speaker and the expertise that comes from combining practical experience with theoretical knowledge.

In summary, then, the example is psychologically a vivid evocation that clarifies the meaning of an idea or problem. When details are given, and when the audience finds an example plausible because of detail or conformity to their experience, it becomes highly effective in creating identification and in involving the audience with the problem. Real examples are stronger than hypothetical ones. To be effective, a hypothetical case must establish its similarity to real-life situations. Examples are stronger when they are relatively detailed and when a series of them is used. Examples are weak as proof because they are single instances that may be atypical and unrepresentative. They are also weak if they are undetailed and if they contradict the experiences of the audience.

Their precise opposite in terms of strengths and weaknesses is statistical or numerical data.

STATISTICS

Here is another excerpt from the article by Bill McKibben in which the author talks about what is happening to population growth:

> Around the world people are choosing to have fewer and fewer children—not just in China, where the government forces it on them, but in almost every nation outside the poorest parts of Africa. Population growth rates are lower than they have been at any time since the Second World War. In the past three decades the average woman in the developing world, excluding China, has gone from bearing six children to bearing four. Even in Bangladesh the average has fallen from six to fewer than four; even in the mullahs' Iran it has dropped by four children. If this keeps up, the population of the world will not quite double again; United Nations analysts offer as their mid-range projection that it will top out at 10 to 11 billion, up from just under six billion at the moment. The world is still growing, at nearly a record pace—we add a New York City every month, almost a Mexico every year, almost an India every decade. But the rate of growth is slowing; it is no longer "exponential," "unstoppable," "inexorable," "unchecked," "cancerous." If current trends hold, the world's population will all but stop growing before the twenty-first century is out. . . .
>
> Will the drop continue? It had better. UN mid-range projections assume that women in the developing world will soon average two children apiece—the rate at which population growth stabilizes. If fertility remained at current levels, the population would reach the ab-

surd figure of 296 billion in just 150 years. Even if it dropped to 2.5 children per woman and then stopped falling, the population would reach 28 billion.

But let's trust that this time the demographers have got it right. Let's trust that we have rounded the turn and we're in the home stretch. Let's trust that the planet's population really will double only one more time. Even so, this is a case of good news, bad news. The good news is that we won't grow forever. The bad news is that there are six billion of us already, a number the world strains to support. One more near-doubling—four or five billion more people—will nearly double that strain. Will these be the five billion straws that break the camel's back? (56)

The United States is a highly technological, scientific society. Accordingly, we use a great many statistics, and we tend to trust numerical measures more than most other kinds of evidence. A *statistic* is a numerical or quantitative measure of scope or of frequency of occurrence. In the material cited above, there are many statistics—the drop in birth rates among women in many countries, the projection that world population will top out at 10 or 11 billion from its current level (now over 6 billion). That calculation is based on the assumption that women in the developing world will soon average two children apiece, and the projection about the incredible population surge that would occur if it stayed at current levels as well as the data about what population would be if the average remained at 2.5 children per woman. Note, again, that these are all measures of size, extent, or frequency of occurrence.

As you will have recognized, most of these statistics are comparisons that enable us to have a sense of their significance. When we know that the average woman in the developing world now has four rather than six children, we have a sense of the size of the drop that has occurred. If we were told only that such women now have four children, we would have little basis for assessing the meaning of that data. That world population will nonetheless nearly double from its current level is apparent from the world's present population of six billion and the estimates that population will stop growing at somewhere around 10–11 billion. The estimates about what world population would be if current levels continued or if child-bearing stabilized at 2.5 children per woman are predictions or extrapolations from present data.

All of these give us a sense of size, scope, and extent. Note, however, that these remain quite remote from us. I do not have a real sense of what it means for the world population to be six billion at present, and I have a hard time imagining just what it will mean when that number doubles. And that is precisely the weakness with statistics. The author has some awareness of that problem, and he uses an important and useful strategy to counteract the remoteness of numerical data. At the end of the first paragraph, he writes that "we add a New York City every month, almost a Mexico every year, almost an India every decade." This is a strategy of translation; instead of giving us numbers (we add some eight million people every month), he substitutes or translates those numbers into something that is more meaningful, more within our experience. The psychological impact of saying that we add a New York City is that it gives us an existential sense of what such growth means, and the idea that we add an India, soon to be the most populous nation in the world, every decade is awe-inspiring. This strategy of translation is one of the most effective ways to counteract the abstraction and remoteness of numbers.

Statistics are strong logically and empirically because they are measures of frequency, but even as proof, they pose some problems. As the subtle cliché puts it, "Figures can't lie but liars can figure." In other words, numbers can be used to distort and misrepresent. At least two questions should be asked about every statistic:

1. What counts as an instance of what is being measured?
2. How was the whole population sampled to obtain these data?

Such problems are less important for the material cited above. In most countries, births and deaths are recorded fairly reliably. But these problems can loom large in other kinds of statistics.

As an example, let us suppose that the state highway department reports speeding as the major cause in one-third of all fatal automobile accidents. It is easy to determine what a fatal auto accident is, but it may be hard to decide just what "speeding" is. Is it exceeding the posted speed limit? If so, how do we know that was happening? Was someone clocking the speed? Is speeding traveling faster than is safe for the conditions? A fatal accident would seem to be proof that the driver exceeded the safe speed, but mechanical problems might cause such an accident even at low speeds. In addition, how do we decide what is the *major* cause? Suppose we know that someone was driving faster than the speed limit but was also legally drunk or on medications that slowed reactions. Which is the major cause? If you ask such questions, you will realize that this statistic is a rough approximation of what state troopers believe is a major factor in serious auto accidents based on their reading of the signs (skid marks, damage, distance traveled after impact, Breathalyzer tests) and on extensive experience.

Other statistics are gathered through survey research, however, the kind of technique through which George Gallup, Louis Harris, Elmo Roper, and others question a random sample whose views are, then, taken to be representative of the views of all Americans "with a margin of error of plus or minus 5 percent" or some similar figure. What is called a "sampling" error occurs when this smaller population—the group questioned—is unlike the larger population it is meant to represent. In the past, the accuracy of the Nielsen ratings of television viewing, for example, was questioned because few African American or Hispanic viewers were included in their samples, far below their representation in the population. In the 1948 election when pollsters predicted that Dewey would beat Truman, for example, one major error seemed to come from sampling that included only people with telephones, people who were, at least in 1948, more affluent and more sympathetic to Republican candidates. A similar error might be made today if we sampled only those with cellular phones or personal computers.

Many cigarette ads illustrate another kind of statistical distortion—the suggestion that a measurable difference makes a difference. Brands of cigarettes have been advertised as having only 1 or 4 or 7 milligrams of "tars" or nicotine, which implies that it is healthier to smoke these brands. There is, however, no evidence of any medically significant advantage from smoking brands with lower levels of these ingredients as currently measured. Smoking any cigarette is bad for one's health. The undesirable effects of smoking may even arise, not from the amount of "tars" or nicotine, but from the products of combustion—carbon dioxide, nitrous oxide, sulfur dioxide, and the like. But the statistic makes it seem "safer" and "better" to smoke some brands than others, and if we fear the effects of smoking but cannot bring ourselves to stop, we may go along with the pretext that a numerical difference makes a medical difference.

The willingness to make such an assumption calls attention to a psychological asset of statistics: the appearance of objectivity and precision, which leads us to treat them as factual and true. Our scientific, technical society reveres the empirical and "objective" so much that, as members of audiences, we are likely to be particularly impressed by statistical evidence.

This psychological strength is offset in part, however, by a psychological problem: Statistics are hard to understand and remember. An audience confronted with a series of statistics is likely to become confused and lost; special efforts must be made to translate large numbers remote from personal experience into more familiar terms. In this case, for example, the author translates the rates of increase in population into entities that have more meaning than numbers alone—"we add a New York City every month, almost a Mexico every year, almost an India every decade." Think how much less vivid it would be if the author used the actual numbers.

You can compensate for the weaknesses of statistical evidence by combining numbers with analogies, another kind of evidence, discussed below. Biologist Stephen Jay Gould, for example, claims that "Joe DiMaggio's fifty-six-game hitting streak is the greatest accomplishment in the history of baseball, if not in modern sport." Gould explains that, despite the belief in "hot hands," or streaks, they just don't exist. They can all be explained statistically; better players have longer runs of success because they are better players, and less talented players have shorter runs. "There is one major exception, and absolutely only one—one sequence so many standard deviations above the expected distribution that it should not have occurred at all: Joe DiMaggio's fifty-six-game hitting streak in 1941. . . . He beat the hardest taskmaster of all, a woman who makes Nolan Ryan's fastball look like a cantaloupe in slow motion—Lady Luck." At this point, Gould has used analogies to make the significance clearer. How hard is it to beat the odds? When compared to Nolan Ryan's fastball, which has given that pitcher one of the winningest records in baseball, it makes his achievements appear to be nothing, as if his fastball had been so slow that it looked like a cantaloupe in slow motion, a pitch even the least talented of us probably could hit.

Gould explains that we have problems appreciating DiMaggio's feat "because we are so poorly equipped, whether by habits of culture or by our modes of cognition, to grasp the workings of random processes and patterning in nature." He argues that we cannot bear to accept the randomness of chance: "We believe in 'hot hands' because we must impart meaning to a pattern—and we like meanings that tell stories about heroism, valor, and excellence." He argues that DiMaggio's accomplishment was "a unique assault upon the otherwise unblemished record of Dame Probability." His feat combined extraordinary luck with great skill. Gould, a biologist, draws an analogy between DiMaggio's accomplishment and the biological entities that interest him:

> The history of a species, or any natural phenomenon that requires unbroken continuity in a world of trouble, works like a batting streak. All are games of a gambler playing with a limited stake against a house with infinite resources. The gambler must eventually go bust. His aim can only be to stick around as long as possible. . . . DiMaggio's hitting steak is the finest of legitimate legends because it embodies the essence of the battle that truly defines our lives. DiMaggio activated the greatest and most unattainable dream of all humanity, the hope and chimera of all sages and shamans: he cheated death, at least for a while.[3]

Several analogies (discussed below) are at work. All attempts, Gould argues, to overcome the laws of probability, the power of chance, are like gambling. Thus, the efforts of species to survive are like a batting streak, and just as the gambler must lose eventually, and the batting streak must end, he implies that species die out. Hence, beating the laws of chance at the gaming table or in the batting box is like beating death—which you can do only for a little while. Notice that these analogies are considerably more powerful from a renowned biological scientist and a student of the statistical lore of baseball (and other sports). Note, too, that the analogies also confer meaning on a pattern, ironically doing just what he has chided us humans for wanting to do!

Incidentally, sports fans are extremely reluctant to give up the belief in "hot hands" and "streaks," which is, in and of itself, a strong bit of evidence of the human need to perceive patterns and to make meaning out of random events, part of the psychological power of statistics.[4]

In the article from the *Atlantic Monthly* cited at the beginning of this chapter, Bill McKibben uses examples to highlight the difficulties of explaining why population growth is slowing. Those examples, that the women in Oman who know about contraception still average six or more children each and the contrast between childbearing by women in Turkey and Japan who use contraceptives at the same rate, call into question the reasons offered by experts for the decline in child-bearing. Note, too, that these problems of explanation emphasize just how speculative the predictions about future population growth really are.

In summary, statistics are a strong form of evidence that you can use to convey how often something happens or the size and scope of a problem. To interpret statistics, you need to know how the raw data were gathered, how measurements were made, what counted as an instance of this event, how sampling was done, and what kinds of error might be involved.

Psychologically, statistics are strong because of the empirical and scientific bias of our society and our respect for objectivity, for "hard cold facts." Despite this general attitude, however, statistics are a difficult form of proof to use effectively. Lists of numbers are hard to understand and remember. Speakers and writers must make special efforts to translate numerical measures into more familiar terms, into proportions and relationships that are within our personal experience. Often this is done through visuals, another form of evidence used in rhetorical acts.

VISUALS

Because of the problem of absorbing and recollecting a series of numbers, you may want to use visual aids when you present statistics. Statistical evidence often makes better sense to both readers and listeners if it is in the form of charts and graphs that depict quantitative relationships in *visual terms*; in effect, you are presenting the same material through two sensory channels. President Reagan, for example, was praised for using charts and graphs innovatively to illustrate his State of the Union addresses, speeches that are not particularly easy to present because they often discuss complex problems and solutions, the kinds of problems and solutions that most often involve statistical evidence. Independent presidential candidate H. Ross Perot used charts and graphs extensively in 1992 in the infomercials in which he discussed the problems of the federal deficit; even with all the charts and graphs, his analysis was difficult for anyone other than economists to interpret and understand, in part because each chart and graph could be seen only for a few seconds. Without the charts and graphs, however, most of what Perot said would have been a mass of indigestible numbers.

Here is an example of a visual aid that tries to translate very large numbers into something meaningful.

FIREPOWER, THEN AND NOW[5]

One bomb represents the firepower unleashed in World War II, nonnuclear as well as the bombs dropped on Hiroshima and Nagasaki: 3 megatons.

Three bombs equal the firepower of the weapons on one U.S. Poseidon submarine: 9 megatons, enough to destroy more than 200 of the largest Soviet cities.

Eight bombs represent the firepower of the weapons on a U.S. Trident submarine: 24 megatons, enough to destroy every major city in the Northern Hemisphere.

The 6,000 bombs below represent the 18,000 megatons of nuclear firepower shared by the United States and the Soviet Union (in 1987).

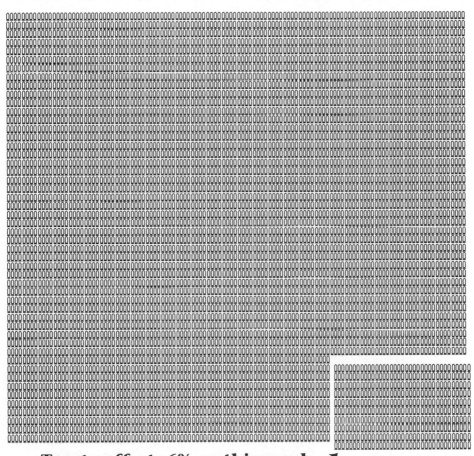

Treaty affects 6% or this much ➚

This pictograph (a chart representing numerical data pictorially) attempts to represent visually the meaning of some statistics. Note that in this case, the numbers are transformed into visual entities in which size is represented by the space occupied by the bombs. It simplifies a mass of information and puts it in a form that lets us make comparisons easily. The size of each little bomb is defined experientially as the amount of firepower unleashed in World War II including the atomic bombs dropped on Japanese cities. The significance of three bombs is defined in relation to armaments—what amount of firepower is available on one Poseidon submarine—and the amount of damage that amount of firepower could do—destroy 200 of the largest cities in what was then the Soviet Union. Eight bombs are also described in this way: the firepower on a single Trident submarine, which is enough to destroy every major city in the Northern hemisphere. Note that "major" isn't defined—it's assumed that the scope is large enough to make that omission insignificant. Finally, we are told just how many of those little bombs there are in the picture below and what that total represents in the firepower of the two major nuclear powers. Finally, one area of the chart is broken off to give us a visual comparison to dramatize how small a part of the total arsenal is covered by the proposed intermediate-range nuclear missile treaty with the then Soviet Union. In addition, that segment is translated into a percentage, another way to help us understand just how small a part it is. This is an excellent example of translating statistical evidence into a visual form that makes such huge numbers more intelligible.

In the article from the *Atlantic Monthly*, the strength of visuals are especially apparent. Pictorial representation is used in an entertaining, efficient way to simplify many complex ideas about depleting natural resources. Here visual evidence takes the form of vibrantly colored modernized drawings, six of which take up the better part of a double-page magazine spread. Each accentuates the tone of urgency in McKibben's plea for conservation. The reader's gaze is drawn to a series of disturbing pictures: a luxurious red queen Anne chair crammed with identical faces all over it; a skeleton of a fish—its guts made to look like smokestacks; a water faucet with four spouts turned on full blast; and the most eye-opening: four missiles increasing in size from bottom to top with the largest two missiles looking like babies! The enthymeme suggested by this picture is a powerful one. It's not nuclear missiles that will destroy us; it's overpopulation! In addition, on every page in the right-hand corner stands an alarm clock with a chunk (a quarter) of its numbers missing—reminding us of McKibben's primary thesis: between now and the year 2050 is "a special moment in history" for us to reverse global warming and its deleterious effects. Visuals are an enthymematic, efficient, and emotional form of evidence. On the other hand, visuals tend to oversimplify and thus distort issues. Increasingly, many scholars argue that we are becoming a society of visual learners. Recognizing that visual rhetoric deserves specialized treatment, Chapter 12 examines its many nondiscursive features.

ANALOGIES

Analogies are likenings or comparisons between things, processes, persons, or events. They come in two varieties: literal analogies (usually simply called comparisons) and figurative analogies (usually called metaphors).

Literal Analogies

Literal analogies focus on the similarities between items that are obviously alike in some ways: two colleges, three hair styles, eight field hockey players, four rivers, and so on. Literal analogies are comparisons among items that are alike in detail and similar in explicit and obvious ways. The demands made on two professional tennis players are similar, for example, and you might compare their records of points on first serves and numbers of unforced errors in order to state that one is more skillful or talented than another. In the essay cited earlier, the author compares the birth rates among women in different countries and world birth rates at different periods.

Such comparisons are made for the purposes of evaluation and prediction. One compares in order to evaluate just how serious and extensive the drop in rates of child-bearing have been. One compares in order to judge which team or player is better or to predict which will be more successful in a future encounter. It is risky, however, to predict a pitcher's success because her success also depends on the skill of her outfield and on the hitting power of her teammates. These complexities suggest the critical factor in the power of literal analogies as proof: the extent of relevant similarities and the presence of relevant differences. As a rule, the greater the number of relevant similarities between two cases, the better the basis for evaluation or prediction; the existence of relevant differences (differences directly related to the evaluation or prediction being made) lessens the strength and force of any claim. Baseball teams are just that—teams. The skill of a pitcher is only one element in its success, and the differences in talent and experience of other members of the teams being compared are significant for evaluating the performance and predicting the success of any one member.

Literal analogies enable us to go from what is known and tested and in operation to what is unknown, untested, and not yet working. In one high crime neighborhood, for instance, traffic patterns are altered to prevent through traffic, and a crime control unit to report suspicious events is set up. The burglary rate drops 45 percent during the year after these changes are made. If we can replicate this success in other neighborhoods, people and property will be much safer. Careful analysis of such a project and determination of how similar—how analogous—any two neighborhoods really are should help us determine whether what worked in the one area will work in another.

Figurative Analogies

The process by which we go from what is known and familiar to what is unknown and unfamiliar is accentuated in the figurative analogy, a comparison of items that are unlike in obvious ways, that are apparently totally different if looked at with literal and practical eyes. The *figurative analogy* asserts a similarity that is metaphoric or that is a similarity in principle. For example, there are no obvious similarities between playing blackjack and batting a baseball except for their common relationship to the workings of chance, and there is no similarity between a baseball and a cantaloupe except their generally round shape. There are no obvious similarities between the earth's capacity to sustain human life and the back of a camel, yet the question, "Will these be the five billion straws that break the camel's back?" dramatizes the threat represented by increasing population.

The figurative analogy is one means by which a concept or problem can be made more vivid and dramatic. A later section of McKibben's article illustrates this process:

> Throughout the 10,000 years of recorded human history the planet—the physical planet—has been a stable place. In every single year of those 10,000, there have been earthquakes, volcanoes, hurricanes, cyclones. . . . But these have never shaken the basic predictability of the planet as a whole. . . .
>
> Among other things, this stability has made possible the insurance industry—has underwritten the underwriters. Insurers can analyze the risk in any venture because they know the

ground rules. If you want to build a house on the coast of Florida, they can calculate with reasonable accuracy the chance that it will be hit by a hurricane and the speed of the winds circling that hurricane's eye. If they couldn't, they would have no way to set your premium—they'd just be gambling. They're always gambling a little, of course: they don't know if that hurricane is coming next year or next century. But the earth's physical stability is the house edge in this casino. As Julian Simon pointed out, "A prediction based on past data can be sound if it is sensible to assume that the past and the future belong to the same statistical universe."

So what does it mean that alone among the earth's great pools of money and power, insurance companies are beginning to take the idea of global climate change quite seriously? What does it mean that the payout for weather-related damage climbed from $16 billion during the entire 1980s to $48 billion in the years 1990–1994? What does it mean that top European insurance executives have begun consulting with Greenpeace about global warming? What does it mean that the insurance giant Swiss Re, which paid out $291.5 million in the wake of Hurricane Andrew, ran an ad in the *Financial Times* showing its corporate logo bent sideways by a storm?

These things mean, I think, that the possibility that we live on a new earth cannot be discounted entirely as a fever dream. (63)

In an effort to explain the changing character of the earth, the author in this case compares insurers to casino owners who are able to make a profit by calculating the odds and making sure that the payouts are smaller than the premiums. The house edge, like the favorable odds built into slot machines and roulette wheels, is the stability of the planet. The point of that comparison is made with a statement from an authority, Julian Simon, who sets forth the basic assumptions underlying predictability. Readers may not be mathematical geniuses; they may not know about the kinds of tables used by insurance companies to calculate odds, but most Americans are now familiar with casinos and gambling, and the figurative analogy makes the point much clearer.

The main weakness of the figurative analogy, however, is that, in logical and empirical terms, it gives no proof, makes no demonstration. But figurative analogies are not all equivalent in rhetorical force; some are stronger and more persuasive than others. As a rule, a figurative analogy is more powerful when it is more comprehensive, that is, when there are many points of similarity. Here, for example, the comparison is powerful because the laws of chance and the rules of predictability are at work in both cases.

In the essay cited above, McKibben uses analogies to appeal for action to reverse the problems that have developed:

If we can bring our various emissions quickly and sharply under control, we *can* limit the damage, reduce dramatically the chance of horrible surprises, preserve more of the biology we were born into. But do not underestimate the task. The UN's Intergovernmental Panel on Climate Change projects that an immediate 60 percent reduction in fossil-fuel use is necessary just to stabilize climate at the current level of disruption. Nature may still meet us halfway, but halfway is a long way from where we are now. What's more, we can't delay. If we wait a few decades to get started, we may as well not even begin. It's not like poverty, a concern that's always there for civilizations to address. This is a timed test, like the SAT: two or three decades, and we lay our pencils down. It's *the* test for our generations, and population is part of the answer. (72)

The analogy of the time allotted to respond to the problems of pollution and global warming to the time allotted to take the SAT is a vivid figurative analogy. For most students, the SAT is a milestone in determining what college they can go to, and it is a somewhat frightening moment when one's performance is vital to one's future. The author hopes that young people especially can respond to that comparison and feel a sense of the pressure we are under to respond to these problems.

Weaker figurative analogies rest on one or few similarities of principle, for example, as illustrated by the comparison of the world's capacity to sustain life and the back of a camel or describing the need for "sinks" to dispose of the special wastes that are developing. Consider how weak or how strong you consider the comparison to the SAT in the above excerpt. Is the comparison strengthened by the contrast drawn between poverty, a recurring and enduring problem, and the special character of the threat posed by global warming?

The strengths of the figurative analogy are, like the power of a metaphor or the force of a slogan, somewhat difficult to describe. When the analogy is a fresh comparison that strikes the audience as highly apt, it has considerable persuasive force. The comparison of DiMaggio's hitting streak to the fate of species, for example, is disturbing and thought-provoking, especially from this source.

In sum, the analogy derives its strength from its originality, its ability to make us see things from a new angle; from its aptness, its capacity to evoke an "aha" reaction; and from its brevity, its ability to crystallize a whole range of problems into a single phrase or image. That, too, is the power of the slogan, the brief phrase that expresses a position or idea in a vivid, unforgettable image. "Pro-Choice" and "Forced Motherhood" struggle against the power of "Right to Life." "A Woman's Place is in the House—and Senate!" turns the stereotypic view of women on its head to express another point of view. This tactic of turning things around to express the opposite view is the best defense against a figurative analogy or slogan in argumentative terms.

EXPERTISE OR AUTHORITY

In some of the material quoted above, an expert's view was cited. In the essay by McKibben many experts are quoted, and excerpts from his essay are good examples of the strengths and weaknesses of this kind of evidence.

Authority evidence is a strong way to bolster a claim and enhance the credibility of the rhetor. The contrast between a lay and an expert witness in a courtroom is a helpful way to define the special function of this kind of evidence. If you or I, as ordinary people or lay witnesses, testify in a court of law, we can testify only to what we have actually seen or heard or know from personal experience. (We give testimony, a form of the example.[6]) We are not allowed to draw conclusions, and lawyers are not allowed to "lead" us, that is, to ask us to draw conclusions or interpret evidence. In contrast, the expert witness comes to court specifically to draw conclusions and interpret raw data. A ballistics expert draws on her experience and training to conclude that two bullets were shot from the same gun; a psychologist draws on her experience with the defendant and on her training to interpret the defendant's mental capacity. The functions of the expert witness are the same functions performed by authority evidence.

Authority evidence appears in two forms in the material we have quoted. In one case, an expert named Julian Simon was quoted about the soundness of predictions. We have no information about his qualifications, and we are likely to accept that statement primarily because it fits our general knowledge about predictability. The second kind of authority is that of the author. This essay is strong evidence of the quality of the research that has been done. In the course of the essay, McKibben writes: "Ten years ago I wrote a book called *The End of Nature*, which was the first volume for a general audience about carbon dioxide and climate change, an early attempt to show that human beings now dominate the earth" (65). McKibben has written half a dozen books about environmental degradation and how to live in ways that are less destructive. His concern for the fate of the earth and the people on it is evidence of one kind of ethos, the demonstration that one has the good of the community at heart.

Evidence from authority, like evidence from statistics, discussed below, can be misused. The commonest sort of misuse is to cite experts in one area as if they were experts in another, which happens often in advertising. You should pay attention to this common distortion problem, for example, when Tiger Woods assesses golf equipment and golf courses. He is not only a winning professional golf player, but an astute analyst of equipment and courses. When advertisers try to suggest that he speaks as an expert on consumer products unrelated to golf, however, I am skeptical. Why should I believe him when he endorses automobiles or watches? What knowledge does he have in those areas? Similarly, I doubt the claims of actors on the benefits of a particular brand of dog food or garden fertilizer, but I would listen seriously to them when they talk about television and film acting because that is where they have demonstrated their abilities in performance. No one is an expert in all areas; the strength of authority evidence as proof is directly related to the authority's degree of expertise in the area in question.

Authoritative evidence is strongest when

1. We know the credentials of the authority—her or his training and experience
2. We know the explicit relationship between the expertise of the authority and the subject
3. We know details about the data used by the authority to make interpretations

Authority evidence is weakened when we do not know details about credentials, when the relationship of the authority to the subject is indirect or unclear, or when we do not know what data, principles, or experiences were used in drawing conclusions or making interpretations.

McKibben is well aware of the strengths and weaknesses of authority evidence and of the need to compare the views of various experts. In one section of his essay, he talks about the difficulties of predicting the impact of population on the world's resources by acknowledging how wrong the Reverend Thomas Malthus was in 1798 when he predicted that the growth of population would outstrip the supply of food. In fact, McKibben notes that there is a whole group of experts who take the opposite point of view:

> This group's intellectual fountainhead is a brilliant Danish economist named Ester Boserup—a sort of anti-Malthus, who is 1965 argued that the gloomy cleric had it backward. The more people, Boserup said, the more progress. Take agriculture as an example: the first farmers, she pointed out, were slash-and-burn cultivators, who might farm a plot for a year or two and then move on, not returning for maybe two decades. As the population grew, however, they had to return more frequently to the same plot. That meant problems: compacted, depleted, weedy soils. But these new problems meant new solutions: hoes, manure, compost, crop rotation, irrigation. Even in this century, Boserup said, necessity-induced invention has meant

that "intensive systems of agriculture replaced extensive systems," accelerating the rate of food production. (59)

Here the expertise is focused on reinterpreting the available historical data to emphasize that "necessity is the mother of invention." As the author points out, these experts have been right so far: Despite dire predictions about the effect of population growth, technological developments have produced increased resources rather than starvation. As a transition, he asks, "Will Malthus still be wrong fifty years from now?" (60) and offers some additional authority evidence:

> In 1986 [Stanford biologist Peter] Vitousek decided to calculate how much of the earth's "primary productivity" went to support human beings. He added together the grain we ate, the corn we fed our cows, and the forests we cut for timber and paper; he added the losses in food as we overgrazed grassland and turned it into desert. And when he was finished adding, the number he came up with was 38.8 percent. We use 38.8 percent of everything the world's plants don't need to keep themselves alive; directly or indirectly, we consume 38.8 percent of what it is possible to eat. "That's a relatively large number," Vitousek says. "It should give pause to people who think we are far from any limits. . . . There's a sense among economists that we're so far from any biophysical limits. I think that's not supported by the evidence." (60)

It's very likely that you have never heard of Peter Vitousek. That he is a biologist is an indicator of his expertise regarding the conditions of life, and that he is connected with Stanford University suggests that he is a person of above average competence. McKibben uses this material to respond to the anti-Malthusians, and this material is more persuasive because the author explains how Vitousek went about calculating how much humans consume—almost 40 percent of what it is possible to consume—before quoting his statement that we are closer to the biophysical limits of our planet than many economists seem to believe. We don't just have to take his word for it; we have some idea of how he reached that conclusion, and if we think that process is sensible, we are more likely to accept the claim that follows.

These contrasting viewpoints emphasize the limits of authority evidence. Both experts are unfamiliar figures; we have no experience with them that allows us to judge their competence. We have only brief references to their areas of expertise and the institutions/nations with which they are associated. Each is interpreting a body of data, and as is so often the case, the experts disagree. In each case, we have some basis for understanding how they arrived at their conclusions. Neither can provide us with definitive evidence; all they can do is suggest the ways in which we might interpret the available evidence. Quite possibly, audience members will choose to believe one or the other based on their prior attitudes on this topic.

Based on these examples, what should you do to use evidence most effectively in your rhetoric? Combine the different forms of evidence so the limitations of one kind are compensated for by the strengths of another—compensate for the impersonality of statistics with the vivid, concrete drama of an example; compensate for the lonely example with more instances buttressed by statistical measures showing frequency of occurrence; compensate for the complexity of data with analyses and interpretations of experts; predict specific cases, as you cannot with statistics, through detailed comparisons. Summarize an essential principle through the figurative analogy; contrast the generalizations of an expert with examples of testimony from people who have actually experienced the problem.

The functions of evidence are three: (1) to prove, (2) to make vivid, and (3) to clarify. To fulfill their functions, they must be combined into larger units, into arguments and organizational patterns, which are the subjects of Chapters 5 and 6.

MATERIAL FOR ANALYSIS

Coincidence? We Think Not![7]
by Scott Ostler

1   Were Babe Ruth and Elvis Presley twins? On the surface, that's a hard case to make. There's the age difference, 40 years. And the separate sets of parents. The keen observer will also note the dissimilarity in appearance. Women wept at the beauty of Elvis's face, while Babe's moonish mug was so nonclassically constructed, it could have stopped a clock in mid-tick.

2   But dig deeper into the lives and lore of America's two greatest pop-culture gods and the similarities are astonishing, beginning with the date they died, August 16—Ruth in 1948 and Presley in 1977. Was there some kind of psychic-spiritual link between the two men who changed our world by swinging their hips just so? You be the judge.

3   Both rose from abject poverty to absolute royalty. Ruth was born in a row house in Baltimore and became the Sultan of Swat. Presley was born in a crude house his father built in Tupelo and became the King.

4   The playful wink was a signature of both. Jimmy Austin, an opposing third baseman who watched many of Babe's home run trots, said, "He'd never pass me without giving me a wink." Were they having fun? Ruth would come back to the dugout after a homer, laughing and boasting, "Baby got his today!" Elvis on stage would break into uncontrollable giggles.

5   They were the end of the world as we knew it. To purists, the Ruth-inspired home run craze did for baseball what the butt-mounted outboard motor might do for Olympic swimming. Preachers and parents recoiled at Presley's body language.

6   Both busted out at 19, Elvis releasing his first record, *That's All Right (Mama)*, for Sun Records and Babe signing with the minor league Baltimore Orioles.

7   Ruth loved music and Presley loved sports. Babe had a booming baritone voice and considered himself a damn fine singer. Elvis enjoyed touch football and full-contact rollerskating scrimmages with his buddies.

8   Guns, guns, guns. Ruth loved to hunt, and he obtained a permit to pack heat, to protect his ever-present wad o' cash. Presley owned many weapons, including a machine gun.

9   They ate like pigs. Early in Babe's career he would down a mid-game snack of hot dogs, peanuts and ice cream on the bench. Elvis's favorite snack was a peanut butter and banana sandwich, fried in a pool of butter. Guess what? They ballooned from sleek young quarter horses—Presley 6' 1" and 185 pounds, Ruth 6'2" and 185, both with broad shoulders and skinny legs—into hippos. Ruth would pork up as heavy as 270 pounds. Presley, between movies, would push 250.

10   Both were relentless in their pursuit of the wine-women-song parlay. They bragged like schoolboys about their sexual conquests and seemed oblivious to the

anguish they caused their wives. Helen Ruth suffered a nervous breakdown and finally left her husband. Elvis was stunned and enraged when his wife, Priscilla, left him for a karate instructor.

11   They delighted in the grand, impulsive gesture. Both gave away Cadillacs as gifts. They were monstrous tippers, massive spenders. Cars? They bought 'em like candy and drove 'em like amusement-park bumper cars. Miraculous healing powers! Parents brought sick children to Presley in hopes that his touch would cure them. When Ruth promised a homer to a gravely injured kid named Johnny Sylvester, then hit three, it was widely believed that Babe had given Johnny the will to live.

12   Each was ruled by a colonel: Ruth by Col. Jacob Ruppert, the Yankees' president, and Presley by Col. Tom Parker, his manager. Nearing death, Babe leaned on a Louisville Slugger for support; the woozy Elvis leaned on a jewel-studded cane. Each died young—Ruth at 53, Presley at 42—and of his own excesses. Babe smoked like a steel mill, sometimes 30 cigars a day, chewed tobacco and dipped snuff and was done in by throat cancer. Elvis spent his final years on a pathetic roller coaster of pills and shots, uppers and downers. He died sitting on a toilet, the King's final throne. Taking stock of what Babe and Elvis gave us, some have tried to measure their legacy in numbers. How many home runs, how many gold records. But how many was never the point. The point was how.

13   Proposed: a holiday, Babe 'n' Elvis Day, August 16. The difference between this and the normal dead-guy holiday would be that instead of taking the day off, everyone would take the day on. Swing from the heels, sing from the heart, live larger, dream bigger, eat more, sleep less, break new ground, break old rules, break a record, cut a record, cut a swath.

14   And as you're trotting around third or leaving the building, don't forget the wink.

Questions for Analysis

1. Itemize all the ways Babe Ruth and Elvis Presley are portrayed as similar. Is this a literal or figurative analogy? Now identify all the ways in which you know they are different. Do similarities outweigh differences? How does the extensive use of analogy in this piece illustrate the strengths and weaknesses of this form of evidence?
2. How does the extensive use of analogies contribute to the tone of the article?
3. How do analogies contribute to both the consummatory and instrumental purposes of the editorial?

EXERCISES

Adapting Evidence to Definitional Strategies

1. The ability to define a term clearly and craftily is a sign of a capable rhetor. It requires knowledge of the various ways in which support material can be utilized. In Figure 4–2 you will find 10 "definitional strategies" that will help you think about using evidence carefully.[8]

    Prepare a one- to two-minute definitional speech designed to *alter perception* in which you carefully unpack a term using three to five definitional strategies. Choose a concept sufficiently large in scope that you can define it in several different ways. Choose a concept that is unfamiliar to your audience or one that has several confusing meanings. Choose a concept that you think your audience needs to know. Consider such words as Wisdom, Justice, Obscenity, Myth, Agape, etc. Consider such ideas as Feminism, Renaissance, Chaos Theory, Postmodernism, Compassionate Conservatism, etc.

Figure 4–2
Definitional Strategies

Name	Function	Example
Dictionary Definition	Defining from a dictionary	"According to Webster's 10th Edition: 'Rhetoric is the art of oratory.'"
Stipulative Definition	Defining in your own particular way	"As many of you know, I like to define rhetoric by its seven P's: rhetoric is discourse that is purposive, poetic, problem-solving, public, propositional, pragmatic, and powerful."
Authoritative Definition	Defining from an expert on the subject	"Aristotle has defined rhetoric as 'the faculty of discovering the available means of persuasion in any given case.'"
Negative Definition	Defining by what it is not	"By the term rhetoric, I do not refer to its pejorative, misunderstood usages such as bombast, hot air, bloviation, mere words, or deceptive speech."
Etymological Definition	Defining from original sources	"*Ethos,* a Greek word and key constituent of rhetoric, comes from two words: ethics and ethnic; hence, rhetoric is always concerned with a speaker's moral conduct and his/her ability to reflect the norms of a given community."
Exemplar Definition	Defining by using examples	"To help you understand the scope of rhetoric, let me share with you some examples: Bill Clinton's Inaugural Address is rhetoric; George Will's political commentary in *Newsweek* is rhetoric; Tracey Chapman's folk music is rhetoric; the Doonesbury comic strip is rhetoric."
Contextual Definition	Defining by tracing its usage through various times in history	"In the 4th century BCE, rhetoric referred to the full range of communicative interaction; in the 1st century distinctions were first made between informative and persuasive speaking; in the 14th century rhetoric became relevant to the sacred sphere; in the 19th century the scientific aspects of rhetoric were studied and rhetoric was transformed into the study of eloquence."
Analogical Definition	Defining by comparing the known with the unknown	"The study of rhetoric is akin to the study of literature; both involve a heightened sensitivity of the power and artistry of words."
Synonym Definition	Defining by words that can be used interchangeably	"Rhetoric is equated with the terms *persuasion, oratory,* and *social influence.*"
Operational Definition	Defining by describing its process or procedures	"Rhetoric is a process involving a source, a receiver, a message, feedback, channel, situation, and noise."

Source: Susan Schultz Huxman, *Public Speaking: A Repertoire of Resources* (New York: McGraw-Hill College Custom Series, 1992).

2. Prepare a four- to five-minute speech designed *to explain* or to create understanding about something unfamiliar to the audience. Plan the speech carefully to run not more than five minutes. Build in, "Are there any questions?" at each strategic point in the process.

The audience is expected to take notes and then to ask the speaker only two kinds of questions: (1) what do you mean? (a request for explanation, clarification, or definition) and (2) how do you know? (a request for data). No one should be allowed to argue with the speaker or to refute claims or challenge evidence; however, active audience participation is essential.

After completing the exercise, discuss problems of clarity (vocabulary, explanation) and audience needs for evidence that speakers did not recognize. Discuss the problems of delivery created when your presentation is interrupted by questions from the audience. Discuss why the speaker needs to solicit questions to make this exercise work (why won't you interrupt when you don't understand or want proof for an assertion? what communication norms are involved?). What factors seemed to make some speakers more effective than others in doing this assignment?

3. Prepare a four- to five-minute speech to *create virtual experience* that mandates the use of visuals. (Your instructor may suggest additional rhetorical purposes.) Consider such topics as the styles of radio disc jockeys, methods of musical arrangement, a detailed statistical analysis, an explanation of a form or map, a comparison of television commercials. Ideally, students should seek to use a variety of visuals: pictures, graphs, charts, audio and videotapes, transparencies, slides, films, power point, demonstration assistants, and others.

4. The importance of visuals in presenting material is the special concern of those who belong to the Demonstrative Evidence Specialists Association, a trade group made up of businesses that provide graphic materials for lawyers and others.[9] The graphics they create range from charts that reduce a complex argument about damages into a simple bottom line that a jury can clearly understand to a-day-in-the-life-of videotapes of severely injured litigants that show the quality of their lives as a result of an accident. Obviously, graphics that can simplify a complex case can also oversimplify, but the need to tell a story in a culture that is now filled with visual images makes graphics an important tool in persuasion.

Those who study jury behavior, however, agree that fancy graphics cannot save a weak case. On the other hand, where both sides have strong cases, graphics might make the difference. To be admissible in court, graphics must conform to the rules of evidence, which are good rules for anyone using visual aids: they must be accurate, relevant, and not overly prejudicial, meaning that their emotional impact must not outweigh their value as proof.

Discuss the physical (e.g., delivery, lights, eye contact), mechanical, and temporal (how much more time they take) problems such aids create. What kinds of data do they make more accessible? Recall the principles of using visual aids discussed in Chapter 3.

5. Consider the following general claims:

The dot-com industry has been built almost overnight on a very shaky foundation; hence, one should not hope for its miracle to live on.

After-school, summer, and other part-time jobs are beneficial to teenagers; hence, local communities should consider ways to encourage employers to hire teenagers.

The diet industry should be regulated because currently too many shady companies use misleading advertisements and provide dangerous advice to their clients.

What kinds of personal experiences can you come up with that would support any of these claims? Using InfoTrac College Edition, locate information about the dot-com industry, jobs for teenagers, and/or the diet industry, and try to gather as much evidence as possible in support of the above claims. What kinds of evidence would you use if you were to defend any of the above positions in front of (1) your communication class; (2) a city council committee investigating the relationships between large, multinational corporations and local communities; (3) a student group dedicated to raising the civic engagement of students on campus; and (4) your family. What considerations should guide your choice? What are the strengths and limitations of each type of evidence?

6. **Portfolio Entry 3: Evidence**
Compare and contrast how your three rhetorical selections use evidence (VASES) to advance their purposes. What are the strengths and weaknesses of each? In one to two pages, work on using critical equations smoothly.

NOTES

1. Aristotle, *Rhetoric*, trans. W. Rhys Roberts (New York: Modern Library, 1954).

2. Bill McKibben, "A Special Moment in History," *Atlantic Monthly*, May 1998, pp. 55–91.

3. Stephen Jay Gould, "The Streak of Streaks," *New York Review of Books*, August 18, 1988, pp. 8–12.

4. See also Thomas Gilovich, *How We Know What Isn't*

So: *The Fallibility of Human Reason in Everyday Life* (New York: The Free Press, 1991).

5. [Minneapolis] *Star Tribune*, September 19, 1987, p. 13A.

6. For a detailed analysis of the many problems with this form of evidence, see Elizabeth F. Loftus, *Eyewitness Testimony* (Cambridge, MA: Harvard University Press, 1980).

7. Reprinted courtesy of *Sports Illustrated*, August 18, 1997, p. 80. Scott Ostler is a columnist for the *San Francisco Chronicle*. © 1997 Time, Inc. All rights reserved.

8. For early work on the value of a "one point speech," see Douglas Ehninger, *Influence, Belief, and Argument* (Glenview, IL: Scott, Foresman, 1974); Bruce Gronbeck, *The Articulate Person*, ed. (Glenview, IL: Scott, Foresman, 1983).

9. See Peter Applebome, "Showing Beats Telling in Many Lawsuits," *New York Times*, January 13, 1989, p. 22Y.

chapter 5

The Resources of Argument

No fact has any meaning by itself. To be significant, to have impact, evidence must become part of an argument, and arguments, in turn, must be combined into larger rhetorical wholes (the subject of Chapter 6). My concern in this chapter is with arguments, a key building block of rhetorical action. Just what is an argument?

Commonly, an argument means a debate or a quarrel because arguments usually express differing viewpoints or disagreements. In a general sense, we can speak of the argument of a novel, referring to the principle or pattern of its development and the kind of experience it attempts to create. This usage reflects an understanding that arguments are structures, ways of organizing material. In this chapter, however, I use argument to refer to the process of giving reasons for or against some position. Thus, for rhetorical purposes, an *argument* is a claim or a conclusion backed by one or more reasons or justifications.

Based on that definition, here are some arguments: Capital punishment should be abolished because it is an ineffective deterrent against violent crime. Teenagers should receive sex education and contraceptive information because they are not yet equipped to be good parents. State lotteries should be abolished because they are a highly regressive and inefficient way to raise revenue. These are arguments because each makes a claim based on a justification or a reason.

Figure 5–1
Reasoning

These examples also illustrate the role of evidence in argument. One appropriate response to these arguments is, How do you know that capital punishment is an ineffective deterrent against rising murder rates? That many or most teenagers engage in sexual intercourse? That teenagers are not equipped to be good parents? That lotteries are regressive and inefficient? And each question must be answered with evidence. Some arguments omit the evidence on which they are based, but all arguments are based on evidence. All imply that evidence exists and could be presented.

The most basic elements of an argument and their relationship can be illustrated as in Figure 5–1. Because evidence was discussed in Chapter 4, I now turn to the other two elements.

CLAIMS

The shape or character of an argument is determined by the kind of claims it makes, the conclusion it draws. *A claim or conclusion* is an assertion. Some examples are: That is a dog. You are in good health. Smoking causes lung cancer. Affirmative action damages the self-esteem of those it is designed to help.

Every claim is an assertion, and every assertion is a claim that goes beyond the facts, beyond what can actually be proved. A claim involves a logical or inferential "leap." Even when you make a claim as simple as "That is a dog," you "jump" to a conclusion based on a few surface characteristics that seem to indicate that this creature is a kind of canine. When we make such a claim, few of us have either the necessary data or the biological expertise to back up our statement by distinguishing canines from other mammals or domestic dogs from coyotes, dingoes, foxes, or wolves.

Even when the person who makes the claim is an expert who has lots of data, such a leap is present. During the summer of 1993, Reggie Lewis, a Boston Celtics basketball player died while shooting baskets with a friend at the team's training center at Brandeis University.[1] Earlier, on April 29, during the opening game of the playoffs,

Lewis had collapsed. After tests conducted by the team physician and a group of a dozen heart specialists, Lewis was found to have cardiomyopathy, a life-threatening condition that would have ended his athletic career. But a second team of physicians at another hospital disputed those findings and concluded that Lewis had a benign neurological condition known as neurocardiogenic syncope, a condition that causes fainting but rarely is fatal. In this case, each team of cardiologists made a leap from the data gathered by their tests to a conclusion about Lewis's health. Each conclusion was informed by empirical evidence drawn from echocardiograms, magnetic resonance imaging of the heart, monitoring of his heart rhythm while he ran a treadmill, and electrical stimulation of his heart to learn whether it was vulnerable to bursts of potentially fatal rhythms. Those test results were interpreted in light of the physicians' long training and years of medical practice establishing how to construe such test results.

Lewis's death was a dramatic and tragic reminder that the physicians' conclusions, like all argumentative claims, are inferential leaps that go beyond the available evidence. Obviously, none of these cardiologists wanted to put Lewis in mortal peril, and which conclusion to accept was a hard choice for the team and the player. Tragically, however, the inferential leap made by the group that Lewis and the Celtics chose to believe was wrong. Note, too, how belief, accepting one claim rather than another, follows self-interest: Lewis did not want to give up a satisfying and lucrative career in professional basketball, and the Celtics did not want to lose their 6'7" captain. The outcome, however, is dramatic evidence of the discrepancy between data (the test results) and the claim (that he did or did not have a life-threatening heart condition).

The special character of an argument is precisely this: that it makes a leap from data to a claim. That is why it is a fundamental building block in rhetorical action. That is also what gives an argument its force, and, as the example shows, it is what makes arguments risky and open to challenge.

REASONS

The leap made in an argument ordinarily is not a blind leap made in ignorance. As indicated in the illustration, we go from evidence or data to a claim via a justification or reason. A reason is an authorization or *warrant* for the leap made in an argument. In other words, reasons are grounds or bases for drawing conclusions. They are justifications for claims.

To illustrate this process, let us return to the example. In making tests, cardiologists gather all kinds of data about the heart—its muscle, its pumping efficiency and that of the vessels that feed it, its performance under stress, and so forth. When the results are in, they are measured against certain standards or norms established for identifying people who have different kinds of heart beat variations and problems. By comparing the data from these tests with these standards, a cardiologist can decide whether or not someone has a life-threatening problem. Several reasoning processes are involved. It is assumed that (1) all reliable tests of heart activity were made; (2) they were made by competent cardiologists using accurate instruments; and (3) the results were compared to standard indicators of a potentially lethal or a relatively benign heart arrhythmia (variations in the rhythm of heartbeats) for persons of the patient's age and physical condition. Each of these is a reason a cardiologist might use to support a conclusion about the health of an individual's heart: all essential tests were made; these tests were made and interpreted by experts; the results were compared to established standards for a given group of people with the characteristics of the individual being tested.

These reasons are related to medicine and cardiology; thus, such reasons are sometimes called *field-dependent* because they belong to a particular field or area of expertise, and they rely on the authority of persons skilled in that field. (Recall that in Chapter 4 an authority was defined as a person thought competent to interpret data and to decide what conclusions could be drawn from it.) That reasons often arise out of the knowledge accumulated in a field of knowledge means that the reasons appropriate for one subject may not be appropriate for another.

ISSUES

An *issue* is a fundamental point in dispute, a question crucial in making a decision, choosing a stance, or selecting a course of action. Most issues fall roughly into these three types: questions of fact, of value, and of policy.[2] Issues distinguish kinds of arguments and reveal the resources of each.

Questions of Fact

A *question of fact* is a dispute about what evidence exists and how it should be interpreted. Several issues about capital punishment, for example, are really questions of fact: Does capital punishment deter others from committing murder? (What evidence of deterrence exists? What is reliable evidence of deterrence? How can it be gathered?) Are a disproportionate number of poor, nonwhites executed, and does the ethnicity of the victim affect such sentencing? (What proportion of capital crimes are committed by poor nonwhites? What kind of data exist about the socioeconomic status and race of executed persons? Are there data to show that those who kill whites rather than nonwhites are more likely to be executed?) What kind of legal representation did those accused of capital crimes receive? (Was that representation competent, and what kind of evidence is needed to establish competence or incompetence?) Such disputes are not simple, as the conflicting evidence about deterrence demonstrates, but they do reflect some fundamental agreements: that deterrence is an important goal; that penalties should be applied without class, ethnic, or other bias; that the ultimate punishment should be applied only after a fair trial in which the defendant receives competent legal representation.

In other words, when you address a question of fact, the issues focus on the quality, accuracy, and adequacy of the evidence. As illustrated above, disputants agree on a common goal—deterrence—and proceed to examine the evidence to determine whether a specific policy, such as capital punishment, meets that goal. The dispute will focus on the amount and quality of evidence and its appropriate interpretation, and most of the warrants will be field-dependent. Authoritative evidence will be particularly important because such evidence allows facts to be interpreted.

Questions of Value

A *question of value*, by contrast, is a dispute about goals, and it reflects a more fundamental disagreement. Some of the issues about capital punishment are questions of value: Should we avenge premeditated murder or obey absolutely the injunction against killing? What are the ethical implications of killing by the state? Is our goal to rehabilitate those who commit crimes or to protect society from murderers? Is our moral standard "better that ten guilty persons go free than that one innocent person die"? Are there circumstances under which murder is justified (such as self-defense or the battered-woman syndrome)? Such issues reflect fundamental commitments, and no single rhetorical act is likely to change them.

Disagreements over values often define target audiences (those who share a fundamental value). They may be a measure of audience hostility, one kind of obstacle or aspect of the rhetorical problem. Conflicts between the values held by individual members of the audience may be a resource for initiating rhetorical action. Such conflicts may be used to provoke individuals to reconsider their priorities and to seek ways to reestablish internal consistency within their value systems.

Values arise from our basic needs, from cultural norms, and from our peculiarities as individuals (see Chapter 8). All of these values are resources for arguments because each value is a reason or justification. Such reasons are not field dependent; they depend on cultural norms and social mores. Reasons or justifications drawn from such values are sometimes called *motivational* because they are grounded in our motives as human beings, as members of a culture, or as unique individuals.[3]

When we are urged to act to ensure our survival, for example, when we are pressed to buy a year's supply of food to protect ourselves against the devastation of nuclear attack, economic depression, or millennial meltdown, a motivational reason is at work. Such reasons are also present in many arguments that appeal to our need for esteem (Vote for George W. Bush or Al Gore because he shares our values) for love (avoid dandruff and be attractive and desirable by using ABC shampoo), and for self-actualization (buy *How to Be a Success in Business*). When arguments appeal to basic needs, cultural values, or to personal achievement, motivational justifications are being used.

Questions of Policy

The issues in *questions of policy* are so universal that they are known as involving stock issues (they are commonplaces, always "in stock"). A policy is a course of action, a procedure that is systematically followed and applied. According to Aristotle, the central issue of what he called deliberative rhetoric, which treats questions of policy, is expediency—that is, "appropriateness to the purpose at hand" or the most efficient and effective means to an end. Stock issues arise from what a rhetor must do to make a good case for changing current policy or the means to achieve our goals now in use. These issues can be stated as follows:

1. Is there a compelling need to change the current policy? To demonstrate this, show that
   a. Someone is harmed or injured.
   b. The harm or injury is of sufficient scope to be of social concern.
   c. The harm or injury is a direct consequence of the policy presently in effect (what has been called inherency).
2. Is there an alternative policy? (More than one may need to be considered.)
3. Is the alternative policy under consideration practical and beneficial?
   a. Do we have the resources and expertise to put it into effect; does it require what we consider an appropriate amount of resources?

b. Will the results of the policy improve the situation or is it likely to have side effects that would make it, on balance, undesirable?

Each of these elements combines questions of fact and questions of value.

A policy is a way of doing something. It is a systematic way of dealing with a particular kind of situation or event. Because we do not assume that change is good in itself, when you advocate policy changes, you assume an argumentative responsibility that is called *the burden of proof*. If you fulfill its requirements, however, as described below, then supporters of current policies are obligated to respond to your arguments and evidence.

First, you must show that someone is harmed (a question of fact and of value). A fact by itself does not demonstrate harm. The fact must be measured against a standard (or value) to show that what exists is harmful. Consider, for example, the startling fact that over 400,000 people in the United States die each year from the effects of smoking, a figure that dwarfs the 58,000+ Americans killed over several years in the Vietnam War. The deaths in the Vietnam War produced national concern and considerable social disruption. The deaths from smoking have been an accepted part of our culture for many years, and, until quite recently, little has been done to reduce those numbers. As these examples illustrate, a claim that some situation is harmful combines data with a justification drawn from a value.

But demonstrating harm is not enough. The harm must have a certain scope or magnitude. This measurement moves from injuries to individuals to harm affecting the well-being of society. A student did this well in a speech arguing that measles vaccinations should be required for all children. She transformed that topic from triviality to significance by citing evidence to show how many unvaccinated children would get the measles, how many of those children would be permanently brain-damaged, and what the cost to society would be. Suddenly a rather unimportant childhood disease that had been quite remote became a significant social problem with important financial implications for each of us.

As these examples suggest, scope or magnitude is usually demonstrated with statistics, but that is not always the case. A single innocent person who is executed through capital punishment is likely to raise serious questions, not only because of the importance of one human life, but also because that one instance is a sign that all the procedures designed to ensure justice were not sufficient to prevent its most serious miscarriage. Similarly, a single nuclear accident like that at Chernobyl in which substantial amounts of radioactive materials were released into the air (something many thought never could happen) may be significant enough to call into question policies governing nuclear power plant construction and maintenance in the republics that used to form the Soviet Union. That single case may move other nations including the United States to provide monetary help to enable these republics to make a transition from closing these plants to developing alternative sources of energy.

But harm and scope are not enough by themselves. You must also demonstrate that these problems are the direct result of the present policy. In other words, you must prove that harm of this magnitude is intrinsic to, an inevitable part of, the current procedure. As an illustration, suppose that, using your current method of study (the policy), you receive a D in nutrition. That grade, clearly harmful, does not automatically mean that you will conclude that your current method of study is at fault. Perhaps you were not adequately prepared for this kind of science course and are really proud that you passed it in spite of your handicap. Perhaps your teacher was unskilled at explaining ideas, inaccessible for conferences, and absentmindedly asked questions on the tests about material that wasn't covered in the text or lectures. Perhaps you were seriously ill during a major part of the semester, and any course you were able to pass was a victory over your health problems. Note that, in these cases, the cause lies outside the policy. Change, if any, needs to occur somewhere else, in your preparation for the course, in the teacher's approach, in your health, but not in your mode of study.

This test is part of a question of policy because no policy is ever presumed to be perfect. All policies are carried out by imperfect humans who have bad days and who can create any number of problems for which the policy itself cannot be held responsible, and all of us have had experience with individuals who seem determined to make some procedure as difficult as possible! As a result, the issue of whether or not the problem is intrinsic to the policy is a demand that you show that it is the policy itself, not the persons who carry it out or some special set of circumstances, that is generating the problem.

If you can demonstrate significant harm, and that the harm is an inevitable part of the current policy, you must still show that an alternative course of action exists. In most cases this is easy—several alternatives will seem obvious. But the issue exists because if we are to change, there must be something to change to. Many students, for instance, do not consider changing the way they study because they are not aware of any alternative. Most students are not taught how to study or exposed to various approaches, and so do not see any other way to do it. Conditions must exist that make change possible. After a certain number of heart attacks, for example, a person no longer has the opportunity to change lifestyle. Given a certain amount of damage, exercises to improve heart action and circulation are no longer possible. Those who mourn the effects of aging are often called up short by someone who says, "Consider the alternative!"

And if you demonstrate that an alternative exists, you still must show that it is practical. That is, you must show that the personnel, expertise, time, money, and materials are available to institute the new procedure. If these resources are not available or difficult to obtain, or if the allocation required is too substantial to gain assent because of its impact on other areas of importance, the policy is not a realistic alternative. If the cost of the policy is too high, we may decide to live with the current level of harm. For example, many students consider the cost involved in following a method of study that would produce an A average too high. They place higher priorities on time spent in recreation with friends or in extracurricular activities such as debate or athletics.

Finally, you must demonstrate that the alternative policy is, on balance, beneficial. This issue reflects a recognition that all policies, no matter how wonderful, have undesirable as well as desirable effects. If we change our procedure, we want to be assured that we shall come out ahead. In the face of data that increasing numbers of Americans are without health insurance, the president may propose measures to Congress, such as programs to provide health care for poor children, that will insure that more people receive adequate health care, but such programs are costly, and they require either additional taxes or shifting appropriations from other programs to this one in order to be put into operation, policies that reduce money for pay to members of the armed forces or other programs. Members of Congress will try to determine, to the extent they can, whether the benefits of reducing the numbers without health care outweigh the evils of higher taxes or lower spending in other areas.

Each of these issues combines questions of fact and questions of value. Questions of harm and scope measure facts against values. Evaluation of the current policy depends on how clearly we can establish that it, rather than other factors, is responsible for the problem. That an alternative policy exists must be demonstrated before we can evaluate its practicality (what costs we are willing to bear combines facts and values) or benefits (evaluation of predicted effects). Policy questions are treated separately here, not because they differ from questions of fact and value, but because certain demands must be met by any rhetor who advocates policy change. The values used to judge these questions may differ among persons or cultures, but these same issues are addressed whenever anyone evaluates policies.

INVENTION

The ancient Greek and Roman rhetoricians called the process of preparing for rhetorical action *invention* (from the Latin *invenire*, to come upon or find). The term reflects their understanding that, ordinarily, rhetors do not create original arguments from scratch, but rather appropriate arguments they discover in their research, in the course of their training, in reports of research by others, in other speeches or essays, in cultural ideas. These arguments are applied to new circumstances, and invention refers to the choice from among available argumentative options. Invention also reflects the creative role of the rhetor in selecting and adapting arguments and evidence in ways best suited to the occasion and audience and to her or his purpose, and in organizing these into an effective whole.

Skillful invention requires that you know yourself and the role you will play, that you know just what audience you are trying to reach, and that you are familiar with the available evidence and arguments and with the cultural history of your subject. Once again, an understanding of your specific rhetorical problem is essential to making wise choices in preparing your materials.

Some clues about the importance of arguments and evidence in rhetoric come from a body of research that is called *persuasive arguments theory*. This research has been done on decisionmaking in small groups, and the results suggest that arguments have more to do with attitude change than peer pressure, the influence of the attitudes of others on the positions we take.[4]

Persuasive arguments theory goes like this. It is estimated that there is a culturally given pool of arguments on an issue (what we have called the cultural history of the subject; see Chapter 9). In order to decide what position to take, individuals sample from this pool of arguments. Arguments vary in availability (the chance that they are known or will come to mind), direction (pro and con), and persuasiveness (impact on, salience for an individual). According to this research, people take positions on issues because of the balance of arguments; that is, they decide where they stand based on the number of pro or con arguments that have force for them that they know about or are exposed to. As a result, novel or unfamiliar arguments become especially important because such arguments may tip the balance and change an individual's attitude. This research also demonstrates the significance of cultural history as part of the rhetorical problem, because, in these studies, attitude change was least likely to occur when all members of the group were familiar with the entire pool of arguments (that is, the entire cultural history of the subject was known to them).

One kind of evidence, citations from trusted and respected authorities, assumes special significance. When individuals encounter an unexpected position in a statement by a recognized authority, they tend to think up arguments that would explain why the authority would take such an unexpected position. These potentially novel arguments, constructed by members of the audience, can also shift the balance and change attitudes. Imagine, for example, that you are a committed conservative with high regard for former U.S. Ambassador to the United Nations Jeane Kirkpatrick. You discover, to your surprise, that she opposes U.S. air strikes against the Iraqis who violate the restricted air space designated by the United Nations. You then think up reasons that she might have for that position (perhaps it is difficult militarily to avoid hitting civilian targets; perhaps the dangers to our pilots are too great; the costs of this policy are escalating and we are not receiving support from our allies, and so on). The arguments you construct will be good reasons for you—sensible, salient, forceful. Such arguments are ideally adapted to their audience (you) and have a unique capacity to influence you.

This research suggests that evidence and arguments with which the audience is unfamiliar are particularly potent because they can prompt those exposed into rethinking a position and alter the balance of arguments to shift opinion. Audiences may construct highly potent novel arguments when confronted with an unexpected stance from a respected authority. The research underlines the rhetorical obstacles created by the cultural history of a subject; that is, attitude change is unlikely when the audience is familiar with the entire pool of arguments. In effect, we tune out when we recognize arguments that are familiar to us.

Some of the reasons that arguments are the building blocks of rhetorical action are now apparent. Arguments are essential units in rhetoric because they combine facts and values to advance claims that express our knowledge, understandings, and commitments. As such, they harness together the power of our knowledge and our values. Arguments are building blocks because they address the fundamental issues of fact and value that are part of all choices. They focus on essentials, the grounds for belief and attitude. They are structures that make sense of the world. For all of these reasons, arguments are powerful rhetorical resources.

Another way of thinking about arguments comes from the theorizing and research of Richard Petty and John Cacioppo.[5] Their *elaboration likelihood model (ELM)* emphasizes self-persuasion—that is, the likelihood that audience members will be stimulated to participate in creating a message, that is, to process or interpret it, to develop, clarify, or embellish it, and consider its implications.

Note that from this perspective a better, stronger argument is one that engages audience members, one that they collaborate in creating, translating it into their own words, attempting to clarify what seems ambiguous, and amplifying what the rhetor has voiced by contributing personal experiences, thinking up relevant questions, and the like. In other words, a good argument is one that the audience digests and makes its own.

According to their research as well as that of others, the single most important variable affecting one's desire or willingness to digest and amplify an argument is personal relevance, that is, the expectation that the issue it addresses is vital or will have significant consequences for one's life. Put differently, personal relevance is the single greatest motivator prompting audience members to involve themselves in a message. That underscores the importance of adapting arguments to the audience and how essential it is to point out the relevance of issues for those you seek to reach and influence.

A number of other variables affect an audience member's propensity and willingness to elaborate. Some people are natural "noodlers" who love to play around with ideas; they are relatively easy to tempt into argumentative engagement. In addition, we are more willing to participate in messages that reflect our values and beliefs, our ways of looking at the world. Obviously, such messages speak to us in familiar language and offer justifications that we already accept as valid. The fields we choose or the professions we practice reflect such preferences: engineers respect statistical proofs and practical applications; economists respond particularly to claims based on economic principles, and so on. For example, the essay "Jesus Was a Feminist" at the end of this chapter illustrates a rhetorical act with a somewhat controversial message addressed to those with strong religious beliefs. In this case, the arguments are based on religious justifications, and personal salience arises out of a body of beliefs and a commitment to living one's life according to certain moral principles. By contrast, even those sympathetic to feminism but reared without much religious training or without strong religious beliefs are likely to be less responsive to this essay and less willing to participate actively in it.

As noted, ELM theory recognizes that persuasion does not occur solely on the basis of the quality of the evidence and the argument. We sometimes use what they call *a peripheral route*, a kind of shortcut, to avoid the hard work involved in exploring the implications of arguments and evidence (see Figure 5–2). Instead of doing the work yourself, for example, you might turn to *Consumer Reports*, a magazine that sells no advertising; on that basis, you might ignore the details of their testing and the assumptions from which they worked and simply look for the bottom line, accepting whatever they say is the best brand of running shoes, which you then go out to buy. In that case, you judge the source and use it as a peripheral cue on which to make a decision, a highly efficient way of making a choice. Arguments themselves may be peripheral cues; for example, we can be influenced by the sheer number of arguments offered—a peripheral cue—in effect, concluding that because there are many reasons given for it, it must be the best choice.

Figure 5–2
Elaboration Likelihood Model (ELM)

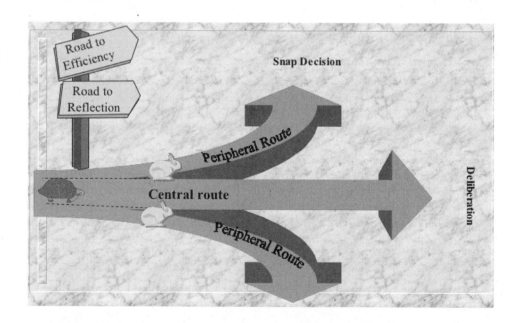

The accumulated evidence of research on persuasion is quite consistent with the ELM view that there is a tradeoff between participating in messages—exploring and evaluating arguments and evidence—and relying on peripheral cues. In general, anything that reduces a person's ability and/or motivation to interpret, test, and amplify issue-relevant arguments also increases the likelihood that simple peripheral cues from the source, occasion, or context will influence the outcome.

Thus far, I have considered arguments as rational structures that make explicit claims backed by reasons and evidence. But arguments, even rational arguments, are often implicit, subtle, and fragmentary, especially when they appear in the statements of real human beings in contrast to neat diagrams in logic textbooks. The most basic kinds of arguments found in rhetoric are outlined in Figure 5–3: (1) *enthymeme*, (2)

Figure 5-3

Reasoning Types (or General Arguments)

Name	Function	Example	Value
Enthymeme	An abbreviated kind of argument. Audiences must complete the argumentative cues provided by the rhetor.	The classic negative campaign ad of 1968, "The Daisy Spot," never explicitly says "Goldwater will push the nuclear button." But audiences draw that conclusion from the sequencing of powerful visual and aural cues (see Ch. 11).	Invites participation Audiences like drawing their own conclusions
Induction/ Deduction	In inductive argument, a rhetor details examples in order to arrive at a larger claim; in deductive argument, a rhetor presents a claim as presumed truth or fact and then proceeds to document how that claim is true.	"I've Been to the Mountain Top" is organized inductively. King gives many brief and poignant examples of civil rights successes before concluding that it is a righteous cause and it is God's will for the movement to prevail. "The Gettysburg Address" is organized deductively. Lincoln begins with an established truth: "all men are created equal." The rest of the address buttresses this truth.	Inductive = seductively draws audiences to accept rhetor's conclusions Deductive = straightforward appearance of logical rigor
Causal	Establish necessary relationships between two phenomena.	DiGiovanni writes in "Kosovo Diary: Madness Visible": "Slobodan Milosevic's rabid speech to the Serb minority in Kosovo on April 24, 1987 . . . set in motion a hideous cycle of nationalism and ethnic hatred, first in Slovenia and Croatia, then Bosnia, and now spiraling wildly out of control in Kosovo."	Adheres to the scientific method
Analogy	Compare two phenomena in order to evaluate, predict, or dramatize the rhetor's point.	Scott Ostler, *Sports Illustrated* writer, composes an entire editorial on the similarities between Babe Ruth and Elvis Presley. "Were Babe Ruth and Elvis Presley twins? . . . Dig deeper into the lives and lore of America's two greatest pop culture gods and the similarities are astonishing."	Adheres to the jurisprudence (courtroom) model

induction/deduction, (3) *causal*, and (4) *analogy*. Here, the attention will focus on enthymemes, argumentative resources that lie outside the field of logic and emphasize the importance of audience participation in the process of persuasion.

ENTHYMEMES

An enthymeme is a rhetorical argument. Ordinarily, it draws a conclusion that is probable rather than certain; it relies on reasons that are culturally or socially accepted; it often is deficient by strict logical standards; and its subject matter usually is concrete and specific rather than abstract. What distinguishes the enthymeme from other arguments, however, is that it is constructed out of the beliefs, attitudes, and values of the audience. An *enthymeme* is an argument jointly created by author and audience. It is an elaborated argument in the ELM sense, and it has force because audience members fill in details or add to the evidence from their experience or supply additional reasons or draw the implications of claims for themselves. A rhetor can plan to try to prompt such processes, but an enthymeme can only be created if readers or listeners participate in it and amplify it.

The concept of the enthymeme comes from the work of Aristotle, but contemporary theorists also refer to the interact or the transact as the minimal unit of communication.[6] Transacts and interacts are concepts that emphasize that you cannot commit a rhetorical act alone. Rhetoric is a transaction (*trans* means across or over or through) or an interaction (*inter* means between or among). Each of us brings a store of experience, feelings, beliefs, values, and concepts to every encounter; these are the raw materials through which we participate in rhetorical action. Note that enthymemic processes are present in all parts of an argument—audience members can collaborate in creating evidence or data, reasons, or claims—or all three!

The actor Patrick Stewart who played the captain on *Star Trek: The Next Generation* has been featured in ads for automobiles. Presumably, like any other individual, he gives a kind of personal testimony applauding a car that he likes. His reaction is no more or less valid than that of any other individual; in fact, because we have no information about his knowledge of mechanics or cars, it is quite a weak endorsement. By contrast, Stewart is a skilled and talented actor, and if he were speaking about acting, he would be an expert to whom we should attend.

But there is a second argument, and its existence is the reason that Stewart is paid handsomely to make these commercials. Although he has played other roles, Stewart is virtually indistinguishable from the character he played in the television series. In the role of captain, he appears calm and authoritative; he is a capable leader, and the adventures through which he leads his crew are associated with the exploration of frontiers, high technology, and life in the future. The automaker assumes that audiences hear, not Stewart, but the captain of the *Enterprise D* giving them advice about the most advanced, even futuristic automotive technology. In this case, no claim is made about his expertise, but it is hoped that audiences will make the assumption just the same.

A now infamous commercial made for the George Bush presidential campaign of 1988 is a more dramatic and controversial example of these two levels of argument.[7] The ad was sponsored and aired by the National Security Political Action Committee and first appeared early in September. It opened with side-by-side pictures of Bush and Michael Dukakis, Bush's Democratic opponent. Dukakis appeared somewhat dishev-

The Enthymeme

What Aristotle calls the enthymeme is a special kind of reasoning that Aristotle believed was the chief characteristic of rhetorical discourse. The word comes from three Greek terms: *en* (meaning "in") + *thumo* (heart or spirit/mind) + *ma* (the result of action). Put differently, something lodges in the heart or spirit of the listener as a result of the act of speaking. What distinguishes rhetorical reasoning is the use of *endoxa*—the opinions, beliefs, ideology, experiences, knowledge of the audience—as the basis for arguments. These can be the premise for the argument, the evidence used as proof, or the warrant that links the premise and conclusion. Of special importance is that this kind of argument relies on the active participation of, or collaboration by, audience members. Here are some examples.

> René Descartes is on a plane. The flight attendant comes down the aisle and asks, "Would you like some peanuts or a soft drink?" He replies, "I think not," and disappears. If you and your classmates laugh, that is an enthymeme. In this case, the punchline and the premise—that the 17th-century French philosopher has survived into an era of jet travel and carbonated beverages—depend on the listener supplying the detail that Descartes was the man who uttered those immortal words, "I think; therefore, I am." (courtesy of Suzanne Daughton)

You can collect examples of enthymemes from popular culture. *The Simpsons,* for example, relies on that kind of inside joke for much of its humor. That is also true of advertising, which first teaches us what we need to know and then omits it in later ads. For example, after a certain amount of exposure, we do not need to be told what product is "The Real Thing."

> A *Far Side* cartoon shows a fork, knife, and spoon in a room. The caption: "In the early days, living in their squalid apartment, all three shared dreams of success. But in the end, Bob the Spoon and Ernie the Fork ended up in an old silverware drawer, and only Mac went on to fame and fortune." (courtesy of Suzanne Daughton)

What makes the cartoon funny?

---

eled in a dark photo; Bush was smiling and well groomed in bright sunlight. As the pictures appeared, an announcer said, "Bush and Dukakis on crime." Then Bush's picture appeared as the announcer said, "Bush supports the death penalty for first-degree murderers." Then came a picture of Dukakis, with these words: "Dukakis not only opposes the death penalty, he allowed first-degree murderers to have weekend passes from prison." At this point a close-up mug shot of William Horton appeared on the screen with the words, "One was Willie Horton, who murdered a boy in a robbery, stabbing him nineteen times." A blurred black-and-white shot of Horton seemingly being arrested was shown with the words, "Despite a life sentence, Horton received ten weekend passes from prison." The words "KIDNAPPING," "STABBING," and "RAPING" in big white capital letters appeared as captions to Horton's mug shot as the announcer said, "Horton fled, kidnaping a young couple, stabbing the man and repeatedly raping his girlfriend." A photo of Dukakis then appeared, as the announcer said, "Weekend prison passes. Dukakis on crime."

There are, once again, two levels of argument. One is a rather simple and explicit argument. The claim: Vote for President Bush rather than his opponent Dukakis. The reason: Their contrasting stands on punishment of criminals. Bush supports the death penalty for first-degree murderers whereas Dukakis approved a weekend prison furlough for a lifer who committed violent crimes while out. The evidence: The sound of the announcer's words voicing Bush's position and the pictures of William Horton with the information about the crimes he had committed to receive a life sentence and that he committed while on a prison furlough.

The second level of argument is subtle and implicit. The ad suggests that the Horton case is typical (it was not), and without identifying him as African American, the photos in the ad feed into fears about rising crime (the fears are greater than the actual crime rate) and racist stereotypes that many whites have about crime by African American men. The ad helps to prompt the creation of that second argument visually through the contrasting photos of a sunny Bush and a shadowy Dukakis, the ugly, threatening mug shot of Horton, the large white letters that underscore the inflammatory words that appear on the screen under Horton's photograph, and the bits of information that can easily be formed into a scenario worthy of becoming a script for a TV movie.

The subtle, second-level argument goes something like this: It would be dangerous to vote for Dukakis. Why? Because one African American criminal committed serious crimes while on a prison furlough. When spelled out in this way, the argument seems a little silly, but the subtle argument is powerful. Racial stereotypes prompt viewers to assume that Horton was typical (in fact, no other first-degree murderer of any ethnicity murdered or raped while on a furlough), and the Horton case triggers fears about violent crime that, as I noted, are greater than the actual crime rate, fears that often have racist overtones. The second level or nondiscursive argument not only illustrates how audiences construct the proofs by which they are persuaded, it shows us a case in which an argument is constructed out of pictures, associations, and stereotyping. The enthymeme, the process of rhetorical argument, involves processes in which we construct both discursive or logical and nondiscursive or nonlogical arguments out of visual and verbal materials.

In other words, rhetorical arguments come into being in the minds of members of the audience through direct and indirect means. In fact, all rhetorical action combines elements that are discursive (logical, formed out of propositions and evidence) and nondiscursive (nonlogical, formed by association, prompted by juxtapositions, frequently visual and nonverbal). In order to understand the nature of argument, we have to step back to take a broader view of rhetorical action.

DIMENSIONS OF RHETORICAL ACTION

As I wrote in Chapter 1, rhetoric is the study of all the processes by which people are influenced. Some of these processes are logical, some are not. The dimensions of rhetorical action reveal the mixture of qualities that are found in it. Each of these dimensions is a continuum; that is, each dimension is formed by a pair of qualities related in such a way that one of them gradually becomes the other. The ends of each continuum represent extreme forms of the same quality or characteristic.

	Discursive (logical links)	**Nondiscursive (nonlogical)**
Purpose	Instrumental .... (a tool)	Consummatory (purpose in action itself)
Argument	Justificatory .... (offers reasons)	Ritualistic (participatory, performative)
Structure	Logical .... (necessary links)	Associative (learned, from personal experience)
Language	Literal .... (describes world)	Figurative (describes internal state)

Evidence	Factual..	Psychological
	(verifiable)	(appeals to needs, drives, desires)

Each dimension focuses on the mixture of qualities involved in each facet of rhetorical action: purpose or argument or structure or language or evidence.

Instrumental-Consummatory

Something instrumental functions as a tool; it is a means to an end. Something consummatory is its own reason for being—the purpose is the action itself; the end is the performance or enactment, "singing sweet songs to please oneself," as in singing in the shower. Most rhetoric is primarily instrumental because it seeks to achieve some goal outside itself: to alter perception, to share information or understanding, to change attitudes, or induce action. But rhetorical action is also consummatory. Bill Bradley spoke at the Democratic National Convention and John McCain spoke at the Republican National Convention in the summer of 2000. Just what they said in their speeches is probably less important than that they were willing to appear at the convention. Their mere willingness to speak at conventions that nominated their primary opponents to be their party's presidential nominee was seen as a willingness to endorse candidates Al Gore and George W. Bush. Similarly, the boasts of victorious athletes during championship competitions are consummatory in celebrating their prowess. They are often instrumental, however, in spurring their opponents to new efforts, a reason that such boasting is discouraged by coaches. These are instances in which instrumental and consummatory purposes are mixed and interrelated.

Some rhetorical acts are primarily consummatory. If you were to attend a football or basketball game at the University of Kansas, you would see the Kansas fans rise and begin to murmur what sounds like a Gregorian chant while waving their arms slowly over their heads. They repeat, at an ever-increasing speed, the words "Rock Chalk. Jayhawk. K.U." Unless you are a member of the University of Kansas community, the words and gestures are meaningless.[8] But if you belong to the community, you chant and wave to affirm or reaffirm your membership in it. There is also an instrumental component. The chant expresses, indirectly, support for Jayhawk athletic teams, which represent the community on these occasions. Because morale affects play, the chant may increase the team's likelihood of winning.

Most rhetorical acts are a combination of these purposes, with the emphasis on instrumental ends. Consummatory purposes are often revealed in introductions and conclusions that express shared values and affirm membership in a community.

Justificatory-Ritualistic

An act that is justificatory gives reasons; it explains why something is true or good or desirable. Ritual refers to the prescribed form or order of an act (usually a ceremony), to the way it is performed. For this reason, ritualistic elements are often nonverbal or involve the sheer repetition of verbal elements, as in a chant. Ritual involves formal practices, customs, and procedures. Rituals do not justify or explain, they affirm and express. Some common ritualistic acts are pledging allegiance to the flag, standing to sing the national anthem, taking communion, or participating in the "Rocky Horror Picture Show." Participating in a ritual requires behaviors such as standing, putting your hand over your heart, kneeling, throwing rice, eating, or drinking. Rituals are performed by members of a community; they are repeated over and over again; the form of their performance is very important. Many Roman Catholics, for example, were dismayed when the Latin liturgy was abandoned; many Protestants were unhappy when the King James Version of the Bible was supplanted by translations using more contemporary language. By contrast, justificatory acts imply an absence of shared belief, which requires the presentation of arguments and evidence. Note that the enthymeme illustrates the degree to which rhetorical action falls between these two extremes.

A vivid example of the use of ritual to make a rhetorical point occurred when women's peace groups in Israel kept a silent vigil every Friday to protest Israeli treatment of Palestinians in the West Bank and Gaza, especially those engaged in the uprising called the *Intifada*. Their action aroused intense responses, which ranged from physical attacks to shouted epithets. These women were accused of being traitors to the Jewish community, but their silent Sabbath vigil was a powerful accusation that many Israelis could not ignore. Ritualistic arguments can also be made positively. The conflict over school prayer, for example, is, in part, a conflict over the force of ritualistic appeal. Just how much pressure is put on a child when a teacher says, "Let us pray," and many of her schoolmates bow their heads?

Logical-Associative

Logical relationships are necessary relationships, such as effect to cause or cause to effect. Logical structures reflect such relationships; they express necessary or asserted connections. By contrast, associative relationships are learned through personal experience or based on cultural linkages or social truths. Associative relationships are based on personal experiences and subjective reactions, but, as illustrated by stereotyping, they can be shared by many individuals.

Associative structure is like juxtaposition—two things are placed in relation to each other, and because they are positioned that way, a relationship is inferred. Rorschach tests are associative, asking individuals to divulge what pops into their minds when they see giant ink blots. Thematic Apperception Tests (TATs), asking individuals to finish stories, are examples of associative structure. Commercials that show beautiful, young, sexy people in attractive locales drinking a soft drink are trying to create associations between the advertised brand and the qualities of the models who appear in the ad. Recently, tobacco companies are being blamed for deaths from smoking, despite warnings on cigarette packages, because of the power of their advertising to prompt links between smoking and health, beauty, and sexual appeal.

Logical structure is ordinarily explicit and overt. Claims are stated as propositions. The connections between ideas are made clear to us, and we can examine claims, evidence, and reasons, testing them against other evidence and the like. Associative structure is usually implicit and oblique. Relationships are suggested to us, indirectly, by juxtaposing ideas or events or pictures, and we test these connections against our personal experience and subjective response. As the ad for the Bush campaign illustrates, logical and associative links can be involved in the same rhetorical act. Note that the associations prompted by juxtapositions can act as substitutes for formal arguments.

The power of arguments based on personal relevance links these two concepts. Prior to the late 1960s, the argument that "if you're old enough to fight, you're old enough to vote" was dismissed as illogical. The qualities needed to fight are quite different from those needed to vote intelligently, so the implied literal analogy was rejected.

During the Vietnam War, however, large numbers of men under the age of 21 were sent to fight in Vietnam, and the argument came to have greater force. Should those who would be asked to risk their lives have a right to choose those who would make that decision? Suddenly, the argument was heard as analogous to "no taxation without representation," the view that no government should have the right to tax you unless you have a vote in deciding who will represent you. Now the analogy was between choosing those who would have the power to take away what is your own, whether it be your property in taxes or your life in war. Note that the same basic argument can be seen as illogical or logical depending on which analogy is emphasized. That choice, of course, was deeply affected by personal relevance, and in 1971, the United States lowered the voting age to 18.

Many of the strategies discussed in Chapter 7 use the resources of language to make associative connections. Repetitions of sounds, words, and phrases create structures based on association. Relationships based on logic are only one kind of form that appears in rhetorical action. Other forms are based on relationships that emulate patterns in nature and in our experience: repetition, crescendo and decrescendo, and the like.[9]

Rhetorical action combines forms based on logic and on association. Both kinds of form prompt the creation of arguments in the minds of listeners. Television advertising is an excellent source of examples of the use of associative form to support claims.

Literal–Figurative

Literal language is prosaic and factual; it is intended to describe the world. Figurative language is poetic and metaphorical, and it reveals the person who uses it. Literal language deals with external reality; in some cases, it can be tested empirically for accuracy. Figurative language reveals the experiences and feelings of the rhetor. One poet calls the moon "the North wind's cookie"; another calls it "a piece of angry candy rattling around in the box of the sky." These statements reveal the feelings of the authors but tell us little about the moon. As critics, we look for metaphors to discover how a rhetor perceives the world. For example, in his famous "I Have a Dream" speech in 1963, Dr. Martin Luther King, Jr., construed civil rights for Americans, including African Americans, as a promissory note and efforts to obtain them as analogous to attempting to cash a check on a substantial bank account and being told that there were insufficient funds. That metaphor captures the sense of legal obligation inherent in fundamental citizen rights and the profound injustice in being told by a bank that you had no right to the money on deposit there for you.

Rhetorical acts combine the literal language of factual statements with metaphors and other poetic devices. In her 1988 keynote address to the Democratic National Convention, Texas Governor Ann Richards used a figurative analogy to describe women's ability to perform well in situations usually associated with men, such as delivering keynote addresses: "After all, Ginger Rogers did everything that Fred Astaire did, she just did it backwards and in high heels." In a 1975 commencement address at Barnard College, playwright and author Lillian Hellman told a story to illustrate the problems that still existed despite some progress toward equal opportunity for women. The story involved a critic, George Brandes, and Henrik Ibsen, the Norwegian playwright who wrote the early feminist play, "A Doll's House," about a woman named Nora who leaves the safety of her marriage to seek her own life after she has discovered how little she was respected by her husband. As Hellman related the story,

They were taking a walk on a wintry day in Oslo. They passed an open park with a great wind blowing through it. The park was empty except for a middle-aged woman sitting on a bench. Ibsen shook his head and said, "Poor lady." Brandes said, "I have always wanted to ask you. What happened to Nora?" Ibsen turned round, pointed back to the lady on the bench and said, "That is Nora."[10]

Chapter 7 explores these and other dimensions of language and their role in rhetorical action.

Factual–Psychological

These qualities of evidence have already been explored in Chapter 4. The factual dimension of evidence can be verified to determine its accuracy or truthfulness. Psychologically, evidence appeals to our needs, drives, and desires. Evidence can be fictive or hypothetical, inducing us to imagine and speculate. Evidence can pander to our prejudices or reflect our opinions and beliefs, which may be wrong. Rhetorical evidence is both data about the world and our perception of the world in terms of ourselves, a process that transforms the "facts" of what exists into instruments for our use and into obstacles that frustrate us.

These continua express the discursive and nondiscursive dimensions of rhetorical action. Although the concept of argument emphasizes discursive or logical processes, rhetorical argumentation includes all kinds of cues that stimulate us to treat our associations as evidence, to construct reasons, to draw conclusions. Many of these cues are nondiscursive. The characteristics of the enthymeme reflect the ways in which rhetorical action combines these dimensions.

Strategies of Proof

Strategies of proof resemble or mimic logical arguments. Through the identification and participation of the audience, they invite the audience to provide material that will justify a claim or conclusion. Figure 5–4 identifies seven common strategies of proof, several of which are illustrated more fully.

Rhetorical Question. A *rhetorical question* is a question to which no answer is expected or to which only one answer can be given. It is an idea put in the form of a question for greater effect. It is a question whose answer is known by the audience. Presidential campaigns often include rhetorical questions. In 1952, Dwight D. Eisenhower said, "The Democrats say you never had it so good. Do you want it any better?" That's a particularly effective rhetorical question because few people would answer no, but it was a highly strategic choice for Ike in this campaign. It allowed the audience to supply the defects of the Democrats so that the heroic leader of the allied forces in Europe in World War II did not have to stoop to making nasty charges. In 1980, Ronald Reagan asked, "Can anyone look at the record of this administration and say, 'Well done'? Can anyone compare the state of our economy when the Carter administration took office with where we are today and say, 'Keep up the good work'? Can anyone look at our reduced standing in the world today and say, 'Let's have four more years of this'?"[11] Once again, the questions need no answer. Note that they also presented Reagan as merely reminding us of what all of us knew (the questions work as enthymemes) rather than as making charges against a sitting president, and that the

Figure 5-4

Strategies of Proof (or Specific Arguments)

Name	Function	Example	Value
Rhetorical Question	Probative, sometimes confrontational way to stimulate the audience to support the rhetor's position	Former Russian President Boris Yeltsin urged Americans to support his plea for mutual cooperation. "After all, what sense does it really make to reinvent the bicycle? Why do we have to pursue parallel efforts doing exactly the same thing in Russia and the United States? Why can't we put our unique expertise together and when I say expertise I mean both research, development and basic and applied research? Why couldn't we join our hands and then we will be able to work miracles?"	Invites audience participation; encourages pseudo-dialogue
A fortiori "to the greater"	A specialized analytical argument that says if something happened in one case how much more likely would it happen in another	Angelina Grimké: " If God punished his own peculiar people [the Jews] for their transgressions of slavery, how much more likely will He subject His wrath on our transgression of slavery."	Logical force
Enumeration	A long list of particulars designed to give overwhelming support to a claim	In Reagan's tribute to the Challenger crew, he said: "There will be more shuttle flights, more shuttle crews and yes, more volunteers, more civilians, more teachers in space. Nothing ends here."	Emphatic proof
Refutation	Rhetors state opposing argument and then show why their opponent's case is flawed	Anglina Grimké says: "It is admitted by some that the slave is not happy under the worst forms of slavery. But I have never seen a happy slave. I have seen him dance in his chains, it is true; but he was not happy. There is a wide difference between happiness and mirth."	Showcases rhetor's expertise
Definition	A rhetor sets the terms for the debate	In an RJR Tobacco campaign on secondhand smoke, one ad reads: "Since we have discussed scientific aspects of the passive smoking controversy in previous messages, we'd like to focus here on the social questions."	Allows rhetor to argue from position of strength
Enactment	Rhetor is living proof of the claim she/he is making	Angelina Grimké argues women are competent, articulate persons capable of bringing about reform in the public arena. Her very presence as a public speaker in 1838 in the great hall in Pennsylvania, her very ability to talk down her detractors, her bold, scolding tone, her eyewitness expertise on slavery, are all visual and aural proof of the claim that she is making.	Difficult to deny because disagreement means you discount the authority of the rhetor
Turning the tables	Taking an opponent's argument and turning it against him/her	The Budweiser Image ad promoting the WNBA uses All-star Cynthia Cooper to disarm those who think disparagingly of women's sports. She compliments two men for their basketball skills with the line: "You play like a girl."	Disarms opposition

questions direct our attention to economic and foreign policy issues, areas in which the Carter administration was particularly vulnerable because of the Americans then held hostage by the Iranians.

A Fortiori. *A fortiori* is a phrase that means "to the stronger," and it is an organizational strategy. It connects two claims so that if we accept the first, it becomes more likely we will accept the second. If it can be shown that a politician betrayed his spouse or a close friend who trusted him, for example, it becomes more plausible that he would betray his constituents. Early in the contemporary women's movement, political scientist Jo Freeman wrote an essay designed to show the subtle forces at work that limit women's achievement by teaching women not to take risks or deviate from traditional patterns. She structured her essay following *a fortiori* principles. The opening sections of the essay document the history of discrimination against women in law, followed by sections that document the effects of socialization on women's ambition. If it can be shown that women are discriminated against overtly in law, it becomes much more plausible that they face covert discrimination based in socialization. Again, the strategy aims at proof. Where arguments are in an *a fortiori* relationship, the claim in the second is made more likely by proof of the first.

Enumeration. *Enumeration* means a bill of particulars is specified, a list of examples is provided. If done well, we are swamped with a mass of details, and each particular or example gains force from all those that have preceded it. In the essay referred to above, feminist Jo Freeman used enumeration as part of her proof to show the effects of socialization on women as reported in studies in the 1950s:

> To understand how most women are socialized we must first understand how they see themselves . . . [one study] showed that women strongly felt themselves to be such things as uncertain, anxious, nervous, hasty, careless, fearful, dull, childish, helpless, sorry, timid, clumsy, stupid, silly, and domestic. On a more positive side women felt they were: understanding, tender, sympathetic, pure, generous, affectionate, loving, moral, kind, grateful, and patient.[12]

This long list of adjectives functions strategically to overwhelm us with evidence of the negative attitudes women have had toward themselves. Note, however, that the list works only if you see these self descriptions negatively. If these are qualities you believe desirable in a "true woman," then the strategy will fail. Note also that enumeration can become a dull laundry list of particulars that bore the audience. That has often occurred in presidential State of the Union addresses.

Refutation. Answering and rebutting the arguments of the opposition is one of the commonest but most important strategies. In an organizational pattern that examines arguments pro and con, it can work strategically to answer questions in the minds of the audience and to inoculate them against competing persuaders. One form of refutation, however, deserves special mention. *Debunking* refutes opposing positions by making fun of exaggerated claims. Debunking is a process of deflating pretense, of shrinking opposing arguments to their "proper" size. It is often done through names that serve as labels. For example, a public speaking text addressed the problems of using slang and jargon, and the authors wrote:

> The observations about the use of slang apply also to the use of the special terminology and jargon of, let us say, sports commentators, the entertainment world as represented in the publication Variety, and such cults as the libbers and the discotheque enthusiasts.[13]

Feminists are being debunked as "libbers" and as extremists and fanatics (a cult). That it is feminists who are being debunked is most evident if we rewrite the paragraph to make the style consistent: "the special terminology and jargon of, let us say, sports jockeys, show biz gossip, and such cults as the libbers and disco freaks." Now each group is treated with equal informality, and all are debunked by unflattering labels.

Once again, note that the strategy depends on the beholder. The strategy is most evident to feminists who resent such chummy labels and is least evident to those who share the authors' views. Note that the list of examples also functions as enumeration.

Definition. Those with experience in debate quickly learn that definitions are strategic. Chapter 4 included a chart of definitional strategies because definitions are critical elements in determining just what must be proved in order to establish a claim. The dialectical definitions discussed earlier are also examples of strategic definitions. *Definitions* explain highly abstract terms, and they are often used in an attempt to change the perceptions of the audience. Bernice Sandler, for example, used this strategy in a 1991 speech at Illinois State University in Normal to explain the meaning of an unfamiliar and technical sociological term.

> At a very early age, boys learn to use girls as what the sociologists call a "negative reference group." In other words, the boys define themselves by comparing themselves favorably to girls, the lesser group, the females. After all, what is the worst thing you can call a little boy? A sissy—which means he is acting like a girl. By teasing girls a boy begins to feel good about himself—he is better than they are, and teasing them makes him feel like a "real boy." Moreover, by putting down girls and females he can get closer to his buddies. They can all put down the girls, and feel better and bigger than the girls. Harassment, and even sexual assault, can be, for many men, the way in which they show other men how "manly" they really are. We see this in its extreme in the case of gang rape, where psychologists have noted that the men are not raping for sexual reasons but are really raping for each other. This is how they show their friends how strong, how virile, how manly, how wonderful they really are.[14]

Sandler's statement combines a number of strategies. It defines by enumerating the various activities that illustrate the meaning of the phrase "negative reference group." The illustrations are arranged in a climax construction that works from the least to the most harmful manifestation, from teasing girls to gang raping them. The phrase, its definition, and the illustrations are all part of an effort to demonstrate the harmful effects of sexism in our society and to make us more willing to intervene to prevent the earliest indications of such attitudes among boys. Note that the final sentence uses the terms "strong," "virile," "manly," and "wonderful" in a sarcastic way.

Other strategies aid the rhetor in making arguments and substantiating claims, but these are the most important. Strategies described here and in Chapter 7 often appear in combination and depend on the participation of the audience.

MATERIAL FOR ANALYSIS

The following essay appeared in the January 1971 issue of *Catholic World*, pp. 177–183. At the time it was written, the author was a faculty member in the religion department of Temple University in Philadelphia. He is the author of a number of related works.[15] The form of the essay is discursively argumentative, setting out a thesis, defining terms, and setting forth the criteria by which the quality of the evidence and reasons, the proof, are to be judged. At the same time, it is targeted to a special kind of audience, one composed of people with deep religious beliefs who are strongly committed to living their lives in imitation of the model set by Jesus Christ, now expressed in the question, What would Jesus do? Because some of the strongest arguments against changing the status of women toward lives of greater opportunity and equality are often justified on the basis of scripture, particularly the epistles of St. Paul, the case that the author makes addresses an important facet of resistance to feminist efforts.

Jesus Was a Feminist
by Leonard J. Swidler[16]

1   *Thesis: Jesus was a feminist.*

2   Definition of terms: By Jesus is meant the historical person who lived in Palestine two thousand years ago, whom Christians traditionally acknowledge as Lord and Savior, and whom they should "imitate" as much as possible. By a *feminist* is meant a person who is in favor of, and who promotes, the equality of women with men, a person who advocates and practices treating women primarily as human persons (as men are so treated) and willingly contravenes social customs in so acting.

3   To prove the thesis it must be demonstrated that, so far as we can tell, Jesus neither said nor did anything which would indicate that he advocated treating women as intrinsically inferior to men, but that on the contrary he said and did things which indicated that he thought of women as the equals of men, and that in the process he willingly violated pertinent social mores.

4   The negative portion of the argument can be documented quite simply by reading through the four Gospels. Nowhere does Jesus treat women as "inferior beings." In fact, Jesus clearly felt especially sent to the typical classes of "inferior beings," such as the poor, the lame, the sinner—and women—to call them all to the freedom and equality of the Kingdom of God. But there are two factors which raise this negative result exponentially in its significance: the status of women in Palestine at the time of Jesus, and the nature of the Gospels. Both need to be recalled here in some detail, particularly the former.

The Status of Women in Palestine

5   The status of women in Palestine during the time of Jesus was very decidedly that of inferiors. Despite the fact that there were several heroines recorded in the Scriptures, according to most rabbinic customs of Jesus' time—and long after—women were not allowed to study the Scriptures (Torah). One first-century rabbi, Eliezer, put the point sharply: "Rather should the words of the Torah be burned than entrusted to a woman. . . . Whoever teaches his daughter the Torah is like one who teaches her lasciviousness."

6   In the vitally religious area of prayer, women were so little thought of as not to be given obligations of the same seriousness as men. For example, women, along with children and slaves, were not obliged to recite the Shema, the morning prayer, nor prayers at meals. In fact, the Talmud states: "Let a curse come upon the man who [must needs have] his wife or children say grace for him." Moreover, in the daily prayers of Jews there was a threefold thanksgiving: "Praised be God that he has not created me a gentile; praised be God that he has not created me a woman; praised be God that he has not created me an ignorant man." (It was

obviously a version of this rabbinic prayer that Paul controverted in his letter to the Galatians: "There is neither Jew nor Greek, there is neither slave nor free, there is neither male nor female; for you are all one in Christ Jesus.")

7   Women were also grossly restricted in public prayer. It was (is) not even possible for them to be counted toward the number necessary for a quorum to form a congregation to worship communally—they were again classified with children and slaves, who similarly did not qualify (there is an interesting parallel to the current canon 93 of the *Codex Juris Canonici* which groups married women, minors, and the insane). In the great temple at Jerusalem they were limited to one outer portion, the women's court, which was five steps below the court for the men. In the synagogues the women were also separated from the men, and of course were not allowed to read aloud or take any leading function. (The same is still true in most synagogues today—canon 1262 of the CIC also states that "in church the women should be separated from the men.")

8   Besides the disabilities women suffered in the areas of prayer and worship there were many others in the private and public forums of society. As one Scripture scholar, Peter Ketter, noted: "A rabbi regarded it as beneath his dignity, as indeed positively disreputable, to speak to a woman in public. The 'Proverbs of the Fathers' contain the injunction: 'Speak not much with a woman.' Since a man's own wife is meant here, how much more does not this apply to the wife of another? The wise men say: 'Who speaks much with a woman draws down misfortune on himself, neglects the words of the law, and finally earns hell. . . .' If it were merely the too free intercourse of the sexes which was being warned against, this would signify nothing derogatory to woman. But since the rabbi may not speak even to his own wife, daughter or sister in the street, then only male arrogance can be the motive." Intercourse with uneducated company is warned against in exactly the same terms. "One is not so much as to greet a woman." In addition, save in the rarest instances, women were not allowed to bear witness in a court of law. Some Jewish thinkers, as for example, Philo, a contemporary of Jesus, thought women ought not leave their households except to go to the synagogue (and that only at a time when most of the other people would be at home); girls ought even not cross the threshold that separated the male and female apartments of the household.

9   In general, the attitude toward women was epitomized in the institutions and customs surrounding marriage. For the most part the function of women was thought [of] rather exclusively in terms of childbearing and rearing; women were almost always under the tutelage of a man, either the father or husband, or if a widow, the dead husband's brother. Polygamy—in the sense of having several wives, but not in the sense of having several husbands—was legal among Jews at the time of Jesus, although probably not heavily practiced. Moreover, divorce of a wife was very easily obtained by the husband—he merely had to give her a writ of divorce; women in Palestine, on the other hand, were not allowed to divorce their husbands.

10   Rabbinic sayings about women also provide an insight into the attitude toward women: "It is well for those whose children are male, but ill for those whose children are female. . . . At the birth of a boy all are joyful, but at the birth of a girl all are sad. . . . When a boy comes into the world, peace comes into the world: when a girl comes, nothing comes. . . . Even the most virtuous of women is a witch. . . . Our teachers have said: Four qualities are evident in women: They are greedy at their food, eager to gossip, lazy, and jealous."

11   The condition of women in Palestinian Judaism was bleak.

The Nature of the Gospels

12   The Gospels, of course, are not the straight factual reports of eyewitnesses of the events in the life of Jesus of Nazareth as one might find in the columns of the *New York Times* or the pages of a critical biography. Rather, they are four different faith statements reflecting at least four primitive Christian communities who believed that Jesus was the Messiah, the Lord and Savior of the world. They were composed from a variety of sources, written and oral, over a period of time and in response to certain needs felt in the communities and individuals at the time; consequently they are many-layered. Since the gospel writer-editors were not twentieth-century critical historians they were not particularly intent on recording *ipsissima verba Christi* [the exact words of Christ], nor were they concerned to winnow out all of their own cultural biases and assumptions. Indeed, it is doubtful they were particularly conscious of them.

13   This modern critical understanding of the Gospels, of course, does not impugn the historical character of the Gospels; it merely describes the type of historical documents they are so their historical significance can more accurately be evaluated. Its religious value lies in the fact that modern Christians are thereby helped to know much more precisely what Jesus meant by certain statements and actions as they are reported by the first Christian communities in the Gospels. With this new knowledge of the nature of the Gospels it is easier to make the vital distinction between the religious truth that is to be handed on and the time-conditioned categories and customs involved in expressing it.

14   When the fact that no negative attitudes by Jesus toward women are portrayed in the Gospels is set side by side with the recently discerned "communal faith-statement" understanding of the nature of the Gospels, the importance of the former is vastly enhanced. For whatever Jesus said or did comes to us only through the lens of the first Christians. If there were no very special religious significance in a particular concept or custom, we would expect that current concept or custom to be reflected by Jesus. The fact that the overwhelmingly negative attitude toward women in Palestine did not come through the primitive Christian communal lens by itself underscores the clearly great religious importance Jesus attached to his positive attitude—his feminist attitude—toward women: feminism, that is, personalism extended to women, is a constitutive part of the Gospel, the Good News, of Jesus.

Women and Resurrection from the Dead

15   One of the first things noticed in the gospels about Jesus' attitude toward women is that he taught them the Gospel, the meaning of Jesus' first appearance after his resurrection to any of his followers was to a woman (or women), who was then commissioned by him to bear witness of the risen Jesus to the Eleven (John 20:11ff.; Matt. 28:9f.; Mark 16:9ff.). In typical male Palestinian style, the Eleven refused to believe the woman since, according to Judaic law, women were not allowed to bear legal witness. As one learned in the Law, Jesus obviously was aware of this stricture. His first appearing to and commissioning women to bear witness to the most important event of his career could not have been anything but deliberate: it was clearly a dramatic linking of a very clear rejection of the second-class status of women with the center of His Gospel, His resurrection. The effort of Jesus to centrally connect these two points is so obvious that it is an overwhelming tribute to man's intellectual myopia not to have discerned it effectively in two thousand years.

16　The intimate connection of women with resurrection from the dead is not limited in the gospels to that of Jesus. There are accounts of three other resurrections in the Gospels—all closely involving a woman. The most obvious connection of a woman with a resurrection account is that of the raising of a woman, Jairus' daughter (Matt. 9:18ff.; Mark 5:22ff.; Luke 8:41ff.). A second resurrection Jesus performed was that of the only son of the widow of Nain: "And when the Lord saw her, he had compassion on her and he said to her, 'Do not weep.' " (Cf. Luke 7:11ff.). The third resurrection Jesus performed was Lazarus', at the request of his sisters Martha and Mary (Cf. John 11). From the first it was Martha and Mary who sent for Jesus because of Lazarus' illness. But when Jesus finally came Lazarus was four days dead. Martha met Jesus and pleaded for his resurrection: "Lord, if you had been here, my brother would not have died. And even now I know that whatever you ask from God, God will give you." Later Mary came to Jesus and said much the same. "When Jesus saw her weeping, and the Jews who came with her also weeping, he was deeply moved in spirit and troubled; and he said, 'Where have you laid him?' They said to him, 'Lord, come and see.' Jesus wept." Then followed the raising from the dead. Thus, Jesus raised one woman from the dead, and raised two other persons largely because of women.

17　There are two further details that should be noted in these three resurrection stories. The first is that only in the case of Jairus' daughter did Jesus touch the corpse—which made him ritually unclean. In the cases of the two men Jesus did not touch them, but merely said, "Young man, I say to you, arise," or, "Lazarus, come out." One must at least wonder why Jesus chose to violate the laws for ritual purity in order to help a woman, but not a man. The second detail is in Jesus' conversation with Martha after she pleaded for the resurrection of Lazarus. Jesus declared himself to be the resurrection ("I am the resurrection and the life."), the only time he did so that is recorded in the Gospels. Jesus here again revealed the central event, the central message, in the Gospel—the resurrection, His resurrection, His being the resurrection—to a woman.

Women Disciples of Jesus

18　There are of course numerous occasions recorded in the Gospels, the Scriptures, and religious truths in general. When it is recalled that in Judaism it was considered improper, and even "obscene," to teach women the Scriptures, this action of Jesus was an extraordinary, deliberate decision to break with a custom invidious to women. Moreover, women became disciples of Jesus not only in the sense of learning from Him, but also in the sense of following Him in His travels and ministering to Him. A number of women, married and unmarried, were regular followers of Jesus. In Luke 8:1ff. several are mentioned by name in the same sentence with the Twelve: "He made his way through towns and villages preaching and proclaiming the Good News of the kingdom of God. With him went the Twelve, as well as certain women . . . who provided for them out of their own resources." (Cf. Mark 15:40f.). The Greek word translated here as "provided for" and in Mark as "ministered to" is *diekonoun*, the same basic word as "deacon"; indeed, apparently the tasks of the deacons in early Christianity were much the same as these women undertook.) The significance of this phenomenon of women following Jesus about, learning from and ministering to Him, can be properly appreciated when it is recalled that not only were women not to read or study the Scriptures, but in the more observant settings they were not even to leave their household, whether as a daughter, a sole wife, or a member of a harem.

Women as Sex Objects

19   Within this context of women being disciples and ministers, Jesus quite deliberately broke another custom disadvantageous to women. There were situations where women were treated by others not at all as persons but as sex objects, and it could be expected that Jesus would do the same. The expectations were disappointed. One such occasion occurred when Jesus was invited to dinner at the house of a skeptical Pharisee (Luke 7:36ff.) and a woman of ill repute entered and washed Jesus' feet with her tears, wiped them with her hair and anointed them. The Pharisee saw her solely as an evil sexual creature: "The Pharisee . . . said to himself, 'If this man were a prophet, he would know who this woman is who is touching him and what a bad name she has.'" But Jesus deliberately rejected this approach to the woman as a sex object. He rebuked the Pharisee and spoke solely of the woman's human, spiritual actions; He spoke of her love, her unlove, that is, her sins, of her being forgiven, and her faith. Jesus then addressed her (it was not "proper" to speak to women in public, especially "improper" women) as a human person: "Your sins are forgiven. . . . Your faith has saved you; go in peace."

20   A similar situation occurred when the scribes and Pharisees used a woman reduced entirely to a sex object to set a legal trap for Jesus. It is difficult to imagine a more callous use of a human person than the "adulterous" woman was put to by the enemies of Jesus [John 8:3–11]. First, she was surprised in the intimate act of sexual intercourse (quite possibly a trap was set up ahead of time by the suspicious husband), and then dragged before the scribes and Pharisees, and then by them before an even larger crowd that Jesus was instructing: "making her stand in full view of everybody." They told Jesus that she had been caught in the very act of committing adultery and that Moses had commanded that such women be stoned to death. (Deut. 22:22ff.) "What have you to say?" The trap was partly that if Jesus said Yes to the stoning He would be violating the Roman law, which restricted capital punishment, and if He said No, He would appear to contravene Mosaic law. It could also partly have been to place Jesus' reputation for kindness toward, and championing the cause of, women in opposition to the law and the condemnation of sin. Jesus of course eluded their snares by refusing to become entangled in legalisms and abstractions. Rather, he dealt with both the accusers and the accused directly as spiritual, ethical, human persons. He spoke directly to the accusers in the context of their own personal ethical conduct: "If there is one of you who has not sinned, let him be the first to throw a stone at her." To the accused woman he likewise spoke directly with compassion, but without approving her conduct: "'Woman, where [are] they [your accusers]? Has no one condemned you?' She said, 'No one, Lord.' And Jesus said, 'Neither do I condemn you; go, and do not sin again."

21   (One detail of this encounter provides the basis for a short excursus related to the status of women. The Pharisees stated that the woman had been caught in the act of adultery and according to the Law of Moses was therefore to be stoned to death. Since the type of execution mentioned was stoning, the woman must have been a "virgin betrothed," as referred to in Deut. 22:23ff. There provision is made for the stoning of *both* the man and the woman, although in the Gospel story only the woman is brought forward. However, the reason given for why the man ought to be stoned was not because he had violated the woman, or God's law, but: "because he had violated the wife of his neighbor." It was the injury of the man by misusing his property—wife—that was the great evil.)

Jesus' Rejection of the Blood Taboo

22   All three of the synoptic Gospels insert into the middle of the account of raising Jairus' daughter from the dead the story of the curing of the woman who had an issue of blood for twelve years (Matt. 9:20ff.; Mark 5:25ff.; Luke 8:43ff.). Especially touching about this story is that the affected woman was so reluctant to project herself into public attention that she "said to herself, 'If I only touch his garment, I shall be made well.' " Her shyness was not because she came from the poor, lower classes, for Mark pointed out that over the twelve years she had been to many physicians—with no success—on whom she had spent all her money. It was probably because for twelve years, as a woman with a flow of blood, she was constantly ritually unclean (Lev. 15:19ff.), which not only made her incapable of participating in any cultic action and made her in some sense "displeasing to God," but also rendered anyone and anything she touched (or anyone who touched what she had touched!) similarly unclean. (Here is the basis for the Catholic Church not allowing women in the sanctuary during Mass—she might be menstruating and hence unclean.) The sense of degradation and contagion that her "womanly weakness" worked upon her over the twelve years doubtless was oppressive in the extreme. This would have been especially so when a religious teacher, a rabbi, was involved. But not only does Jesus' power heal her, in one of His many acts of compassion on the downtrodden and afflicted, including women, but Jesus also makes a great to-do about the event, calling extraordinary attention to the publicity-shy woman: "And Jesus, perceiving in himself that power had gone forth from him, immediately turned about in the crowd, and said, 'Who touched my garments?' And his disciples said to him, 'You see the crowd pressing around you, and yet you say, "Who touched me?" ' And he looked around to see who had done it. But the woman, knowing what had been done to her, came in fear and trembling and fell down before Him and told Him the whole truth. And He said to her, 'Daughter, your faith has made you well; go in peace, and be healed of your disease.' " It seems clear that Jesus wanted to call attention to the fact that He did not shrink from the ritual uncleanness incurred by being touched by the "unclean" woman (on several occasions Jesus rejected the notion of ritual uncleanness), and by immediate implication rejected the "uncleanness" of a woman who had a flow of blood, menstruous or continual. Jesus apparently placed a greater importance on the dramatic making of this point, both to the afflicted woman herself and the crowd, than He did on avoiding the temporary psychological discomfort of the embarrassed woman, which in light of Jesus' extraordinary concern to alleviate the pain of the afflicted, meant He placed a great weight on the teaching this lesson about the dignity of women.

Jesus and the Samaritan Woman

23   On another occasion Jesus again deliberately violated the then common code concerning men's relationship to women. It is recorded in the story of the Samaritan woman at the well of Jacob (John 4:5ff.). Jesus was waiting at the well outside the village while His disciples were getting food. A Samaritan woman approached the well to draw water. Normally a Jew would not address a Samaritan, as the woman pointed out: "Jews, in fact, do not associate with Samaritans." But also normally a man would not speak to a woman in public (doubly so in the case of a rabbi). However, Jesus startled the woman by initiating a conversation. The woman was aware that on both counts, her being a Samaritan and being a woman,

Jesus' action was out of the ordinary for she replied: "how is it that you, a Jew, ask a drink of me, a woman of Samaria?" As hated as the Samaritans were by the Jews, it is nevertheless clear that Jesus' speaking with a woman was considered a much more flagrant breach of conduct than His speaking with a Samaritan, for John related: "His disciples returned, and were surprised to find him speaking to a woman, though none of them asked, 'What do you want from her?' or, 'Why are you talking to her?'" However, Jesus' bridging of the gap of inequality between men and women continued further, for in the conversation with the woman He revealed himself in a straightforward fashion as the Messiah for the first time: "The woman said to him, 'I know that Messiah is coming.' . . . Jesus said to her, 'I who speak to you am he.'"

24   Just as when Jesus revealed Himself to Martha as "the resurrection," and to Mary as the "risen one" and bade her to bear witness to the apostles, Jesus here also revealed Himself in one of his key roles, as Messiah, to a woman—who immediately bore witness of the fact to her fellow villagers. (It is interesting to note that apparently the testimony of women carried greater weight among the Samaritans than among the Jews, for the villagers came out to see Jesus: "Many Samaritans of that town believed in him on the strength of the woman's testimony. . . ." It would seem that John the Gospel writer deliberately highlighted this contrast in the way he wrote about this event, and also that he clearly wished to reinforce thereby Jesus' stress on the equal dignity of women.)

25   One other point should be noted in connection with this story. As the crowd of Samaritans was walking out to see Jesus, Jesus was speaking to His disciples about the fields being ready for the harvest and how He was sending them to reap what others had sown. He was clearly speaking of the souls of men, and most probably was referring directly to the approaching Samaritans. Such exegesis is standard. It is also rather standard to refer to others in general and only Jesus in particular as having been the sowers whose harvest the apostles were about to reap (e.g., in the Jerusalem Bible). But it would seem that the evangelist also meant specifically to include the Samaritan woman among those sowers for immediately after he recorded Jesus' statement to the disciples about their reaping what others had sown he added the above mentioned verse: "Many Samaritans of that town had believed in him on the strength of the woman's testimony. . . ."

Marriage and the Dignity of Woman

26   One of the most important stands of Jesus in relation to the dignity of women was His position on marriage. His unpopular attitude toward marriage (cf. Matt. 19:10: "The disciples said to him; 'If such is the case of a man with his wife, it is not expedient to marry.'") presupposed a feminist view of women; they had rights and responsibilities equal to men. It was quite possible in Jewish law for men to have more than one wife (this was probably not frequently the case in Jesus' time, but there are recorded instances, e.g., Herod, Josephus), though the reverse was not possible. Divorce, of course, also was a simple matter, to be initiated only by the man. In both situations women were basically chattels to be collected or dismissed as the man was able and wished to; the double moral standard was flagrantly apparent. Jesus rejected both by insisting on monogamy and the elimination of divorce; both the man and the woman were to have the same rights and responsibilities in their relationship toward each other (cf. Mark 10:2ff.; Matt. 19:3ff.). This stance of Jesus was one of the few that was rather thoroughly assimilated by the Christian Church (in fact, often in an over-rigid way concerning

divorce—but, how to understand the ethical prescriptions of Jesus is another article), doubtless in part because it was reinforced by various sociological conditions and other historical accidents, such as the then current strength in the Greek world of the Stoic philosophy. However, the notion of equal rights and responsibilities was not extended very far within the Christian marriage. The general role of women was *Kirche, Kinder, Küche*—and only a suppliant's role in the first.

The Intellectual Life for Women

27 However, Jesus clearly did not think of woman's role in such restricted terms; she was not to be limited to being *only* a housekeeper. Jesus quite directly rejected the stereotype that the proper place of all women is "in the home," during a visit to the house of Martha and Mary (Luke 10:38 ff.). Martha took the typical woman's role: "Martha was distracted with much serving." Mary, however, took the supposedly "male" role: she "sat at the Lord's feet and listened to his teaching." Martha apparently thought Mary was out of place in choosing the role of the "intellectual," for she complained to Jesus. But Jesus' response was a refusal to force all women into the stereotype; he treated Mary first of all as a person (whose highest faculty is the intellect, the spirit) who was allowed to set her own priorities, and in this instance had "chosen the better part." And Jesus applauded her: "it is not to be taken from her." Again, when one recalls the Palestinian restriction on women studying the Scriptures or studying with rabbis, that is, engaging in the intellectual life or acquiring any "religious authority," it is difficult to imagine how Jesus could possibly have been clearer in his insistence that women were called to the intellectual, the spiritual life just as were men.

28 There is at least one other instance recorded in the Gospels when Jesus uttered much the same message (Luke 11:27ff.). One day as Jesus was preaching a woman from the crowd apparently was very deeply impressed and, perhaps imagining how happy she would be to have such a son, raised her voice to pay Jesus a compliment. She did so by referring to His mother, and did so in a way that was probably not untypical at that time and place. But her image of a woman was sexually reductionist in the extreme (one that largely persists to the present): female genitals and breasts. "Blessed is the womb that bore you, and the breasts that you sucked!" Although this was obviously meant as a compliment, and although it was even uttered by a woman, Jesus clearly felt it necessary to reject this "baby-machine" image of women and insist again on the personhood, the intellectual and moral faculties, being primary for all: "But he said, 'Blessed rather are those who hear the word of God and keep it!'" Looking at this text it is difficult to see how the primary point could be anything substantially other than this. Luke and the tradition and Christian communities he depended on must also have been quite clear about the sexual significance of this event. Otherwise, why would he (and they) have kept and included such a small event from all the years of Jesus' public life? It was not retained *merely* because Jesus said blessed are those who hear and keep God's word, but because that was stressed by Jesus as being primary in comparison to a woman's sexuality. Luke, however, seems to have had a discernment here and elsewhere, concerning what Jesus was about in the question of women's status that has not been shared by subsequent Christians (nor apparently by many of *his* fellow Christians), for, in the explanation of this passage, Christians for two thousand years did not see its plain meaning—doubtless because of unconscious presuppositions about the status of women inculcated by their cultural milieu.

God as a Woman

29   In many ways Jesus strove to communicate the notion of the equal dignity of women. In one sense that effort was capped by his parable of the woman who found the lost coin (Luke 15: 8ff.), for here Jesus projected God in the image of a woman! Luke recorded that the despised tax-collectors and sinners were gathering around Jesus, and consequently the Pharisees and scribes complained. Jesus, therefore, related three parables in a row, all of which depicted God's being deeply concerned for that which was lost. The first story was of the shepherd who left the ninety-nine sheep to seek the one lost—the shepherd is God. The third parable is of the prodigal son—the father is God. The second story is of the woman who sought the lost coin—the woman is God! Jesus did not shrink from the notion of God as feminine. In fact, it would appear that Jesus included this womanly image of God quite deliberately at this point for the scribes and Pharisees were among those who most of all denigrated women—just as they did the "tax-collectors and sinners."

30   There have been some instances in Christian history when the Holy Spirit has been associated with a feminine character, as, for example, in the Syrian *Didascalia* where, in speaking of various offices in the Church, it states: "the Deaconess however should be honored by you as the image of the Holy Spirit." It would make an interesting investigation to see if these images of God presented here by Luke were ever used in a Trinitarian manner—thereby giving the Holy Spirit a feminine image. A negative result to the investigation would be as significant as a positive one, for this passage would seem to be particularly apt for a Trinitarian interpretation: the prodigal son's father is God the Father (this interpretation has in fact been quite common in Christian history); since Jesus elsewhere identified himself as the Good Shepherd, the shepherd seeking the lost sheep is Jesus, the Son (this standard interpretation is reflected in, among other things, the often-seen picture of Jesus carrying the lost sheep on his shoulders); the woman who sought the lost coin should "logically" be the Holy Spirit. If such an interpretation has existed, it surely has not been common. Should such lack of "logic" be attributed to the general cultural denigration of women or the abhorrence of pagan goddesses—although Christian abhorrence of pagan gods did not result in a Christian rejection of a male image of God?

Conclusion

31   From this evidence it should be clear that Jesus vigorously promoted the dignity and equality of women in the midst of a very male-dominated society: Jesus was a feminist, and a very radical one. Can his followers attempt to be anything less—*De Imitatione Christi?*

Questions for Analysis

1. What is the special role of authority evidence in this essay? How can the use of authority in the essay help you to understand its strengths and limitations?
2. Identify the warrants or justifications that the author uses to move from data to claims. What do they reveal about field-dependent reasons or warrants? How might these reasons have force for those who are not members of the target audience?
3. The essay appeared in a journal targeted to Roman Catholics. Is the essay less effective for Christians who are members of other denominations? Do comments about

attitudes toward women in Judaism at the time of Jesus limit the essay's appeal for contemporary practicing Jews?

4. The author provides quite a bit of detail; however, are readers expected or required to provide additional details that would not be known to those outside the target audience? How much of this argumentation is enthymematic?

EXERCISES

1. Figure 5–5 showcases examples of persuasive strategies that have been identified as *fallacies*—that is, as appeals or tactics used by rhetors that invite audiences to behave in ways that are less than rational. In each case, consider the kinds of argument that each mimics and then discuss just how to distinguish between what would be considered a proper (logical or ethical) use of this tactic and what would not. Contrary to some traditional ways of studying argument, fallacies are not treated here as uniformly unethical or improper. Try telling an editorial columnist not to use fallacies, and see how many readers she'll keep. For example, name-calling mimics the strategy of definition. When is a label descriptive and defining, and when does it become an instance of name-calling? Your discussion can be focused more specifically if you collect and discuss examples of these strategies from newspaper, radio, and television programming from current political campaigns or other disputes over policy, such as welfare reform, mandatory sentencing, and the like.

2. In the editorial "Vouchers a Threat to Public Schools" by Joe Murray of the *San Francisco Examiner*, identify how arguments and fallacies work together. Specifically, consider these points:
   a. How do analogical arguments work in this piece? How does enumeration of the analogies contribute to the tone and purpose of the piece?
   b. How are rational and psychological appeals evident in the analogical argument?
   c. Does the reasoning by analogy turn into a slippery slope fallacy? Explain. What other fallacies do you detect?
   d. What enthymemes can you make from this piece? Is there a causal argument? Is the editorial arranged inductively or deductively?
   e. There are many strategies of proof (or specific arguments) in this piece. Try to identify at least four. Consult Figure 5–4 in this chapter for help.

Vouchers a Threat to Public Schools[17]

1   Gov. George W. Bush wants vouchers for Texas parents who had rather educate their children in private schools or home schooling.

2   Nowadays it seems that whatever George W. Bush wants, he gets. From what I read, if and when he decides he wants to be president, he'll get elected.

3   Maybe then he'll want school vouchers nationwide.

4   Deregulation of public education; Is that what we're talking about? If so, hold the phone.

5   I happen to have an opinion about public education: that no other institution has contributed more to democracy in America.

6   And now we're going to whittle it down into a bunch of splinter groups?

7   People who want their kids to go to private or church schools, or who want to school them at home, think they ought to be able to spend their tax money for education the way they please. After all, it's *their* kids.

8   That sort of argument may sound like it makes sense. The truth is, it's talking silly.

9   You might as well argue that people whose kids are out of school, or people who never had children, shouldn't have to pay school taxes, that government should give back their money so they can spend it as best benefits them.

10   But that's not the issue, what's best for you or what's best for me. Rather, it's what's best for America.

11   Every citizen has an investment in public education. Our nation's children represent our nation's future. As they succeed, we all succeed. It's not by luck that America enjoys the most advanced technology and healthiest economy.

12   You like the idea of school vouchers? Then why not these ideas:

13   Park vouchers for parents who'd rather take their children to Disneyland instead of public parks.

14   Road vouchers for motorists who prefer toll roads to the public highway system.

15   Water vouchers for those of us who drink bottled water instead of city water.

16   Zoo vouchers for animal lovers who enjoy their own personal menagerie over the public zoo. (With eight dogs and two cats, I could use the money.)

17   Protection vouchers for private police and firemen who would come to the aid of only those who subscribe to their services.

Figure 5-5

Argumentative Fallacies

Name	Function	Example
Straw Argument	Presents the weakest point of an opponent's position as if it were the strongest.	Why should we support affirmative action? All these people want is a quota system.
Begging the Question	A speaker assumes as already proven the very point he or she is trying to prove.	Everyone ought to be free, because it is a real value in a society when there is liberty for all.
Non Sequitur	Arguments that advance claims that do not logically follow from the premises.	She must wear Levi's—she's got sex appeal.
Appeal to Ignorance	An argument that a speaker asks the audience to accept solely because it has not been proven false.	No one can prove there was any vote buying in the last election; thus, there clearly was none going on.
Argumentum ad Populum	Assumes that just because a position is popular, it must be good and right.	Both presidential candidates supported keeping Elian Gonzales with his Miami relatives rather than returning him to his father in Cuba because many Americans saw it as the patriotic thing to do.
Faulty Cause and Effect	Asserts a cause-and-effect relationship where one may not exist.	Since sexually transmitted diseases (std) go up when beer is cheap, if we tax beer, std's will go down.
Appeal to Inertia	Assumes that what has been practiced since anyone can remember, must necessarily be true, right, and good.	My great-grandfather was a Republican, I'm a Republican, therefore, you should be a Republican.
False Analogy	When two things are compared that are not alike in significant ways.	Why should car makers complain about working more than ten hours a day? After all, professors work at least that many hours a day without any apparent harm.
Name-Calling	Substitutes name calling for discussing the issues.	The Strategic Defense Initiative is called "Star Wars"; The Estate Tax is called "The Death Tax." The teaching of evolution is called "secular humanism"; The Death Penalty is called "barbarism."
False Dilemma	Presenting only two options as if they are the only two that exist.	Senator Smith is either lying about campaign financing or he is covering it up.
Hasty Generalization	A position that has been reached based on insufficient grounds.	Asians are a studious people.
Glittering Generalities	Feel-good phrases that seek immediate agreement.	Democrats are committed to peace, prosperity, and equality for all.
Guilt or Glory by Association	Transfers positive or negative feelings from a known phenomenon to a product, group, person, or idea.	George W. sometimes shows a blank Dan Quayle look, sometimes speaks with the creative grammar of George Sr., and has the worldview of Ronald Reagan.
Slippery Slope	If we allow this one thing to happen, we will soon see many other things we don't want to happen.	Tighter gun control legislation will ultimately mean a complete erosion of the 14th Amendment and the slow but systematic, disarming of the citizenry.

Source: Susan Schultz Huxman, *Public Speaking: A Repertoire of Resources* (New York: McGraw-Hill College Custom Series, 1992).

18 And, while we're at it, arms vouchers for militia groups who don't trust the U.S. military to defend the nation.

19 Why not, indeed? Because it's silly, that's why.

20 But the proposals for school vouchers aren't silly. Such ideas, proposed by such leaders as Gov. Bush, are serious—a serious threat to our public education system.

21 You want to home-school your children? Fine.

22 You want to send your children to private schools? Fine.

23 But not at the expense of our public schools.

3. Using InfoTrac College Edition, locate Bill Clinton's speech, "We are on the right track" (as cited in *U.S. News & World report*, October 14, 1996, p. 24). What is the issue that Mr. Clinton is addressing? Is it a question of fact, value, or policy? Keeping in mind the continua outlined in Chapter 5, trace the dimensions of the speech as a piece of rhetorical action. How does the speech construct its appeal? How much does it rely on discursive and how much on nondiscursive links? Do you see a connection between those aspects of the speech and the speech's context or the audience's ability to recognize the personal relevance of the argument?

4. **Portfolio Entry 4: Argument**
Compare and contrast how your rhetorical selections use general and specific arguments to advance their purpose. Do you see argumentative fallacies? In two or three pages, use critical equations (c+p+a) to formulate your answers.

NOTES

1. Lawrence K. Altman, "Autopsy Expected to Give Answers," *New York Times*, July 29, 1993, p. B7; Dave Anderson, "Lewis's Death on Celtics' Conscience," *New York Times*, July 29, 1993, p. B6.

2. Aristotle classified issues into four types: being (fact or conjecture), quantity (scope or definition), quality (value, mitigating circumstances), and procedure (including jurisdiction). See *On Rhetoric: A Theory of Civic Discourse*, trans. George A. Kennedy (New York: Oxford University Press, 1991), p. 273, 1417b.21–28.

3. For a discussion of the complex interrelationship between our basic biological needs and their cultural modification through language, see Kenneth Burke, "Definition of Man," *Language as Symbolic Action* (Berkeley: University of California Press, 1966), pp. 3–24.

4. See Eugene Burnstein and Amiram Vinokur, "Testing Two Classes of Theories about Group-Induced Shifts in Individual Choice," *Journal of Experimental Social Psychology* 9 (March 1973): 123–137, and "What a Person Thinks upon Learning He Has Chosen Differently from Others: Nice Evidence for the Persuasive-Arguments Explanation of Choice Shifts," *Journal of Experimental Social Psychology* 11 (September 1975): 412–426. Also see Amiram Vinokur and Eugene Burnstein, "Effects of Partially Shared Persuasive Arguments on Group-Induced Shifts: A Group-Problem-Solving Approach," *Journal of Personality and Social Psychology* 29 (March 1974): 305–315; and Amiram Vinokur, Yaacov Trope, and Eugene Burnstein, "A Decision-Making Analysis of Persuasive Argumentation and the Choice-Shift Effect," *Journal of Experimental Social Psychology* 11 (March 1975): 127–148. A critique of this theory is found in Glenn S. Sanders and Robert S. Baron, "Is Social Comparison Irrelevant for Producing Choice Shifts?" *Journal of Experimental Social Psychology* 13 (July 1977): 303–314.

5. Richard E. Petty and John T. Cacioppo, *Communication and Persuasion: Central and Peripheral Routes to Attitude Change* (New York: Springer-Verlag, 1986).

6. B. Aubrey Fisher and Leonard Hawes, "An Interact System Model: Generating a Grounded Theory of Small Groups," *Quarterly Journal of Speech* 57 (December 1971): 444–453; C. David Mortenson, *Communication: The Study of Human Interaction* (New York: McGraw-Hill, 1972), especially pp. 14–21, 376–377.

7. For a more detailed analysis of this ad, see K. H. Jamieson, *Dirty Politics* (New York: Oxford University Press, 1992), pp. 12–42.

8. They are also meaningless to many K.U. students who do not know that the waving arms symbolize waving wheat or that "rock chalk" refers to quarries in which skeletons of prehistoric animals were discovered by K.U. geologists, whose students originated the chant.

9. Kenneth Burke, "Psychology and Form," *Counter-Statement* (Berkeley: University of California Press, 1968), pp. 29–44, discusses form as the psychology of the audience. Kinds of form and their appeal are discussed on pp. 124–149.

10. Lillian Hellman, "Commencement Address at Barnard College," *Women's Voices in Our Time:*

Statements by American Leaders, ed. Victoria DeFrancisco and Marvin D. Jensen (Prospect Heights, IL: Waveland Press, 1994), p. 20.

11. "Acceptance Speech," *New York Times*, July 18, 1980, p. A8.

12. "The Building of the Gilded Cage," in Karlyn Kohrs Campbell, *Critiques of Contemporary Rhetoric* (Belmont, CA: Wadsworth, 1972), p. 165. The study cited was that by Edward M. Bennett and Larry R. Cohen, "Men and Women: Personality Patterns and Contrasts," *Genetic Psychology Monographs* 59 (1959): 101–155.

13. Donald C. Bryant and Karl R. Wallace, *Fundamentals of Public Speaking*, 5th ed. (Englewood Cliffs, NJ: Prentice-Hall, 1976), pp. 320–321.

14. Bernice Sandler, "Men and Women Getting Along: These Are the Times That Try Men's Souls," in

Contemporary American Speeches, 7th ed., ed. Richard L. Johannesen, R. R. Allen, and Wil A. Linkugel (Dubuque, IA: Kendall/Hunt, 1992), pp. 228–229.

15. Leonard J. Swidler, *Women in Judaism: The Status of Women in Formative Judaism* (Metuchen, NJ: Scarecrow Press, 1976); *Biblical Affirmations of Women* (Philadelphia: Westminster Press, 1979). With Arlene Swidler, he has edited *Women Priests: A Catholic Commentary on the Vatican Declaration* (New York: Paulist Press, 1977).

16. From *Catholic World,* January 1971, pp. 177–183. Reprinted by permission of *Catholic World.*

17. Joe Murray, "Vouchers a Threat to Public Schools," *Wichita Eagle*, March 19, 1999, p. 11A. Reprinted by permission.

chapter 6

The Resources of Organization

"Organizational patterns just provide a nice backdrop for an essay or speech."

"It doesn't really matter what organizational pattern you choose."

"No one can see an organizational pattern, so it is not central to an audience."

Like many beginning critics or public speakers, you may share some of these *misconceptions* about the importance of choosing an appropriate organizational pattern for your rhetorical acts. How you organize rhetoric is not a matter for casual attention. It is integrally related to the type of audience you are addressing, the clarity of your thesis, and the cogency of your arguments. In fact, this chapter will argue that organization itself makes a statement to your audience about what they need to know. In short, organization is a kind of argument. It is a process of structuring materials so that ideas are clear and forceful for readers or hearers. Ideally, the pattern of development should reflect a consistent point of view on a subject, clarify the relationships among ideas, and make a case effectively. That's a tall order! And that is exactly why organizational patterns should not be considered inconsequential.

As noted earlier, Aristotle wrote: "There are two parts to a speech; for it is necessary [first] to state the subject and [then] to demonstrate it. . . . Of these parts, the first is the statement [*prothesis*], the other is the proof [*pistis*]" (1414a.30-1).[1] This is good advice for starters, but, as Aristotle also recognized, you need to adapt your ideas to an audience. My purpose is to show you how thinking strategically about organization assists rhetors in adapting ideas to people. First, I talk about formulating a thesis and developing an outline. Second, I discuss the three basic types of organizational structure, their function and strategic value. Third, I identify some more in-depth pointers about introductions and conclusions that help you adapt these to your audience.

THE THESIS

The key to organizing ideas rhetorically is a clear central idea or thesis. A good thesis statement has these qualities:

1. *It is a simple sentence* (states one and only one idea). For example, "Heavy television viewing inclines children toward violence and stereotyping" is a problematic thesis, especially for a short essay or speech, because it involves two quite distinct claims that are related only indirectly. Either claim by itself would take a good bit of time to develop.
2. *It is a declarative sentence* (a statement, assertion, or claim—e.g., Mandatory sentencing for drug-related crimes should be abolished) or an imperative sentence, a command (e.g., Join the National Organization for Women!).
3. *It limits your topic* (narrows your subject). The standard for limiting has to be vague—what you can manage in the time or space you will have. This reinforces the first point, but note that even one of the two claims above about television might be too large for a short rhetorical act.
4. *It suggests your purpose* (implies the kinds of response you want)—understanding, belief, or action.
5. *It is a capsule version of everything you will say or write.* That is, it should sum up your purpose, and everything in the rhetorical act should be related to it.

Please note that you may never state your thesis quite as bluntly as it appears in your outline, but the central idea ought to be clear to your audience when you have finished.

OUTLINING

An outline is a visual representation of the relationships among the ideas you will present. Accordingly, it is a useful tool for testing the consistency of your approach and the strength of your case. To understand how this can be, consider this outline skeleton:[2]

I. Your thesis or central idea
   A. Your first main point (subordinate to I; coordinate with B)
      1. Subpoint of and subordinate to A; coordinate to A.2
      2. Subpoint of and subordinate to A; coordinate to A.1
   B. Your second main point (subordinate to I; coordinate with A)
      1. Subpoint of and subordinate to B; coordinate to B.2
        a. Subpoint of and subordinate to B.1; coordinate to B.1.b
        b. Subpoint of and subordinate to B.1; coordinate to B.1.a
      2. Subpoint of and subordinate to B; coordinate to B.1

This outline form says many things. First, that there is one central, all-inclusive idea, Roman numeral I. In a speech or essay, this would be the thesis. It says that this central idea is divided into two relatively equal parts, letters A and B. It says that A and B are divided into two parts, but that the idea expressed at B.1 requires fuller development, perhaps for more detailed explanation or proof. Overall, this format indicates which ideas are larger and which are smaller, which ideas are parts of other ideas, which ideas will receive special emphasis.

In this outline, A and B are main points, A.1 and A.2 and B.1 and B.2 are subpoints, and B.1.a and B.1.b are sub-subpoints. Notice, however, that in each case, a larger idea is subdivided into two parts. If the content of the outline reflects the form, these subdivisions should have three characteristics. They should be:

1. *Subordinate*, that is, they should be ideas of smaller scope than the claim they support or explain.
2. *Coordinate*, that is, the subdivisions should be of relatively equal scope and importance.
3. *Mutually exclusive*, that is, they should cover different aspects of the larger idea; their content should not overlap.

For example, here is the basic outline of a speech given by a student who was an advocate for the disabled:

I. The segregation of physically and/or mentally disabled children in U.S. schools must end.
   A. Integration teaches the very young to accept others' differences.
      1. Placing children together early in life decreases biases against the disabled.
      2. Among children who were exposed to minority populations during their school years, this acceptance lasted a lifetime.
   B. Disabled and "normal" children learn from each other if educated together.
      1. Disabled children learn how to behave appropriately in a normal social setting where the majority is not disabled.
      2. "Normal" children learn that although some people in our society are different, they are still valuable.
      3. "Normal" children learn how to behave appropriately around the disabled and how to aid in caretaking.
   C. Including disabled children in regular classrooms offers them a brighter future.
      1. Inclusion develops positive self-concepts.
      2. Inclusion develops higher level cognitive skills.
      3. Inclusion in all schools would cause future decision makers to realize all that disabled people are capable of accomplishing.

Note that each main point is *subordinate* because each identifies a particular benefit of integrating disabled and nondisabled children. Each point is roughly *coordinate* in covering bases for increased acceptance, mutual learning, and the beneficial effects for the disabled. Most points are mutually exclusive, though there is a bit of overlap because the higher cognitive skills discussed under point C are presumably part of what disabled children learn from interaction with their nondisabled schoolmates, but that is normal in a rhetorical act of this type. The main points are not stated in parallel fashion, but the subpoints under C are laid out in that way.

Another student argued for the legalization of marijuana working from this outline:

I. Marijuana (hemp) should be legalized.
  A. Hemp is very beneficial for the environment.
    1. It reseeds itself in forests.
    2. Oil from hemp seeds has many commercial uses, particularly as a substitute for petroleum.
    3. Fibers in the stem can be used for textiles.
      a. Natural fibers are less damaging than synthetics to the environment.
      b. Hemp fibers are stronger than cotton fibers.
  B. Hemp has important medical uses.
    1. Extracts from its leaves can be used to aid cancer, multiple sclerosis, and AIDS patients as a painkiller and to stimulate appetite, e.g., following chemotherapy.
  C. Hemp has important nutritional uses.
    1. After the oil is removed from the seeds, a substantial amount of protein remains.
      a. Hemp seeds have more protein than soybeans.
      b. Hemp seeds are more nutritious than alternatives for animal feed.
  D. Marijuana is a far less dangerous drug than alcohol, which is legal.
    1. Alcohol is addictive, with high social costs in lost productivity and highway deaths.
    2. Alcohol is a health hazard.
      a. It destroys brain cells.
      b. It destroys liver cells, causing cirrhosis.
    3. The effects of marijuana are small.
      a. It lowers sperm count.
      b. Like other cigarettes, smoking it contributes to lung cancer.
      c. In some cases, heavy use causes memory loss.

Again, each point is subordinate; each sets forth a reason for legalization. The points are relatively coordinate in exploring environmental, medical, nutritional benefits and comparing the ill effects of a legal drug, alcohol, to marijuana. The fourth point shifts ground slightly. The earlier points talk about absolute benefits, the last explores comparative benefits, which are actually comparative harms.

Main points such as these develop, divide, explain, and prove the thesis. Main points can explain just what the thesis means. Main points can try to demonstrate the truth of the thesis. The subdivisions of a thesis or of any point in an outline usually answer one of these questions:

- What do you mean?
- How do you know?
- How does it work?
- Why?

In other words, there is a necessary relationship between a main point and its subdivisions. For example:

1. Capital punishment should be abolished. (Why?)
   (Because) A. It does not deter would-be murderers.
   (How do you know?)

1. Comparisons of similar jurisdictions reveal that those with capital punishment have murder rates as high as those without.
2. Most murders are crimes of passion and lack the thought and planning that might make a deterrent effective.

In other words, an outline is (1) a way to plan how you will develop your ideas, (2) a way to lay them out so you can examine the relationships among them, and (3) a way to make relationships among ideas clear to your audience.

Although some outlines need not be composed of sentences, it is essential that rhetorical outlines be sentence outlines. The reason is simple. The building blocks of rhetoric are arguments, and arguments only exist in sentences. A claim must be an assertion, a declarative sentence; and summaries of evidence and statements of justification (reasons or warrants) require expression in sentences. Accordingly, you cannot make the sort of outline you need or use the outline to test the coherence of your ideas unless you use sentences.

Here is an outline that served as the basis for an excellent short speech:

I. Traumatic shock is a dangerous condition for which every injured person should be treated. (thesis; purpose is to alter perception of the condition known as shock and to create understanding in order to affect behavior.)
(Why? Because)
   A. Traumatic shock is potentially fatal. (What do you mean?)
      1. Shock is a substantial reduction in the vital functions of the body caused by a decrease in the volume of circulating blood. (defines and explains shock)
      2. If shock is allowed to persist, the person will die. (details results of shock on an injured person)
      (Why treat every person?)
   B. Traumatic shock can result from almost any injury.
      1. Common household accidents can produce shock.
      2. Psychological factors may speed the onset of shock.
   C. There are no reliable indications of the presence of shock.
      1. The symptoms of shock can be misinterpreted or misunderstood.
      2. A person can experience shock without showing any of the usual symptoms.
   D. Treatment of shock is simple. (feasibility)
      1. Keep the person in a prone position.
      2. Keep the person warm but not overheated.
      3. Try to reduce contributing psychological factors by reassurance.

This outline leaves out a number of things that happened in the actual presentation. But the outline is strong because it divides the topic and explains its dimensions, and the main points prove that the thesis is true (if A and B and C and D, then I must follow). In effect, the outline says you treat every injured person for shock because shock is life-threatening, it can result from any injury, you can't tell whether or not it is present, and it is relatively easy to treat.

FORMS OF ORGANIZATION

There are three basic ways to develop your thesis, central idea, or major claim: through *sequence structures*, *topical structures*, and *logical structures*. Each of these general patterns can be varied in several ways, and all three patterns may be used to develop parts of a single piece of rhetoric.

Sequence Structures

Chronological sequence organizes an idea in terms of its development through time or in a series of ordered steps (Figure 6–1). This may involve division in terms of historical periods or by phases or stages. Chronological organization argues that this topic is best understand in terms of how it develops or unfolds through time, or that you cannot achieve a goal without following a certain sequence. The most obvious form of chronological structure follows historical development. For example:

I. Contemporary feminism has gone through a series of ideological changes.
   A. Until 1968, it was a relatively conservative, reformist movement.
   B. From 1968 until 1977, it divided into conservative and radical factions.
   C. Since the Houston Conference of 1977, the factions have unified into a less conservative but highly political coalition.
   D. Following the Anita Hill–Clarence Thomas hearings in 1991, political activity escalated.
   E. During the late 1990s, a backlash developed that produced what some call "post-feminism."

Chronological organization is also used to develop the steps or stages in a process. For example:

I. Follow a sequence in preparing for rhetorical action.
   A. Choose your subject.
   B. Research available materials.
   C. Select a thesis.
   D. Structure your ideas.
   E. Produce a first draft (orally from notes or in writing).
   F. Edit your work through rewriting or oral practice (rehearsal).

Figure 6–1
Sequence Structures

Sequence	Function	Example	Value
Chronological	Treats a subject by tracing its development over time	To explain the seven steps to performing CPR	Well suited for "how to" speeches Amplifies a subject Presumes little audience knowledge
Narrative	Treats a subject in story form	To formulate the belief that diligence pays, with a timely version of Little Red Hen	Teaches in nonlogical ways Induces audience participation Transcends cultural barriers
Spatial	Treats a subject in a directional pattern	To explain what the new science building will look like by giving a simulated guided tour of the first three floors	Helps audiences visualize subject Audiences can anticipate sequence

Organizational patterns that develop ideas historically or processually are common in rhetoric, but another, less common form of sequence structure is *spatial structure*. Spatial sequence organizes an idea in terms of its development through direction or space. This may involve moving from left to right or top to bottom to describe a building, an outfit, a geographical site, or a surgical procedure. For example, an architect must give presentations all the time that follow this sequence. She must explain the blueprint of a building project by giving a simulated guided tour of each floor. Beauty consultants sell makeovers by starting with options for eyebrows and ending with variations of lip liner. Geologists explain the intricacies of earth layers in this way. Spatial sequence argues that audiences must visualize and anticipate the directional progression of ideas for them to be memorable. Like a time sequence, a directional sequence requires a rigid adherence to its operating principle. Once you begin a time or directional developmental line to your topic, you must be faithful to that form to fulfill the expectations of your audience.

A third, highly poetic sequence structure that is impossible to outline occurs when ideas are shaped into a *narrative sequence*. When a speaker or writer tells a story to make a point, he or she argues ever so subtly. Because stories entertain by inviting audience participation we sometimes forget that they do more than create virtual experience; they work to alter perceptions and even initiate action. An example of such a story is James Thurber's "The Little Girl and the Wolf," one of his *Fables for Our Times*. The story relies on cultural history in two ways. First, it adopts the form of the fable, a story with a moral, most familiar from Aesop's fables or Jesus' parables, and it assumes that we are already familiar with this form. Second, it assumes our familiarity with the plot of the fairy tale about Little Red Riding Hood, which it revises and parodies.

The Little Girl and the Wolf
by James Thurber[3]

One afternoon a big wolf waited in a dark forest for a little girl to come along carrying a basket of food to her grandmother. Finally a little girl did come along and she was carrying a basket of food. "Are you carrying that basket to your grandmother?" asked the wolf. The little girl said yes, she was. So the wolf asked her where her grandmother lived and the little girl told him and he disappeared into the wood.

When the little girl opened the door of her grandmother's house she saw that there was somebody in bed with a nightcap and nightgown on. She had approached no nearer than twenty-five feet from the bed when she saw that it was not her grandmother but the wolf, for even in a nightcap a wolf does not look any more like your grandmother than the Metro Goldwyn Mayer lion looks like Calvin Coolidge. So the little girl took an automatic out of her basket and shot the wolf dead.

Moral: It is not so easy to fool little girls nowadays as it used to be.

This revision is humorous because it pokes fun at the original story, but it also forces us to look anew at the old story and to consider the unstated moral that it implies. In the original story, Little Red Riding Hood is naive, incapable of defending herself against the evil in the world, and she, like her grandmother before her, is eaten by the wolf. Only when a hunter comes to their rescue can she and her grandmother be saved. Neither the story and the moral of either version can be reduced to outline form. They are nondiscursive or nonlogical structures, and they follow a different pattern of development. This pattern is followed by most stories, dramas, and jokes, and it looks something like this:

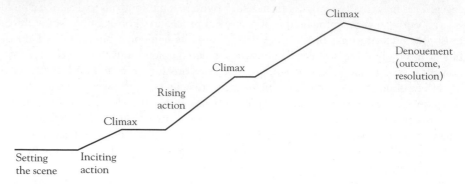

James Thurber's fable follows this pattern. The first paragraph sets the scene and alerts us that this is a retelling of a familiar fairy tale about a little girl, a wolf, and a grandmother; it introduces us to the wolf and the threat he implies, and to the other main characters in the familiar story. The inciting action is the appearance of the little girl. There is rising action as the wolf and she carry on a brief dialogue, which escalates the possible threat. A new pattern of rising action begins when the little girl arrives at her grandmother's house, sees that there is someone in her grandmother's bed, and recognizes that it is not her grandmother. The climax, the height of the conflict, occurs when she takes an automatic out of her basket and kills the wolf. The resolution or denouement is the moral, a comment that interprets the meaning of the story.

This story is a useful illustration for several reasons. First, as a fable, it is intended to teach and persuade. Second, it teaches and persuades in an entirely nondiscursive way. There are no arguments, and no data are presented. The story is wholly outside logical and empirical reality. If it teaches us and gains our assent, it does so because it is a revision that exploits our familiarity with the original story of Little Red Riding Hood. The humor arises out of our surprise at what happens in this version and in response to the highly original figurative analogy and a point made by the second meanings lurking in "little girls" and "wolves." It also works because it teaches by contrast, forcing us to think about the assumptions in the original story. How could we ever have believed that a little girl would mistake a wolf for her grandmother? Why did we assume that the little girl wouldn't have prepared herself to cope with the dangers of the forest?

Good stories have certain qualities. They follow certain patterns and develop through details that we can see or imagine, and the plot has universality or general application (fairy tales deal with the hopes and fears of all of us; fables such as those of Aesop comment on common human failings, made more palatable by being presented as the failings of animals, e.g., the stories of the fox and the grapes or the dog in the manger). They usually develop one or more characters with whom we can identify or they describe a situation in which we can imagine ourselves. They are organized around a conflict that increases in intensity so that we are drawn into the story and come to care about how it is resolved or "comes out." The rhetorical strength of many stories comes from their *verisimilitude*, that is, their formal resemblance to events and persons in our world of experience. In this case, the verisimilitude arises out of the story's resemblance to a familiar tale, out of a structure that follows the familiar form of the fable, and situations in which wolves wait to prey upon little girls.

A work that is structured as a dramatic narrative exploits the literary and poetic resources of language or the plot lines with which we are familiar. On the simplest level, such a story is an extended example, with all of the strengths and weaknesses of this kind of evidence, but dramatic narratives have compensating strengths. They can reach out to the audience to prompt identification and participation. They are easy to follow and pleasing, and so invite involvement. In a dramatic narrative, we are invited to share the point of view of the narrator, to imagine ourselves in the experiences described. The rhetor's claim is expressed as a series of concrete experiences or dramatic encounters, and the conclusion is the meaning of the tale. If the story is well constructed, it is hard to reject such "claims." They become part of our experience, not simply an idea or an argument.

Narrative-dramatic development is less common than other forms of organization in rhetorical discourse, but when it appears, it illustrates these resources. The most famous examples are the parables of Jesus, stories he told to illustrate truths. "Toussaint L'Ouverture," a speech delivered many times by the abolitionist orator, Wendell Phillips, is a rare instance of an entire speech organized in this way.[4] It is the story of the Haitian leader and revolutionary, whose life is detailed in order to demonstrate that former slaves deserve full citizenship. The story itself is strong proof because a single contrary instance is enough to disprove a "biological law." If one person of African descent is clearly a human being of superior abilities, descendants of Africans as a group cannot be biologically inferior or incapable of all the rights and privileges of personhood and citizenship. But the story steps outside the usual antislavery–proslavery argumentation to involve us in the life and hopes and tragedy of one person. We share his experiences; we identify with him. Phillips's speech transcends the obstacles of cultural history and engages his listeners and readers in a more direct and participatory way.

There are more recent examples. Rachel Carson's *Silent Spring*[5] is often credited with initiating environmental activism with its vivid evocation of a world polluted by DDT. The film *Saving Private Ryan* memorialized the sacrifices of American soldiers in World War II and revived interest in that period. A series of films about the war in Vietnam, *Apocalypse Now, Coming Home, Born on the Fourth of July,* and *Platoon* among others, helped Americans to come to terms with the costs of that war and the sacrifices of U.S. soldiers. Movie director Oliver Stone's film *J.F.K.* was his way of arguing the controversial position that there was a conspiracy behind the assassination of President Kennedy. In each of these cases, a dramatic narrative transcends the obstacles created by cultural history or diminishes hostility toward a controversial group or idea or reaches across the chasm of cultural differences to create identification between rhetor and audience. Incorporating a detailed example into a speech is one way to use the resources of narrative.

You should choose some form of sequence structure if you wish to emphasize development over time or in steps or stages. It is a good choice if the audience knows little of your subject, because it is a pattern ideally suited to provide background and to develop relationships among events. It is also a kind of structure easily adapted to hold the attention of the audience because it emphasizes progress through time, completion of a process, or movement toward a climax.

Topical Structures

Topical structures develop a subject in terms of parts or perspectives (Figure 6–2). Sometimes the divisions are integral *parts* of the subject, such as the executive, judicial, and legislative branches of the U.S. government. Frequently, however, the topics are familiar *perspectives* we take on many subjects—the economic, legal, and social implications of, say, affirmative action programs in the automobile industry, or of discontinuing federally funded programs to create jobs for inner city youth, or of ending welfare programs. In other words, the outline above about legalizing marijuana is a rather typical example of a topical outline. Note that the student considers marijuana/hemp in terms of environmental, medical, and food benefits. Similarly, in the outline on integrating disabled students into regular classrooms, the argument develops by topics of accepting differences, learning from each other, and improving the future of the disabled.

Topical organization is ideally suited for selecting some parts of a subject for discussion or emphasis. For example, a contemporary feminist wants to talk about the forms of social control that limit the options open to women. Because there are many forms of social control, she must narrow her focus and select only some forms for discussion. Her outline might look like this:

I. U.S. women suffer from overt and covert social controls.
    A. The laws control women overtly.
        1. Marriage laws have been the most oppressive controls.
        2. So-called protective labor legislation has limited access to jobs, promotions, and higher wages, with effects that persist.
        3. The Supreme Court has refused to extend Fourteenth Amendment protections to women.
    B. Socialization controls women covertly.
        1. A female child is reared to believe that she is limited.
        2. Education discourages women from many fields of endeavor.
        3. Popular culture reinforces stereotypes and gender-related limitations.[6]

Figure 6–2
Topical Structures

Topical	Function	Example	Value
Parts	Treats a subject by subtopics	To explain the three basic shots in tennis: forehand, backhand, half-court volley	Flexibility Emphasis Narrowing
Perspectives	Treats a subject by familiar divisions	To explain the economic, legal, and social implications of affirmative action	Familiarity of perspectives

In this case, topical organization structures main points A and B in relation to the thesis as well as A.1 and 2 and 3 and B.1 and 2 and 3. Under A, the rhetor selects three kinds of laws for attention. Under B, she discusses three elements of socialization: child-rearing, education, and popular culture.

Topical organization can explore natural divisions of a subject (fiction and nonfiction, regular and cable television, print and electronic media, for example). It can explore selected parts of a subject (soap operas and situation comedies as outstanding examples of kinds of television programming). Or it can apply familiar perspectives to a subject (the legal, economic, psychological, social, and medical aspects of state-run lotteries or mandatory sentences or nuclear power).

Because there usually is no necessary relationship between the points in a topical structure, this kind of organization can also be put to nondiscursive use. In such a case, the work develops associatively, in a manner analogous to the structure of the lyric poem by exploring the aspects of an attitude or feeling. Such organization is uncommon in rhetorical acts, but it can be highly effective, as illustrated by Elizabeth Cady Stanton's speech, "The Solitude of Self," found in the Materials for Analysis in Chapter 9. When topical organization is used well, it divides a subject into parts that seem appropriate to the audience, parts that reflect a clear appraisal by the rhetor of what is important, what is typical. In addition, these parts should be arranged into some sort of hierarchy so we move from one point to another with a sense of progression. The outline on legalizing marijuana, for example, could be rearranged into a crescendo or climax pattern moving from smaller benefits to larger ones.

The outline on the social control of women works differently. The development and proof of point A, that women are overtly discriminated against in law, prepares us for point B, that they are subtly controlled through socialization. If we assent to point A, we are far more likely to assent to point B; the relationship between the two ideas is *a fortiori*: if the first is true (overt discrimination by law), how much more likely it is that the second is true (covert discrimination in socialization).

Topical structure is an ideal pattern for narrowing a broad subject to a manageable size. It is also a method of emphasis by which you can indicate what parts of a subject are most important.

Logical Structures

Logically linked structures assert that ideas or situations stand in some necessary relationship to each other (Figure 6–3). These patterns express processes of *cause and effect* or define a *problem and its solution*. As you might guess, such organization often is used to develop questions of policy. The relationship between questions of policy and logically linked structure is illustrated by most television commercials (commercials ask you to change policy by buying a new product or by switching brands or to resist the appeals of competing products). Many ads are little problem-solution dramas. For example, a man in a commercial is shown anxiously discussing the lack of interest his girlfriend is showing. His friend suggests the solution of a toothpaste for sparkling teeth and sweet breath. We then see the man with his sexy girlfriend in a scene that leaves no doubt that his romantic problems are over. In other words, if you have a problem being attractive to someone, solve it by brushing with Brand X toothpaste.

Here is an example of a problem-solution outline:

Figure 6-3
Logical Structures

Logical	Function	Example	Value
Causal	Treats a subject by showing a cause and effect relationship	To explain the effects of deforestation and its three principal causes	Reflects necessary, not arbitrary, relationships Streamlines subject
Problem-Solution	Treats a subject in two parts—the first showing harm and scope, the second showing remedy	To initiate the action of random drug testing of students at registration	Ideal for policy speeches Capitalizes on cognitive dissonance theory

I. A state lottery can provide essential funding for education.
   A. The need for new buildings, additional teachers, and special education programs makes major state expenditures indispensable.
   B. Providing the needed funds requires raising property taxes or offering a lottery.
      1. Polls indicate that voters will not support school bond issues based on property taxes for education.
      2. Polls indicate that voters support state-run lotteries.
   C. Therefore, if educational needs are to be met, a state-run lottery must be instituted.

In this case, the thesis implies a goal (providing the resources needed to offer high quality education to all children) and indicates that there are just two alternative courses of action to raise the funds to reach it. Point A states the problem or need, and B indicates that two alternatives are available to raise the needed revenues. Point B.1 eliminates one alternative, and point B.2 indicates popular support for the proposal (which requires statutory action), leaving the alternative advocated in the thesis.

Many speeches combine topical and logical structure, as in this detailed outline for a speech.

The State as Bookie

I. State-run lotteries should be abolished.
   A. Lotteries are not a painless and effective way to raise money for education.
      1. Lotteries are not a significant part of state revenue.
         a. In 1995, the average lottery contribution to state revenue was only 3.32 percent of the state's total revenue; in Montana, the lottery contributed only .9 percent (Peter Keating in *Legalized Gambling: For and Against*, ed. Rod Evans and Mark Hans, 1998, pp. 107–110).
         b. In the year 2000, officials expect that California's lottery will contribute about $877 million on sales of nearly $2.6 billion to

schools, which is only a fraction of their cost: the state will spend some $28 billion on K–12 schools, the lottery provides only 3 percent of the total education budget (*Los Angeles Times*, April 19, 2000).

2. Lotteries are an inefficient way to raise revenues: "A typical tax imposed by a state requires just a nickel to raise a dollar; lotteries require between 10 and 40 cents" (Gerald Bracey, executive director of the Alliance for Curriculum Reform, *Phi Delta Kappan*, December 1995: 322).

B. Lotteries have been sold to the public as funding to subsidize popular civic needs like education and the environment, but lottery revenues just replace other sources of funding.

1. Lotteries have not supplemented education funding.

   a. In Alabama, the lottery proposed in 1999 by Governor Siegelman was intended to increase state support by providing additional funds for scholarships; however, needy students who qualify for federal tuition grants would have the value of those grants deducted from lottery-funded scholarships (*Black Issues in Higher Education*, September 2, 1999: 10).

   b. Instead of supplying extra funds to education, a 1997 study by Donald E. Miller and Patrick Pierce of St. Mary's College shows that states are likely to decrease education funding after enacting a lottery: "States are likely to *decrease* their growth of spending for education upon operating a lottery designated for that purpose. Furthermore, the decrease in the rate of growth is a long-term function of lottery adoption that occurs regardless of revenue generated by the lottery" (*State and Local Government Review*, vol. 29, 1997: 34–42).

2. In Minnesota, the public was told that 60 percent of the profits would go to the state's general fund and 40 percent would go to the Environment and Natural Resources Trust Fund, an endowment to protect the state's natural resources and environment.

   a. Instead, the state's general fund gets about 73 percent of the lottery profits, and the trust fund receives only about 27 percent.

   b. According to Doug Smith in the Minneapolis *Star Tribune*, February 23, 2000: "Far less money goes to the environment or natural resources than many people believe because of how the lottery was established in 1988. Though it took in an eye-popping $392 million in fiscal 1999, only about $11.6 million was spent on environmental and natural resource programs."

C. Legalized gambling is the most regressive form of taxation devised and unfairly places the burden of taxation on those least able to afford it.

1. According to John L. Mikesell, lottery sales actually increase with increases in unemployment, suggesting that it is the unemployed who play the lottery. In the *National Tax Journal*, March 1999, pp. 165–171, he wrote that lottery sales increase "by about 0.17 percent for each one percent increase" in unemployment; "for instance, an increase in unemployment from 4 to 5 percent would be associated with around a 4.25 percent increase in quarterly lottery sales."

2. Nationally, *The Economist* of June 26, 1999, reported that "Lottery players with household incomes under $10,000 spend three times as much on lottery tickets as those with incomes over $50,000; indeed, 5 percent of ticket buyers account for 50 percent of total sales."

3. In a 2000 study of the Texas state lottery, Lamar University professor Donald Price and Boise State University professor Shawn Novak discovered that games with the smallest and most immediate payoffs were the most regressive; moreover, instant games have "heavier participation by members of minority groups and less participation by college graduates" (*Public Finance Review,* January 2000: 91).

4. In Florida, "[t]here are three times as many lottery outlets in the poorest neighborhoods, where the state allows tickets to be sold at liquor stores, pawn shops and payday lenders. Factoring in income, the poorest and least-educated Floridians are spending seven times as much as the best-educated and wealthiest" (*St. Petersburg Times,* December 14, 1999).

5. According to Stephen J. Simurda, associate director of the U.S. Gambling Research Institute and professor of journalism at the University of Massachusetts, "5 percent of lottery players account for 54 percent of revenues," and "Black Americans spend an average of $998 a year on lottery tickets, while whites spend $210" (*The Nation,* June 28, 1999: 8).

D. Legal games do not drive out illegal gambling or eliminate crime.

1. It is estimated that illegal gambling increases when games are legalized because it offers gamblers better odds than the state-run version.

   a. According to Consumers Research Magazine, the probability of winning a typical lotto game is one in 7,059,052 whereas the odds of being "dealt a royal flush on the opening hand in a poker game are one in 649,739 (*Consumers Research Magazine,* March 1996: 22).

   b. There is evidence that operators of illegal numbers games take bets on states' daily numbers games (David Nibert, *Hitting the Lottery Jackpot: Government and the Taxing of Dreams,* 2000, p. 58).

2. In the rush to promote gaming, states risk corruption and an increase in crime.

   a. G-tech, a national firm that runs 29 of the 38 state lotteries in the United States and controls a 70 percent share of the world lottery market, has been found to exercise illegal influence in politics.

      (1) In Texas, Ben Barnes, a former lieutenant governor, was paid 3.2 million by G-tech in a single year to lobby for a renewal of the firm's contract to oversee the Texas lottery (*The Economist,* February 8, 1997, p. 33).

      (2) In California, A G-tech lobbyist was tried for bribing lawmakers; state lottery director Sharon Sharp, who had been referred to as "our gal" on a hidden tape recorder, had handed G-tech the California contract without opening the process to competitive bidding; in Georgia, lottery director Rebecca Paul called a secret meeting with G-tech when its bid to run the lottery came in $50 million above the low bidder (*Washington Monthly,* December 1999, p. 15).

b. Lotteries also can lead to an increase in crime.

    (1) Lotteries have been used to launder money; citing a federal agent's comments to the *Boston Globe*, *People Weekly* reported: "It's not uncommon for wise-guys to buy [winning] lottery tickets to explain to the IRS where there money comes from" (*People Weekly*, August 19, 1991: p. 88).

    (2) A 1990 study by John Mikesell and Maureen A. Pirog-Good found that states with lotteries had a 3 percent higher property crime rate than states without them (*American Journal of Economics and Sociology*, 1990: 7–18).

E. Lotteries are not harmless; "dreams" and "fun" come at high costs.

    1. Lotteries foster irresponsible thinking about money.

        a. States do not just offer an opportunity to gamble; they promote these games aggressively in order to increase revenue; if they don't, sales decline. Lotteries spend $400 million on advertising, putting them "among the largest advertisers in the country" (Michael J. Sandel in *The New Republic*, March 10, 1997: 27).

        (1) To succeed, such advertising promotes the lottery as a better investment than saving or education or hard work.

            (a) As Nicholas Thompson argues in a 1999 issue of the *Washington Monthly*, states often "try to sell sloth as a way to convince potential customers that a lottery offers a free ride to the high life"; for example, a 1996 Massachusetts lottery ad contrasted two ways to get rich; one option: "Start studying at about seven years old, real hard. Then grow up and get a good job. From then on, get up at dawn every day. Flatter your boss. Crush competition ruthlessly. Climb over the backs of co-workers. . . . Do this every day for 30 years, holidays and weekends included. By the time you are ready to retire, you should have your money." The second option was "two lottery tickets" (*Washington Monthly*, December 1999: 14).

    2. There is evidence that lotteries are linked to compulsive gambling.

        a. In a series of articles for the *Boston Globe*, David M. Halbfinger and Daniel Golden reported on the numbers of compulsive gamblers who play state lotteries.

        (1) A 1996 survey conducted in New York found that 9 percent of lottery players and 14 percent of keno players were compulsive gamblers at some point in their lives (*Boston Globe*, February 11, 1997: A1).

        (2) Dr. Lance Dodes, Director of the Center for Problem Gambling at Mt. Auburn Hospital in Cambridge, Massachusetts, estimates that 40 percent of his patients play lotteries (*Boston Globe*, February 12, 1997: A1).

        b. As reported in *Insight on the News*, in 1999, the National Gambling Impact Study Commission, headed by Republican Representative Frank R. Wolf and former Senator Paul Simon, issued a report criticizing state lotteries for their role in pathological gambling and suggesting a mandatory tax on lottery and other gambling profits that would subsidize treatment for compulsive gambling (September 20, 1999: 27).

The thesis of this outline is a policy statement urging abolition of state lotteries. Points A and B state arguments made in their favor, which are then attacked. Point C appeals to an unstated value, fairness in taxation, to point to undesirable qualities of lotteries. Point D is like A and B in stating and attacking pro arguments; point E argues that lotteries erode fundamental civic values. In other words, the main points are formed around what the rhetor believes are the major arguments for and against state lotteries. Note also that the full sentences in the outline enable you to read the outline and get a rather complete sense of what a speech or essay developed from it might say and that it includes references to the evidence to be used. In a sense, such an outline becomes the notes from which you could write a first draft of an essay or begin to practice your speech. Note, however, that the outline has not been adapted to create an introduction or conclusion nor has it been shaped for a particular target audience. As you think about adapting such material to an audience, consider what you might use to attract attention, and what might leave an indelible impression on the audience in your conclusion.

Cause-effect structure is a variation of problem-solution. Note that causal arguments are asserted or attacked in the above outline on state lotteries. Cause-effect structure ordinarily focuses on the first *stock issue* of a question of policy, the need for a change. Emphasis is placed on effects (the scope of the harm) and their cause (intrinsic to the current policy). For example,

I. High rates of minority unemployment are caused, in part, by a lack of skills.
   A. Education in urban ghettoes and in the rural South does not provide basic reading and arithmetic skills.
   B. Few vocational training programs are available.
   C. Minorities are denied access to union apprenticeship programs.
   D. Federal programs do not teach marketable skills.

Once again, this outline combines topical and logical structure. The thesis asserts a cause-effect relationship, but the main points are a topical list of the major causes of the problem—lack of skills.

As these examples illustrate, logical structures are ideal for treating questions of policy. It allows you to meet the requirements for defending a change of policy, and it can be used to explore causal relationships. In all cases, logical structures reflect necessary relationships between ideas or events.

Each form of organization is a kind of argument. Each structure offers a particular kind of perspective on a subject. You can combine these different forms in a piece of rhetoric, but in each case, you should choose the kind of structure best suited to the kind of argument you are trying to make.

ADAPTING STRUCTURE TO THE AUDIENCE

In the early part of this century, U.S. philosopher John Dewey published a book entitled *How We Think*.[7] The book laid out the *stages in reflective thinking*, the processes by which we recognize problems and then go about solving them. These stages included

1. Perceiving a felt difficulty or recognizing that a problem exists
2. Analyzing the problem, including attempts at definition
3. Exploring possible solutions and evaluating them
4. Selecting the best solution
5. Discovering how to implement the selected course of action

Dewey's analysis reflects the stock issues of a question of policy, especially in stages 2, 3, and 4. But the first and last steps are additions, and they are clues to one kind of structural adaptation that needs to be made in presenting material to an audience. Step 1 is introductory; it establishes the facts and values that suggest that we ought to be concerned about something, that we ought to find out what sort of problem this is and whether and how it can be solved. Step 5 goes beyond the stock issues to ask how can we go about setting in motion the change we have decided would be a good one. It concerns concrete action, for example, how do we go about getting Ralph Nader or Pat Buchanan on the ballot in our state now that we have decided that the solution to our political woes is this third-party candidate?

Dewey's book was probably the stimulus for *the motivated sequence* that Alan H. Monroe developed.[8] This structural form illustrates the adaptation of logical organization for presentation to an audience. The steps in the motivated sequence are as follows:

1. *Attention*: call attention to the problem; in Dewey's terms, make the difficulty felt.
2. *Need*: demonstrate that a need exists (that is, develop the first issue of a question of policy to prove there is harm, of significant scope, arising out of current practice).
3. *Satisfaction*: show the audience that the need can be met (that is, that there is a practical and beneficial alternative policy).
4. *Visualization*: describe vividly and concretely what will happen if the problem is or is not solved (that is, picture good or bad consequences).
5. *Action*: call for immediate action from the audience; show them how to bring about the solution.

The motivated sequence is based upon *cognitive dissonance theory*, a theory of persuasion first proposed by psychologist Leon Festinger.[9] As the terms "cognitive (thought) and "dissonance" (imbalance) suggest, a rhetor's task is to create psychological discomfort by showing that a major problem exists. Then the rhetor's task is to create "consonance" (balance) by suggesting a remedy (a policy) that will solve the problem. The theory asserts that persuasion is more likely to occur if you first experience dissonance because psychological discomfort motivates the acceptance of a new belief or action (Figure 6–4).

As you examine this sequence, you will see that steps 2 and 3 develop the stock issues of a policy question. In other words, the motivated sequence is a form of logical organization that is appropriate only for advocating a course of action. Steps 1, 4, and 5, however, are structural elements designed to adapt materials for presentation to an audience. Step 1 precedes the thesis in order to involve the audience in the subject. Step 4 is designed to increase the motivation of the audience by vividly depicting what their world will be like with or without the policy proposed. In ads for exercise machines or diet aids, for example, "before" and "after" photographs are juxtaposed to perform this function. Step 5 presumes that the audience needs specific instructions on how to bring a solution about—where to go, what to do, who to write or call, and so on. It is designed to bring the proposed policy or course of action closer to reality. In

Figure 6-4
*The Motivated
Sequence and
Cognitive
Dissonance
Theory*

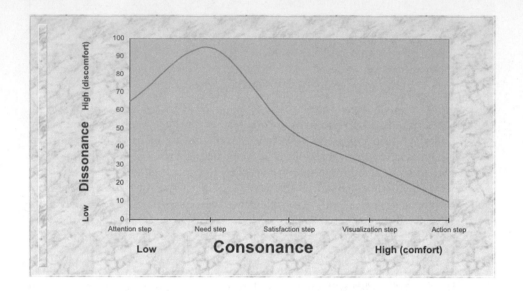

sales, it becomes the closing. Steps 4 and 5 also require additions to the outline forms described above. They require special sections that make your ideas vivid and concrete and that give the audience assistance in implementing policy change.

The motivated sequence is an excellent pattern to follow in adapting logical organization for presentation to an audience, but all rhetorical action requires similar adaptations. At a minimum, it is necessary to begin with an introduction and to end with a conclusion.

Introductions

The basic functions of an introduction that you learned from Chapter 3 are to gain attention, to create accurate expectations in the audience for what follows, and to suggest the relationship between the subject and the audience. These functions are good general touchstones for anyone preparing for rhetorical action. But the introduction also serves a vital purpose in overcoming the rhetorical obstacles that you face on any given occasion. For this reason, the introduction is the first attempt to cope with these difficulties. The choices a rhetor makes should be guided by the answers to these questions:

1. *What is the relationship between the rhetor and the audience?* Do they share many experiences and values, or is the rhetor seen as an alien or outsider?
2. *What is the attitude of the audience toward the subject and purpose?* Will the audience perceive the subject as overworked and complex or as fresh, vital, and intelligible? Is the reaction to the purpose likely to be hostile and indifferent or sympathetic and interested?
3. *What is the rhetor's relationship to the subject?* Is she or he an expert or an interested amateur?

As these questions indicate, introductions should be adapted to the attitude of the audience toward your subject and purpose, to the relationship between you and your audience, and to the relationship between you and your subject. It is in light of these considerations that you need to gain attention, create accurate expectations, and develop connections between the subject and the audience.

Kenneth Burke wrote, "Only those voices from without are effective which can speak in the language of a voice within."[10] His statement emphasizes the importance of *identification* between a rhetor and audience and emphasizes the role that the rhetor plays as a context for the message. One of the most important functions of an introduction, therefore, is to create common bonds between author and audience, that is, to overcome the perception that the rhetor is different, not like the members of the audience. Very often, personal experience is used to create connections and to establish common grounds. Here, for example, is part of an introduction Maryland Senator Barbara Mikulski used in a speech titled "The American Family" in the summer of 1988 speaking in Atlanta, Georgia.[11] Notice how she moves from introducing herself in ways that make her distinctive to identifying herself with the subject and reaching out to a broad general audience:

> Fellow Americans. My name is Barbara Mikulski. I come from Baltimore, Maryland. I love the Orioles, Chesapeake Bay crabs, and I love my family.
>
> I grew up in a large family and still live in the old neighborhood. I know my neighbors. I've got two sisters and I'm Aunt Barb to six nieces and nephews.
>
> So I know a lot about the family. I know the American dream begins with the family.
>
> It's nurtured around the kitchen table, at the family barbecue, Thanksgiving dinner and Sunday church. It grows on the family farm, thrives at the neighborhood block party, builds new strength at the suburban PTA meeting.

This part of the introduction indicates that Senator Mikulski thought the first and major obstacle she faced would be the perception of the audience that she was not like them and that, because she was unmarried and childless, she couldn't talk about this topic. If she was going to say anything about the American family that they were going to hear, she had to create a relationship between them and her and establish that she had the personal experience and values that made her an appropriate speaker on this subject. The introduction acknowledges differences, but it aims at creating identification, a combination of shared values and personal experiences.

But she had more work to do before she could begin to develop her point of view. After pointing out that some families have to cope with terrible problems, she said:

> But family life should be more than just coping and making ends meet; more than just pinching pennies and dipping into the nest egg. If there is anything that concerns the American family today it is this—our government hasn't caught up with the new facts of American family life. Families have changed, so why can't Washington?
>
> *New fact:* Mom's working. Nearly 65 percent of all mothers are working. Part-time. Full time. All the time. Keeping the family together. Making ends meet. Making America more prosperous.
>
> Working mothers need affordable day care and the pay they deserve. Too often they can't get either.

This part of the introduction is an attempt to make a transition from shared views toward a more controversial area. She starts with problems and economic struggles, which often push women into the workforce, then states a fact that shocks the audience into recognizing the extent of changes, and then links that change first to women's hard work and then to shared values—keeping the family together, making enough to pay the bills, and, in the process, producing goods and services that are part of the nation's well-being. Then, and only then, does she move to the more controversial claims, for affordable day care and the pay they deserve (note that she doesn't say equal pay or comparable worth—her stand is ambiguous). These moves begin to alter perception of the problem and to lessen audience resistance to her proposals.

Ads, especially advocacy ads, are good examples of techniques to gain attention. In the *New York Times Magazine* of June 18, 2000, the American Civil Liberties Union had an ad seeking support. The headline on the ad read: "Thanks to Modern Science 17 Innocent People Have Been Moved from Death Row. Thanks to Modern Politics 23 Innocent People Have Been Removed from the Living." The center of the ad is the picture of a man strapped in the electric chair. The opening paragraph read:

> On April 15, 1999, Ronald Keith Williamson walked away from Oklahoma State Prison a free man. An innocent man. He had spent the last eleven years behind bars. "I did not rape or kill Debra Sue Carter," he would shout day and night from his death row cell. His voice was so torn and raspy from his pleas for justice that he could hardly speak. DNA evidence would eventually end his nightmare and prove his innocence. He came within five days of being put to death for a crime he did not commit. (101)

Note that different kinds of evidence are attention-getting. The headline exploits a dramatic contrast and statistics; the opening paragraph uses a dramatic example. As you think about preparing an introduction, look at the evidence you have gathered and consider which of it might work as introductory material.

Introductions may be composed of almost any of the resources available to a rhetor—examples, visuals, analogies, statistics, quotations from authority, a literary reference, personal experience, explanation, description, and so forth. What an introduction needs to do in a given case depends on the specific obstacles you face. You always need to gain attention, create appropriate expectations, and seek to involve the audience with your subject. But how you accomplish these depends on the audience's attitude toward your subject and purpose, your relationship to the audience, and the nature of your expertise on the subject.

Conclusions

You should remember from Chapter 3 that a good basic conclusion (1) summarizes the major ideas that lead to the claim that is your thesis, and (2) fixes the specific purpose in the audience's mind. In addition, the conclusion ought to be both an ending and a climax. It should be an ending in the sense that it provides a sense of closure, a feeling of completion. Rhetorical action should end, not just stop or peter out. A conclusion can be an ending in the simplest and most obvious way—as a summary that recalls the processes by which rhetor and audience drew a conclusion. Unless the act is unusually short or the structure is very simple, a review of the arguments is highly desirable and probably necessary. If you doubt this advice, listen closely to some television commercials and note the amount of repetition that occurs even in these relatively short bits of rhetoric.

Ideally, the conclusion ought also to be the climax or emotional highpoint, and the material in the conclusion should epitomize (typify, embody) the thesis. Such a conclusion might include a story that captures the essence of what you are saying. It might present a metaphor or analogy that represents the idea. Obviously, a literary allusion or quotation, a citation from an authority, or other kinds of resources might be used as well. Here is an example from a speech by Katherine Davalos Ortega, then Treasurer of the United States, at the West Point Savings Bond Kickoff on April 21, 1988:[12]

> But through all the years and all the changes, one thing has not changed. That is the idea behind bonds—the notion that patriotism and profit are teammates, that because we co-operate in selling bonds, our country will be able to better compete in a world where the economic race is to the swift. At the ancient Olympic games, kings ran side by side with soldiers—the only prize a modest wreath of olives. Yet the name of the victor would be inscribed with the immortals.
>
> Today you put your name on the passport to America's future. And in doing so, you make our common journey uncommonly successful. Because you enter the competitive ranks, we all run faster. Because of this room full of winners, American wins. Thank you very much.

Ortega appeals to the long history of Savings Bonds and using alliteration links patriotism to personal profit. She uses an athletic metaphor—teammates, running a race—and reinvigorates it through an allusion to the early Olympic games and echoes the words of the Bible ("the race is not to the swift"—Ecclesiastes 9:11). At this point she mixes her metaphors, referring to the bonds as a "passport" related to our national "journey," after which she returns to her original metaphor. She praises the audience for running the race, calling all of them winners, and reaffirming that their willingness to participate contributes to U.S. success. This is not an eloquent conclusion—the metaphor is too familiar, and its power is weakened by the metaphoric mixture. The Olympics allusion is undeveloped, which lessens its force. But overall, she summarizes her main point, makes the idea more vivid through imagery, and praises the audience, all of which contribute to her goal.

On January 19, 1988, JoAnn Zimmerman, then lieutenant governor of Iowa and a nurse, spoke to the Iowa Nurses Association on their Legislative Day.[13] She began by defining "political," then told detailed stories about Florence Nightingale's many political activities. This is how she ended her speech:

> Florence Nightingale understood how to make things happen. Unfortunately our nursing history stresses her origination of modern nursing practice and education and gives little space to the tremendous amount of time and energy she spent "politicking!"
>
> I give you this story of modern nursing for you to understand the importance of influencing the political world. Please understand the political world is also the work world, your place of practice.
>
> Clara Barton also learned to use the political process in gaining funds for her work.
>
> Mary Breckenridge, the founder of the frontier nursing service, Wendover, Kentucky, also understood the importance of gaining the support of a political network.
>
> In 1935, the Maternity Center Association and the Lobenstein Midwifery Clinic applied to the State of New York to consolidate under the name of Maternity Center Association.
>
> Early private registries eventually turned to the public sector to validate our profession in a codified registry—a legal certification.
>
> Many of our predecessors have understood the art [and] practice [of] influence. We, too, must unify, choose some major priorities upon which we can agree and move to solidify our position as a profession. Our bickering and divisions will destroy our ability to apply political pressure. As our numbers shrink in the nursing shortage, we *must*, must understand this is the

time to move forward as a profession! It is imperative that we become involved in the political process, attend the local caucus, or vote in the primary, and develop resolutions to shape the political party platforms! We can have our say and make it count!

Based on the text of the speech, an important part of the rhetorical problem as Zimmerman saw it was persuading nurses in the association to become politically involved and to convince them that their involvement could have an effect. These are important elements of the problem created when audiences are not sure their actions can produce change. In addition, it appears that she believed many nurses might see such activity as inappropriate for them. Accordingly, she turned to an important role model, the originator of nursing as a profession, to demonstrate the importance of political activity from the very beginning. In the conclusion, she refers to other role models, Clara Barton, founder of the American Red Cross, and Mary Breckenridge, a role model for nurses on the frontier. These examples are intended to reinforce the need for and the efficacy of political action for her audience. Notice that the supporting material in the speech, the detailed examples from the life of Florence Nightingale, and the undeveloped examples in the conclusion are adapted to this particular audience and will have special force for them. These are women that nurses would like to emulate professionally. Zimmerman is arguing that they should be imitated in other ways—by engaging in political activity. Note that this purpose is consistent with the speaker, who is herself an example of a nurse who has become active in politics, and with the occasion, a day on which the nurses focus on issues related to legislation, that is, political issues.

The ACLU ad cited earlier ends in a rather conventional way:

> Even those who support capital punishment are finding it increasingly more difficult to endorse it in its current form. Capital punishment is a system that is deeply flawed—a system that preys on the poor and executes the innocent. It is a system that is fundamentally unjust and unfair. Please support our efforts to have a moratorium on further executions declared now. Support the ACLU.

The beginning of the conclusion rehearses what the authors hope you as a reader will be feeling and thinking. That is followed by an appeal based on the stock issue of *inherency*—it is the system, not individual cases, that is flawed. Note the dramatic language: "preys on the poor and executes the innocent." That kind of language is more typical in conclusions because audiences find emotional appeals more acceptable after a case has been made. Note the appeal to values: the legal system should be just and fair. Lastly, there is an appeal to support a specific effort and then to support the organization that is leading the fight for that cause.

Finally, here is the conclusion to the speech that Elizabeth Cady Stanton made at the first woman's rights convention at Seneca Falls, New York, in 1848. The speech was long and complex, setting forth arguments to respond to all of the major justifications offered for women's special and limited place. At the end, she wished to rouse her listeners to action, and she said:

> "Voices" were the visitors and advisers of Joan of Arc. Do not "voices" come to us daily from the haunts of poverty, sorrow, degradation and despair, already too long unheeded. Now is the time for the women of this country, if they would save our free institutions, to defend the right, to buckle on the armor that can best resist the keenest weapons of the enemy—contempt and ridicule. The same religious enthusiasm that nerved Joan of Arc in her work

nerves us to ours. In every generation God calls some men and women for the utterance of truth, a heroic action, and our work to-day is the fulfilling of what has long since been foretold by the Prophet—Joel 2:28: "And it shall come to pass afterward, that I will pour out my spirit upon all flesh, and your sons and your daughters shall prophesy." We do not expect our path will be strewn with the flowers of popular applause, but over the thorns of bigotry and prejudice will be our way, and our banners will beat the dark storm-clouds of opposition from those who have entrenched themselves behind the bulwarks of custom and authority, and who have fortified their position by every means, holy and unholy. But we will steadfastly abide the result. Unmoved we will bear it aloft. Undaunted we will unfurl it to the gale, for we know that the storm cannot rend from it a shred, that the electric flash will but more clearly show to us the glorious words inscribed upon it, "Equality of Rights."[14]

At the time of this speech, women were not allowed to speak in public, and when they married, they ceased to exist in law—they could not sue or bear witness, own property, including their own earnings, and had no guardianship rights in their children. Cady Stanton knows that it will be very difficult for women to pay the costs in ridicule or to face the intense hostility of most men and women to their cause. She seeks to raise their morale, to give them courage to pursue this cause. She does so in the high style of nineteenth-century U.S. public address, but her appeal is powerful, particularly to an audience with deep religious commitments. Joan of Arc is a model of a woman who stepped out of her traditional place in order to pursue a moral cause; the words of the prophet Joel foresee a time when women will speak for moral causes. She also ends with an appeal to the nation's fundamental values. Thus, in the face of what she knows will be great obstacles, she energizes her audience with religious and patriotic appeals that may enable them to withstand fierce resistance.

These examples illustrate the basic functions that conclusions should perform. They are competent, real illustrations of experienced public speakers trying to end their rhetorical acts effectively.

ADAPTING YOUR OUTLINE TO THE AUDIENCE

If you were to follow the form of your outline in presenting your ideas to the audience, your rhetorical action would be presented through *deduction*, which means starting from a general conclusion and moving to illustrations and applications of it. In fact, all outlines are deductive in starting from a thesis and moving to its divisions. But such a pattern may not be the ideal way to present your ideas under all circumstances. For example, if an audience is hostile to your purpose, or if the subject is controversial, announcing your thesis (forewarning) might stir up resentment and prevent the audience from hearing or considering your ideas. In such a case you might want to present your ideas inductively.

Deductive Structure

The advantages of presenting your ideas in deductive order, as in your outline, are that (1) such a structure avoids ambiguity and possible misinterpretation, and (2) such a procedure is perceived as honest and straightforward. The disadvantages are that hostility may be created or increased by a blunt statement of the thesis and by a failure to acknowledge opposing viewpoints or arguments. The problems of hostility can be handled to some extent through the introduction. The clarity of this pattern is a strong advantage. As you will note below in the section on two-sided structure, it is possible to incorporate a deductive approach into a two-sided presentation of the pro and con arguments on an issue. In all cases, however, your choice of the pattern in which you present your materials should be a conscious one that you make after having considered carefully the obstacles that you face and the strengths and weaknesses of alternative modes of presentation.

Inductive Structure

Logically, *induction* is a process of going from specifics to a general conclusion. In fact, in traveling from data or evidence to a claim, induction involves the "leap" described in Chapter 5. You will probably follow such a pattern of thinking in the preparation of your speech or essay. But it would be strange indeed if you were to operate inductively while you were speaking to or writing for an audience. That would mean that you were drawing your conclusions and deciding on your thesis at the same moment you were presenting them to the audience. As a thoughtful rhetor, you will have reached conclusions before you present your ideas to an audience. An inductive structure, however, is an attempt to recreate for the audience the process by which you arrived at your conclusions. Obviously, you cannot replicate that process exactly. But you might shorten and streamline the process you went through while giving the listener or reader a sense of how you came to draw the conclusions you are advocating.[15] The inductive format has several advantages. It is likely to increase audience involvement, as they will participate more directly in the processes by which conclusions are drawn. This form of presentation also minimizes hostility. The audience has fewer opportunities to disagree, fewer chances to dispute the positions taken by the author. But there are disadvantages. Inductive presentation takes more time or space for development. Also, unless the audience participates very actively—listens acutely or reads intently— they may miss the point, fail to draw the conclusion, and misunderstand your purpose.

Two-Sided or Refutative Structure

As described, an outline is a brief or series of arguments developing reasons for taking one position rather than another. But many subjects of rhetorical action are controversial issues. There will be arguments on both sides that need to be considered and examined. When speaking about such an issue, you might wish to use *refutative structure* by exploring the opposing arguments as part of the process of explaining why you have decided to advocate another position. In effect, you look at the pool of available arguments in order to show that the weight of the evidence and of available arguments falls on one side or the other. A two-sided presentation also can present you as a mediator who has examined more extreme positions and who seeks to find a compromise between them.

Two-sided or refutative structure is also more appropriate for certain audiences. A two-sided presentation allows you to incorporate refutation into your presentation. That is essential under several conditions:

1. When you know that the audience is familiar with opposing arguments or will be exposed to competing persuaders
2. When a one-sided presentation may motivate the audience to seek out opposing views
3. When a one-sided view of an issue may need to be corrected
4. When your opposition is also a significant part of your audience

In the first situation, opposing arguments are already in the minds of the audience or they soon will be. As a result, it is essential that you respond to questions they have in their minds or that you prepare them for the arguments they will hear from competing persuaders. When arguments already exist in the minds of audience members, you ignore them at your peril, as they are competing with you whether you know it or not (note how this is done in the outline attacking state lotteries). When the audience will eventually be exposed to opposing arguments, you can *inoculate* them by suggesting weaknesses in the arguments, which will make them less susceptible to the appeals of competing persuaders. Without such inoculation, the arguments of opponents may become the novel arguments that shift the balance and alter opinion.

As discussed in more detail in Chapter 8, there are three conditions in which audiences seek information that challenges their beliefs or values: when audience members are of generally higher levels of education, when the information is very useful, and when the audience members' history of exposure leads them to believe they have heard a biased or one-sided presentation. Thus, two-sided presentations are desirable with knowledgeable audiences—a slanted or one-sided presentation can create a desire on the part of the audience for competing information. That is particularly true when the position you take is extreme or unusual. If you claim that ingesting almonds cures AIDS but don't acknowledge contradictory views, you may drive your audience to seek out competing medical studies. If you claim that there is no evidence that smoking is dangerous to health or that the amount of cholesterol in foods we eat has no effect on heart condition, you are likely to send your audience off to competing persuaders to look at the opposing evidence. At a minimum, you will need to qualify your claims. At best, you will acknowledge opposing arguments.

Finally, there are situations in which those holding opposing views are part of your target audience. One of the finest examples of two-sided or refutative structure is an essay on the birth of the "Black Power" slogan written by Dr. Martin Luther King, Jr.[16] King's opposition included more militant civil rights activists who were using the slogan and a more militant approach to civil rights protest. But those same people were part of his primary audience, because he sought to reconcile these competing groups and to unify the effort for civil rights. However successful his efforts at persuasion might have been, he would have failed if he had not demonstrated to his opponents that he understood their position and respected it. As a result, the essay is both a persuasive statement for a nonviolent approach and a moving statement of why the slogan and a more militant approach became attractive to civil rights workers. The essay is so balanced that it is an excellent source of information about the motivation of more militant civil rights groups. Despite his fair treatment of the opposition, King makes a powerful case for his own point of view. But a two-sided presentation was ideally suited to the conditions in which he found himself: competing with those whom he needed to persuade. When your opposition is also your audience, not only must you make a two-sided presentation, but you must also present opposing arguments fairly and sympathetically.

A Mercury Drop, a Deadly Lesson

by Helen O'Neill[17]
The Wichita Eagle, September 14, 1997, p. 1A
Lyme, N.H.

1 It was just a drop of liquid, just a tiny glistening drop. It glided over her glove like a jewel.

2 Scientist Karen Wetterhahn knew the risks: The bad stuff kills if you get too close. She took all the precautions working with mercury in her Dartmouth College lab—wearing protective gloves and eye goggles, working under a ventilated hood that sucks up chemical fumes.

3 So on that sunny day in August 1996, when she accidentally spilled a drop, she didn't think anything of it. She washed her hands, cleaned her instruments and went home.

4 It was just a drop of liquid, just a tiny glistening drop.

5 At first, friends thought she had caught a stomach bug on her trip to Malaysia. It wasn't until she started bumping into doors that her husband, Leon Webb, began to worry. Karen, always so focused, always so sure of her next step, was suddenly falling down as if she were drunk.

6 In 15 years together, she had never been sick, never stopped working, never complained. Leon was stunned when she called for a ride home from work. Over lunch a few days later, Karen confided to her best friend, Cathy Johnson, that she hadn't felt right for some time. Words seemed to be getting stuck in her throat. Her hands tingled. It felt like her whole body was moving in slow motion.

7 "Karen," Johnson said as she drove her back to the college, "we've got to get you to the hospital."

8 "After work," Karen promised, walking unsteadily into the Burke chemistry building for the last time.

9 That night, Leon drove her to the emergency room. It was Monday, Jan. 20, 1997, five months since she had spilled the drop in the lab.

10 Just a single drop of liquid. Yet somehow it had penetrated her skin.

11 By the weekend, Karen couldn't walk, her speech was slurred and her hands trembled. Leon paced the house. "Virus" seemed an awfully vague diagnosis for symptoms that were getting worse every day.

12 "It's mercury poisoning," Dr. David Nierenberg said. "We have to start treatment immediately."

13 Leon hung up with relief. At last, they understood the problem. Now maybe they could fix it.

14 It seemed impossible to believe that anything could be wrong with Karen Wetterhahn, one of those quietly impressive individuals whose lives seemed charmed from the start.

15 Serious and hardworking, she excelled at everything she turned to— science or sailing or skiing. She grew up near Lake Champlain in upstate New York in a family so close that when she and her only sister became mothers, they named their daughters after each other: Charlotte and Karen.

16   Karen was always the brilliant one of the family, the one who would do great things. And she did, becoming the first female chemistry professor at Dartmouth, running a world-renowned laboratory on chromium research, devoting herself to her work.

17   It was important work, the kind that could lead to cures for cancer and AIDS. Karen thrived on it. She loved nothing more than experimenting with a chemical, figuring out its bad side and how it breaks down living things.

18   In the often cutthroat world of scientific research and ideas, where work is judged in academic journals and egos are as enormous as intellects, Karen stood out. Other professors would send their students to her office just to meet her. Talk to Karen, they would say. See how you can balance the demands of work and life, and still be on top of your field.

19   The only place on Earth more precious than her lab was the dark cedar house that Leon, a mason, had built with his own hands. Home was Karen's haven, her retreat from the rarefied halls of Ivy League academia.

20   Here, in the pretty village of Lyme, at the top of a hill at the end of a dirt road, she would listen to rock music—heavy metal was her favorite—and tend her garden.

21   Here, science came second to 12-year-old Charlotte's baby rabbits, 14-year-old son Ashley's mountain bikes, Todd the goat, and Dillon the pony.

22   At home, she would throw great neighborhood parties by the pool, or gather up the family and drag them off to the golf course, or the tennis court, or Ashley's hockey game.

23   "We never knew she was a world-famous scientist," one neighbor said afterward. "She was just Char and Ashley's mom."

24   Mercury poisoning.

25   Karen beamed when she heard the news. Finally, something she understood. Something she could explain. They would feed her fat white nasty-tasting pills that would flush the poison out of her system. Science would cure her, she told her husband, giddy with excitement as she sat in bed surrounded by her children and her notes.

26   "Karen was happy, so I was happy," Leon says now. "We just didn't know."

27   How could they have known? Back in January, virtually nothing was known about the extraordinary dangers of dimethylmercury, the rare man-made compound Karen had spilled. Scientists didn't know it could seep through a latex glove like a drop of water through a Kleenex. Doctors didn't know it could break down the body over the course of a few months, slowly, insidiously, irreversibly.

28   Above all, no one knew how to stop its deadly progress, as it cut off her hearing, her speech, her vision, reducing her body to a withered shell.

29   Today, because of Karen, the world knows so much more.

30   Quicksilver, as mercury is called, has long played a sinister game of seduction with science. One of the world's oldest metals, it comes in various forms—some that heal, some that kill. Dimethylmercury, a colorless liquid that looks like water but is three times heavier, is far more toxic than other forms—the kind used in thermometers and batteries and medicine. It's made purely for research and is rarely used.

31   Aug. 14, 1996. Just one shimmering drop. Now, six months later, Karen's body was riddled with it.

32   Karen was the one who remembered the spill. It nagged away at her in the hospital as she underwent CT scans and spinal taps and tests for everything except chemical poisoning.

33   But I work with mercury, she said. Shouldn't I be tested for the bad stuff?

34   The results plagued the doctors even more: Why had it taken so long for the symptoms to show? What kind of brain damage had already occurred? Had anyone else been exposed? Was she contagious?

35   And the question that still stings Leon's heart, the one that still seems almost obscene: "Does your wife have any enemies?"

36   "Enemies!" he whispers incredulously through tears. "Karen didn't have enemies. Everyone loved her."

37   She was easy to love, this tall athletic woman with the deep infectious laugh. Comfortable to talk to. Always there for students, colleagues and friends.

38   And for Leon.

39   In some ways, they seemed an unlikely match: Leon, 40, the son of a Vermont dairy farmer who decided early on that masonry was more profitable than milking cows, and Karen, 48, the daughter of a chemist, the brilliant teacher and scholar. They had an easy comfort with each other. She would watch him coach Charlotte's basketball team; he would accompany her on lecture trips to Italy, Norway, and Hawaii.

40   He always knew her work was important but, since the accident, he has made an effort to really understand it. Today, he can recite her resume almost by heart: the awards she won as a doctoral student at Columbia, the Women in Science mentoring program she started at Dartmouth, the $7 million federal grant she won to study toxic metals.

41   She didn't talk much about work at home, except the grant, the largest in the college history. "She was so proud of that," he says.

42   The mercury research she was doing with Harvard and MIT was just something on the side, Leon explains. Chromium was Karen's real area of expertise.

43   He shakes his head at the irony. Who could have imagined that the builder would eventually learn more than the scientist about the perils of dimethylmercury?

44   Others were learning, too. At Dartmouth Medical Center, Dr. David Nierenberg scoured the medical literature for clues about how to treat his colleague and friend. A mile away in his campus office, two doors down from Karen's, John Winn, head of Dartmouth's chemistry department, grabbed every paper on mercury he could find.

45   The more her colleagues read, the more their hearts sank.

46   There was only one documented case of dimethylmercury poisoning this century, a Czech chemist in 1972 who had suffered the same symptoms as Karen and died. A handful of people had been exposed directly to pure methylmercury, another toxic mercury compound, and died. More well-known mercury poisoning epidemics, like those in Iraq in the 1970s and Japan in the 1950s, involved exposure to foods contaminated by methylmercury.

47   There was no telling whether dimethylmercury would act the same way.

48   Karen herself was beginning to understand. There was a desperate look on her face as she pointed to the clock when it was time to take her pills.

49   Still, she kept up a brave face, kept saying not to worry.

50   "Even if I don't fully recover, maybe I'll get well enough to ride again," she whispered to her horse-riding friend and fellow scientist, Jacqueline Sinclair.

51   And when the hospital psychologist asked whether she was depressed, she smiled. Wouldn't you be? she replied.

52   That was Jan. 31, three days after the diagnosis. A week later, Karen was transferred to Massachusetts General Hospital for a massive blood transfusion that nearly killed her. Leon was pacing at home again, torn between honoring his wife's wish not to alert her parents and the feeling that she was sinking faster than she knew.

53   The phone rang. The nurse said Karen wanted to talk to her son. From her hospital bed, the mother struggled. She drooled and moaned and the words just wouldn't come. Ashley waited uncomfortably. He didn't like the sounds. He didn't like the silence. "Hi, Mom," he coaxed, loud so she might hear. It was useless. The nurse ended the torture and took the phone.

54   "She just wanted to say goodnight," Ashley says, bowing his head to hide the tears when he remembers the last time he talked to his Mom. "She couldn't even say goodnight."

55   Others remember final moments, too, although everything was happening so fast they didn't seem like good-byes at the time. But friends could see the toll on the scientist's mind and body. They could see her faith fading, even as she continued to talk about being back on her feet for her new spring course. The day the ambulance came to take her to Massachusetts, she cried uncontrollably.

56   "I think that's when she knew," says Nadia Gorman, remembering how she tried to comfort her friend and colleague as she wondered whether she would ever talk to her again. "There was a feeling of total tragedy in the air."

57   In the ambulance, Karen told Cathy Johnson for the first time in their 15-year friendship that she loved her. In the hospital, she struggled to point to the letters "N" and "H" on her alphabet board. Leon nodded. He promised that, whatever the outcome, he would take her home, to New Hampshire.

58   "As a non-scientist, I couldn't comprehend it all," says Provost Jim Wright, Karen's friend and former boss.

59   Doctors didn't have answers either. They turned to Thomas Clarkson at the University of Rochester in New York, who had set up clinics in Iraq during the epidemic there in the 1970s, when hundreds of people died after eating mercury-poisoned bread.

60   His lab stopped everything to help, testing Karen's hair and blood samples, ordering a batch of dimethylmercury to begin its own tests.

61   "I felt such a sense of helplessness," Clarkson says. "Here was one of the world's most distinguished scientists, and I was looking at this woman dying realizing there is nothing the scientific or medical communities can do."

62   Karen's lab was shut down. Her family, students and co-workers were tested. Her hospital room was checked for airborne mercury from her breath. Federal environmental and health agencies were alerted, as was the state health department. Her car and clothes and house were sniffed with mercury-detectors.

63   E-mails flew around campus, and around the country. Students emptied libraries of books on mercury, staying up all night to translate obscure research papers, seizing on any sliver of information they could find.

64   Scientists and doctors around the world offered their services.

65   "It was an extraordinary outpouring," Nierenberg says.

66   But Karen was slipping too fast to appreciate it. Ten days after the diagnosis, on Feb. 7, she fell into a coma in Massachusetts. Leon told the doctors he was taking her home.

67   Back at Dartmouth, her family kept vigil by her bedside, her parents and sister talking to her as her body thrashed and moaned. Leon plastered the walls with cards and photographs: Karen on the golf course, at Disney World with the kids, lunch with her friends Cathy and Nadia, shaking hands with President Clinton at graduation ceremonies in 1996.

68   Just a tiny drop of poison. And she was fighting it with all her might.

69   It became too difficult for the children to visit. Even friends stayed home, waiting for the phone call that would tell them it was over.

70   Her husband stroked her face. Her sister and her best friend washed her hair. Doctors tried treatments never attempted on humans before.

71   But they couldn't save her from the poison. On June 8, it took her life.

72   "She didn't suffer," Ashley told his eighth-grade class the next day. "She just stopped breathing."

73   It was 10 months since she had spilled the drop in the lab, four months after she had slipped into a coma.

74   Karen Wetterhahn's death was as extraordinary as her life and, in many ways, just as important.

75   While she could still speak, she urged doctors and scientists to learn everything they could from her accident and to warn the world about the dangers.

76   The world has already learned so much. It learned that the gloves that were supposed to protect her actually acted as a conductor to the poison. It learned that dimethylmercury, so easy to order in research catalogs, is more deadly than anyone had imagined. Saddest of all, it learned that by the time the symptoms showed, it was too late.

77   There is much more to learn, as scientists and doctors study her case. There will be studies and papers, symposiums and tributes. There may even be new federal regulations and mandatory blood tests for scientists who work with heavy metals. There is talk of banning dimethylmercury for good.

78   Her funeral took place on a hot summer day to the strains of a flute and a choir singing "Be Not Afraid."

79   In the packed college chapel, the sense of betrayal was as powerful as the sense of loss. Colleagues wept as they eulogized a modern-day Madame Curie who had sacrificed her life to her cause.

80   What good was pushing back the boundaries of human knowledge, they cried, if they had to bury one of their own?

81   Alone and bewildered, Leon sat in the front pew, looking out of place in his dark funeral suit, tears streaming down his face.

82   It all seemed like a dream, he says later. No, he corrects himself—a nightmare.

83   He picks up the picture of Karen working in her lab, a study of intensity in her goggles and gloves, staring at her test tubes and vials.

84   "She loved her work," he says. "It made her happy."

85   She couldn't have known the risks. She couldn't have known how bad the bad stuff really was. Truth is, no one knew.

86   Just a tiny drop of liquid. Sweet-smelling. Dense. Deadly.

Questions for Analysis

1. "A Mercury Drop" is an unusual rhetorical act. Although it reads like a gripping piece of literature it is really a front-page newspaper story. Helen O'Neill is an AP reporter, and this column ran in many newspapers across the country. What makes it newsworthy?
2. Trace the ways in which narrative structure unfolds in this speech. Why is this organizational pattern a strategic choice given the subject?
3. How does narrative structure interact with evidence and language to give the reader an intimate glimpse of the fated scientist?
4. How are our perceptions of scientists altered after reading this act?
5. What rhetorical purposes does this act fulfill?

EXERCISES

1. Two-sided presentations: Prepare a speech or write an essay organized to present two sides of a controversial topic. Select one of these obstacle as your focus;
   a. Inoculating the audience against the arguments of competing persuaders or refuting the major arguments of the opposition.
   b. Moderating the views of extremists, for example, urging extreme conservatives to moderate their demands on politicians, urging abortion foes to permit abortions in cases of rape, incest, or where there is a threat to the mother's life, or urging pro-choice advocates to limit their appeals to the first trimester, and the like.
   c. Presenting arguments from another perspective to an audience likely to be familiar with only one side of an argument, such as minority or women's points of view to majority/male audiences.
   d. Acknowledging the justice of arguments on both sides while taking a point of view, for example, acknowledging the problems of censorship while arguing that the linkage of sex and violence in pornography is more significant, or acknowledging the evils of pornography while arguing that the evils of censorship are more significant.
      Focus attention on the strengths and weaknesses of this form of organization and attempt to locate the particular rhetorical situations in which it is likely to be most effective.
2. Prepare a two- to three-minute storytelling speech to create virtual experience. Be sure your story follows the narrative-dramatic form and is plausible. See Appendix Form for storytelling speech for assignment specifics.
3. Prepare a six- to eight-minute policy speech to initiate action. Use the motivated sequence and capitalize on cognitive dissonance. See Appendix Form "Speech to Initiate Action" for assignment specifics.
4. Divide into groups. Each group will be asked to design a brief outline of major points on the topic "McDonald's" using a different organizational pattern assigned by your instructor to advance your group's claims. Designate someone from your group to present your case. What do you learn about the way structure complements purpose? How is the value of each organizational pattern realized in your group's use of it?
5. Think about an ad that you know well. Does it conform to the motivated sequence? In what ways? Share your observations with the class.
6. Create copy for a one-minute radio spot on why students should attend your college or university. Use the motivated sequence to structure your ad. Vote for a class winner.
7. There are topics that hardly stir controversy, yet they deserve revisiting. Take, for instance, the issue of road safety. Even though most of us might agree that the behaviors we encounter on the roads are far from perfect, we may still not feel a sense of urgency in addressing the issue. Go to your InfoTrac College Edition database and locate the article "It Won't Happen to Me: Unrealistic Optimism or Illusion of Control?" by Frank P. McKenna (*British Journal of*

Psychology 84, no. 1 [1993]: 12). The article suggests that there is a discrepancy between the actual, statistical risk of being injured on the road and people's perceptions about that risk. Imagine that you are a member of a government task force working to educate the public about road safety. As McKenna suggests, the challenge of this project is that you would have to battle not just the audience's current misperceptions but also the significance of their driving habits and their varying degrees of emotional investment. Consider various ways in which you could organize your speech if your were going to speak to (1) parents, (2) teenagers learning to drive, (3) suburban commuters who have never been involved in a car accident, and (4) people who have been involved in a car accident.

Find information in the InfoTrac College Edition database about recent antismoking campaigns in the United States and abroad. What kinds of issues need to be taken into consideration when a message is transported into a different cultural, institutional, or community context? How are these considerations integrated into the structure of the campaign's message? Compare and contrast the campaigns described in the various articles in the database, which appear under the key words "anti-smoking campaign."

8. **Portfolio Entry 5: Organization**
Examine your rhetorical acts for the type of organizational pattern they use. How do these organizational patterns illustrate the value of such patterns as indicated in chapter reading? How does the organizational pattern advance the purpose of the act? Is one pattern more striking than others in advancing the cause? Why? Explain in one to two pages.

NOTES

1. *On Rhetoric: A Theory of Civic Discourse,* trans. George A. Kennedy (New York: Oxford University Press, 1991), p. 273.

2. Rhetorical acts inevitably violate ordinary outline form because they are unified by a single central idea, the thesis or specific purpose. In all of the illustrative outlines here, Roman numeral I. indicates the thesis.

3. *Fables for Our Time* (New York: Harper & Bros., 1940), p. 5. Reprinted by permission.

4. *American Speeches,* ed. W. M. Parrish and Marie Hochmuth (New York: Longmans, Green, 1954), pp. 311–332.

5. New York: Summit Books, 1977.

6. See Jo Freeman, "The Building of the Gilded Cage," *The Second Wave: A Magazine of the New Feminism* 1 (Spring 1971): 7–9, 33–39.

7. (Boston: D.C. Heath, 1910).

8. *Principles and Types of Speech,* 2d ed. (Glenview, IL: Scott, Foresman, 1939). Both were probably influenced by Francis Bacon's *Advancement of Learning* in which he developed the concepts underlying faculty psychology and in which he wrote that "the duty and office of rhetoric is to apply reason to the imagination for the better moving of the will."

9. *A Theory of Cognitive Dissonance* (Evanston, IL: Row, Peterson, 1957).

10. *A Rhetoric of Motives* (1950; reprint ed., Berkeley: University of California Press, 1969), p. 39.

11. Text of speech provided by office of Senator Barbara Mikulski.

12. Text of speech provided by the office of the Honorable Katherine D. Ortega, Treasurer of the United States.

13. Text courtesy of Lieutenant Governor JoAnn Zimmerman's office.

14. Elizabeth Cady Stanton, "Speech at the Seneca Falls Convention, 1848," *Man Cannot Speak for Her: Vol. 2: Key Texts of the Early Feminists,* ed. K K. Campbell (Westport, CT: Greenwood Publishing, 1989), pp. 69–70.

15. An exceptionally fine example of this is Virginia Woolf's *A Room of One's Own* (1929; reprint ed., New York: Harbinger, 1957).

16. "Black Power," the second chapter of King's book, *Where Do We Go From Here: Chaos or Community?* (New York: Harper and Row, 1967). It is reprinted in Robert L. Scott and Wayne Brockriede, *The Rhetoric of Black Power* (New York: Harper and Row, 1969), pp. 25–64.

17. Reprinted with permission of Knight Ridder/Tribune Information Services.

chapter 7

The Resources of Language

The language of a rhetorical act may be casual (It just blew my mind . . .) or formal (Four score and seven years ago, . . .), vague (Play it loud!), or precise (Only 2 calories in an 8 oz. glass), figurative (Using a different fat-free sauce on this Reuben would be like using steak sauce on salmon), or literal (Compare Teletire's cut prices on these performance radial tires), but whatever its style and whatever strategies are used, language is a powerful and significant resource.

However else it may be defined, rhetoric is the art of using symbols. All the resources of rhetorical action have their foundation in language. Given its importance, the student of rhetoric needs to understand the characteristics of language that allow it to play such a special role in rhetorical action.

THE CHARACTERISTICS OF LANGUAGE

In its ordinary sense, language refers to verbal symbol systems such as Sindebele or Hmong. Language also includes other symbol systems based on space, movement, sound, pitch, time, color, and so on. In their most developed forms, such symbol systems are dance, music, sculpture, painting, architecture, and the like. Through symbol systems, we order our experiences and assign them meaning. Instead of being bombarded by billions of distinct stimuli, language enables us to make sense of the chaos so that we can perceive and respond to a world of recognizable objects and events.

There are three primary dimensions of language: *naming*, *abstracting*, and *negating*.

Naming

The first dimension of language is naming—the process by which we notice, recognize, and label certain elements or qualities in ourselves and in our world. Names permit us to identify and isolate significant events. For this reason, the vocabulary of an individual or a community is a rough index of what is or has been important to that person or group, a relationship reflected in the "verbal ability" sections of college entrance examinations.

Naming is a process of ordering the world and of focusing our attention. A name does not label one single thing but a category of relatively similar objects or events. As labels that refer to categories, names permit us to ignore the differences among objects and events and to lump them together into groups to which we can respond similarly. If you identify an object as a "chair," for example, you respond to it as a humanly created object with arms or a back, intended for a category of actions labeled "sitting," and ignore the unique characteristics of this particular chair. If this process of labeling and responding is to work well, however, there must be standards to determine when a particular object, person, or event may be included in a particular category—that is, when it may properly be labeled with a particular name. Such standards are set by definitions.

A definition specifies the essential qualities that something must have to be labeled in a particular way in a given linguistic community. Definitions collected in dictionaries give words a special meaning called *denotation*. People do not learn meanings from dictionaries, however. They learn meanings in situations, by having experiences with words and with the persons, events, and objects to which words are applied. In these real, concrete situations, people not only learn denotative meanings, they learn to associate the feelings they experience in these situations with the words. Such meanings are called *connotations* (con = together with, notate = to mark or note), and they refer to the associations a word calls up.

Recently, a graduate student named Lin-Lee Lee gave me a chapter of her dissertation on the 1996 presidential election in the Republic of China. She reported that presidential candidate Chen Li-an had urged Taiwanese citizens to view each of their homes as a *baldachin*. I went to the dictionary, knowing that my student had searched for an English counterpart to a distinctive Chinese noun. A baldachin (or baldachino) is a canopy of cloth or wood or stone used to protect the image of a saint or an altar in a procession or in a church. When I read the definition, I was delighted; it was an apt metaphor for a candidate whose campaign emphasized moral values. I then recalled seeing the word in churches I had visited in Italy. The following Sunday in my *New York Times*, there it was again in a review in the Arts and Leisure section. Accordingly, in this case, baldachin not only refers to a protective religious canopy but it also means one of the unusual words that crop up when a foreign student is struggling with translation, an apt metaphor for the importance of moral values in the home, my experiences with such canopies in Italy, and a good example to use in this book explaining how connotative meanings develop. If you remember the word, one part of your connotative meaning will be related to reading about it in this book.

Semanticists (students of meaning) say that meaning is in people, not in things or even in words. The connotative meanings associated with all symbols illustrate this idea. They also show that names are not just factual or descriptive. Words are labels for our experiences so that names are valuative as well as descriptive. Meanings include subjective qualities such as associations and connotations.

Names are valuative at the most basic levels because they are signs of interest and relevance. If you already knew the meaning of baldachin, for example, your knowledge would indicate past experience with the word. You may have encountered it in a church or novel, you may be a student of religious architecture or pageantry, you may even have run across it in the dictionary. But it is unlikely the term produces strong reactions, because it is unlikely to be a word that you associate with intense or disturbing experiences.

Contrast *baldachin* with *masturbation*. The latter term is, for many, associated with disquieting sexual feelings and taboos. (Consider that a U.S. Surgeon-General was forced to resign her post after suggesting that masturbation should be taught to teenagers as an alternative to more dangerous and consequential forms of sexual activity!) In a class on the psychology of sex at the University of Kansas students asked their professor not to use that word because it was so upsetting. The students decided they preferred *self-pleasuring*. Denotatively, masturbation and self-pleasuring are identical, but connotatively they are not. Masturbation calls up many highly charged associations, but self-pleasuring, a less familiar term, is unlikely to have been used to label forbidden feelings and behaviors. As a result, hearing and using it are less disturbing. Recently, Pfizer, the drug company that markets Viagra, "insisted on calling the problem 'erectile dysfunction,' and not 'impotence.'" A successful marketing campaign involves managing the pitfalls of connotation: "Part of that is giving them [potential customers] language that is not emotionally charged," said David Brinkley, the worldwide team leader for Viagra at Pfizer.[1]

When we speak of loaded language, we are referring to words that provoke strong feelings; the person who hears or reads them has vivid, intense associations because of emotion-laden experiences with them. No term understood by a person is simply neutral or factual. It is always bound up with experiences and will always contain evaluations resulting from feelings associated with those experiences. In some cases, however, the response is so strong that it interferes with communication. For many people, it is not possible to talk calmly about abortion or rape or condoms or homosexuality or AIDS. Think, for example, about euphemisms that we use in order to talk about such subjects as death, money, and sexual intercourse, among others. Euphemistic terms are one strategy we use to avoid such intense reactions.

Connotations change. For example, at the beginning of the 1960s *Negro* had positive connotations as a term of respect and *black* was a term of disrespect. In the course of that decade, protestors changed those connotations so that Negro was associated, negatively, with persons who sought approval from whites and who were ashamed of their culture, their past, and their physical characteristics. By contrast, *Black*, now capitalized, became associated with racial pride. *African American* is now the preferred term (formerly, but no longer, hyphenated) because it has become associated with ethnic history and ethnic pride.

Naming, the first dimension of language, enables us to order, call attention to, focus, define, and evaluate. Names have denotative meanings, found in dictionaries, that define the accepted conditions for their use. Names have connotative meanings that reflect our experiences and associations with a term and its use. The connotations of terms can change for us as individuals and for us as members of a culture as our experiences with terms change.

Abstracting

The second dimension of language is abstracting. *Abstracting* is a process of leaving out details; the most basic kind of abstracting occurs with names. As a title for a category, names leave out all the distracting details. You call what you sit in a desk, ignoring its color, the gum underneath the seat, the initials carved in its surface or inscribed in ink, the difference between it and the desks your professors have in their offices. The most basic element in abstracting is omission—leaving out or ignoring details in order to treat different objects in similar ways.

Abstracting moves us farther and farther from concrete, specific details. In fact, we can go on and on leaving out more and more details. The word *abstract* is defined as "not concrete or specific, without reference to a specific instance, theoretical, not easily understood, abstruse." That definition alerts you to problems in communication that arise from abstracting. As we move farther from concrete detail, an idea or concept becomes more and more difficult to grasp and the chances of misunderstanding increase. Abstracting is also a major linguistic resource, however.

Symbols are abstractions that permit us to talk about an absent world. We write books about the remote past, most of whose details have vanished; we read books and talk about places we have never seen; we argue about a future that is outside our experience; we explore concepts we can never see or touch. Here is an example of abstracting as a process of including more and more experience but omitting more and more detail.

Most abstract	5.	All of the activities and experiences involved in obtaining knowledge and skills.	"An education"
	4.	All of the activities, academic and nonacademic, of this institution.	"The university"
	3.	All classes offered to students leading to degrees at this institution.	"The curriculum"
	2.	All of the classroom experiences on T, Th at 9:30 in Elliott 111, Spring 2002.	"Rhetoric 535"
Least abstract	1.	Concrete experiences with the individuals now in this classroom.	Abstracted by labels such as "students" and "teachers"

Even at the most concrete level in the here and now, abstraction occurs. It occurs as we label our experiences, as for example, when we ignore individual differences and label people as "students" and "teachers." As we move up each level, we include greater amounts of experience as we omit more and more details. Level 2 lumps together many hours of varied activity under a single label. Level 3 lumps together all the courses offered to students and orders them into one giant pattern. And so on.

The advantages of abstracting are evident; they enable us to combine, for thinking and talking, ever-larger areas of experience while ignoring varied and complex detail. As we move up the ladder of abstraction, it becomes more and more difficult to understand these abstractions—they are farther and farther from our personal experience. It is also easy to ignore significant differences—to forget that students differ in background, age, social skills, verbal ability, maturity, and so on, and to treat them stereotypically, as if they were all identical. Abstraction allows us to manipulate great hunks of the world verbally; it tempts us to forget that these chunks are made up of highly varied concrete events, objects, and individuals. The capacity of language to abstract permits us to talk about the absent, the past, and the future, and it allows us to conceptualize ideas such as love, truth, beauty, and rhetoric that lie far beyond our concrete experience.

Abstracting is a powerful source of identification and has great potential to prompt participation. Politicians exploit this potential by speaking in less concrete, more general terms hoping that listeners will interpret such language in different ways, enabling them to appeal to diverse groups. Many of us may believe that change is needed and respond to a politician who says that, as many voters did to Bill Clinton's statements about health care in 1992, only later to discover that the politician's idea of change and the listeners' ideas of change were quite different. Is anyone opposed to "family values," for example? But what does the person espousing them really mean by that phrase? Reducing or eliminating abortion? Opposing sex education in schools? Providing family leave to parents of newborn or newly adopted children? Providing tax write-offs for child-care services? All of these might be part of whatever someone might mean by that phrase.

Negating

Negating is the third dimension of language. Definitions are based on negating because when we say what something is, we are also saying what it is not. The rhetorical power of negation is reflected in the Judeo-Christian cultural heritage. As the Ten Commandments state, "Thou shalt not . . ." But negation is very tricky, because such prohibitions imply their opposites. Whenever you say to a child, "Don't . . . ," and describe some proscribed action, you are, at the same time, suggesting an enticing possibility! Thus, even positive commands imply their opposite, suggesting the option not to do whatever it is that we are being told to do.

Negation also is involved in abstracting. To abstract is to omit (negate) details and ignore (negate) differences. In fact, the ability to use symbols at all requires an understanding of negation. Whatever a name is, it is *not* what it stands for. "Cat" is a bit of black ink or a few sound waves, not this sable-colored, furry creature that meows and purrs, bites and scratches, grooms by licking, and adores its catnip toy.

Negation underlies all comparisons and contrasts, including those involved in literal and figurative analogies. As discussed in Chapter 4, literal analogies allow us to evaluate and to predict. But comparisons are also involved in definitions.

A dialectical definition defines by contrast. If you wish to define capitalism, for example, you might compare it to socialism and conclude that what is distinctive about it is the private ownership of the means of production. Such a definition uses socialism as a perspective through which to look at capitalism; it ignores similarities and emphasizes differences. We can also compare capitalism and democracy. In this case, the focus shifts to assumptions made about individuals. Capitalism presumes that some will have more economic power (capital) while democracy affirms the right of each individual, regardless of economic or other differences, to an equal voice in how he or she is governed. If we compare capitalism and feudalism, the focus shifts to the reciprocal obligations of liege lord and vassal and the absence of such mutual obligations between capitalist/employer and laborer/employee. Comparisons between capitalism and communism might emphasize the difference between production controlled by the market and production determined by state planning. In each case negation, in the form of contrast, directs our attention and shapes the definition that results. Dialectical definitions are effective ways to delineate the specific meanings of highly abstract terms.

Negation is also the basis for the figurative analogy and for metaphorical language generally. The moon is not "the North Wind's cookie" or "a piece of angry candy" or "a ghostly galleon tossed upon cloudy seas" as it has been described by poets. We can understand and use such metaphors precisely because we recognize that they are not literally true. This form of the negative extends the range of our symbols to include comparisons between anything and anything. In addition, the negative allows us to use irony (to say one thing but mean something else), develop satire and parody, and speak in a sarcastic tone.

These, then, are the three fundamental dimensions of language: the capacities to *name*, to *abstract*, and to *negate*. From them come all the powers of language to influence our perceptions and our attitudes. And from them arise the specific resources of style and strategy.

STYLE

Style is what is distinctive about the language of a rhetorical act. The style of an act can vary. It can be more or less formal, more or less precise, more or less literal, and more or less redundant, for example.

Formality

Whenever we speak or write, we make certain assumptions about what kind of language is appropriate to the situation at hand. Basically, this amounts to deciding how formal or informal to be. Rhetorical style ranges from the formality of a presidential address or a scholarly article on the one hand to the informality of a newspaper article or a conversation with a friend on the other. Generally speaking, as style becomes more informal it becomes more conversational or colloquial.

Informality may be a way of identifying with those to whom you appeal or from whom you seek support. Barbara Christmas, a 1992 candidate seeking to represent Georgia's First District in Congress, talked the talk of those from whom she sought support. She presented herself to voters, "Remember, ah'm just a country girl from Tattnall County. . . . No way ah'm against gun controls. . . . Ah grew up with a gun rack in the pickup truck. . . . Ah'm no ultraliberal feminist. Ah'm a traditional—but progressive—woman." Christmas received support from the National Organization for

Women but she also is the daughter of a retired warden of the Reidville state penitentiary, and she commented, "Y'see, that way I built this incredible Good Ol' Boy network of my own? . . . A network of law-enforcement people, state troopers, sheriffs, lawmakers? They all know I'm all right." In other words, the language she used reflected real links to the community she wanted to represent, and her accent and her colloquial style were reminders of them.[2]

The factors influencing the degree of formality are those that will be discussed in Chapters 8, 9, and 10 as parts of the rhetorical problem: the audience, the purpose, and the rhetor. Whatever is serious and important will be presented in a more formal style. The more authoritative the rhetor is or wishes to appear, the more formal the style. The relationship between rhetor and audience also affects formality. Formal prose creates distance between rhetor and audience while informality minimizes distance.

The differences between formal and informal prose are chiefly matters of grammar, sentence structure, and vocabulary. Formal prose is strictly grammatical and uses complex sentence structure and a lofty or technical vocabulary. Informal prose is less strictly grammatical and uses short, simple sentences and ordinary, familiar words. Informal style may include sentence fragments and some colloquialisms or slang.

How formal or informal should you be? Obviously the answer depends on your subject and purpose, the role you will play, and your relationship to your audience. Most public rhetorical action observes conventional niceties of grammar, is modestly complex in sentence structure, and avoids an excessive use of colloquialisms (words or phrases found more frequently in conversation than in writing). That is, it is relatively formal, although the rhetor must determine just where on the continuum from highly formal to informal a particular rhetorical occasion should be placed.

Precision

Language can be highly precise, specific, and verifiable, or it can be ambiguous and vague. Precise language expresses ideas clearly and distinctly. It is exact and sometimes technical. Ambiguous language is open to more than one interpretation, and vague language is inexplicit and indefinite. For the most part, good style aims for precision and avoids ambiguity.

Precise language is a symptom that a rhetorical act is emphasizing empirical evidence and logical proof. Only clearly stated arguments can be evaluated logically; only exact statements are capable of verification. Precision in language indicates purpose and reflects the rhetor's assumptions about the audience. More complex, technical subjects require the use of formal, technical vocabulary. In addition, precision reflects the expertise of the speaker or writer.

Some apparently precise terms, however, can be highly ambiguous. Many advertisements illustrate how technical words can confuse and mislead. For instance, a brand of skin care lotion advertises itself as "oxygen therapy," although all skin is constantly exposed to oxygen in the air, and no externally applied product can introduce oxygen into skin cells. Similar instances can be drawn from military jargon. "Collateral damage" in the Gulf War, for example, referred to Iraqi civilians killed unintentionally by missiles or bombs that missed their primary target. In such a case, apparently precise terms turn out to be vague, even deceptive. This phrase took on grim connotations when Timothy McVeigh referred to the children killed by the bomb he placed at the Murrah Federal Building as "collateral damage."

The persuasive advantages of vagueness are illustrated in many advertisements. Commercials tell us that a brand of heating and air conditioning is an "Rx prescription for home comfort," that we should "Just do it," that a particular makeup "acts like skin care" or that "X is more than a mouthwash." These are *pseudo-claims*, statements that sound like conclusions, but assert nothing. What is a prescription for home comfort? What should we "just do"? What does it mean to "act like skin care" (like washing one's skin? like putting on lotion?)? More *what* than a mouthwash?[3] In these cases, imprecise statements are used as cues to suggest arguments to or evoke memories in viewers, and if the ads are successful, viewers participate to embellish these statements to create arguments—*enthymemes*—in their minds.

Some imprecision in language is inevitable. No word (except some proper nouns) refers to only one thing. The abstraction of language makes ambiguity inevitable. We need some vague terms such as middle-aged to refer to conditions that have no definite boundaries. We require the ambiguity of euphemism (substituting an inoffensive term, e.g., passed away or self-pleasuring, for ones considered offensively explicit) to deal with some highly controversial, emotionally charged subjects. We need figurative language to make concepts vivid and to enlarge the bases for comparison.

Stylistic precision is good for complex subjects and for exact proof. Precision implies that the rhetor is expert. The ambiguities of abstraction, euphemism, and figurative language are important resources for persuasion, but at the same time they open wide vistas for confusing, misleading, and deceiving audiences.[4]

Literalness

The style of a rhetorical act can vary in its use of figurative or metaphorical language. Figurative language grasps and defines the intangible qualities of experience. Such language can be used to explain or illustrate a difficult concept. Although it may not be verifiable, it involves another kind of precision—the vividness of immediate sensory experience. In a parody of the clichés mouthed to college graduates, Tom Lehrer wrote a song that told them, "Soon you'll be sliding down the razor blade of life." Such an image is painfully vivid.

Figurative language holds our attention. An ad headline says, "Rekindle your love affair with New York. Our new guide will provide a few sparks," and if you've enjoyed New York city in the past, the metaphor may be enough to induce you to read the smaller print and, perhaps, seek out a guide to help you to savor it even more. Like the figurative analogy, the metaphor connects what is known and familiar with what is unknown and unfamiliar.

Metaphors reflect attitudes. If life is a dance, it follows a pattern and is influenced by individual artistry. If life is a chess game, it is a competitive struggle of wits. If life is a crap game, it is ruled by chance. If "life is a banquet and most poor suckers are starving to death," as Patrick Dennis's Auntie Mame claimed, then it's time to dig in and eat up!

Metaphors evaluate. Sensory images express our values. Bad books are dry. A conservative refers to "hemophiliac" liberals bleeding for every cause; liberals, on the other hand, sometimes call conservatives cold and heartless.

There is an ongoing tension between literal and figurative language in rhetorical action. Literal language is more precise and exact, but it often is less vivid and engaging. Literal language is part of accurate description and an effort to produce careful proof. Metaphorical language enlivens ideas and arouses participation. Rhetoric is made effective by both.

Redundancy

Style varies in its use of repetition or restatement. Advice to writers usually suggests that they aim for economy of language, avoiding wordiness and circumlocutions. The amount of repetition needed depends on the complexity of the subject and argument and on the knowledge of the audience.

Oral style, whether in live public speeches or in radio and television commercials, differs from written style. Most commercials repeat their claims at least three times and usually many more. Highly creative ads restate their central idea in several amusing ways, frequently in oral, visual, and nonverbal terms. All repeat the product's name many times over. Engaging ditties and the attractive faces and graceful or humorous actions of skilled actors help to relieve the monotony.

Oral style must be more redundant. Because you can reread material and pause to think between paragraphs, a writer need not repeat and restate, at least not as often. But listeners do not have such options. Accordingly, successful speaking requires internal summaries, transitions connecting ideas, repetition of the major steps in the argument, and the like. Such redundancy increases both comprehension and impact for listeners. Used in print, such devices become irritating under all but the most unusual circumstances.

No other quality so consistently distinguishes oral and written style. Both oral and written rhetoric range along the other dimensions. Both can be highly formal or informal. Both reflect the possibilities of precision and ambiguity, although formulations demanding the most precision appear in writing. Both exploit the possibilities of figurative language and require literal expression for careful proof. Because oral style is often related to informality, it is likely to be more personal, with greater use of personal pronouns. But the impersonality and formality of presidential addresses indicate that such qualities are not an inevitable part of oral discourse.

Evaluating Style

Good style is clear, vivid, appropriate, and consistent.

Clarity. To say that style has clarity is to say that it is immediately intelligible to the audience. There is no delay in understanding it; no translation is required. The vocabulary is familiar to the audience, the syntax meets the norms of listeners and readers, and the discourse develops according to a pattern that can be followed easily. (See "Just a Drop" at the end of Chapter 6.) Obviously, if you write or speak on a technical subject, however, all of your language will not be immediately clear to most audiences, who will not be experts. The standard simply requires that unfamiliar terms and concepts be defined and illustrated so they can be understood by nonexperts or by members of the audience you are addressing. No rhetorical act can achieve its goals if it leaves the audience puzzled, confused, at sea.

Vividness. Good style is vivid. It comes alive. It makes us see and hear and imagine and feel. It creates virtual experience. Vividness is essential to catch and hold the attention of the audience, a prerequisite to successful rhetorical action. It also speaks to the psychological dimension of proof—we must give assent, not just recognize facts. Vivid style depicts, dramatizes, personifies, and describes. It employs the resources of language to focus and emphasize, to make ideas memorable. Vivid style fills our eyes, noses, ears, and mouths with associations and enriches the connotations of words and ideas with sights, smells, sounds, tastes, and memories.

Figurative language holds our attention and surprises us. In a review of the *Selected Letters of Rebecca West,* Francine Prose quoted from an account of a talk by the editor Frank Harris. West wrote: "His manner was foully offensive: a barking arrogance with oily declensions at the points where he was moved to speak of the necessity of the artist to feel pity and love—awful passages as though the Sermon on the Mount had kittened, and these were its progeny."[5] In those words one hears the voice and attitude of the speaker Frank Harris; in addition, one hears the intense reaction of the writer and critic. The coined verb is a shock—a vivid evocation through metonymy of sloppy sentimentality!

Appropriateness. Like all other elements of rhetorical action, style is contingent on the audience, subject and purpose, occasion, and rhetor. Your style should reflect the formality of the occasion and the seriousness of your purpose. It should be suitable for the complexity of the subject, and it should be adapted to the expertise and attitudes of the audience and to them as members of a linguistic community. Your style must be appropriate to you—to your expertise on the subject, to your relationship to the audience, to the persona you present in this situation.

These statements reflect general admonitions to apply your analysis of the rhetorical problem to stylistic choices. The Material for Analysis sections at the ends of the chapters provide models for rhetorical analysis; and the choices made by these specific speakers and writers should be used to refine these comments.

Consistency. Good style is consistent. All elements fit together so your discourse is a unified whole. Your language should reflect your tone, your persona, your purpose, and your relationship to the audience. Style may vary, but avoid contradictions among the elements of your rhetoric or major shifts in your perspective.

The importance of consistency should focus special attention on introductory statements. Opening lines establish tone and create expectations. As a result, stylistic choices made at the outset become important commitments for the statements that follow.

Strategies are one route by which speakers and writers achieve some of their stylistic goals.

STRATEGIES

A *strategy* is a plan of action, a maneuver designed to overcome the obstacles in a particular rhetorical situation. Strategies are part of rhetorical invention. They are discovered or found in your materials as you prepare for rhetorical action, and they are part of the creativity of your role as a rhetor. Strategies are used to cope with controversial and complex issues, with hostile and skeptical audiences, and with difficulties in establishing your credibility and expertise as a source. Every rhetorical situation is as different as every athletic competition, and successful persuasion, like successful play, involves assessing the obstacles you face and the resources at your disposal.

Many of the resources already discussed can and should be used strategically. Evidence should be selected and presented strategically to speak to the audience, to refute competing persuaders, to present your subject and perspective clearly. Each organizational pattern is a strategic way of unfolding a position. The arguments you select should be chosen strategically for the response you seek and the audience you want to reach. Introductions and conclusions are particularly important as strategic responses to the rhetorical problem. In the speeches and essays you analyze, consider how speakers and writers have used opening and closing statements to respond to the obstacles in a particular situation.

Despite the strategic character of most rhetorical choices, specific strategies are usually devices that exploit the capacities of language. Although their purposes overlap, strategies are designed to assist in proof, to make ideas vivid, and to create connotations. All strategies require participation by the audience and illustrate that rhetorical action is jointly constructed by rhetor and audience.

Strategies to Animate and Vivify

Nearly all strategies catch and hold attention and, in that sense, make ideas more vivid, but some strategies have this as their chief function. They are intended to make people and events come alive before our eyes, to create virtual experience by allowing us to see and hear and feel what the rhetor is talking about.

Description. Providing the detail that makes a scene or person come alive before our eyes is the function of description. It creates the sensation that you are there watching events as they occur. An editorial by physician Mark DePaolis describes in detail a videotape of the procedures involved in liposuction, with narration, to warn readers about this method of removing fat from thighs or abdomen. According to his report of the videotape, after areas of the patient's body are marked for removal, a sharp metal tube like a curtain rod is inserted under the skin, and

> "the powerful suction machine is turned on." . . . Suffice it to say that the tube is moved back and forth in "a piston-like motion" to suck up the fat. . . . Meanwhile, the patient's skin, which has evidently grown accustomed to those fat deposits, is putting up a valiant fight to keep them. This requires several burly assistants to keep the patient on the table while the surgeon works. . . . In the next hideous scene, as the narrator puts it, "fat can be seen moving through the transparent tube. . . . No more than 2,000 ccs are removed at any one time," the doctor says finally, showing us what looks like an extremely heavy two-liter soda bottle. . . . The tube is removed, the incision is sewn shut and several miles of gauze is wrapped around the patient. This is to hide the fact that her thighs now look like gallons of ice cream with one scoop taken out. . . .
>
> After seeing this tape, "liposuction" has moved to the top of my "don't do" list, underlined and with several added stars.[6]

Note that the description incorporates figurative analogies ("like a curtain rod"; "piston-like"; "like gallons of ice cream with one scoop taken out") and emotive language that reflects his reaction ("suffice it to say"; "hideous"). He also personifies the fatty deposits, which he describes as "putting up a valiant fight" not to be removed, a struggle intensified by describing the assistants who are holding the patient down as "burly." He translates the statistic 2,000 ccs by explaining that that is an amount that would fill a two-liter bottle of soda. These details help to create virtual reality and, he hopes, deter us from considering this procedure.

Dr. Helen Broinowski Caldicott, a founder of the group Physicians for Social Responsibility, was a nuclear freeze activist, whose work for a freeze culminated rhetorically with "This Beautiful Planet," the annual Phi Beta Kappa oration, delivered during Commencement Week of 1981 to an audience of 700 in Sanders Theatre at Harvard University. *Harvard Magazine* called the speech "powerful" and "chilling" (July–August 1981:50, 52, 53). Based on a series of articles published in the *New England Journal of Medicine*, she described the horrors of nuclear war in vivid detail, as adapted to a Cambridge, Massachusetts, audience:

> A 20 megaton bomb is equal to 20 million tons of TNT. That is four times the collective size of all bombs dropped during the Second World War. It is a small sun. It explodes with the heat of the sun. It will do this to Boston: it will carve out a crater about half a mile to a mile wide and 300 feet deep. . . . Every human being within a radius of six miles from the hypocenter will be vaporized. . . . Concrete and steel will burn. Out to a radius of 20 miles, most people will be dead. . . . If you happen to glance at the blast from 35–40 miles away, the flash would instantly burn the retina and blind you. It will create a fire storm of 15,000 to 30,000 square miles . . . creating a holocaust fanned by hurricane winds, so if you were in a fallout shelter, you would be pressure cooked and asphyxiated as the fire used all the oxygen.[7]

Dr. Caldicott uses descriptive language to make statistics vivid and real. The literal analogy to the bombs dropped in World War II helps us to grasp the existential size of a 20-megaton bomb. The figurative analogy to a small sun give us a sense of its brightness, which is heightened by her description of what would happen should a person be unfortunate enough to look at the blast even from a distance of over 30 miles away. It is plausible that there would be a firestorm, like that seen during powerful forest fires, that would cover many square miles. Its power and devastation are heightened by comparing the winds to those in a hurricane, and the lack of safety in a fallout shelter is made vivid by the analogy to what happens to food in a pressure cooker and the reminder of how much oxygen such a fire would consume. Here description serves primarily to dramatize the size and impact of a catastrophic event.

Another function of description comes from an earlier event. A great deal of controversy was aroused when the Walker Report labeled the behavior of Chicago police officers at the 1968 Democratic National Convention as a "police riot." Most Americans view police officers as helpful protectors and believe that if they misbehave, they must have been provoked. In combatting such attitudes, the Walker Report used eyewitness accounts such as this one to describe the kinds of confrontations that occurred between Chicago police and antiwar demonstrators:

> A federal legal official relates an experience of Tuesday evening.
> I then walked one block north where I met a group of 12–15 policemen. I showed them my identification and they permitted me to walk with them. The police walked one block west. Numerous people were watching us from their windows and balconies. The police yelled profanities at them, taunting them to come down where the police would beat them

up. The police stopped a number of people on the street demanding identification. They verbally abused each pedestrian and pushed one or two without hurting them. We walked back to Clark Street and began to walk north where the police stopped a number of people who appeared to be protesters, and ordered them out of the area in a very abusive way. One protester who was walking in the opposite direction was kneed in the groin by a policeman who was walking towards him. The boy fell to the ground and swore at the policeman who picked him up and threw him to the ground. We continued to walk toward the command post. A derelict who appeared to be very intoxicated, walked up to the policeman and mumbled something that was incoherent. The policeman pulled from his belt a tin container and sprayed its contents into the eyes of the derelict, who stumbled around and fell on his face.[8]

This instance illustrates the convergence of evidence and strategy. The cited material is testimony (an eye-witness account) that provides a series of examples of police behavior. Because the eye witness is described as "a federal legal official," his observations shift toward authority evidence rather than mere testimony: He may be competent to judge what is improper behavior, and his status gives his report greater credibility. But the descriptive details give this evidence its force. The police "yell," "taunt," "abuse," and "push." As described, the attack on the "boy" is wholly unprovoked, and because it is an attack on a *boy*, it is doubly offensive (note that the police officer's ability to pick him up and throw him to the ground lends credence to this label). The description gives us the sense of walking down the street with this group and watching what occurs. We come to see the events as the observer does and to judge them, unfavorably, with him. Such descriptions are particularly effective ways to induce readers to participate in creating the proofs by which they are persuaded. Note that these are the verbal counterparts of the visual images from Somalia, Bosnia, Rwanda, and Afghanistan that have horrified Americans and energized efforts to aid the suffering.

Depiction is an intensified form of description. To represent in picture or sculpture or to portray in detail is what depiction literally means. It is a particularly vivid form of description, and it usually involves dramatization, presenting material as a story, a drama of characters in conflict. If successful, it should create virtual experience. Woman suffragist Anna Howard Shaw used detailed examples in refuting arguments of antisuffragists. In a speech delivered in New York in 1915, for instance, she responded to the argument that if women voted, it would cause conflict and destroy happy homes. In her words,

> Then they will tell you all the trouble that happens in the home. A gentleman told me that in California,—and while he was talking I had a wonderful thing pass through my mind, because he said he and his wife had lived together for twenty years and never had a difference of opinion in the whole twenty years, and he was afraid if women began to vote that his wife would vote differently from him and then that beautiful harmony which they had had for twenty years would be broken, and all the time he was talking I could not help wondering which was the idiot,—because I knew that no intelligent human beings could live together for twenty years and not have differences in opinion. All the time he was talking I looked at that splendid type of manhood and thought, how would a man feel being tagged up by a little woman for twenty years saying, "me too, me too." I would not want to live in a house with a human being for twenty hours who agreed with everything I said. The stagnation of a frog pond would be hilarious compared to that. . . . Now it may be that the kind of men . . . that the anti-suffragists live with is that kind, but they are not the kind we live with and we could not do it. Great big overgrown babies! Cannot be disputed without having a row! While we

do not believe that men are saints, by any means, we do believe that the average American man is a fairly good sort of fellow.[9]

The overall strategy is refutation of the argument that voting will cause friction between spouses. To do so, she tells the story in some detail of a particular man who raised this objection so that her listeners can assess the objection in a particular case. This depiction is rather unusual, because it also includes a description of what goes on in Shaw's mind as she listens to what he says, through which she invites us to join her in treating this objection as absurd, and she dramatizes that absurdity by imagining the wife going around after the husband saying, "me too, me too." The comments following the story are important because the depiction of this man is an effort to isolate him, to present him as a special case, quite unlike other men who can tolerate differences of opinion without starting a row. Isolating this man as unusual allows Shaw to help to create the audience of male agents of change that she must persuade in order to obtain the ballot for women. Consider how pleasing for men to see themselves as she describes them and how effective this must have been in creating a role that her male auditors would have been happy to play, a role that would make them more likely to support suffrage. She not only refutes but also debunks fears about political conflicts between spouses as unrealistic, which is more effective as the story she tells is real, not hypothetical. Note, too, that strategies often come in groups. Depiction here includes refutation, a figurative analogy, and an effort to create the audience—to invite them to see themselves in ways that are helpful to her purpose. The example also is a vivid case of Shaw's ability to use humor that debunked her opposition while making them laugh. Finally, this example is from a stenographic record of a stump speech, and the informal style and the small grammatical errors reflect its extemporaneous delivery and its orality.

The most famous example of depiction in rhetorical literature occurs in a speech by Senator Daniel Webster of Massachusetts given in reply to Senator Robert Y. Hayne of South Carolina in 1830. The crux of the debate was the issue of slavery and the power of the federal government to regulate it. Hayne advocated state nullification, that is, that states should have the right to nullify acts of the federal government, and Webster argued that this doctrine must inevitably lead to war. But Webster chose to make his case, not through logical argument, but through depicting what must happen if a state should nullify a federal law. He used the tariff law and nullification by South Carolina as his example:

> We will take the existing case of the tariff law. South Carolina is said to have made up her opinion upon it. . . . She will, we must suppose, pass a law of her legislature, declaring the several acts of Congress, usually called the tariff laws, null and void, so far as they respect South Carolina, or the citizens thereof. So far, all is a paper transaction, and easy enough.

> (*At this point, Webster has set the scene for his depiction.*)

> But the collector at Charleston is collecting the duties imposed by these tariff laws. He, therefore, must be stopped. The collector will seize the goods if the tariff duties are not paid. The State authorities will undertake their rescue, the marshal, with his posse, will come to the collector's aid, and here the contest begins.

> (*The depiction includes a drama, and Webster prepares us for conflict.*)

> The militia of the State will be called out to sustain the nullifying act. They will march, Sir, under a very gallant leader; for I believe the honorable member [Hayne] himself com-

mands the militia of that part of the State. He will raise the nullifying act on his standard, and spread it out as his banner! It will have a preamble, setting forth, that the tariff laws are palpable, deliberate, and dangerous violations of the Constitution! He will proceed, with his banner flying, to the custom-house in Charleston,

> All the while,
> Sonorous metal blowing martial sounds.

Arrived at the custom-house, he will tell the collector that he must collect no more duties under any of the tariff laws. . . . But, Sir, the collector would not, probably, desist, at his bidding. He would show him the law of Congress, the treasury instruction, and his own oath of office. He would say, he should perform his duty, come what might.

Here would ensue a pause; for they say that a certain stillness precedes the tempest. The trumpeter would hold his breath awhile, and before all this military array should fall on the custom-house, collector, clerks, and all, it is very probable some of those composing it would request of their gallant commander-in-chief to be informed a little upon the point of law; for they have, doubtless, a just respect for his opinions as a lawyer, as well as for his bravery as a soldier. . . . They would inquire, whether it was not somewhat dangerous to resist a law of the United States. What would be the nature of their offence, they would wish to learn, if they, by military force and array, resisted the execution in Carolina of a law of the United States, and it should turn out, after all, that the law was constitutional? He would answer, of course, Treason. No lawyer could give any other answer. . . . How, then, they would ask, do you propose to defend us? We are not afraid of bullets, but treason has a way of taking people off that we do not much relish. How do you propose to defend us? "Look at my floating banner," he would reply; "see there the nullifying law!" Is it your opinion, gallant commander, they would then say, that, if we should be indicted for treason, that same floating banner of yours would make a good plea in bar? "South Carolina is a sovereign State," he would reply. That is true; but would the judge admit our plea? "These tariff laws," he would repeat, "are unconstitutional, palpably, deliberately, dangerously." That may all be so; but if the tribunal should not happen to be of that opinion, shall we swing for it? . . .

Mr. President, the honorable gentleman would be in dilemma, like that of another great general. He would have a knot before him which he could not untie. He must cut it with his sword. He must say to his followers, "Defend yourselves with your bayonets"; and this is war,—civil war.[10]

This excerpt from Webster's speech is justly famous as an outstanding example of the depiction of a hypothetical encounter, and like many strategies, it combines animation and demonstration. As proof, it spells out the consequences of Hayne's position, but the proof depends on the plausibility of the scene for the listener. It is highly effective refutation that shows that, contrary to Hayne, state nullification means civil war. The humor of the depiction debunks Hayne's position, reduces it to absurdity. Webster also uses an allusion to the story of Alexander the Great cutting the Gordian knot as a figurative analogy to illustrate that Hayne's position must end in violence. Webster's depiction is structured as a drama. He sets the scene, presents characters, sets forth the conflict, presents the dialogue between Hayne and his militia, and even provides the theatrical spectacle of banners and trumpets. The conflict within the doctrine, dramatized in the dialogue, escalates to a climax, which is followed by a denouement that draws his conclusion: "This is war,—civil war."

The detail Webster provides is worth noting. The marshall and his posse, supporting the federal customs collector, confront Hayne and the state militia. The acts of the collector are detailed. The dialogue between Hayne and the militia men spells out the internal contradiction in Hayne's position.

Webster might easily have chosen to set forth these consequences in a logical argument, but depicting this scene animated his claim, a process that was essential if civil war was to be averted. He attempted to create virtual experience, to allow his audience to imagine a scene in all its detail, so that they would perceive, in human terms, the results of Hayne's position.

Personification and Visualization. Closely allied to description and depiction are the strategies of personification and visualization. Personification represents an object or an abstract idea as if it were a human being or had human capacities. Advertisers personify products as characters or cartoon figures, such as the Energizer bunny or "scrubbing bubbles." The longevity of a battery or the power and gentleness of a cleaning agent cannot be seen or experienced directly. The strategy of personification attempts to overcome this problem. Visualization puts an idea into visual form. A long-running series of commercials showed someone drinking a glass of iced tea and then falling backward into a swimming pool. The ad visualized what you might experience if you drank a glass of cold, refreshing iced tea.

Enactment. When there is enactment the speaker or writer is proof of the claim that she or he is making. Enactment is both proof and a way to present evidence vividly. For example, Representative Barbara Jordan gave the keynote address at the Democratic National Convention in 1976. In her speech she said, "And I feel that, notwithstanding the past, my presence here is one additional piece of evidence that the American dream need not forever be deferred."[11] That she, an African American woman, had achieved the stature to be asked to give the address was proof that minorities and women can reach the highest levels of achievement in the United States. A similar move was made by Geraldine Ferraro in her nomination acceptance address in 1988, and in Ruth Bader Ginsburg's 1993 speech accepting nomination to be an associate justice of the Supreme Court. Enactment is powerful evidence because members of the audience see and hear the evidence for themselves, directly. The references to the mob in Angelina Grimké's 1838 speech (the rhetorical act you will analyze in the next chapter) are another example. This form of proof is particularly vivid—it is alive in front of and around the audience!

Other Animating Strategies. Alliteration, assonance, rhyme, and rhythm are some of the ways of arranging words so that ideas and phrases become more vivid and memorable. *Alliteration* is the repetition of initial consonants, a strategy advertisements and speeches use effectively. In a speech urging adoption of his budget on August 3, 1993, President Clinton spoke of opponents of his plan as "guardians of gridlock." Columnist William Safire, a former White House speechwriter well known for using alliteration, commented: "I would have added an alliterative advance adjective 'grim,' to convey a full nattering-nabob-of-negativism flavor," noting that current speechwriters are more restrained."[12]

Assonance is the repetition of a vowel sound, and it produces a kind of rhyme. In his inaugural address, for example, John F. Kennedy spoke of "the steady spread of the deadly atom." The repetition made the phrase memorable and the creeping vowel seemed to mirror the creeping danger.

Actual *rhymes* occur less frequently in both oral and written rhetoric. Interesting contemporary examples appear in the speeches of Jesse Jackson. For example, in the opening remarks of his 1988 address to the Democratic National Convention, Jackson capitalized on the "Jesus Loves Me" song by saying: "When I look out at this convention, I see the face of America: Red, Yellow, Brown, Black and White. We are all precious in God's sight—the real rainbow coalition." Later in the speech he said: "Leadership must reverse the arms race. At least we should pledge no first use. Why? Because first use begets first retaliation. And that's mutual annihilation." And still later, he added: "I'm tired of sailing my little boat, far inside the harbor bar. I want to go out where the big ships float, out on the deep where the great ones are. And should my frail craft prove too slight for waves that sweep those billows o'er, I'd rather go down in the stirring fight than drowse to death at the sheltered shore."

Such rhymes not only make ideas vivid, but they also work to change the attitudes of the reader. Note that such rhymes appear in popular rap songs and in raps used in advertisements, suggesting their power to engage us and be memorable.

Parallelism is a strategy that creates rhythm in prose. It can also enhance the precision of language and create an impression that the rhetor thinks in a very orderly fashion. Perhaps the most famous example is the repeated "I have a dream . . ." in Dr. Martin Luther King, Jr.'s, famous speech of that name. Like King's speech, it may take the form of a series of sentences or paragraphs, all of which begin with the same phrase. In his inaugural address, for example, John F. Kennedy addressed his statements, "To those old allies, . . . To those new states, . . . To those peoples in the huts, . . . To our sister republics . . ." He began each of his statements addressed to adversaries with the phrase, "Let both sides . . ." Such parallelism creates patterns that are easy for listeners to follow, and such patterns help fix ideas in our minds. They are particularly well suited to oral rhetoric.

Parallelism can also create contrast and emphasis. *Antithesis* is a kind of parallelism that contrasts one idea with another. Two examples in contemporary speeches have proved particularly memorable. In 1960 John F. Kennedy said, "Ask not what your country can do for you: Ask what you can do for your country." In 1964 Barry Goldwater accepted the Republican nomination for the presidency and said, "I would remind you that extremism in the defense of liberty is no vice! And let me remind you also that moderation in the pursuit of justice is no virtue!" Republican strategist William Kristol rang a change on this in 1994 when he said of health care reform, "we should make clear now that there will be no deal. 'Obstructionism,' when it comes to protecting our health care system, is no vice."[13] As these examples illustrate, rhetoric builds on prior rhetoric, and the memorable antithesis remains a resource. Antitheses juxtapose two ideas, and the contrast not only defines the speaker's position more clearly; it animates it with emphasis.

Climax constructions are also a form of parallelism. In a climax construction, repetition builds to a high point of excitement or tension, a climax. The conclusion of the last speech of Dr. Martin Luther King, Jr., discussed in Chapter 2, is an excellent example.

Finally, recall that parallelism also appears in patterns of organization. Ideally, main points in an essay or speech will be stated in parallel form so that major ideas will stand out for the reader or listener. Once again, these are only some of the strategies that can be used to make ideas vivid.

Strategies to Change Connotations

The strategies described in this section are directed at our attitudes. They are attempts to change associations so that we will become more positive or negative toward an idea or position. Successful rhetorical action changes verbal behavior. Our speech reflects our perceptions, understandings, and attitudes, and if these change, our speech will change. But the reverse is also true: If we change the way we talk, changes in perception and attitude will follow.

The preceding statement is highly controversial although the protest movements of Blacks and Chicanos (or Latinos or Hispanics or *La Raza*) illustrate the power of a name change to mobilize a social movement.[14] The argument is at the heart of disputes over whether or not the pronoun "he" or the word "man" can function generically to include both men and women. Feminists present examples to show that they cannot, as in "Man, being a mammal, breast-feeds his young." Or "All men are mortal; Sophie is a man; therefore, Sophie is mortal." They also argue that shifts in words, such as the use of chair or chairperson, and in pronouns, "s/he" or "he and she," raise consciousness about the sexism of our society.[15] In all these cases, all the parties involved behave as if the words we use are very, very important.

Labeling. The commonest strategy used to alter attitudes is labeling, and it is often related to debunking. A label is a name or epithet chosen to characterize a person or thing. Republican President George W. Bush calls himself "a compassionate conservative," in an effort to capture the positive associations of both those terms. His opponent in the 2000 Republican primaries, Senator John McCain of Arizona, referred to his drive for the nomination as "The Straight Talk Express," an effort to characterize himself as someone who would speak the truth rather than pander to audiences. As the examples illustrate, labels work by creating associations.

At the beginning of the early woman's rights movement of the nineteenth century, women activists were told that if they spoke in public, they would be "unsexed," that is, they would lose their femininity. In the 1960s, at the beginning of the contemporary women's movement, women activists were called lesbians or dykes, once again implying that women who sought to improve their status were not feminine, not real women. These are powerful attacks because success for women has been defined as attracting a male and marrying, which presumably places a high value on traditional femininity. Note that even those contemporary advertisements that show women in settings outside the home continue to reinforce the beauty myth, present women as sex objects, and show women primarily in the role of mother, all of which reinforce traditional concepts of femininity.[16] Accordingly, being attacked as unfeminine is a strong deterrent to feminist identification and activism.

Slogans. Labels expanded become slogans. They are highly effective because they condense into a single phrase or sentence a whole world of beliefs and feelings. This power to sum up is illustrated in phrases such as "the American dream," "the personal is political," "black is beautiful," and "rugged individualism." They are powerful unifiers because, although individuals have their own ideas of just what they mean, the level of abstraction is such that disputes over meaning are avoided. Because of their broad appeal, they are especially attractive to advertisers and politicians who seek to reach the widest possible audiences. An effective slogan draws together a whole world of ideas in a short, cleverly expressed phrase or sentence. Advertisers seek such catchphrases: "The un-cola." "Just do it." "Everything you always wanted in a beer. And less." Every political campaign manager tries to find such a slogan, because, in a short, memorable phrase, it can sum up many associations and evoke strong reactions.

Metaphors. Many labels and slogans are also metaphors. Figurative language not only makes ideas vivid but it also changes our attitudes toward them, and it clarifies meaning. A particularly famous example comes from the speech Booker T. Washington made at the Atlanta Exposition in 1895. Washington, an African American, tried to allay the hostility of whites while urging them to support the economic and educational development of his people. The metaphor he used illustrates how metaphors can clarify, vivify, and change connotations. He said, "In all things that are purely social we can be as separate as the fingers, yet one as the hand in all things essential to mutual progress."[17]

In his famous "I have a dream" speech of 1964, Dr. Martin Luther King, Jr., translated the issues of civil rights into terms every listener could understand. He said: "In a sense we have come to our nation's Capitol to cash a check. When the architects of our republic wrote the magnificent words of the Constitution and the Declaration of Independence, they were signing a promissory note to which every American was to fall heir. . . . Instead of honoring this sacred obligation, America has given the Negro people a bad check; a check which has come back marked 'insufficient funds.' But we refuse to believe that the bank of justice is bankrupt."[18] The idea of civil rights is abstract, and many statements about it were now known and familiar. The imagery King used made the abstract concrete and familiar to all his hearers, yet the metaphor was original, making his appeal fresh and vivid. Elizabeth Cady Stanton's speech, "The Solitude of Self" (a rhetorical act you will analyze in Chapter 9), is an extended illustration of the use of *metonymy*, that kind of trope that finds a physical counterpart for abstract notions, such as a heart for the idea of love.

Allusion. Closely related to metaphors are allusions to items from our shared cultural knowledge, such as references to history, the Bible, Greek and Roman mythology, Shakespeare's plays or other works of literature, or to elements of popular culture such as television programs, films, comic books, or national advertising.

When he was running for the governorship of Minnesota in 1998, Jesse Ventura needed to counter the charge that he was unprepared for that office. He had not completed college, and his resumé consisted chiefly of his experiences as a professional wrestler and a talk-show host on a local radio station. Bill Hillsman, an advertising genius who also prepared the ads that helped Senator Paul Wellstone to beat incumbent Rudy Boschwitz in 1992, prepared an ad that showed a flesh-colored Jesse Ventura in the position of Rodin's famous sculpture, *The Thinker,* which is among the most familiar sculptures in existence. Against the sound of classical music, and introduced by large classical lettering, of "THE BODY," the voiceover recited his personal history as a Navy SEAL, union member, volunteer high school football coach, outdoorsman, husband of 23 years, and father of two children. As the camera panned to the statue/ Jesse Ventura's face, the letters "THE MIND" appeared and the voiceover indicated his positions: "A man who will fight to return Minnesota's budget surplus to the taxpayers. A man who will fight to lower property and income taxes. A man who does not accept money from special interest groups. A man who will work to improve public schools by reducing class sizes." At this point, the camera zoomed back to show us the entire statue with the words "Jesse Ventura Our Next Governor" superimposed on it. At that point, the camera zoomed in on Ventura's face, and he smiled and winked.

The ad exploits the ambiguity of Rodin's statue, which presents a beautiful male body in a position of deep thought. It subtly counteracts voters' tendency to think of Ventura solely as a body, a wrestler, and writes a different meaning on his past by listing facts about his life (note that it omits his history as a wrestler). Then, exploiting the statue as an expression of intellectual effort, the ad presents the positions Ventura presumably has arrived at after thoughtful deliberation. The end of the ad—the smile and the wink—invite us not to take all this too seriously while inviting us in a warm and charming way to participate in the ad and reject efforts by opposing candidates to suggest that Ventura is not qualified.

Much of this process is nondiscursive. Our familiarity with Rodin's statue means that we already have its dual meaning in our mind, which makes it easy to extend it to candidate Ventura. The ad is also discursive, providing basic information about Ventura and about his positions. Visually and musically, the ad is highbrow—a famous sculpture viewed against the sound of classical music. The ending counteracts that quality with the smile and the wink, letting us all know that Jesse is a regular guy. Consider how much more effective this rebuttal is than another ad that provided the information without the metaphorical and visual appeal of this version of the statue.

Biblical materials are also a common source of allusion. Such materials are frequently used to demonstrate that God is on our side or we are doing God's will. In defending U.S. involvement in Vietnam, for example, Richard Nixon said, "Let historians not record that when America was the most powerful nation in the world we passed on the other side of the road and allowed the last hopes for peace and freedom of millions of people on this earth to be suffocated by the forces of totalitarianism."[19] The allusion is to the story of the good Samaritan, and it was intended to convince us that in Vietnam we were behaving as good neighbors.

Allusions can be used to perform acts that would not be acceptable to an audience if they were done directly and explicitly. Most audiences, for example, do not take kindly to being threatened. Yet, in what is surely one of the most controversial of all Fourth of July addresses, on July 5 in 1852 the African American abolitionist orator Frederick Douglass used the story of Samson in Judges 16:23–30 to threaten the audience:

> The Fourth of July is yours, not mine. You may rejoice, I must mourn. To drag a man in fetters into the grand illuminated temple of liberty, and call upon him to join you in joyous anthems, were inhuman mockery and sacrilegious irony. Do you mean, citizens, to mock me by asking me to speak today? If so, there is a parallel to your conduct. And let me warn you that it is dangerous to copy the example of a nation whose crimes, towering up to heaven, were thrown down by the breath of the Almighty, burying that nation in irrevocable ruin![20]

If you know the story of Samson (stripped of his prodigious strength by the cutting of his hair, captured by the Philistines, blinded, taken to Gaza, brought to the temple for sport on the feast day of their god Dagon, praying for strength, pulling down the temple, and killing more Philistines in death than he had in life), there are powerful parallels between it and the situation of Frederick Douglass on July 5, 1852. If you do not know the story, you may not recognize the allusion, much less feel its impact. Allusions work only if the audience recognizes them and can fill in the necessary details.

Biblical allusions are powerful if they are familiar, because our culture is Judeo-Christian, and many persons accept the Bible as the word of God. For contemporary readers, that is only half the problem. To appreciate the parallels one must know biographical facts about Douglass (an escaped former slave speaking in Rochester, New York, at a time when slavery was still a fact in much of the country). These problems illustrate the limitations of allusions, which depend for their impact on knowledge in the minds of the audience.

Identification. Finally, the strategy of identification uses language to create positive associations between the rhetor and the audience; it suggests shared experience or common viewpoints. Speakers and writers traditionally identify ties of kinship, shared beliefs, and common experience as ways to create bonds between themselves and the audience.

On June, 18, 1992, Russian President Boris Yeltsin addressed a convocation at Wichita State University in Wichita, Kansas. Here is how he attempted to link himself to his audience in his speech entitled, "Why Kansas? Free People, Broad Smiles."

> Now, you can ask me, why the hell did you come to Kansas? Not New York, Chicago, or LA.; I mean there is a profound reason for this. I have been studying your history. I've been reading some very important briefing papers on this, and I think I know something about the history of the state of Kansas.
>
> I think this state is called a first in freedom, first in bread state, is that correct? I think . . . it is also important to know that your grandfathers and great-grandfathers played a very important role in the history of the United States. They were the people who courageously fought slavery, not only here, but throughout the United States.
>
> So I came to Kansas, to see that bread, to see those free, freedom-loving people. On my way to Wichita University I saw some very beautiful fields of wheat out there not far from the university. And Senator Dole told me that the average yield here is about 60 bushels per acre.
>
> While it took us some time to convert that into kilograms and tons, but I guess if we compare that in Russia, the yield would be seven, maybe eight, bushels. And just think that 75 years ago, Russian farmers had the same yield back in my country. So this is what our communist system did to us. And this (is) why we have destroyed that system, and there is no coming back. . . .
>
> I do know that you have problems; I do know that you are going through hardships in certain areas. But I have seen on my way to the university here, I've seen some very beautiful people. People who live here in Wichita, Kansas. And I think I saw here what people call the broad American smile. Those people were smiling at me. But they were not smiling at me personally; I think they were smiling at the people whom I represent.
>
> Thank you very much for coming. I want to say good luck to you ladies and gentlemen and dear friends. Good luck to the United States of America. To Wichita. To the state of Kansas. And thank you very much again for giving this beautiful welcome to the first freely elected Russian president who came to the United States and visited the state of Kansas. Thank you.[21]

Consider the many ways in which Yeltsin links himself to his audience, using praise, humor, shared beliefs, and state history, among other things.

Similarly, when then Philippine President Corazon Aquino addressed a joint session of the U.S. Congress on September 18, 1986, she began by making a personal connection to the audience. She said: "Mr. Speaker, Senator [Strom] Thurmond, distinguished Members of Congress, three years ago I left America in grief to bury my husband, Ninoy Aquino. I thought I had left it also to lay to rest his restless dream of Philippine freedom. Today, I have returned as the President of a free people."[22] She was able to personalize and dramatize the remarkable, peaceful revolution through which the Philippines returned to a democratic system.

Aquino reinforced her links to the U.S. audience through repeated allusions to President Abraham Lincoln's second inaugural address, which was delivered close to the end of the Civil War when it was clear that the Union would prevail. She needed to persuade members of Congress and President Reagan that she would seek to reconcile the supporters of defeated President Ferdinand Marcos and that she would take a tough stand to resist the military efforts of communist guerrillas who still opposed her presidency. Responding to the first concern, she said: "As I came to power peacefully, so shall I keep it. That is my contract with my people and with God. He had willed that the blood drawn with the lash shall not, in my country, be paid by blood drawn by the sword but by the tearful joy of reconciliation." She appropriated Lincoln's words to make a powerful promise not to exact revenge from Marcos's supporters.

Later in the speech, she again used Lincoln to defend her willingness to seek a peaceful resolution to the guerrilla conflict that threatened her newly elected democratic government. She said:

> I will not stand by and allow an insurgent leadership to spurn our offer of peace and kill our young soldiers, and threaten our new freedom.
>
> Yet, I must explore the path of peace to the utmost, for at its end, whatever disappointment I meet there, is the moral basis for laying down the olive branch of peace and taking up the sword of war. Still, should it come to that, I will not waver from the course laid down by your great liberator:
>
> "With malice towards none, with charity for all, with firmness in the right as God gives us to see the right, let us finish the work we are in, to bind up the Nation's wounds, to care for him who shall have borne the battle, and for his widow and for his orphans, to do all which may achieve and cherish a just and lasting peace among ourselves and with all Nations."
>
> Like Lincoln, I understand that force may be necessary before mercy. Like Lincoln, I don't relish it. Yet I will do whatever it takes to defend the integrity and freedom of my country.

The strategy of appealing to shared values was now directed to a new purpose. By linking Lincoln to a policy that first seeks mercy and reconciliation rather than a military struggle, Aquino effectively preempted objections that she was not taking a hard enough line against the guerrillas. Thus, what began as a strategy to create identification became a strategy through which she could refute those who opposed her policy. What Aquino did also might be described as a strategy of appealing to cultural values, an appeal through which she sought to change the audience's feelings about her, increasing her ethos.

Figure 7–1 captures many of the language strategies discussed in this chapter. Pay particular attention to the function and example used to illustrate each. Use it as a handy resource in constructing your own rhetorical acts.

These are some of the strategies available for rhetorical action. Strategies are techniques that use language to prove, vivify, and alter attitudes. Each of these functions is a central element in rhetoric. Strategies provide important resources for rhetors to overcome obstacles in a rhetorical situation.

Figure 7–1
Language Strategies

Name	Function	Example
Metaphor	Creates an image by comparing two dissimilar things that share certain properties.	Columnist Ellen Goodman characterizes cell phones as "the boom boxes of the 90's," as "a status symbol on a par with the S.U.V.," and as "promoting a verbal gated community."
Metonymy	Idea evoked or named by means of a term designating some associated notion, often more concrete.	Referring to royal authority as "the sceptre" or to military action as "the sword," or the heart in "I ♥ NY."
Onomatopoeia	The tendency in certain words to imitate by their very sound the actions they symbolize.	Words such as buzz, hiss, bump, meow, trudge. Budweiser ad: "Waaas Uuuuuup?"
Parallelism	Using the same initial wording in a sequence of statements or phrases in order to add emphasis, order, and climax to an idea.	MLK: "If I had sneezed . . . If I had sneezed . . . If I had sneezed."
Antithesis	The succinct juxtaposition of opposing expressions to make an idea more memorable, distinctive, and sloganistic.	President John F. Kennedy said in his inaugural address: "Ask not what your country can do for you, but what you can do for your country."
Rhyme	The repeating of the final vowel and consonant sound of words to imprint a key message of your speech either for emphasis or as a mnemonic device to help your audience remember important points.	Johnny Cochran, defense attorney in the O. J. Simpson trial, reminded jurors: "If it doesn't fit, you must acquit."
Depiction	Choose highly descriptive, sensory words to catch the interest of your audience.	Janine DiGiovanni describes the plight of Kosovo refugees: "It is cold in the factory but Mehije wears only a sweater, muddy bedroom slippers and thin cotton socks, pink ones. She has a long, messy plait running down her back."
Personification	A representation or abstraction of an inanimate object or idea that is endowed with personal or human qualities.	The Energizer Bunny, Scrubbing Bubbles, Mr. Clean.
Alliteration	Repeats the initial consonant sounds in words. Alliteration captures attention and makes for clever slogans.	Spiro Agnew's referring to the press as: "nattering nabobs of negativism."
Slogan	Slogans are wise, compact sayings that summarize the beliefs of a people.	Susan B. Anthony: "Resistance to tyranny is obedience to God." Nike ad: "Just Do It." Causes: "It's a life, not a choice." "Think Globally, Act Locally."
Allusion	Indirect references to our shared cultural knowledge, such as the Bible, Greek and Roman Mythology, or our history.	To defend U.S. involvement in Vietnam, Richard Nixon said: "Let historians not record that when America was the most powerful nation in the world we passed on the other side of the road and allowed the last hopes for peace and freedom of millions of people on this earth to be suffocated by the forces of totalitarianism."
Identification	Use of language to create perceived similarity between rhetor and audience; includes humor, stroking, and appeal to shared values.	While at Wichita State University, then Russian President Boris Yeltsin humored and honored the student body: "Now you can ask me why the hell did you come to Kansas? Not New York, Chicago, or Los Angeles? I mean there is a profound reason for this. I have been studying your history. I know something about the history of the state of Kansas. I think the state is called a first in freedom, first in bread state. Is that correct? So I came to Kansas to see that bread, to see those free freedom-loving people."
Labeling	A name or epithet chosen to characterize a person or thing.	Republican presidential candidate John McCain labeled his campaign "The Straight Talk Express." His challenger in the primary, George W. Bush, labeled his campaign "Compassionate Conservatism." Pundits labeled George W. "Dubya" to distinguish him from his father. McCain was labeled a "war hero."

In 1852, the Rochester, New York, Ladies Anti-Slavery Society invited one of the city's most famous residents, Frederick Douglass, a former slave, to deliver the Fourth of July oration. Douglass accepted, and on July 5, 1852, he delivered one of the most memorable antislavery discourses in U.S. history. The speech illustrates vividly the ways in which the speaker responded to the rhetorical problem and used all of the resources available to him, including all of the resources of language.

What to the Slave Is the Fourth of July?
by Frederick Douglass[23]

1 FELLOW-CITIZENS—Pardon me, allow me to ask, why am I called upon to speak here to-day? What have I, or those I represent, to do with your national independence? Are the great principles of political freedom and of natural justice, embodied in that Declaration of Independence, extended to us? and am I, therefore, called upon to bring our humble offering to the national altar, and to confess the benefits and express devout gratitude for the blessings resulting from your independence to us?

2 Would to God, both for your sakes and ours, that an affirmative answer could be truthfully returned to these questions! Then would my task be light, and my burden easy and delightful. For who is there so cold, that a nation's sympathy could not warm him? Who so obdurate and dead to the claims of gratitude, that would not thankfully acknowledge such priceless benefits? Who so stolid and selfish, that would not give his voice to swell the hallelujahs of a nation's jubilee, when the chains of servitude had been torn from his limbs? I am not that man. In a case like that, the dumb might eloquently speak, and the "lame man leap as an hart." [Isa. 35:6]

3 But such is not the state of the case. I say it with a sad sense of the disparity between us. I am not included within the pale of this glorious anniversary! Your high independence only reveals the immeasurable distance between us. The blessings in which you, this day, rejoice, are not enjoyed in common. The rich inheritance of justice, liberty, prosperity and independence, bequeathed by your fathers, is shared by you, not by me. The sunlight that brought light and healing to you, has brought stripes and death to me. This Fourth of July is yours, not mine. You may rejoice, I must mourn. To drag a man in fetters into the grand illuminated temple of liberty and call upon him to join you in joyous anthems, were inhuman mockery and sacrilegious irony. Do you mean, citizens, to mock me, by asking me to speak today? If so, there is a parallel to your conduct. And let me warn you that it is dangerous to copy the example of a nation whose crimes, towering up to heaven, were thrown down by the breath of the Almighty, burying that nation in irrevocable ruin! I can to-day take up the plaintive lament of a peeled[24] and woe-smitten people!

4 By the rivers of Babylon, there we sat down. Yea! We wept when we remembered Zion. We hanged our harps upon the willows in the midst thereof. For there, they that carried us away captive, required of us a song; and they who wasted us required of us mirth, saying, Sing us one of the songs of Zion. How can we sing the Lord's song in a strange land? If I forget thee, O Jerusalem, let my right hand

forget her cunning. If I do not remember thee, let my tongue cleave to the roof of my mouth. [Psa 137:1–6]

5   Fellow-citizens, above your national, tumultuous joy, I hear the mournful wail of millions! Whose chains, heavy and grievous yesterday, are, to-day, rendered more intolerable by the jubilee shouts that reach them. If I do forget, if I do not faithfully remember those bleeding children of sorrow this day, "may my right hand forget her cunning, and may my tongue cleave to the roof of my mouth!" To forget them, to pass lightly over their wrongs, and to chime in with the popular theme, would be treason most scandalous and shocking, and would make me a reproach before God and the world. My subject, then, fellow-citizens, is AMERICAN SLAVERY. I shall see this day and its popular characteristics from the slave's point of view. Standing there identified with the American bondman, making his wrongs mine. I do not hesitate to declare, with all my soul, that the character and conduct of this nation never looked blacker to me than on this 4th of July! Whether we turn to the declaration of the past, or to the professions of the present, the conduct of the nation seems equally hideous and revolting. America is false to the past, false to the present, and solemnly binds herself to be false to the future. Standing with God and the crushed and bleeding slave on this occasion, I will, in the name of humanity which is outraged, in the name of liberty which is fettered, in the name of the constitution and the Bible which are disregarded and trampled upon, dare to call in question and to denounce, with all the emphasis I can command, everything that serves to perpetuate slavery—the great sin and shame of America! "I will not equivocate; I will not excuse"; I will use the severest language I can command; and yet not one word shall escape me that any man, whose judgment is not blinded by prejudice, or who is not at heart a slaveholder, shall not confess to be right and just.

6   But I fancy I hear some one of my audience say, "It is just in this circum-stance that you and your brother abolitionists fail to make a favorable impression on the public mind. Would you argue more, and denounce less; would you persuade more, and rebuke less; your cause would be much more likely to succeed." But I submit, where all is plain there is nothing to be argued. What point in the anti-slavery creed would you have me argue? On what branch of the subject do the people of this country need light? Must I undertake to prove that the slave is a man? That point is conceded already. Nobody doubts it. The slaveholders them-selves acknowledge it in the enactment of laws for their government. They acknowledge it when they punish disobedience on the part of the slave. There are seventy-two crimes in the State of Virginia which, if committed by a black man (no matter how ignorant he be), subject him to the punishment of death; while only two of the same crimes will subject a white man to the like punishment. What is this but the acknowledgment that the slave is a moral, intellectual, and responsible being? The manhood of the slave is conceded. It is admitted in the fact that southern statute books are covered with enactments forbidding, under severe fines and penalties, the teaching of the slave to read or to write. When you can point to any such laws in reference to the beast of the field, then I may consent to argue the manhood of the slave. When the dogs in your streets, when the fowls of the air, when the cattle on your hills, when the fish of the sea, and the reptiles that crawl, shall be unable to distinguish the slave from a brute, then will I argue with you that the slave is a man!

7   For the present, it is enough to affirm the equal manhood of the Negro race. Is it not astonishing that, while we are ploughing, planting, and reaping, using all

kinds of mechanical tools, erecting houses, constructing bridges, building ships, working in metals of brass, iron, copper, silver, and gold; that, while we are reading, writing and ciphering, acting as clerks, merchants and secretaries, having among us lawyers, doctors, ministers, poets, authors, editors, orators and teachers; that, while we are engaged in all manner of enterprises common to other men, digging gold in California, capturing the whale in the Pacific, feeding sheep and cattle on the hillside, living, moving, acting, thinking, planning, living in families as husbands, wives and children, and, above all, confessing and worshiping the Christian's God, and looking hopefully for life and immortality beyond the grave, we are called upon to prove that we are men!

8   Would you have me argue that man is entitled to liberty? That he is the rightful owner of his own body? You have already declared it. Must I argue the wrongfulness of slavery? Is that a question for Republicans? Is it to be settled by the rules of logic and argumentation, as a matter beset with great difficulty, involving a doubtful application of the principle of justice, hard to be understood? How should I look to-day, in the presence of Americans, dividing, and subdividing a discourse, to show that men have a natural right to freedom? Speaking of it relatively and positively, negatively and affirmatively. To do so, would be to make myself ridiculous, and to offer an insult to your understanding. There is not a man beneath the canopy of heaven that does not know that slavery is wrong *for him*.

9   What, am I to argue that it is wrong to make men brutes, to rob them of their liberty, to work them without wages, who keep them ignorant of their relations to their fellow men, to beat them with sticks, to flay their flesh with the lash, to load their limbs with irons, to hunt them with dogs, to sell them at auction, to sunder their families, to knock out their teeth, to burn their flesh, to starve them into obedience and submission to their masters? Must I argue that a system thus marked with blood, and stained with pollution, is wrong? No! I will not. I have better employment for my time and strength than such arguments would imply.

10   What, then, remains to be argued? Is it that slavery is not divine; that God did not establish it; that our doctors of divinity are mistaken? There is blasphemy in the thought. That which is inhuman, cannot be divine! Who can reason on such a proposition? They that can, may; I cannot. The time for such argument is passed.

11   At a time like this, scorching irony, not convincing argument, is needed. O! Had I the ability, and could I reach the nation's ear, I would, to-day, pour out a fiery stream of biting ridicule, blasting reproach, withering sarcasm, and stern rebuke. For it is not light that is needed, but fire; it is not the gentle shower, but thunder. We need the storm, the whirlwind, and the earthquake. The feeling of the nation must be quickened; the conscience of the nation must be roused; the propriety of the nation must be startled; the hypocrisy of the nation must be exposed; and its crimes against God and man must be proclaimed and denounced.

12   What, to the American slave, is your 4th of July? I answer; a day that reveals to him, more than all other days in the year, the gross injustice and cruelty to which he is the constant victim. To him, your celebration is a sham; your boasted liberty, an unholy license; your national greatness, swelling vanity; your sounds of rejoicing are empty and heartless; your denunciation of tyrants, brass fronted impudence; your shouts of liberty and equality, hollow mockery; your prayers and hymns, your sermons and thanksgivings, with all your religious parade

and solemnity, are to Him, mere bombast, fraud, deception, impiety, and hypocrisy—a thin veil to cover up crimes which would disgrace a nation of savages. There is not a nation on the earth guilty of practices more shocking and bloody than are the people of the United States, at this very hour.

13   Go where you may, search where you will, roam through all the monarchies and despotisms of the Old World, travel through South America, search out every abuse, and when you have found the last, lay your facts by the side of the everyday practices of this nation, and you will say with me, that, for revolting barbarity and shameless hypocrisy, America reigns without a rival.

Questions for Analysis

1. What language strategies do you see in this speech? How do they contribute to tone? Persona?
2. What is the structure of this speech? What kinds of arguments are embedded in the structure?
3. A Fourth of July speech is designed to venerate the nation, its heroes; it is designed to be uplifting, inspiring, and patriotic. Why does Douglas violate these expectations? What purpose is he trying to achieve?
4. How does the speech indicate the author's awareness of the rhetorical obstacles that he faces? (For a detailed discussion of obstacles, see Chapters 8, 9, and 10.)

EXERCISES

1. Fill-in-the-blank exercise. Choose the correct language strategy (as illustrated in chapter readings) for each sentence below.
   a. "America: Love It or Leave It"; "Just Do It"; "Question Authority"; "Have you hugged your kids today?" "Shit Happens." These are examples of _____ language strategy?
   b. "Ask not what your country can do for you, but what you can do for you country" (JFK) is an example of _____ language strategy?
   c. "We've come from disgrace to amazing grace"; "Doctors are now more concerned with public health than personal wealth" (Jesse Jackson) are examples of _____ language strategy?
   d. "Take it from me, Mr. Clean, I am a cleanser with scrubbing bubbles" is an example of _____ language strategy?
   e. "Peter Piper picked a peck of pickled peppers" is an example of _____ language strategy?
   f. "If I had sneezed, I wouldn't have been here in 1961 . . . If I had sneezed I wouldn't have been able to tell a nation about a dream I'd had . . . if I had sneezed . . . " (MLK) is an example of _____ language strategy?
   g. "The steady spread of the deadly atom" (JFK) is an example of _____ language strategy?

   h. "I will lift up my voice like a trumpet and tell the people of their transgressions"; "Deluded beings they know not what they do" (A. Grimké) are examples of _____ language strategy?
   i. "There will be more shuttle flights, more shuttle crews, more volunteers, more civilians, more teachers in space" (Reagan) is an example of _____ language strategy?

2. Bring the lyrics to your favorite song, or jot down the words of a memorable bumper sticker, billboard or poem. What language strategies are at work? Why must these forms of rhetoric exploit the resources of language?

3. Language strategies and delivery work hand in hand to accentuate the artistic dimensions of rhetoric. Practice reading aloud from a Dr. Seuss book or a Mother Goose Nursery Rhyme book. How do rhyme, rhythm, alliteration, onomatopoeia, work with rate, pitch, volume and vocal variety to create a memorable piece of rhetorical action?

4. What is the correct word for an unshaven man, wearing shabby clothes, lying on a pile of cartons in an off-street alley and drinking from a bottle hidden in a paper bag? Consider the following terms: a person on welfare, a panhandler, a homeless person, a hobo, a

skid row "wino," a beggar, a pauper, a drunkard. Using these terms as keywords, find articles in the InfoTrac College Edition database. Do you see a connection between the term being used by the writers and what they perceive as the causes for the person's condition?

Conduct research in InfoTrac College Edition about attitudes toward rich and powerful people. Consider terms such as tycoon, country club elite, chief executive officer (CEO), corporate leader. Judging by the vocabulary used in the articles, can you draw conclusions about the writers' political biases, convictions, or commitments?

When rhetors hold a claim with limited evidence or with some reservations, it is best for them to state their conclusions somewhat tentatively. This can be done with the use of qualifiers, words that indicate the degree of certainty they have in their claims. Locate articles in the InfoTrac College Edition database that use the words "probably," "likely," or "marginally" in their titles. Then locate articles that use the word "certainly" in their title. Do you see a relationship between the use of qualifiers and the power of the articles' arguments? Does the use of qualifiers constrain the scope of the arguments (i.e., making them tentative, or more or less committed, more or less ambiguous); or, on the contrary, does the use of qualifiers boost the credibility of the writers as well-educated people who recognize the possibility of exceptions?

5. **Portfolio Entry 6: Language**
   What resources of language are used strategically in your rhetorical acts? Are they particularly well-crafted in the use of words or not? What might explain why some selections use word choice better than others? Answer in two pages.

NOTES

1. Gina Kolata, "Impotence Is Given Another Name," *New York Times*, April 18, 2000, p. D6.

2. Frances X. Clines, "Showing the Good Ol' Boys How to Play Their Own Game," *New York Times*, September 25, 1992, p. A18. These efforts are not always successful; Christmas did not win the election.

3. For almost 100 years, ads for Listerine claimed that the product prevented colds and sore throats. It does not. In 1977 the court upheld the Federal Trade Commission requirement that the next ten million dollars of Listerine's regular advertising include the corrective statement, "Listerine will not prevent colds or sore throats or lessen their severity" (*Warner-Lambert Co.* v. *FTC*, 562 F.2d 762 [1977]).

4. See M. Lee Williams, "The Effect of Deliberate Vagueness on Receiver Recall and Agreement," *Central States Speech Journal* 31 (Spring 1980): 30–41, for empirical evidence about the advantages and disadvantages of precision and vagueness.

5. *Lingua Franca*, April 2000, pp. 30–31.

6. Mark DePaolis, "A Power-Tool Approach to Weight Loss," [Minneapolis] *Star Tribune*, July 16, 1993, p. 19A.

7. "This Beautiful Planet," Phi Beta Kappa Oration. *Speak Out*, ed. Herbert Vetter. (Boston: Beacon Press, 1992), pp. 85–93.

8. Daniel Walker, "A Summary of the Walker Report," in *Counterpoint: Dialogue for the 70s*, ed. Conn McAuliffe (Philadelphia: J.B. Lippincott, 1970), p. 153.

9. Anna Howard Shaw, "The Fundamental Principle of a Republic," in *Man Cannot Speak for Her: Key Texts of the Early Feminists*, vol. 2, ed. K. K. Campbell (Westport, CT: Greenwood Press, 1989), p. 451.

10. Daniel Webster, "Reply to Hayne," in *Famous Speeches in American History*, ed. Glenn R. Capp (Indianapolis: Bobbs-Merrill, 1963), pp. 57–58.

11. *New York Times*, July 15, 1976, p. 26.

12. *New York Times*, August 5, 1993, p. A15. Safire was the author of the line "nattering nabobs of negativism," which was used in a 1969 speech by then Vice President Spiro Agnew to characterize those who opposed the Vietnam War.

13. *New York Times*, July 3, 1994, p. E3.

14. See Karlyn Kohrs Campbell, "The Rhetoric of Radical Black Nationalism," *Central States Speech Journal* 22 (Fall 1971): 151–160; Richard J. Jensen and John C. Hammerback, "Radical Nationalism among Chicanos: The Rhetoric of José Angel Gutierrez," *Western Journal of Speech Communication* 44 (Summer 1980): 191–202.

15. See, for example, Wendy Martyna, "Beyond the 'He/Man' Approach: The Case for Nonsexist Language," *Signs: Journal of Women in Culture and Society* 5 (Spring 1980): 482–493.

16. See Anthony J. Cortese, *Provocateur: Images of Women and Minorities in Advertising* (Lanham, MD:

Rowman & Littlefield, 1999); John B. Ford and Michael S. Latour, "Contemporary Female Perspectives of Female Role Portrayals in Advertising," *Journal of Current Issues and Research in Advertising* 18 (Spring 1996): 81–95; M. A. Masse and K. Rosenblum, "Male and Female Created They Them: The Depiction of Gender in the Advertising of Traditional Women's and Men's Magazines," *Women's Studies International Forum* 11 (1988): 127–144. For broader analyses of how advertising and mass media treat women, see Erving Goffman, *Gender Advertisements* (Cambridge, MA: Harvard University Press, 1976); Jean Kilbourne, *Can't Buy My Love: How Advertising Changes the Way We Think and Feel* (New York: Simon & Schuster/Touchstone Book, 1999), and Liesbet van Zoonen, *Feminist Media Studies* (London: Sage Publications, 1994).

17. Booker T. Washington, "Atlanta Exposition Address," *Famous Speeches in American History*, ed. Glenn Capp (New York: Bobbs-Merrill, 1963), p. 115. Washington may have heard this metaphor in a speech President Rutherford B. Hayes delivered in 1880 at Hampton Institute, where Washington was on the faculty.

18. "I Have A Dream. . . ." in *Selected Speeches from American History*, ed. Robert T. Oliver and Eugene E. White (Boston: Allyn and Bacon, 1966), pp. 291–292.

19. Speech delivered November 3, 1969, *Congressional Record*, Vol. 115, Part 24, pp. 32784–32786.

20. *The Frederick Douglass Papers: Series One: Speeches, Debates, Interviews: Volume 2: 1847–54,* ed. John W. Blassingame (New Haven: Yale University Press, 1982), pp. 359–388. Cited material is on p. 368.

21. Text of speech given at Wichita State University, June 18, 1992.

22. Corazon Aquino's speech was published in *Democracy by the Ways of Democracy: Speeches of President Corazon C. Aquino: Official Visit to the United States of America, September 15–24, 1986* (Manila: Philippine Information Agency, National Printing Office, 1986). It is also found in the *Congressional Record,* II 7073–7075.

23. Reproduced from Douglass's autobiography, *My Bondage and My Freedom* (New York: Miller, Orton & Mulligan, 1855), pp. 441–445.

24. The *Oxford English Dictionary* defines *peeled* as "stripped of possessions, plundered, reduced to destitution."

chapter 8

Obstacles Arising from the Audience

A problem is the gap between what you have and what you want. In rhetorical action, a rhetor confronts an audience that perceives, understands, believes, or acts in one way and wants that audience to perceive, understand, believe, or act in another way. The *rhetorical problem* is an umbrella concept that covers all of the obstacles rhetors face. Part Three examines *obstacles* arising from the audience (Chapter 8), from the subject (Chapter 9), and from the rhetor (Chapter 10).

In practice, of course, obstacles arising from audience, subject, and rhetor cannot be isolated so neatly. For example, suppose that your subject was the history of oats as a cash crop. Even if your purpose were merely informative (and not efforts to increase the acreage devoted to raising oats), you would have a fairly hard time holding the interest of audiences made up of teenagers or lawyers. But your rhetorical problem would be much smaller if your audience was a group of midwestern farmers, preferably sprinkled with dedicated horse breeders and trainers (oats is the best grain to feed horses). In other words, whether or not your subject and purpose create obstacles depends partly on the nature of your audience. In fact, obstacles are only obstacles if the audience perceives them that way.

Think of these three aspects of the rhetorical problem as forming a triangle (Figure 8–1). The interrelationships among the aspects symbolized by the triangle can be expressed in three questions:

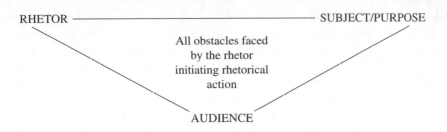

Figure 8-1
The Rhetorical Problem

RHETOR ———————————————————— SUBJECT/PURPOSE

All obstacles faced
by the rhetor
initiating rhetorical
action

AUDIENCE

1. What will be necessary to induce the audience to take part in rhetorical action?
2. What does the subject/purpose demand of the audience?
3. What demands are made on the credibility (ethos) of the rhetor by the subject/purpose and the audience?

Beginning rhetors tend to make two common errors in thinking about audiences. First, they assume that most audiences (particularly classmates, friends, colleagues) are just like themselves, with the same experiences, values, religious beliefs, political preferences, and life goals. They are shocked to discover—within the same culture or community or even in the same communication class—wide divergences in belief. But people do differ. All audiences, even close friends, need explanation, adaptation, and effort to see the importance and significance of the issue and the purpose.

Your assumption that members of the audience are just like you, the rhetor, takes several specific forms. Sometimes, for example, you might take for granted that those you address are, like you, rational, impartial, interested, informed, and concerned. Although people can be all of these some of the time, we are also creatures of deep feeling who are, at the same time, likely to be apathetic toward issues of great importance to others. And your audiences are people. As a rhetor, you must treat them as many-faceted and not assume they are well informed and curious unless you make an effort to provide information and arouse curiosity. In this sense, you create or construct your audience—you provide the materials that enable them to become the ideal respondents to your message.

The second common error rhetors make is to transform the audience into vicious monsters eagerly waiting to jeer at them and to discredit their messages. Assuming that those for whom you write or speak are different from you can help when you try to imagine yourself as a member of the audience. But this feeling can be carried too far. Audience members are like you. Although not identical, they have needs and fears similar to yours. You and they have many values in common. Generally, an audience can share your experience and come to understand a differing point of view.

To be successful as a rhetor requires that you induce the audience to participate, indeed, to collaborate in creating the rhetorical act. You and the audience must identify with each other and come to some kind of common understanding if the message you produce is to be a communication. With some experience, you will discover that one of your assets as a rhetor is your individuality—your special experiences, biases, and fallibilities, especially as you are able to recognize them and share them with the audience.

Your goal as a rhetor, then, is to avoid both these errors: to recognize differences between yourself and members of the audience and yet create common bonds between you from what you do share. In other words, prepare your rhetorical act to overcome the obstacles represented by these differences.

Beliefs about persuasion are also relevant to the rhetorical obstacles arising from the audience. At various times in U.S. history we have demonstrated our fears of the power of persuasion. We have banned certain books and movies as heretical or obscene and have forbidden self-styled Nazis and Communists to speak in certain forums, as if exposure to a book, a movie, or a speech could cause good Christians to lose their faith and become ravening sex fiends, or patriotic Americans to become traitors or converts to a dramatically different ideology. As this chapter will indicate, normal people are not transformed by a single rhetorical act. Audiences, in fact, show considerable resistance to persuasion in all forms. Indeed, considering all of the obstacles to persuasion that arise from audiences, you may well marvel that any persuasion ever occurs.

THE AUDIENCE

There are at least four ways to understand what is meant by an "audience." An audience can be (1) those exposed to the rhetorical act, the *empirical audience*; (2) the *target audience*, the ideal audience at whom the act is aimed; (3) the *agents of change*, or VIP audience, those who have the capacity to do as the rhetor wishes, who can make changes; and (4) the role the audience is invited to play by the rhetor, the *created audience*.

The Empirical Audience

In the most simple sense, the audience is all those exposed to the rhetorical act, whether it be in a face-to-face encounter or through the print or electronic media. Obviously, if people do not encounter the rhetorical act, nothing can occur. The channels through which rhetorical acts are transmitted select and limit the potential empirical audience. An essay printed in *Ms*, a feminist magazine, reaches a relatively small audience of subscribers and others—at a friend's house or the women's clinic—who pick up the magazine and read it. Those who read *Ms* are likely to be different from those who read *Ebony*, a magazine targeted at African Americans, or *Road and Track*, a magazine for car lovers. A rhetor who wishes to reach the appropriate audience must try to find the channel that will expose her or his ideas to the ideal or target audience.

The Target Audience

Realistically, you cannot address everyone. All rhetorical acts are shaped and planned to reach people with certain characteristics. These people are the target audience. They are the ones most likely to be responsive to the issue and capable of acting on it (agents of change, discussed below). The target audience is likely to share basic assumptions with the rhetor; ideally, they have common experiences and shared longings. Patterns of television advertising illustrate this concept. For example, the demographic analyses of television viewers made by the Nielsen Company indicate that a large proportion of viewers of network news are older people (over age 45). Accordingly, if you watch the news on any broadcast network, you will see advertisements for such products as laxatives, denture adhesives, and vitamins because older viewers are thought more likely to suffer from constipation, have loose false teeth, or need vitamin supplements. Similarly, razor blades and after-shave lotions are advertised on broadcasts of football games because Nielsen studies indicate that a majority of viewers of such programming is male. In each case, the ads are targeted at audiences most likely to have needs these products can fill.

The Agents of Change

Only some members of your potential audience have the capacity to do what you desire—to buy an expensive product, to provide a service, or to enact a change in policy. You should target those who have the power to act, those with the political ability, the economic power, the numbers, or the social influence to alter the situation. Effective rhetors aim their messages at those who can do what they desire—who have the political power (the vote), the economic power (the money), or the numbers (to march, petition, vote) or other resources (expertise, technology, or whatever) to act. We often refer to such influential persons as VIPs—very important persons.

Such a description of the audience seems to make it a power elite, but other factors are also at work. Advertisers, for example, have learned that they can be effective if they reach those who can influence the agents of change. Pokémon cards, monster-shaped vitamins, sugar-coated cereals, toys, and video games are advertised on children's television programs although few children make independent purchasing decisions.[1] Children, however, can influence the decisions of their parents. The agents of change are not only those with the power to act but also those who can influence them. Lobbyists and constituents may not be able to vote on legislation, but they can influence members of the House and Senate.

The Created or Constructed Audience[2]

Rhetorical action is participatory; it involves a reciprocal relationship between those involved in it. Just as the rhetor plays a role and takes on a persona, audiences are invited to play roles and take on one or more personas. Advertising, for example, creates scenarios that are appealing and invite us to imagine ourselves playing roles in them. Playing roles in these scenarios, however, require us to purchase products. Cosmetic ads invite viewers to imagine themselves as glamorous, seductive women with long, bouncy hair (buy our shampoo), glistening lips (buy our lipstick or lip gloss), and sultry eyes with long dark lashes (buy our eye shadow and mascara). If and only if we can be prompted to see ourselves in such roles will we buy the products they advertise.

The importance of creating the audience, of inviting them to play a role, is illustrated by the challenges posed by female audiences. An audience must not only have the power to act, but it must also believe that it has that power. A number of studies seem to indicate that women, especially young women, have low self-esteem and lack confidence in their ability to succeed in areas not traditionally identified as female.[3] In fact, they can act as agents of change. As they have demonstrated, they can sue for admission to all-male institutions; they can use affirmative action to gain entry to areas from which women have been excluded; they can start businesses as well as vote, work as volunteers, and donate money to candidates; they can write letters to influential people and outlets; they can influence businesses through purchasing decisions; they can form groups that will influence school policy, television programming, and police actions. They can run for office and be elected. But they can do these things if and only if they come to believe that they can. Following the Anita Hill–Clarence Thomas

Figure 8–2
*Audience-Related
Rhetorical
Obstacles*

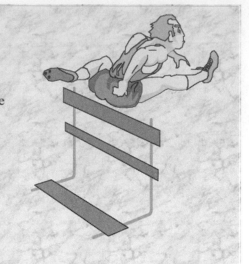

**■ Audience-Related
Obstacles**

- inattention
    - ■ insulated from exposure
- misperception
    - ■ stereotyping/distortion
- lack of motivation
    - ■ no salience
- inertia
    - ■ resistance to
    change/powerless

hearings in 1991, for example, a record number of women ran for office, and women more than doubled their contributions to women political candidates. Their economic power to affect political campaigns had always been there, but the hearings mobilized many of them to exercise it. The so-called consciousness-raising groups in the women's liberation movement can be seen as transforming women into audiences—that is, into people who believe that they can act effectively to become agents of change.

In other words, if a rhetorical act is to have any chance of succeeding, audience members must participate in it from beginning to end. They must perceive its ideas accurately and internalize the "virtual experience" presented. They must see the information and arguments as coming from an informed and trustworthy source,[4] and the rhetorical act as relevant to their needs. In addition, the audience must see the purpose of the act and the means to achieve it as consistent with their values, and they must come to believe that they can take action, here and now, that can reasonably be expected to achieve the goal desired. These requirements suggest the dimensions and the facets of the obstacles that arise from the audience.

The common kinds of *audience-related rhetorical obstacles* (Figure 8–2) are

1. Inattention
2. Misperception and misinterpretation
3. Lack of motivation
4. Inertia

INATTENTION OBSTACLES

Although you may not appreciate it, as a student you are in a rare and highly privileged rhetorical situation: you have a captive audience. Your teacher is paid to read and comment on your essays or to listen and evaluate your speeches, and your classmates are required to attend class. Unlike most rhetors, you do not need to struggle to gather an audience, to have your name recognized, or to gain media coverage.

College teachers also have more or less captive audiences. Yet as a college professor, I compete directly in any given lecture with the university, throwaways, and local newspapers, letters from parents and friends, and assignments for other classes. When students use laptops in class, I compete with e-mail and with sites on the Internet. Until students read my syllabus regarding classroom policies, I must also compete with the annoyance of cell phones and pagers.

And like all other rhetors I compete indirectly with the hundreds of eager persuaders our students encounter daily: newspaper editorials and letters to the editor; television, radio, and magazine advertising; telephone and door-to-door solicitors; billboards; political candidates; family and friends. If this bombardment does not create resistance to persuasion by its sheer volume, it may outclass me in slickness or entertainment quality. Although I come in three dimensions and the mass media persuaders do not, and though I am in "living color," I cannot make eight retakes, do a dissolve, edit the tape, or cut to an animated cartoon when attention flags.

If my students could choose whether or not to come to class, I would encounter another audience-related obstacle. Let us call it limited or *selective exposure*. Audiences selectively expose themselves to messages and selectively attend to those they see or hear. Students do this to some degree in their choices of electives. In other words, audiences control their exposure to rhetorical acts. In general, we tend to expose ourselves to messages that meet our physical, psychological, or social needs. The young woman about to be married suddenly begins to seek out *Bride* magazine; the student faced with the need to buy a car suddenly seeks out *Consumer Reports* for information on reliability and repairs to maximize her purchase. We routinely read those publications and watch those programs that reflect our general interests and styles. The messages we encounter here are likely to be reassuring and reinforcing. If you are an investor or running a small business, you are likely to read the *Wall Street Journal*, and its editorial columns are likely to take positions congenial to people like you, for example, opposing an "employer mandate" in proposed health care reforms. If you are such a person, you are less likely to read *Mother Jones* and be exposed to editorials and articles with strong commitments to environmentalism, some parts of which may be costly to businesses. In other words, our patterns of viewing and reading are related to topics and subjects important to satisfying our needs for information and advice, and these patterns tend to expose us primarily to supportive or unchallenging viewpoints. When faced with a choice, however, especially an important choice, we seek out wider sources of information. We watch debates among prominent candidates and deliberately expose ourselves to conflicting views. In other words, our interests and needs limit our exposure to rhetoric, and to some extent, such limits filter in messages that are supportive or reassuring. You know this from your own experience. Although they hear both sides represented, committed conservatives are more likely to watch and listen to such programs as *Crossfire* where the conservative viewpoint is well and strongly represented. (If you want to avoid hearing opposing views, you can turn to Rush Limbaugh.) Such exposure is pleasant because it does not threaten our views, and it reinforces our sense that we have made the right choices. On the other hand, as these examples indicate, ordinarily we do not avoid exposure to alternative points of view.

As a rhetor, however, you need to know that under certain circumstances people actively seek out information that conflicts with what they know and with views that challenge their own. At least three factors significantly modify the commonsense picture just presented: the audience's level of education, the usefulness of the information to be presented, and the audience's history of exposure. One early study concluded: "Clearly the most powerful known predictor of voluntary exposure to mass communications of an information or public-affairs sort is the general factor of education and social class."[5] Put simply, people with more education and higher incomes choose to expose themselves to more news and information on public affairs in the mass media. They buy more magazines and newspapers; they watch more public affairs programs on radio and television (and they can more easily afford cable hookups that give them access to more outlets); they are more likely to be active in groups that spread such information; they are more likely to have personal computers and use the Internet for information, entertainment, and shopping. In fact, education and social class may be a more significant factor in exposure than ideological agreement.

As suggested above, another factor influencing exposure is the immediate usefulness of the information to the recipient; in some studies, subjects preferred what they saw as more useful information to what they saw as less useful, regardless of which of these supported their previous beliefs.[6] Ideological differences or a lack of shared beliefs and attitudes are serious barriers, but ones that can be breached by relevance, that is, if the recipients see a direct, personal use for the information provided now.

Finally, past exposure to the issue influences a person's reaction to future exposure in ways that are not necessarily related to the compatibility of beliefs. Some studies have found that when individuals initially were exposed to one-sided or biased information, they later preferred opposing information regardless of whether it supported their initial position.[7] Such studies, along with others indicating tolerance for and interest in new and challenging data, suggest that it would be a mistake to assume that audiences will not read or listen to information that conflicts with their beliefs and attitudes.

The first challenge you face as a rhetor in relation to an audience, then, is gaining and maintaining attention. As indicated here, the individual rhetor competes for attention with many other persuaders and meets obstacles having to do with the selection of messages by members of the audience. A tendency to be exposed to information compatible with our interests and needs and, hence, views we already hold is balanced by the generally high level of interest in information evident among the more educated and affluent, by a desire for useful information, and by a desire for opposing information if the initial exposure seems to have been one-sided or biased.

MISPERCEPTION AND MISINTERPRETATION OBSTACLES

Selective perception names a second kind of audience-related obstacle you face. It refers to the human ability to function rather like a radio—to tune one channel in and another out, turn the volume down or up, fade the sound in and out, or turn the set off entirely. We do not "perceive" all the stimuli to which we are exposed—we would go crazy if we did. We sort out what we believe is relevant, for example, and ignore the rest. The basis for this ability remains largely a mystery. There is evidence, however, that our attitudes influence what we perceive and how we interpret it.

Attitudes

No one has ever seen an attitude. *Attitude* is a concept developed by researchers to describe some of the mental (emotional/affective and rational/cognitive) processes and behaviors of human beings. The concept is particularly difficult because it is complex, and not all researchers agree on how to define attitudes or on whether and how they can be distinguished from *beliefs* and *values*.

Attitudes are likes or dislikes, affinities for or aversions to situations (liking to speak publicly or hating to talk on the phone), events (weddings), objects (motorcycles), people (children), groups (Methodists), or any identifiable aspect of one's environment (humidity). Attitudes are a mental readiness or a predisposition to react that influences a fairly large class of one's valuative responses consistently or over a significant period of time.

Attitudes are expressed in statements like these: I don't like big parties; I love ice cream; I like assertive people; the *New York Times* is the best newspaper in the United States. Presumably, as a result of direct experience (at parties, eating ice cream, making choices, reading many newspapers) and other kinds of learning (from school, parents, and peers, among others), people develop valuative categories so they are prepared to respond, favorably or unfavorably, with varying degrees of intensity (strongly or mildly favorably or unfavorably) to the items they encounter.

Attitudes are relatively generalized (they tend to refer to categories or classes rather than to individual items), and they are enduring (they persist over time). They also are learned. People probably learn likes and dislikes as they learn nearly everything else, and they categorize their valuative experiences in order to simplify the world. If you have an aversion to cats, for example, it is likely that you were frightened or scratched by a cat as a child or had a reaction to cat dander or have a parent, friend, or sibling with a strong dislike. In most cases, the attitude will apply to most or all cats, and probably if you dislike them today, you will continue to dislike them next week and next month, although change is possible based on new experiences and learning.

In addition, your aversion to cats would probably influence reactions to related areas: to cat shows, to cat owners, to prohibitions against pets in apartments, and so on. Obviously, the rhetor who tries to alter audience attitudes like this one or whose purposes run counter to intensely held attitudes of audience members will run into trouble. Attitudes are learned over a period of time from experiences or credible sources; they are reinforced by later experiences; they are also patterns of response that make it easier to cope with the world. This rhetorical problem is compounded because attitudes influence what we perceive and how we interpret it.

A famous study of the influence of attitudes on perception used a particularly controversial football game between Dartmouth and Princeton as its raw material. The researchers showed students from both schools the same film of the game and tested their perceptions of who broke the rules how many times and in what ways. From the test results, you might have thought the two groups of students had seen two different events. For example, Princeton students "saw" the Dartmouth team break the rules more than twice as many times as the Dartmouth students "saw" their team do so. The researchers concluded that the same data transmitted in the same way create different experiences in different people, and that the significance of an event depends on the purposes different people bring to it and the assumptions they have about the purposes of other people involved. They wrote: "It is inaccurate and misleading to say that different people have different 'attitudes' concerning the same 'thing.' For the 'thing' simply is not the same for different people whether the 'thing' is a football game, a presidential candidate, Communism, or spinach."[8]

You can probably think of many similar examples from the sports world in which partisanship strongly influences what the fans see. And such responses are not surprising, given the nature of attitudes. For example, in the third inning of the second game of the 1991 World Series, Minnesota Twins first baseman Kent Hrbek tagged out Atlanta Braves center fielder Ron Gant at first base. Braves fans contended that the 258-lb. Hrbek used a "rasslin' move" to knock the 172-lb. outfielder off the base and record the inning-ending out. Hrbek himself expressed the view of the Minnesota fans: "I thought it was pretty obvious what happened. . . . He was the one with the momentum. If I wasn't there, he probably would have wound up in the dugout. I just held the tag on him."[9] The Twins fans wanted them to beat the Braves; the Braves fans wanted them to win; each team's fans perceived what happened through the lenses of their desires.

And what happens in sports can easily happen in other areas. An attitude is a readiness to respond favorably or unfavorably. It represents an expectation of favorable or unfavorable qualities and behaviors. In other words, we tend to "see" the qualities and behaviors in objects, events, persons, and so forth that we expect to be there. Accordingly, our attitudes influence our perceptions and our interpretations of events.

Beliefs

The influence of attitudes on perception and interpretation suggests that there is a close relationship between information and evaluation. A *belief* is a judgment about what is true or probable, real or likely. Beliefs may refer to the past (guns were involved in 10,976 murders in 1998, more than any other weapon), the present (rape and sexual assault are still increasing in the United States), or the future (so many guns already are owned by Americans that gun control legislation cannot reduce their role in violent crime). They may assert a causal relationship (negative attitudes toward women are reinforced in televised entertainment programming) or evaluate the credibility of sources of information (seeing is believing; Secretary of State Colin Powell is an expert on U.S. foreign policy; Alan Greenspan, Federal Reserve Director, is an expert on the U.S. economy; the speaker knows what she's talking about).

Insofar as attitudes are learned from our own experiences or those of others, they are based on beliefs, on what we consider true, or likely. For example, if you strongly dislike dogs, you probably believe that they bite many people each year, that they often bite without provocation, and that they are the source of some serious diseases of children. These beliefs not only describe dogs, as you may see them, but also predict future situations.

Note that insofar as attitudes rest on beliefs, they can be influenced by future learning. Hence, the rhetor who wants to change attitudes tries to alter perception (and beliefs) through "virtual experience." Conversely, as the Dartmouth–Princeton and Twins–Braves examples show, attitudes influence perception in ways that undermine this process, and even conflicting information can be perceived as compatible with the perceiver's attitudes.

Decoding

Attitudes influence perception and interpretation so strongly that rhetors cannot be sure their audiences will perceive information as they do. In fact, the interpretation of information and argument is a problem with all audiences, however well intentioned they may be. *Decoding* is a term used to refer to this interpretive process by which listeners or readers translate and interpret messages from outside, assign meanings, determine relationships, and draw out implications.

Audiences obviously find decoding hard to do. Thus, much of the impact of a rhetorical act is lost unless rhetors make special efforts to organize material, to state conclusions, and to show the relationships among ideas. In one study, for example, an audience of bright college students became confused when conclusions were not stated explicitly. Other studies confirm this finding.[10] The rhetorical problem is that the audience resists or botches decoding unless claims are presented clearly and made explicit. At a minimum, the rhetor must state conclusions, organize materials clearly, and provide transitions that show relationships if the audience is to interpret what is being said accurately.

The Elaboration Likelihood Model (ELM). As first introduced in Chapter 5, researchers Richard Petty and John Cacioppo have developed a theory they call the *elaboration likelihood model (ELM)*[11] because it emphasizes the central role of the audience in persuasion. Their theory, as its name implies, focuses on the likelihood that audience members will be stimulated not only to attend to and decode a message but also to develop or elaborate it—that is, to process or interpret it, to amplify, clarify, or embellish it, and to consider its implications. By this standard, the most effective rhetorical act is one that produces the greatest amount of cooperative message building by members of the audience. Under ideal circumstances, audience members collaborate with the rhetor in creating the discourse by which they are influenced.

ELM is useful in understanding the role of the audience in persuasion. As a theory, ELM postulates two routes through which persuasion occurs: *a central route* and *a peripheral route*. The central route is rationalistic and argumentative, that is, it is directly related to cooperative message-building prompted by the quality of the argument and the evidence on which it rests. Based on many research studies, it seems that changes in attitude that occur via this route require more work, more thought, on the part of the reader or listener; however, research studies also suggest that attitude changes resulting from this process last longer, are more resistant to counterpersuasion from opponents, and are more predictive of actual behavior. In other words, a good case can be made for the importance of argument and evidence if audience members respond to, participate in, and collaborate in creating a message that is initiated by a rhetor.

As its label suggests, the peripheral route is less direct; mostly, we use it for purposes of efficiency—we cannot investigate thoroughly all issues on which we must make decisions. Some snap judgments are necessary. Decisions made via this route are shortcuts; instead of the hard work involved in interpreting the argument and evidence, we use some element in the persuasive context or situation as a cue or sign by which to assess the message. It could be linked to the person who carries it—positively or negatively. It could be linked to a belief system with which audience members agree or disagree. Whatever the association, it allows audience members to make a relatively simple leap from the cue to the position being advocated; for example, someone who is intensely disliked supports a position that is rejected because of that association—that is, because of feelings about the source (e.g., "If Rush Limbaugh favors it, it must be bad—or good").

According to this research, the most important variable affecting audience members' willingness to work at this special kind of decoding—the motivation actively to participate in and interpret a persuasive message—is its *personal relevance*, that is, a belief that the topic or issue is vital and will affect them personally. The greater its possible personal consequences for the audience, the greater will be the importance of forming an opinion based on the most accurate and complete information. As one author can attest, younger women are less likely to work at understanding messages about osteoporosis, for example, but women who are approaching menopause are likely to pay close attention to messages about the pros and cons of estrogen- or hormone-replacement therapy; in fact, they may even seek out such messages! That's unfortunate because younger women need to eat foods with lots of calcium (and do weight-bearing exercises) to build up their bone mass, which is the best protection against bone loss later in life. When there are immediate and vital personal consequences, people are likely to be motivated to engage in the mental work—the interpretation and decoding—necessary to evaluate the true merits of a proposal. This strongly suggests the importance of showing why your message is vital for those you hope to reach.

The willingness to collaborate in creating the rhetorical act is also affected by one's worldview. Those who view the world legalistically, such as lawyers, for example, find messages that are justified on legalistic grounds to be more persuasive, whereas those who see the world in religious terms are more likely to be persuaded by messages that are justified on religious or moral grounds. The essay "Jesus Was a Feminist," found at the end of Chapter 5, is likely to be more persuasive to those with strong religious commitments who see the Bible as a primary authority and Jesus as a model for ideal behavior than to those who do not share these beliefs.

In sum, the ELM model suggests that there is a tradeoff between the brainwork involved in participating in messages—exploring and evaluating arguments and evidence—and the importance of peripheral or external cues. In general, anything that reduces someone's ability and/or motivation to interpret and amplify issue-related arguments also increases the likelihood that external cues in the source, message, recipient, or context may affect response. On the other hand, all of us use such peripheral cues to make a great many decisions because we haven't the time or inclination to scrutinize all the arguments and evidence relevant to every choice we have to make. For example, one might buy bleach or laundry detergent impulsively by the color of the bottle or box, but make a detailed study of evaluations of cars in *Consumer Reports* and other outlets before spending thousands of dollars on a new one.

LACK OF MOTIVATION OBSTACLES

Needs

People act for reasons. They pursue goals, they are motivated, they try to satisfy their needs. The significant role of needs and goals has already been indicated by people's willingness to expose themselves to messages containing information they believe will be useful to satisfy needs. What are these "needs"? Among the many catalogs of human needs, one of the most useful was developed by Abraham Maslow.[12] Maslow, a psychologist, postulates what now is referred to as *Maslow's hierarchy of needs*. His hierarchy or ranking premise suggests that some needs may be more intense and basic than others. The most fundamental and intense needs are *physiological*—needs for food, water, sleep, and protection from exposure. Only when these are relatively well satisfied do needs for *safety* (stability, order, freedom from violence and disease) begin to domi-nate. When these, in turn, are relatively well met, needs for *love and acceptance* (affec-tion, giving and receiving love, touching and being touched) emerge. And when these are satisfied, needs for *esteem* (recognition, respect from others and for ourselves) sur-face. Finally, when all of these are relatively well met, the need for *self-actualization*—to be all that one is capable of being, to develop one's unique potential—becomes dominant. All humans experience all of these needs and seek to have them met. This pyramid of needs can help us to understand the successes and failures of some kinds of rhetorical processes. We may wonder why parliamentary democracy has not attracted more Third World nations, but most citizens of these countries do not have their physiological and safety needs met. They need to find ways to meet the needs at the more basic levels of the pyramid, whereas democracy is an ideology that emphasizes satisfying individual needs for esteem and self-actualization, needs nearer to the top of the pyramid.

Likewise, the successes of charismatic and mystical religious movements should not be too surprising in our culture. We are a nation of transients (one of four families moves every five years) with a diminishing sense of community; our families are a less stable source of love and acceptance—at present, one of every two marriages ends in divorce. In such a climate, a community of believers becomes very attractive; if no one else loves you or cares for you, God does. The vogue for books on self-development in the 1980s reflected a society in which the basic needs of many people were relatively well met so that interest focused on self-actualization; the changed conditions of the 1990s shifted interest to therapeutic books on how to cope with the results of changing economic conditions, changing marital roles, or how to deal with stress. In the twenty-first century, increasing investment in the stockmarket has made books on buying stocks and on handling wealth more popular.

Because the concept of "needs" focuses on deprivation and because it does not take into account the extent to which our needs are modified by socialization and accul-turation, values also need to be considered.

Values

Attitudes, our predispositions to respond favorably or unfavorably to elements of the environment (including invitations to rhetorical action), are influenced not only by beliefs about what is true or probable but by goals or values. Like attitude and belief, *value* is a construct describing a pattern of human behavior. It cannot be touched or seen. Values are usually defined as judgments about what is moral (good or right), im-portant (worthy, significant), or beautiful (moving, expressive, pleasing), or as funda-mental preferences for certain ends (such as equality, freedom, self-actualization) or for certain modes of conduct (such as honesty, courage, or integrity). In other words, val-ues express strong, basic, and very general views of how one should act or what goals one should seek (what goals are worthy of seeking). The ideal of self-government, for example, strongly implies that all citizens should enter into policy deliberations and should involve themselves actively in discourse related to choosing those who repre-sent them in government. These are views that positively value rhetorical action.

Values seem to arise from three sources: our biology, our cultures, and our distinc-tive qualities as individuals. These sources suggest the relationship between values and needs. Some values arise from biological needs or genetic characteristics (birds need to fly; salmon need to swim upriver to spawn). Despite the many catalogs in psychological works or Maslow's hierarchy of needs (leading to a hierarchy of motives), there is no list of needs that satisfactorily describes human motivation. Consider Maslow's hierarchy. It cannot explain artists who are driven to paint or sculpt even though they cannot buy enough food to eat and are scorned by others. Nor can it explain religious figures, such as Mother Teresa or Dorothy Day, who devote their lives to acting altruistically. Maslow himself recognized these exceptions and discussed the problems involved in establishing any needs as basic or in describing motivation as arising from deprivation. As he noted, rats seem to run mazes as fast out of curiosity as out of hunger, thirst, or sex drive.

Obviously, human beings need nutrition, safety, shelter from exposure, and affection, but we have modified these needs culturally and socially—creating a second source of values. The Masai of Africa, for example, seem to thrive on a diet composed largely of the milk and blood of their cattle, a diet that would nauseate most Americans. Dwellers in tropical and even Mediterranean climates meet part of their sleep needs by the siesta, a practice unintelligible to those from more temperate climates. In other words, what begin as organic or biological needs are shaped by culture and society.

In every community, there are norms about what is good and proper to eat, and what is a delicacy to one group may be revolting to another. Values arise, then, not only from biological requirements but also from the norms of the groups we belong to, groups ranging in size from the nation to the gang on the block. Group values are expressed in such statements as, "That is unpatriotic or disloyal." "This is the Chinese way." "Seventh Day Adventists are vegetarians." "That's sissy." These values, affecting every facet of life, are so fused with biological needs that no one can say just where biology stops and socialization begins.

A third source of values is idiosyncrasies, the unique qualities of the individual. Each of us is physiologically different. If you have an unusually acute sense of smell, you may have a strong aversion to many perfumes; if tobacco smoke gives you headaches, you may support regulations creating smoke-free areas. Epileptics place a special value on sleep (seizures are more likely if they are deprived of it). Those who suffer from migraines dislike strobe lights and avoid television programs with lots of jump cuts because these can provoke headaches. Some people have intense aesthetic needs, some have few sexual needs, some relish food, and others eat only to survive. As you will note from these examples, such individual values are refinements or modifications of cultural values and biological needs. Values arising from the special qualities of individuals may account for some unusual responses to rhetorical efforts. Individual values are also a source of variation in the importance or priority given to a particular social value.

Attitudes, our predispositions to respond, are a product of values and beliefs. The emotive and affective component of attitudes (reflecting our desires) and goals comes from our values; the cognitive component of values (based on information and inference) comes from our beliefs. Clearly, however, these concepts and the processes they represent are inseparable because evaluations are based on what we believe to be true, and our evaluations, in turn, influence what we perceive and how we interpret its *salience*, or relevance in our lives. In sum, as a rhetor you must recognize that lack of motivation will likely plague your audience unless you can answer the question posed at the beginning of this chapter: What will be necessary to induce the audience to take part in rhetorical action? by saying: I know my audience's needs and values.

INERTIA OBSTACLES

The concept of *inertia* is by now a familiar one. Inertia is the tendency of an object to continue doing whatever it has been doing—to rest if it has been resting, to move in a straight line unless disturbed by an outside force, and so on. When applied to people, inertia refers to an audience's resistance to the rhetor's purpose. Inertia is a complex psychological matter, but from a rhetorical viewpoint, it usually has to do with resisting demands on our time and energies or with a feeling of powerlessness. Audiences will resist changing their ideas and ignore calls to action unless the proposed action is both vital enough to engage their energies as well as within their capabilities, capable of being done here and now, and has a reasonable chance of being effective.

The problem of persuading people to practice "safer sex" is illustrative. Many sexually active people have not used condoms in the past; as a result, "safer sex" involves a change in behavior. Condoms cost money, and buying them can be embarrassing and expensive, especially for many teenagers. Accordingly, those promoting safer sex provide condoms free of charge to make using them easier and try to convince the sexually active not only that they face life-threatening dangers from unprotected sex but also that using condoms is easy, effective, and consistent with sexual pleasure.

Those who write about attitudes argue that they have three parts: cognitive (beliefs), affective (values), and behavioral. Attitudes do not exist apart from behaviors, but the relationship between them is complex. There is no simple correlation between an attitude and a particular behavior. One can agree that unprotected sexual intercourse is dangerous, for example, and behave in various ways. One can act as if that belief had nothing to do with you—as if only gay males were at risk, screening out data about increasing risks to heterosexuals and women. One can believe in the danger but also espouse the value that premarital sex is wrong (value). Taking precautions would contradict that value. In such instances, if sex occurs, pregnancy, a sexually transmitted disease, or exposure to the HIV virus (leading to Acquired Immune Deficiency Syndrome or AIDS) are risked, perhaps as punishment for flouting the value. Or, one can carefully plan to enjoy sexual activity safely. Attitudes and behaviors either correlate very poorly, or people's reported attitudes differ from their actual attitudes.

Just as attitudes can influence behaviors, so behaviors can also influence attitudes. Studies comparing listening to a speech or reading an essay by someone else with composing one's own speech or essay or with recording the arguments made by others are illustrative. In the studies, even for those hostile to the specific purpose of the speech or essay, there was considerable change in attitudes with greater participation.[13] Advertisers who promote contests in which participants write "Why I like X in 25 words or less" are using behavior to influence attitudes. This process is sometimes called self-influence, and it may occur because the people involved try to make their attitudes consistent with their behaviors.

At a minimum, an action is a commitment, often a public commitment, to an attitude. It expresses the recipients' participation in the persuasive process and involves them in the process of influence. Participation in the rhetorical act may be a most effective way of influencing attitudes, and inducing a specific action may be just the reinforcement needed to ensure that a belief will persist. In all cases, as mentioned above, rhetorical acts that propose specific, feasible, and immediate actions for the audience will be the most successful.

These, then, are the rhetorical obstacles arising from the audience: inattention, misperception and misinterpretation, lack of motivation, and inertia. Thankfully, most rhetors never have to face all these obstacles simultaneously. Those that do rarely succeed in combatting them all. A marvelous exception was the courageous true story of a woman named Angelina Grimké. Her compelling story and impassioned speech constitute the material for analysis.

MATERIAL FOR ANALYSIS

Angelina Grimké (1805–1879) was an unlikely reformer. Born into privilege in 1805 in Charleston, South Carolina, to a wealthy slaveholding family, Angelina had every comfort imaginable. She was the youngest of 14 kids, educated by private tutors, raised as a devout Episcopalian, and doted on by her parents and siblings. And yet she was restive. She and her older sister Sarah were particularly disturbed by the practice of slavery. So, even though the laws of South Carolina forbade teaching slaves to read or write, the sisters created an underground school on their own plantation. Angelina's diary describes these sessions with supreme satisfaction. "The light was put out, the keyhole screened, and flat on our stomachs, with the spelling book under our eyes, we defied the laws of South Carolina." The girls were discovered by their father and severely lectured. Rather than give up and be dutiful children, they ran away, took up residence in Philadelphia, and joined the Quakers and the antislavery cause. Here, in 1836, at the age of 31, Angelina published a letter entitled "*Appeal to the Christian Women of the South*" wherein she urged southern women to do the unthinkable: "to persuade your husband, father, brothers, and sons that slavery is a crime against God and man." That sentiment was considered heretical. As pamphlets were disseminated in South Carolina, the Charleston authorities warned Angelina that she would be arrested if she ever returned to her hometown, and the postmaster burned copies of the "letter."

Undaunted, Angelina discovered public speaking, even though in the 1830s it was considered unseemly for women to speak to men in public places. In 1837, in Amesbury, Massachusetts, Angelina engaged in a series of debates on the slavery question—the very first public debates between a man and a woman in the United States.

But a hot May evening in Philadelphia in 1838 became the setting for Angelina's swan song in her struggle for human rights. Two days after her marriage to Theodore Weld, a fellow reformer in the antislavery cause, Angelina accepted an invitation to speak at the dedication of Pennsylvania Hall—a splendid structure with the motto "Virtue, Liberty, Independence" carved in gold letters over the stage. In publicity leading up to the event, she was denounced in the papers by the Massachusetts clergy as "a Godless woman," a "he-woman," even "the devil incarnate." Before the ceremonies could unfold, an angry, howling mob formed in the streets. When a black woman, Maria Chapman, got up to introduce Angelina Grimké, the crowd inside booed and yelled; the mob outside threw bricks and rotten tomatoes through the windows. Maria fainted and the crowd erupted with laughter and ridicule. Calmly, Angelina arose from her seat, gazed around the large hall with such unnerving intensity the crowd momentarily quieted. She began: "Men, brethren, and fathers—mothers, daughters, and sisters, what came ye out for to see? A reed shaken with the wind? Is it curiosity merely, or a deep sympathy with the perishing slave, that has brought this large audience together?" At this, someone yelled: "Fire." People ran. Heavy stones thudded against the windows. Angelina Grimké kept speaking. She continued: "Deluded beings! They know not what they do. Do you ask: What has the North to do with Slavery? Hear it—hear it. Those voices without tell us that the spirit of slavery is here!" Amidst the hostile crowd, Angelina spoke for over an hour. Later that evening, the mob burned the new hall to the ground.

Address at Pennsylvania Hall, 1838[14]
by Angelina Grimké

1   Men, brethren and fathers—mothers, daughters and sisters, what came ye out for to see,? A reed shaken with the wind? [Matt. 11:7] Is it curiosity merely, or a deep sympathy with the perishing slave, that has brought this large audience together? (*A yell from the mob without the building.*) Those voices without ought to awaken and call out our warmest sympathies. Deluded beings! "they know not what they do" [Luke 23:34]. They know not that they are undermining their own rights and their own happiness, temporal and eternal. Do you ask, "what has the North to do with slavery?" Hear it—hear it. Those voices without tell us that the spirit of slavery is here, and has been roused to wrath by our abolition speeches and conventions: for surely liberty would not foam and tear herself with rage [Mark 9:18], because her friends are multiplied daily, and meetings are held in quick succession to set forth her virtues and extend her peaceful kingdom. This opposition shows that slavery has done its deadliest work in the hearts of our citizens. Do you ask, then, "what has the North to do?" I answer, cast out first the spirit of slavery from your own hearts, and then lend your aid to convert the South [Matt. 7:5]. Each one present has a work to do, be his or her situation what it may, however limited their means, or insignificant their supposed influence. The great men of this country will not do this work; the church will never do it . A desire to please the world, to keep the favor of all parties and of all conditions, makes them dumb on this and every other unpopular subject. They have become worldly-wise,[15] and therefore God, in his wisdom, employs them not to carry on his plans of reformation and salvation. He hath chosen the foolish things of the world to confound the wise, and the weak to overcome the mighty [1 Cor. 1:27-28].

2   As a Southerner I feel that it is my duty to stand up here to-night and bear testimony against slavery. I have seen it—I have seen it. I know it has horrors that can never be described. I was brought up under its wing: I witnessed for many years its demoralizing influences, and its destructiveness to human happiness. It is admitted by some that the slave is not happy under the *worst* forms of slavery. But I have never seen a happy slave. I have seen him dance in his chains, it is true; but he was not happy. There is a wide difference between happiness and mirth. Man cannot enjoy the former while his manhood is destroyed, and that part of the being which is necessary to the making, and to the enjoyment of happiness, is completely blotted out. The slaves, however, may be, and sometimes are, mirthful. When hope is extinguished, they say, "let us eat and drink, for to-morrow we die" [Isa. 22:13]. (*Just then stones were thrown at the windows,—a great noise without, and commotion within.*)

3   What is a mob? What would the breaking of every window be? What would the levelling of this Hall be? Any evidence that we are wrong, or that slavery is a

good and wholesome institution? What if the mob should now burst in upon us, break up our meeting and commit violence upon our persons—would this be anything compared with what the slaves endure? No, no: and we do not remember them "as bound with them" [Heb. 13:3], if we shrink in the time of peril, or feel unwilling to sacrifice ourselves, if need be, for their sake. (*Great noise.*) I thank the Lord that there is yet left enough to feel the truth, even though it rages at it—that conscience is not completely seared as to be unmoved by the truth of the living God.

4   Many persons go to the South for a season, and are hospitably entertained in the parlor and at the table of the slave-holder. They never enter the huts of the slaves; they know nothing of the dark side of the picture, and they return home with praises on their lips of the generous character of those with whom they had tarried. Or if they have witnessed the cruelties of slavery, by remaining silent spectators they have naturally become callous—an insensibility has ensued which prepares them to apologize even for barbarity. Nothing but the corrupting influence of slavery on the hearts of the Northern people can induce them to apologize for it; and much will have been done for the destruction of Southern slavery when we have so reformed the North that no one here will be willing to risk his reputation by advocating or even excusing the holding of men as property. The South know it, and acknowledge that as fast as our principles prevail, the hold of the master must be relaxed. (*Another outbreak of mobocratic spirit, and some confusion in the house.*)

5   How wonderfully constituted is the human mind! How it resists, as long as it can, all efforts made to reclaim from error! I feel that all this disturbance is but an evidence that our efforts are the best that could have been adopted, or else the friends of slavery would not care for what we say and do. The South know what we do. I am thankful that they are reached by our efforts. Many times have I wept in the land of my birth, over the system of slavery. I knew of none who sympathized in my feelings—I was unaware that any efforts were made to deliver the oppressed—no voice in the wilderness was heard calling on the people to repent and do works meet for repentance [Isa. 40:3; Matt. 3:3]—and my heart sickened within me. Oh, how should I have rejoiced to know that such efforts as these were being made. I only wonder that I had such feelings. I wonder when I reflect under what influence I was brought up, that my heart is not harder than the nether millstone [Psa. 95:8; Heb. 3:15]. But in the midst of temptation I was preserved, and my sympathy grew warmer, and my hatred of slavery more inveterate, until at last I have exiled myself from my native land because I could no longer endure to hear the wailing of the slave. I fled to the land of Penn; for here, thought I, sympathy for the slave will surely be found. But I found it not. The people were kind and hospitable, but the slave had no place in their thoughts. Whenever questions were put to me as to his condition, I felt that they were dictated by an idle curiosity, rather than by that deep feeling which would lead to effort for his rescue. I therefore shut up my grief in my own heart. I remembered that I was a Carolinian, from a state which framed this iniquity by law. I knew that throughout her territory was continual suffering, on the one part, and continual brutality and sin on the other. Every Southern breeze wafted to me the discordant tones of weeping and wailing, shrieks and groans, mingled with prayers and blasphemous curses. I thought there was no hope; that the wicked would go on in his wickedness, until he had destroyed both himself and his country. My heart sunk within me at the abominations in the midst of which I had been born and educated. What

will it avail, cried I in bitterness of spirit, to expose to the gaze of strangers the horrors and pollutions of slavery, when there is no ear to hear nor heart to feel and pray for the slave. The language of my soul was, "Oh tell it not in Gath, publish it not in the streets of Askelon" [2 Sam. 1:20]. But how different do I feel now! Animated with hope, nay, with an assurance of the triumph of liberty and good will to man, I will lift up my voice like a trumpet, and show this people their transgression [Isa. 58:1], their sins of omission toward the slave, and what they can do towards affecting southern mind [*sic*], and overthrowing Southern oppression.

6   We may talk of occupying neutral ground, but on this subject, in its present attitude, there is no such thing as neutral ground. He that is not for us is against us, and he that gathereth not with us, scattereth abroad [Matt. 12:20]. If you are on what you suppose to be neutral ground, the South look upon you as on the side of the oppressor. And is there one who loves his country willing to give his influence, even indirectly, in favor of slavery—that curse of nations? God swept Egypt with the besom of destruction [Isa. 14:23] and punished Judea also with a sore punishment, because of slavery. And have we any reason to believe that he is less just now?—or that he will be more favorable to us than to his own "peculiar people?" (*Shouting, stones thrown against the windows, &c.*)

7   There is nothing to be feared from those who would stop our mouths, but they themselves should fear and tremble. The current is even now setting fast against them. If the arm of the North had not caused the Bastille of slavery to totter to its foundation, you would not hear those cries. A few years ago, and the South felt secure, and with a contemptuous sneer asked, "Who are the abolitionists? The abolitionists are nothing"—Ay, in one sense they were nothing, and they are nothing still. But in this we rejoice, that "God has chosen things that are not to bring to nought things that are" [1 Cor. 1:28]. (*Mob again disturbed the meeting.*)

8   We often hear the question asked, "What shall we do?" Here is an opportunity for doing something now. Every man and every woman present may do something by showing that we fear not a mob, and, in the midst of threatenings and revilings, by opening our mouths for the dumb and pleading the cause of those who are ready to perish.

9   To work as we should in this cause, we must know what Slavery is. Let me urge you then to buy the books which have been written on this subject and read them, and then lend them to your neighbors. Give your money no longer for things which pander to pride and lust, but aid in scattering "the living coals of truth" [Isa. 6:6–8] upon the naked heart of this nation,—in circulating appeals to the sympathies of Christians in behalf of the outraged and suffering slave. But, it is said by some, our "books and papers do not speak the truth." Why, then, do they not contradict what we say? They cannot. Moreover the South has entreated, nay commanded us to be silent; and what greater evidence of the truth of our publications could be desired?

10   Women of Philadelphia! allow me as a Southern woman, with much attachment to the land of my birth, to entreat you to come up to this work. Especially let me urge you to petition. Men may settle this and other questions at the ballot-box, but you have no such right; it is only through petitions that you can reach the Legislature. It is therefore peculiarly your duty to petition. Do you say, "It does no good?" The South already turns pale at the number sent. They have read the reports of the proceedings of Congress, and there have seen that among other petitions were very many from the women of the North on the

subject of slavery. This fact has called the attention of the South to the subject. How could we expect to have done more as yet? Men who hold the rod over slaves, rule in the councils of the nation: and they deny our right to petition and to remonstrate against abuses of our sex and of our kind. We have these rights, however, from our God. Only let us exercise them: and though often turned away unanswered, let us remember the influence of importunity upon the unjust judge [Luke 18:1–6] and act accordingly. The fact that the South look with jealousy upon our measures shows that they are effectual. There is, therefore, no cause for doubting or despair, but rather for rejoicing.

11 It was remarked in England that women did much to abolish Slavery in her colonies.[16] Nor are they now idle. Numerous petitions from them have recently been presented to the Queen, to abolish the apprenticeship with its cruelties nearly equal to those of the system whose place it supplies. One petition two miles and a quarter long has been presented. And do you think these labors will be in vain? Let the history of the past answer. When the women of these States send up to Congress such a petition, our legislators will arise as did those of England, and say, "When all the maids and matrons of the land are knocking at our doors we must legislate." Let the zeal and love, the faith and works of our English sisters quicken ours—that while the slaves continue to suffer, and when they shout deliverance, we may feel the satisfaction of *having done what we could*.

Questions for Analysis

1. Angelina Grimké speaks to all four audience types in this speech: empirical, target, agents of change, and created. Find passages in the speech to support each audience conception.
2. Identify the ways in which Angelina Grimké experiences all four audience obstacles: inattention, misperception, lack of motivation, and inertia.
3. Prophets are individuals who are "chosen"; they are high authority figures who have "a direct line" to the Almighty. Prophets tend to be courageous and tested. Their duty is to lead a people from their destructive path to a righteous path (recall how Dr. Martin Luther King, Jr., played this role). How does Grimké assume the role of a prophet? What audience obstacles does this role overcome? Why is it a risky role for her to play? How does it relate to the tone of the speech?
4. Locate the following kinds of argument in Grimké's speech: rhetorical questions, analogy, enactment, a fortiori, refutation, and turning-the-tables. What obstacles do these arguments help Grimké overcome?

EXERCISES

1. In the paragraphs below, identify the most likely audience obstacles (choose from inattention, misperception, lack of motivation, inertia):
   a. A college student attempts to persuade her speech class that horrible injustices exist in Iraq. She is concerned that her subject holds little salience for this group.
   b. An ad agency is given an account with Royal Caribbean Cruise Lines to create a mass mailing campaign targeted at corporate executives. The ad agency is concerned, however, that their mailer will be wrongly viewed as "just another flimsy sales pitch."
   c. Angelina Grimké wants to share her compelling story of the horrors of slavery, but she is constrained by the presence of a disruptive audience and a loud, angry mob of detractors outside. She wonders if she can even be heard.

d. MTV wants to launch an educational "Rock-the-Vote" campaign designed to get its young listeners to register to vote. Those producing the radio spots are concerned that if their listeners have never taken part in the electoral process, they may be inclined to resist any message for the simple reason that registering involves a behavioral change.

2. The 1999 Nielsen ratings revealed the widespread problem that inattention can be for network programmers and the advertising that supports them. Fully 75 percent of Americans polled do not stay with a program for its duration. Even the most popular program, *ER*, recorded that 53 percent of their viewers turned away at some point in the show. What do you think sitcoms and dramas must do to recapture an easily distracted public? (source: ABC News, July 30, 1999).

3. For this exercise, design an interviewing schedule (a series of planned and interrelated questions on a subject) and use it to interview three persons on the subject of your rhetorical act: a student, a professor, and a community member. Do not interview friends or roommates; try to interview complete strangers.

The exercise has three purposes: (1) to give you experience with the problems involved in developing questions that elicit accurately what others know, believe, and feel; (2) to give you experience in creating an atmosphere in which others are willing to tell you what they know, believe, and feel; and (3) to provide you with information about the knowledge, beliefs, and attitudes of others to help you adapt a rhetorical act to a general or heterogeneous audience.

The intent of the interviews is to gather information that would help you, as a rhetor, prepare a rhetorical act more likely to be attended to and to be influential for a general audience. You are attempting to discover the causes of resistance to your purpose and the sorts of obstacles you might face. You are also trying to find out what bases there are for appeals that might cause this audience to give your point of view a fair and open hearing. In order to be an effective interviewer, you need to be well informed on the subject yourself.

You need to plan an opening that introduces you, indicates what you are doing and why, introduces the subject, and tells the person to be interviewed how much time will be involved and why it is important that he or she participate. Plan a series of questions that progress through the areas of the subject you think most important. Begin with basic questions to determine just what the person knows. Plan a closing that expresses appreciation and that will end the interview comfortably.

Problems to be avoided: not knowing the questions well enough and/or reading them mechanically, lack of warmth and eye contact suggesting disinterest, speaking too softly or too quickly, rushing the interview so that answers are superficial, apologizing, asking biased questions, suggesting answers if the person hesitates, mentioning how others answered, taking too many notes, and taking too much for granted (such as how much the person knows about the subject or how familiar he or she is with the vocabulary of your topic).

a. Turn in a copy of the questions you used, together with an evaluation of them as a means of getting useful and accurate information about knowledge, beliefs, and attitudes.

b. Briefly evaluate your strengths and weaknesses as an interviewer and indicate what kinds of things were successful and unsuccessful in creating an atmosphere in which people were willing to be interviewed and to take the questions seriously. What places were the best for doing the interviews?

c. Briefly evaluate the information you obtained in terms of using it for a rhetorical act on this subject for a general audience. Indicate what assumptions were confirmed or disconfirmed; consider how your class differs from this wider audience; indicate some ways you might proceed that you think would be effective in gaining a hearing for your point of view.

4. A trend in on-line communication is to make retail Web sites more interactive and thus more influential. Locate the article "Smart Websites" (*African Business*, February 2002, p. 23, [1]) in the InfoTrac College Edition database for an illustration of this trend. Pick a commercial Web site on the World Wide Web or consider the InfoTrac College Edition on-line database system. How do these Web tools create their audience? Who is their empirical audience? Who is their target audience? How do they identify and appeal to their agents of change? Finally, what role do they invite the audience to play? How is a Web site similar to and different from a speech in its relationship to its audience? How are the obstacles arising from the audience similar or different?

5. **Portfolio Entry 7: Audience Obstacles**
Identify and explain the audience obstacles that are evident in your rhetorical acts. Using relevant elements of descriptive analysis, detail how each rhetor tries to combat these audience obstacles. Is one more successful than another? Explain in one to two pages.

NOTES

1. According to professor of marketing James U. McNeal at Texas A&M University, as reported in an article in *American Demographics* in April 1998, children under 12 spent more than $24 billion of their own money in 1997, while directly influencing the spending of $188 billion more. He estimates that by 2001, children's spending may reach $35 billion. "In the 1990s, children aged 2–14 directly influenced about $5 billion in parental purchases," McNeal wrote. "In the mid-1970s, the figure was $20 billion, and it rose to $50 billion by 1985. By 1990, kids' direct influence had reached $132 billion, and in 1997, it may have peaked around $188 billion. Estimates shown that children's aggregate spending roughly doubled during each decade of the 1960s, 1970s, and 1980s, and tripled so far in the 1990s." Reported by Miriam H. Zoll, "Psychologists Challenge Ethics of Marketing to Children," American News Service, April 5, 2000 <http://www.mediachannel.org/originals/kidsell.shtml>. Accessed June 6, 2002.

2. Edwin Black, in "The Second Persona," *Quarterly Journal of Speech* 56 (April 1970): 109–119, discusses the persona of the audience. See also Michael McGee, "In Search of the People," *Quarterly Journal of Speech* 61 (October 1975): 235–249.

3. See K. K. Campbell, "The Rhetoric of Women's Liberation: An Oxymoron," *Quarterly Journal of Speech* 59 (February 1973): 74–86, for evidence of some changes in women's self-images produced by contemporary feminism. See "The Glass Half Empty: Women's Equality and Discrimination in American Society," a report by the NOW Legal Defense and Education Fund, New York City, 1994, for data on young women's attitudes. In addition, a 1991 study by the American Association of University Women, "Shortchanging Girls, Shortchanging America," found substantial problems of self-esteem among teenage women. See also Peggy Orenstein, *School Girls: Young Women, Self Esteem and the Confidence Gap* (New York: Doubleday, 1994).

4. This part of the rhetorical problem is the subject of Chapter 10.

5. D. O. Sears and J. L. Freedman, "Selective Exposure to Information: A Critical Review," *Public Opinion Quarterly* 31 (1967): 175. See also I. L. Janis and L. Mann, *Decision Making: A Psychological Analysis of Conflict, Choice and Commitment* (New York: Free Press, 1977).

6. L. K. Canon, "Self-confidence and Selective Exposure to Information," in *Conflict, Decision and Dissonance*, ed. L. Festinger (Stanford, CA: Stanford University Press, 1964); J. L. Freedman, "Confidence, Utility and Selective Exposure: A Partial Replication," *Journal of Personality and Social Psychology* 2 (1965): 778–780.

7. J. L. Freedman and D. O. Sears, "Selective Exposure," in *Advances in Experimental Social Psychology*, vol. 2, ed. L. Berkowitz (New York: Academic Press, 1965); D. O. Sears and J L. Freedman, "Effects of Expected Familiarity with Arguments upon Opinion Change and Selective Exposure," *Journal of Personality and Social Psychology* 2 (1965): 420–426; D. O. Sears, J. L. Freedman, and E. F. O'Connor, "The Effects of Anticipated Debate and Commitment on the Polarization of Audience Opinion," *Public Opinion Quarterly* 28 (1964): 617–627.

8. A. Hasdorf and H. Cantril, "They Saw a Game: A Case Study," *Journal of Abnormal and Social Psychology* 49 (1954): 133.

9. Jeff Lenihan, "South Riled About Hrbek's Push," *Star Tribune*, October 22, 1991, p. 6C.

10. The original study was done by C. I. Hovland and W. Mandell, "An Experimental Comparison of Conclusion Drawing by the Communicator and the Audience," *Journal of Abnormal and Social Psychology* 47 (July 1952): 581–588, and its findings have been confirmed in subsequent studies. The results emphasize the importance of the thesis, organization, and transitions in your rhetoric; they are the subject of Chapter 6, on the structuring of a rhetorical act.

11. Richard E. Petty and John T. Cacioppo, *Communication and Persuasion: Central and Peripheral Routes to Attitude Change* (New York: Springer-Verlag, 1986).

12. Abraham Maslow, *Motivation and Personality* (New York: Harper, 1954).

13. O. J. Harvey and G. D. Beverly, "Some Personality Correlates of Concept Change Through Role Playing," *Journal of Abnormal and Social Psychology* 63 (1961): 125–130.

14. The comments in parentheses are by the contemporary reporter and describe the scene inside and outside the hall during the speech. Biblical allusions are identified in brackets. The text is from *History of Pennsylvania Hall, Which Was Destroyed by a Mob on the 17th of May 1838*, ed. Samuel Webb (1838), pp. 123–126.

15. The character of Worldly-Wise appears in John Bunyan's *Pilgrim's Progress* (originally published 1683; printed in the United States in 1789), the story of a man struggling to find salvation despite many obstacles and temptations.

16. "Anti-slavery reached its climax in the 1830s, sending over 4,000 petitions to Parliament during three separate sessions, a feat unequalled by any other national movement. . . . Women began to petition en masse at the beginning of the 1830s. . . . In 1833 a single petition of 187,000 'ladies of England—a huge featherbed of a petition' was hauled into Parliament by four sturdy members" (Seymour Drescher, "Public Opinion and British Colonial Slavery," in *Slavery and British Society, 1776–1846*, ed. James Walvin, Baton Rouge: Louisiana State University Press, 1982, pp. 30, 33).

chapter 9

Obstacles Arising from the Subject and Purpose

lthough audience obstacles are central in an analysis of the rhetorical problem, *subject and purpose obstacles* are almost equally important. Actually, of course, the problems discussed here arise out of the interrelationship between the audience and the issue: the subject the audience must consider and the purpose, the response that the rhetor wishes to evoke from the audience. Again, no subject is without interest for some audience, and no subject is of interest to everyone.

To give you a feeling for the kind of rhetorical problem discussed in this chapter, consider this paragraph from the essay on global warming by Bill McKibben cited several times in chapter 4. At this point the author is exploring the conflicting views of experts, some of whom are positive, some fearful, about the carrying capacity of the earth:

> But we can calculate risks, figure the odds that each side may be right. Joel Cohen made the most thorough attempt to do so in *How Many People Can the Earth Support?* Cohen collected and examined every estimate of carrying capacity made in recent decades, from that of a Harvard oceanographer who thought in 1976 that we might have food enough for 40 billion people to that of a Brown University researcher who calculated in 1991 that we might be able to sustain 5.9 billion (our present population), but only if we were principally vegetarians. One study proposed that if photosynthesis was the limiting factor, the earth might support a trillion people; an Australian economist proved, in calculations a decade apart, that

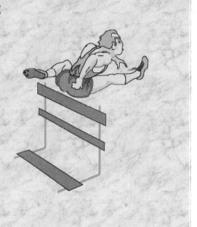

Figure 9-1
Subject-Related Rhetorical Obstacles

- **Subject-Related Obstacles**:
  - Complexity
    - no firsthand experience
    - too difficult to understand
  - Cultural History
    - taboos on subject
    - boredom/overkill
  - Cost
    - too much time, money, effort
  - Control
    - lack of enforcement

we could manage populations of 28 and 157 billion. None of the studies is wise enough to examine every variable, to reach by itself the "right" number. When Cohen compared the dozens of studies, however, he uncovered something pretty interesting: the median low value for the planet's carrying capacity was 7.7 billion people, and the median high value was 12 billion. That, of course, is just the range that the UN predicts we will inhabit by the middle of the next century. (62–63)[1]

The complexity of this issue arises from several sources. One is that there are so many variables involved that it is almost impossible to predict accurately the carrying capacity of the earth. In addition, experts disagree widely. Finally, all of this involves fairly sophisticated mathematical models that are the bases of the prediction. In the face of that kind of complexity, audience members are likely to feel overwhelmed and abandon the subject.

The obstacles facing anyone writing about global warming are great indeed—the audience's limited personal experience, the formidable technical and scientific vocabulary as well as the disagreements among experts, and the mind-boggling statistics. Obstacles of this sort arise from the subject and from the rhetor's purpose. In this chapter, I discuss the four "c's" of subject and purpose obstacles (Figure 9–1).

SUBJECT-RELATED OBSTACLES

There are two major obstacles created by subjects or topics: resistance created by *complexity* and resistance created by the *cultural history* of the issue.

Complexity

Some subjects are complex or, more to the point, the audience sees them as complex. In such cases, you will meet a special kind of audience resistance that is definitely a barrier to joint rhetorical action. (Of course, there might also be an obstacle in your own capability to handle certain kinds of complex subjects. Even if you were speaking from personal experience, the preparation time would be far longer. But let's assume you can handle the subject.)

Subjects are complex or seem so under these conditions:

1. They are remote from the audience's personal experience.
2. They require technical knowledge or some other kind of special expertise.
3. They are bound up with many other difficult issues.

That is, audiences resist participation in rhetorical acts for which they have no touchstone in their ordinary lives. They are uncomfortable with subjects demanding decisions that they do not feel competent to make, and they are often overwhelmed by subjects with broad ramifications.

Subjects that lie outside the personal experiences of the audience create special difficulties. The audience feels unfit to make judgments. This is the case with most foreign policy decisions. Despite a great increase in world travel by Americans, few of us have been in Afghanistan and even fewer have been in sub-Sarahan Africa or have had experiences that would make us feel comfortable about deciding military or economic policies for those areas. By contrast, farmers have considerable experience with acreage allotments, storage facilities, insecticides, crop failure, and the like, and bring a good deal of familiarity to decisions on such issues. Women who have delivered children in hospitals have experience they bring to proposals for birthing rooms; parents have had personal experiences with teachers relevant to educational decisions; and so forth. But when a subject is outside our personal experience, we are at the mercy of others. We have to rely on data gathered by others and on interpretations made by experts. Because experts rarely agree, we must try to decide who is more reliable. And since we have to rely on others, we are more vulnerable to manipulation: It is easier to fool those without personal experience because they have no basis on which to test the data or claims of others. That is one reason we feel helpless about foreign policy decisions and why we can be deceived more easily about what really happened in Rwanda or Kashmir or Somalia or Kosovo.

Subjects are also complex when they require technical knowledge or a special kind of expertise. Subjects that demand a lot of economic knowledge from the audience are particularly dangerous. Making decisions about global warming, for example, demands many kinds of knowledge from audience members. People must know something about the factors influencing agricultural production and causing salinization and the creation of deserts. They need to know about factors affecting population growth, and they have to be able to understand the dynamics created by special kinds of pollution. Audiences faced with such demands are likely to resist participation—unless their livelihoods, say as owners of ski resorts, have been directly affected by climatic changes—because basic information is outside their personal competence. In such a situation, rhetors must become educators, and under such circumstances, they are likely to use the entire range of rhetorical purposes in a persuasive campaign. Rhetors will begin by creating virtual experience, including altering the audience's perception of its own competence. This will be followed by efforts to explain that link and interpret the data. Only then can rhetors try to formulate beliefs in the audience about such things as the degree to which different kinds of pollution are responsible for diminishing the ozone layer, the responsibility of businesses and government for the levels of pollution, how pollution-eliminating technology can be paid for, and what kinds of regulation are needed to prevent this problem from worsening.

Subjects like global warming also are complex because they are bound up with many other difficult issues with broad ramifications. Decisions about pollution controls cannot be separated from issues of rapid transit, highways, car manufacture and costs, agriculture, and the losses of jobs and comforts in altering our lifestyle. The result is a sense that the problem is so large and its implications so extensive that no one can understand it or begin to solve it.

The history of the civil rights movement illustrates the complexity of a problem with broad ramifications. Initial efforts to attack the denial of civil rights involved eliminating clearly defined evidences of oppression—segregated waiting rooms, water fountains, and bathrooms, and barriers to voter registration, for example. When these basic battles were largely won, however, other issues emerged that were not so easy to define or solve: providing quality education, decent housing, and good jobs. Housing cannot be separated from employment nor employment from education. Hence, in order to solve one problem, all the problems apparently have to be solved. Such efforts take time and involve cultural dislocations (reflected, for example, in disputes over school busing and integration plans), and clear evidence of progress may be hard to see.

In summary, a subject may create obstacles because of its real or its perceived complexity. A subject is complex when the audience has no firsthand experience with it, when technical knowledge or special expertise is required, and when the subject is part of an interrelated set of problems or issues.

Cultural History

The second set of obstacles arising from the subject has its roots in events that happened long before you take the stage. Let us call them the *subject's cultural history* to indicate that the obstacles come from ideas or concepts about the subject formed during past discussions in your culture. Obstacles arising from cultural history include these:

1. Boredom or indifference owing to familiarity with existing arguments
2. Closed minds about public discussion of some taboo topics
3. Conditioned responses to emotionally loaded subjects
4. Conflict with cultural values

No subject exists in a void. Every subject has a context and meaning consisting of past experience with the subject and the issues surrounding it. This context is the residue of past rhetorical action. It is the subject's cultural history. If your topic has a long and rich cultural history, beware! Here is an example of the problems for change created by cultural history. Consider how the author tries to combat the rich cultural history that is associated with our national anthem:

The Star-Spangled Earache: What So Loudly We Wail
by Caldwell Titcomb[2]

1   Not so long ago Representative Andrew Jacobs Jr. of Indiana filed a bill to replace "The Star-Spangled Banner" with "America the Beautiful" as our national anthem. Many people have long advocated just such a change, and for a number of reasons the bill deserves wide support.

2   "The Star-Spangled Banner" has been the official national anthem only since March 3, 1931. Most people assume that it has been the anthem virtually

from time immemorial and that it is thus now sacrosanct. But clearly there is nothing wrong with supplanting something that has been in effect for only 50-odd years.

3   The music is by an Englishman, John Stafford Smith (1750–1836), who wrote it as a drinking song for a London social club, the Anacreontic Society. Is our nation so poverty-stricken that we must rule out home-grown music?

4   The tune is a constant stumbling block. Technically, it covers a span of a twelfth—that is, an octave plus a perfect fifth. Not only is it difficult for the general public to sing, but it has repeatedly caused trouble even for professional opera singers. Some people assert that this problem could be solved by selecting the right key for performance. But the point is that *all* 12 possible keys are poor. No matter what the key, the tune goes either too high or too low (and both, for some people). What's more, the tune is irregular in its phrasing and does not always fit the text well. In "Whose broad stripes," for instance, assigning "broad" to a tiny sixteenth note is bad.

5   Finally, Francis Scott Key's poem (1914) is not suitable. It is of low quality as poetry, and its subject matter is too specific and too militaristic, dealing with a one-day incident in a war. Are glaring rockets and bursting bombs the essence of the nation? I wonder how many people have really read through all four stanzas and thought about the words. The third stanza is particularly offensive: "Their blood has wash'd out their foul footsteps' pollution./ No refuge could save the hireling and slave/ From the terror of flight or the gloom of the grave." When a bank celebrated the last Independence Day by buying a full page in the *New York Times* to print the tune and text of the anthem, not surprisingly the dreadful third stanza was entirely omitted. The poem has little to recommend it except for the single line, "The land of the free and the home of the brave."

6   Why not choose "America the Beautiful" in its place?

Consider, for a moment, why such a change might be resisted and the kinds of arguments that might be mounted in defense of retaining the present national anthem. Are virtually all such arguments examples of our attachment to cultural history?

Capital punishment is another kind of example. The death penalty for certain crimes (usually murders) has been defended and attacked so often that the arguments on both sides almost have become clichés. Virtually any audience will have been exposed to them before. Everyone has heard the argument that capital punishment deters people from committing murder (the deterrence argument), and everyone also knows the counterargument—that most murders are committed in the heat of passion when the part of the mind affected by deterrents is simply not in control. On and on go the arguments and counterarguments—from cruel and unusual punishment, unequal protection of the law (many more nonwhites and poor people are executed than whites and the wealthy), the likelihood of rehabilitation to the haunting possibility of executing the innocent. Death, as one anti–capital punishment argument reminds us, is so final.

Because everyone knows these arguments, the first obstacle you face may be *boredom*. Thus, unless you can find a fresh approach to the subject, you might be better off avoiding it. You might argue that the issues are far from settled. Recently, the Governor of Illinois suspended executions after investigations by a group from Northwestern University exonerated convicts on death row and revealed the incompetence of the attorneys who had been assigned to defend those facing capital charges. Public argument about the death penalty reminds us that even much-argued, familiar issues can become lively once again, particularly when new and disturbing evidence of its misuse emerges. Note that this is an illustration of the dynamics of persuasive arguments theory.

Another rhetorical obstacle that may lurk in a subject's history is a *taboo* against discussing it. Consider, for example, almost any subject having to do with sexuality in the United States, dramatically illustrated by public policy disputes over the prevention and treatment of AIDS (acquired immune deficiency syndrome). The virus causing AIDS is spread primarily through sexual contacts, and AIDS cases in the United States initially appeared predominantly among the gay male community. As a result, AIDS involved two areas considered taboo by many—sexual acts and homosexuality, and policy makers and physicians found it hard to discuss, and actions to enhance prevention and to improve treatment were adopted slowly. Even now, with more detailed information about AIDS all over the world and an increasing number of cases caused by heterosexual contacts, proposals to provide sex education in elementary schools and condoms to high school students in order to provide safer sex remain controversial. Despite a rising incidence of AIDS among African Americans, most churches that serve these communities have resisted supporting such programs because of strong religious taboos against homosexuality and public discussion of sexual behavior; recently, that is changing. Many of us seem to want to deny that teenagers or preteens are sexually active and find blatant reminders of their sexuality deeply disturbing, even when providing condoms that, if used, would protect them from sexually transmitted diseases and AIDS and lower rates of abortion by preventing unwanted pregnancies. Discussion of issues such as pornography, venereal disease, rape, incest, and wife-battering arouse resistance among some audiences. Some of these taboos are breaking down, the subjects are beginning to be aired, and the victims are beginning to get help. But if you talk about these subjects, you must choose your audiences and your words carefully, or minds will be so tightly closed against you that no rhetorical action can occur, not even the sharing of basic data.

The cultural history of a subject may also include *highly charged emotional reactions*. Most taboo subjects have such emotional loads. Arab-Israeli relations are highly charged subjects in Jewish and Arab communities; racism and its remedies, and homosexual rights generally or policies toward gays and lesbians in the military are hot-button issues in the United States. These topics produce intense emotional reactions in audiences. If you choose such a subject, you can expect to face several obstacles falling under the general headings of conditioned responses and closed minds.

One sure sign of a "hot" subject is to have a loaded slogan associated with it. In recent debates over legalized abortion in the United States, opponents have chanted "right to life." This slogan not only provokes a strong conditioned response and effectively closes minds to any discussion, but in any debate it puts the opponents in the position of defenders of life and the proponents of legalization in the position of murderers. Thus, proponents have been forced to come up with a slogan of their own, "pro-choice" (or sometimes "voluntary motherhood"), which moves the debate to different ground.

With any such emotionally loaded subject, your problem is to structure the discussion so issues can be treated apart from predictable and intense emotional responses—in short, to open closed minds, if only a little way.

Closely related to highly charged emotional reactions is the intense resistance created by subjects that are in conflict with revered cultural values. Anyone who chooses energy conservation as a subject will have to contend, for example, with the U.S. love affair with the automobile. Independence and personal autonomy have been ultimate goods in our culture for many decades; their value is part of our history. Bigger was better, greater speed and power were symbols of personal power and wealth, and driving bigger, faster, and more powerful cars and SUVs that used more gas was a symbol of success. Faced with rising gas prices, some now argue for a return to smaller cars; others argue that we should pressure OPEC to increase oil production, which would lower gas prices, and reduce the federal tax on gasoline to make it even more affordable. Others, of course argue for policies to encourage the construction and use of rapid transit systems. But until such energy-sensitive values establish themselves, efforts to persuade people to limit their energy consumption, to pollute less, and to protect the environment will run head-on into the value of independence and the long cultural history of the automobile as the symbol of success. And if minds are not actually closed to policies to conserve energy through lessening driving, they are certainly resistant, as reflected in today's rising sales of trucks, vans, and SUVs, most of which are gas guzzlers.

The second major set of rhetorical obstacles arising from your subject and purpose, then, lie in what I have called cultural history. Specifically, they are boredom, taboos, and emotional loads and the closed minds that can result, and conflicts with cultural values.

PURPOSE-RELATED OBSTACLES

As a rhetor, you will not just be dealing with a subject; you will also be trying to induce a certain kind of participation from the audience. The kind of response that you seek may create obstacles. The two kinds of obstacles that arise from rhetorical purposes are resistance to the *cost* of responding and audience perception that it has no *control* over the issue in question (audience members do not see themselves as agents of change).

Cost

Just what is the audience expected to do, and what is the cost in time, energy, money, inconvenience, or ridicule? The greater such costs to audience members, the smaller the chance that they will do what you ask. If you are typical college students, some of you smoke and few of you exercise enough, and many of you eat lots of junk food. In the face of medical evidence, no one argues that smoking is good for your health, that exercise is unnecessary, or that junk food will lengthen your life. Why, then, do so many Americans smoke, live sedentary lives, and eat junk food? The answer is that doing otherwise would cost them too much—too much agony or at least considerable discomfort to quit smoking, too much sustained thought and effort to fit exercise into their way of life, and too much loss of pleasure from withdrawal from butter-drenched popcorn and french fries. Thus, if your purpose is to change any one of these habits, you will meet solid obstacles in the form of the costs the audience sees in what you are suggesting. In fact, no single rhetorical act is likely to achieve this kind of purpose, although Americans are extremely vulnerable to advertising for products that promise that you can stop smoking without discomfort, exercise painlessly, or lose weight without changing eating habits. Smoking clinics, exercise programs, and diet groups that do succeed have long-term contact with participants and supply consistent support from people struggling with similar problems or toward similar goals.

Time is another cost that may obstruct your rhetorical purpose. It is much faster (and easier) to write a check to a political candidate than to telephone all the Democrats, Republicans, or Independents in a precinct; this telephoning, in turn, is easier than going door to door to distribute literature and discuss a candidate. The greater the time, the energy, or the commitment demanded by your purpose, the greater the resistance you will meet.

Still other costs may be involved in your purpose—costs in money and expertise. Your audience may not have to contribute either one directly but may feel the burden in other ways, such as higher taxes or smaller amounts of money or expertise available for other projects.

Finally, cost is closely related to cultural values; these are the social costs of some subjects and purposes. Some beliefs bring down ridicule and other social sanctions on the believers. Because all of us want to be liked and respected by our friends, neighbors, and family, a subject or purpose that would separate us exacts a cost that few are willing to pay, and then, only if the rewards are substantial. For example, nineteenth-century woman's rights activists recognized that what came to be called the "bloomer" costume was both healthy and comfortable. Its loose harem-style pants under knee-length skirts were far better for parenting or housework than fashionably long dresses whose skirts trailed in the dirt and weighed up to 20 pounds and whose narrow waists, cinched by stays, cut off breath and circulation. Yet even the most stalwart gave up the bloomer costume because the ridicule heaped on them was so consistent and so great that it threatened their cause. Similarly, it is hard for a Roman Catholic to espouse pro-choice on abortion, a car manufacturer to support rapid transit, or an evangelical Christian to endorse the Supreme Court decision outlawing prayer in public schools. There are exceptions, of course, but those who take such stances often pay a high social price.

The rhetorical problem of cost, then, measures the price the audience must pay in time, energy, inconvenience, and commitment, money and expertise, or social pressure for going along with your purpose. The more your purpose demands from the audience in such costs, the greater will be your rhetorical problem.

Control

The second obstacle arising from purpose I shall call *control*—that is, the audience's perception that it has at least some control over the outcome, whether or not its members believe they can effect changes. Obstacles arise when members of the audience cannot see what they as individuals can do, or do not believe that their actions will have any appreciable effect—in short, when they feel they have no control. Many Americans, for example, fail to vote because they think their votes make no difference—all politicians are alike, no one vote counts, they don't know how to nominate and elect officials who will do what they want, and so forth. Such feelings illustrate the rhetorical problem of control.

Lack of a sense of control can have other undesirable side effects. Some commentators, for example, have argued that because antiabortion activists have not been able to prevail through nonviolent tactics, some have come to accept violence, including the condoning of the murders or attempted murders of physicians who perform abortions. Deep commitment plus loss of control may lead to extremism.

Problems of control are closely related to problems of the audience—specifically, the audience as agents of change and as created through rhetorical action (see Chapter 8). If rhetors are to overcome obstacles to control, they must ensure that rhetorical action engages those who are or can be agents of change. But the obstacles to control that exist in the perceptions of the audience are difficult to overcome. How does one convince women who are socialized to passivity and deference that they should take the initiative? How does one counteract generations of social influence that has taught African American children that they are inferior and ugly? Given the presidential power to deploy hundreds of thousands of troops prior to the vote, how does one convince members of Congress to vote against an authorization to invade Haiti or Afghanistan or to defend Kuwait or Kosovo? The rhetorical efforts of politicians, religious leaders, protesters, and reporters writing and speaking on the "war on terrorism" are examples of attempts to overcome the obstacle of control or to empower the audience.

Obstacles related to control—and also to cost—exist for all audiences. It is easier to act once and be done with it than to commit yourself to a long-term course of action. If an audience feels unable to make a long-term commitment, it may refuse to act at all. Usually, it is easier to act alone than to organize a group. If a rhetorical act demands group action, individual audience members may not believe that others will join them in the effort. It is also easier to act if a problem is relatively limited and sharply defined than if the problem is complex and calls for varied and sustained actions.

Rhetorical obstacles arising from control are partly a function of the characteristics of the audience. If rhetors are to overcome problems of control, they must not only target the audience carefully, but they must also see that the target audience includes agents of change or those who can influence agents' decisions.

Obstacles arising from purpose are related to obstacles arising from the subject. For example, the problem of control will be greater if the issue is diffuse and complex, and if its ramifications are so great that achieving results requires the concerted and varied efforts of a large group of people over a long period of time.

MATERIAL FOR ANALYSIS

Elizabeth Cady Stanton (1815–1902) was the best known and most persistent advocate of woman's rights in the nineteenth century, with a career that began at the age of 25 and did not abate until she was 87. Even during her lifetime, she was called "the foremost American woman intellectual of her generation." Newspapers called her "America's Grand Old Woman" at the time of her death. She was the champion of a host of causes, including abolitionism, temperance, and labor reform, but most notably she was a crusading figure for woman's rights, broadly conceived. She was a founder of the American Equal Rights Association, the National Woman's Loyalty League, and the National Woman Suffrage Association. She was the first woman to run for the United States Congress.

Moreover, her speaking and writing output was prodigious. From 1869 to 1881, Cady Stanton lectured for the New York Lyceum Bureau, often traveling to 30 cities in six weeks and speaking once daily. Her fees of $3,000 per year gave her enough income to provide higher education for her seven children. Her oratory was described as "the fire of genius" delivered in a "soothing alto voice" of "unshakable conviction" with a "logical incisiveness that left audiences spellbound and somewhat intimidated." Her journalistic career began early with the writing of a regular column for *The Lily*. She became editor of *The Revolution* (1868–1870), assisted in editing the three volumes of *The History of Woman Suffrage* (1881, 1886), and edited and wrote parts of the controversial *The Woman's Bible* (1895, 1898).

"The Solitude of Self" was delivered by Cady Stanton three times over a three-day period, first to the House Committee on the Judiciary on January 18, 1892, then before the NAWSA convention on January 20, and finally to the Senate committee on woman suffrage later that day. The speech was reprinted in the *Woman's Journal* and the *Congressional Record*. It evoked intense reactions from all three audiences. Susan B. Anthony called it "the strongest and most unanswerable argument and appeal made by the pen or tongue for the full freedom and franchise of women." Frederick Douglass said: "After her—silence."[3]

The speech was indeed the climax of a career of advocacy that began at the first woman's rights convention at Seneca Falls in July of 1848, and it is unlike any other speech that she delivered. In her many appearances before state legislative committees and committees of the U.S. Congress, Cady Stanton argued forcefully and directly using all kinds of evidence and made powerful cases for woman's rights and the passage of a woman suffrage amendment. Legislators tired of hearing the same arguments, so this speech may have been an effort to respond to problems created by familiarity. Cady Stanton was 76 at the time of the speech, a well-known public advocate who had been described in the press a year earlier as "looking as if she should be the Lord Chief Justice with her white hair puffed all over her head, and her amiable and intellectual face marked with lines of wisdom."[4] The speech deals with high level abstractions; consider the strategies she uses to transform them into lived experience, and how she addresses members of her audience.

The Solitude of Self[5]

1 The point I wish plainly to bring before you on this occasion is the individuality of each human soul; our Protestant idea, the right of individual conscience and judgment; our republican idea, individual citizenship. In discussing the rights of woman, we are to consider, first, what belongs to her as an individual, in a world of her own, the arbiter of her own destiny, an imaginary Robinson Crusoe, with her woman Friday on a solitary island.[6] Her rights under such circumstances are to use all her faculties for her own safety and happiness.

2 Secondly, if we consider her as a citizen, as a member of a great nation, she must have the same rights as all other members, according to the fundamental principles of our government.

3 Thirdly, viewed as a woman, an equal factor in civilization, her rights and duties are still the same; individual happiness and development.

4 Fourthly, it is only the incidental relations of life, such as mother, wife, sister, daughter, that may involve some special duties and training. In the usual discussion in regard to woman's sphere, such men as Herbert Spencer, Frederick Harrison and Grant Allen, uniformly subordinate her rights and duties as an individual, as a citizen, as a woman, to the necessities of these incidental relations, neither of which a large class of women may ever assume. In discussing the sphere of man, we do not decide his rights as an individual, as a citizen, as a man, by his

duties as a father, a husband, a brother or a son, relations he may never fill. Moreover, he would be better fitted for these very relations, and whatever special work he might choose to do to earn his bread, by the complete development of all his faculties as an individual.

5   Just so with woman. The education that will fit her to discharge the duties in the largest sphere of human usefulness will best fit her for whatever special work she may be compelled to do.

6   The isolation of every human soul, and the necessity of self-dependence, must give each individual the right to choose his own surroundings.

7   The strongest reason for giving woman all the opportunities for higher education, for the full development of her faculties, forces of mind and body; for giving her the most enlarged freedom of thought and action; a complete emancipation from all forms of bondage, of custom, dependence, superstition; from all the crippling influences of fear—is the solitude and personal responsibility of her own individual life. The strongest reason why we ask for woman a voice in the government under which she lives; in the religion she is asked to believe; equality in social life, where she is the chief factor; a place in the trades and professions, where she may earn her bread, is because of her birthright to self-sovereignty; because, as an individual, she must rely on herself. No matter how much women prefer to lean, to be protected and supported, nor how much men desire to have them do so, they must make the voyage of life alone, and for safety in an emergency, they must know something of the laws of navigation. To guide our own craft, we must be captain, pilot, engineer; with chart and compass to stand at the wheel; to watch the winds and waves, and know when to take in the sail, and to read the signs in the firmament over all. It matters not whether the solitary voyager is man or woman; nature, having endowed them equally, leaves them to their own skill and judgment in the hour of danger, and, if not equal to the occasion, alike they perish.

8   To appreciate the importance of fitting every human soul for independent action, think for a moment of the *immeasurable* solitude of self. We come into the world alone, unlike all who have gone before us; we leave it alone, under circumstances peculiar to ourselves. No mortal ever has been, no mortal ever will be like the soul just launched on the sea of life. There can never again be just such a combination of prenatal influences; never again just such environments as make up the infancy, youth and manhood of this one. Nature never repeats herself, and the possibilities of one human soul will never be found in another. No one has ever found two blades of ribbon grass alike, and no one will ever find two human beings alike. Seeing, then, what must be the infinite diversity in human character, we can in a measure appreciate the loss to a nation when any large class of the people is uneducated and unrepresented in the government.

9   We ask for the complete development of every individual, first, for his own benefit and happiness. In fitting out an army, we give each soldier his own knapsack, arms, powder, his blanket, cup, knife, fork and spoon. We provide alike for all their individual necessities; then each man bears his own burden.

10   Again, we ask complete individual development for the general good; for the consensus of the competent on the whole round of human interests, on all questions of national life; and here each man must bear his share of the general burden. It is sad to see how soon friendless children are left to bear their own burdens, before they can analyze their feelings; before they can even tell their joys and sorrows, they are thrown on their own resources. The great lesson that nature

seems to teach us at all ages is self-dependence, self-protection, self-support. What a touching instance of a child's solitude, of that hunger of the heart for love and recognition, in the case of the little girl who helped to dress a Christmas tree for the children of the family in which she served. On finding there was no present for herself, she slipped away in the darkness and spent the night in a open field sitting on a stone, and when found in the morning was weeping as if her heart would break. No mortal will ever know the thoughts that passed through the mind of that friendless child in the long hours of that cold night, with only the silent stars to keep her company. The mention of her case in the daily papers moved many generous hearts to send her presents, but in the hours of her keenest suffering she was thrown wholly on herself for consolation.

11   In youth our most bitter disappointments, our brightest hopes and ambitions, are known only to ourselves. Even our friendship and love we never fully share with another; there is something of every passion, in every situation, we conceal. Even so in our triumphs and our defeats. The successful candidate for the presidency, and his opponent, each has a solitude peculiarly his own, and good form forbids either to speak of his pleasure or regret. The solitude of the king on his throne and the prisoner in his cell differs in character and degree, but it is solitude, nevertheless.

12   We ask no sympathy from others in the anxiety and agony of a broken friendship or shattered love. When death sunders our nearest ties, alone we sit in the shadow of our affliction. Alike amid the greatest triumphs and darkest tragedies of life, we walk alone. On the divine heights of human attainment, eulogized and worshipped as a hero or a saint, we stand alone. In ignorance, poverty and vice, as a pauper or criminal, alone we starve or steal; alone we suffer the sneers and rebuffs of our fellows; alone we are hunted and hounded through dark courts and alleys, in by-ways and highways; alone we stand in the judgment seat; alone in the prison cell we lament our crimes and misfortunes; alone we expiate them on the gallows. In hours like these we realize the awful solitude of individual life, its pains, its penalties, its responsibilities; hours in which the youngest and most helpless are thrown on their own resources for guidance and consolation. Seeing, then, that life must ever be a march and a battle, that each soldier must be equipped for his own protection, it is the height of cruelty to rob the individual of a single natural right.

13   To throw obstacles in the way of a complete education is like putting out the eyes; to deny the rights of property, like cutting off the hands. To deny political equality is to rob the ostracized of all self-respect; of credit in the market place; of recompense in the world of work; of a voice in those who make and administer the law; a choice in the jury before whom they are tried, and in the judge who decides their punishment. Shakespeare's play of "Titus Andronicus" contains a terrible satire on woman's position in the 19th century. Rude men (the play tells us) seized the king's daughter, cut out her tongue, cut off her hands, and then bade her go call for water and wash her hands.[7] What a picture of woman's position! Robbed of her natural rights, handicapped by law and custom at every turn, yet compelled to fight her own battles, and in the emergencies of life to fall back on herself for protection.

14   The girl of sixteen, thrown on the world to support herself, to make her own place in society, to resist the temptations that surround her and maintain a spotless integrity, must do all this by native force or superior education. She does

not acquire this power by being trained to trust others and distrust herself. If she wearies of the struggle, finding it hard work to swim up stream, and allows herself to drift with the current, she will find plenty of company, but not one to share her misery in the hour of her deepest humiliation. If she tries to retrieve her position, to conceal the past, her life is hedged about with fears lest willing hands should tear the veil from what she fain would hide. Young and friendless, she knows the bitter solitude of self.

15   How the little courtesies of life on the surface of society, deemed so important from man towards woman, fade into utter insignificance in view of the deeper tragedies in which she must play her part alone, where no human aid is possible!

16   The young wife and mother, at the head of some establishment, with a kind husband to shield her from the adverse winds of life, with wealth, fortune and position, has a certain harbor of safety, secure against the ordinary ills of life. But to manage a household, have a desirable influence in society, keep her friends and the affections of her husband, train her children and servants well, she must have rare common sense, wisdom, diplomacy, and a knowledge of human nature. To do all this, she needs the cardinal virtues and the strong points of character that the most successful statesman possesses. An uneducated woman trained to dependence, with no resources in herself, must make a failure of any position in life. But society says women do not need a knowledge of the world, the liberal training that experience in public life must give, all the advantages of collegiate education; but when for the lack of all this, the woman's happiness is wrecked, alone she bears her humiliation; and the solitude of the weak and the ignorant is indeed pitiable. In the wild chase for the prizes of life, they are ground to powder.

17   In age, when the pleasures of youth are past, children grown up, married and gone, the hurry and bustle of life in a measure over, when the hands are weary of active service, when the old arm chair and the fireside are the chosen resorts, then men and women alike must fall back on their own resources. If they cannot find companionship in books, if they have no interest in the vital questions of the hour, no interest in watching the consummation of reforms with which they might have been identified, they soon pass into their dotage. The more fully the faculties of the mind are developed and kept in use, the longer the period of vigor and active interest in all around us continues. If, from a long-life participation in public affairs, a woman feels responsible for the laws regulating our system of education, the discipline of our jails and prisons, the sanitary condition of our private homes, public buildings and thoroughfares, an interest in commerce, finance, our foreign relations, in any or all these questions, her solitude will at least be respectable, and she will not be driven to gossip or scandal for entertainment.

18   The chief reason for opening to every soul the doors to the whole round of human duties and pleasures is the individual development thus attained, the resources thus provided under all circumstances to mitigate the solitude that at times must come to everyone. I once asked Prince Kropotkin, a Russian Nihilist,[8] how he endured his long years in prison, deprived of books, pen, ink and paper. "Ah!" said he, "I thought out many questions in which I had a deep interest. In the pursuit of an idea, I took no note of time. When tired of solving knotty problems, I recited all the beautiful passages in prose and verse I had ever learned. I became acquainted with myself, and my own resources. I had a world of my own, a vast empire, that no Russian jailer or Czar could invade." Such is the value of liberal

thought and broad culture, when shut off from all human companionship, bringing comfort and sunshine within even the four walls of a prison cell.

19   As women often times share a similar fate, should they not have all the consolation that the most liberal education can give? Their suffering in the prisons of St. Petersburg; in the long weary marches to Siberia, and in the mines, working side by side with men, surely call for all the self-support that the most exalted sentiments of heroism can give. When suddenly roused at midnight, with the startling cry of "Fire!" "Fire!" to find the house over their heads in flames, do women wait for men to point the way to safety? And are the men, equally bewildered, and half suffocated with smoke, in a position to do more than try to save themselves? At such times the most timid women have shown a courage and heroism, in saving their husbands and children, that has surprised everybody.

20   Inasmuch, then, as woman shares equally the joys and sorrows of time and eternity, is it not the height of presumption in man to propose to represent her at the ballot box and the throne of grace, to do her voting in the State, her praying in the church, and to assume the position of High Priest at the family altar?

21   Nothing strengthens the judgment and quickens the conscience like individual responsibility; nothing adds such dignity to character as the recognition of one's self-sovereignty; the right to an equal place, everywhere conceded; a place earned by personal merit, not artificial attainment by inheritance, wealth, family and position. Seeing, then, that the responsibilities of life rest equally on man and woman, that their destiny is the same, they need the same preparation for time and eternity. The talk of sheltering woman from the fierce storms of life is the sheerest mockery, for they beat on her from every point of the compass, just as they do on man, and with more fatal results, for he has been trained to protect himself, to resist, and to conquer. Such are the facts in human experience, the responsibilities of individual sovereignty. Rich and poor, intelligent and ignorant, wise and foolish, virtuous and vicious, man and woman; it is ever the same, each soul must depend wholly on itself.

22   Whatever the theories may be of woman's dependence on man, in the supreme moments of her life, he cannot bear her burdens. Alone she goes to the gates of death to give life to every man that is born into the world; no one can share her fears, no one can mitigate her pangs; and if her sorrow is greater than she can bear, alone she passes beyond the gates into the vast unknown.

23   From the mountain-tops of Judea long ago, a heavenly voice bade his disciples, "Bear ye one another's burdens"; but humanity has not yet risen to that point of self-sacrifice; and if ever so willing, how few the burdens are that one soul can bear for another! In the highways of Palestine; in prayer and fasting on the solitary mountain-top; in the Garden of Gethsemane; before the judgment-seat of Pilate, betrayed by one of his trusted disciples at his last supper; in his agonies on the cross, even Jesus of Nazareth, in those last sad days on earth, felt the awful solitude of self. Deserted by man, in agony he cries, "My God, my God, why hast thou forsaken me?" And so it ever must be in the conflicting scenes of life, in the long, weary march, each one walks alone. We may have many friends, love, kindness, sympathy and charity, to smooth our pathway in everyday life, but in the tragedies and triumphs of human experience, each mortal stands alone.

24   But when all artificial trammels are removed, and women are recognized as individuals, responsible for their own environments, thoroughly educated for all positions in life they may be called to fill; with all the resources in themselves that

liberal thought and broad culture can give; guided by their own conscience and judgment, trained to self-protection, by a healthy development of the muscular system, and skill in the use of weapons of defence; and stimulated to self-support by a knowledge of the business world and the pleasure that pecuniary independence must ever give; when women are trained in this way, they will in a measure be fitted for those hours of solitude that come alike to all, whether prepared or otherwise. As in our extremity we must depend on ourselves, the dictates of wisdom point to complete individual development.

25   In talking of education, how shallow the argument that each class must be educated for the special work it proposes to do, and that all those faculties not needed in this special walk must lie dormant and utterly wither for want of use, when, perhaps, these will be the very faculties needed in life's greatest emergencies! Some say, Where is the use of drilling girls in the languages, the sciences, in law, medicine, theology? As wives, mothers, housekeepers, cooks, they need a different curriculum from boys who are to fill all positions. The chief cooks in our great hotels and ocean steamers are men. In our large cities, men run the bakeries; they make our bread, cake and pies. They manage the laundries; they are now considered our best milliners and dressmakers. Because some men fill these departments of usefulness, shall we regulate the curriculum in Harvard and Yale to their present necessities? If not, why this talk in our best colleges of a curriculum for girls who are crowding into the trades and professions, teachers in all our public schools, rapidly filling many lucrative and honorable positions in life?

26   They are showing, too, their calmness and courage in the most trying hours of human experience. You have probably all read in the daily papers of the terrible storm in the Bay of Biscay, when a tidal wave made such havoc on the shore, wrecking vessels, unroofing houses, and carrying destruction everywhere. Among other buildings, the woman's prison was demolished. Those who escaped saw men struggling to reach the shore. They promptly, by clasping their hands, made a chain of themselves, and pushed out into the sea, again and again, at the risk of their lives, until they had brought six men to shore, carried them to a shelter, and done all in their power for their comfort and protection.

27   What special school training could have prepared these women for this sublime moment in their lives? In times like this, humanity rises above all college curriculums, and recognizes nature as the greatest of all teachers in the hour of danger and death. Women are already the equals of men in the whole realm of thought, in art, science, literature and government. With telescopic vision they explore the starry firmament and bring back the history of the planetary spheres. With chart and compass they pilot ships across the mighty deep, and with skilful fingers send electric messages around the world. In galleries of art the beauties of nature and virtues of humanity are immortalized by them on canvas, and by their inspired touch dull blocks of marble are transformed into angels of light. In music they speak again in the language of Mendelssohn, Beethoven, Chopin, Schumann, and are worthy interpreters of their great thoughts. The poetry and novels of the century are theirs, and they have touched the keynote of reform, in religion, politics and social life. They fill the editor's and professor's chair, and plead at the bar of justice; walk the wards of the hospital, and speak from the pulpit and the platform. Such is the type of womanhood that an enlightened public sentiment welcomes today, and such the triumph of the facts of life over the false theories of the past.

28   Is it, then, consistent to hold the developed woman of this day within the same narrow political limits as the dame with the spinning-wheel and knitting-needle occupied in the past? No! No! Machinery has taken the labors of woman, as well as man, on its tireless shoulders, the loom and the spinning-wheel are but dreams of the past; the pen, the brush, the easel, the chisel, have taken their places, while the hopes and ambitions of women are essentially changed.

29   We see reason sufficient in the outer conditions of human beings for individual liberty and development, but when we consider the self-dependence of every human soul we see the need of courage, judgment and the exercise of every faculty of mind and body, strengthened and developed by use, in woman as well as man.

30   Whatever may be said of man's protecting power in ordinary conditions, amid all the terrible disasters by land and sea, in the supreme moments of danger, alone woman must ever meet the horrors of the situation. The Angel of Death even makes no royal pathway for her. Man's love and sympathy enter only into the sunshine of our lives. In that solemn solitude of self, that links us with the immeasurable and the eternal, each soul lives alone forever. A recent writer says:

> I remember once, in crossing the Atlantic, to have gone upon the deck of the ship at midnight, when a dense black cloud enveloped the sky, and the great deep was roaring madly under the lashes of demoniac winds. My feeling was not of danger or fear (which is a base surrender of the immortal soul) but of utter desolation and loneliness; a little speck of life shut in by a tremendous darkness. Again I remember to have climbed the slopes of the Swiss Alps, up beyond the point where vegetation ceases, and the stunted conifers no longer struggle against the unfeeling blasts. Around me lay a huge confusion of rocks, out of which the gigantic ice peaks shot into the measureless blue of the heavens; and again my only feeling was the awful solitude.

And yet, there is a solitude which each and every one of us has always carried with him, more inaccessible than the ice-cold mountains, more profound than the midnight sea; the solitude of self. Our inner being which we call our self, no eye nor touch of man or angel has ever pierced. It is more hidden than the caves of the gnome; the sacred adytum of the oracle; the hidden chamber of Eleusinian mystery,[9] for to it only Omniscience is permitted to enter.

31   Such is individual life. Who, I ask you, can take, dare take on himself the rights, the duties, the responsibilities of another human soul?

Questions for Analysis

1. Of the four subject/purpose obstacles (complexity, cultural history, cost, and control), which plague Cady Stanton's speech? How?
2. Omission is sometimes a strategy to combat a subject or purpose related obstacle. Why do you think Stanton never mentions the words "woman suffrage," "the vote," and "a federal amendment" or other policy language?
3. How does Stanton use evidence to appeal to her audience on psychological grounds? What audience and subject obstacles does she help combat with these evidentiary choices?
4. What resources of language give this speech its haunting tone? Which contribute to its purpose of altering perception? What language strategy dominates the speech and why is this effective?

5. Why do you suppose there is no proper introduction or conclusion to this speech? What does this violation of structure say about the nature of the target audience?

EXERCISES

1. In the passages below, identify the most likely subject/purpose obstacles (choose from complexity, cultural history, cost, control):
   a. You have been given six minutes to summarize for your introductory economics class the difference between preferred stock and common stock.
   b. As coordinator of the athletic department, you have been asked to approach local alumni for significant (six figures) financial contributions to the program.
   c. As the public relations coordinator for Planned Parenthood, you are launching a community information campaign in a predominantly Catholic neighborhood on a form of birth control, Norplant, now available at your clinic.

2. The class is divided into two groups. One group prepares a list of topics that they consider most of their classmates would find uninteresting, such as technical or specialized subjects. The other group prepares a list of topics that they think will arouse intense hostility from two or more class members, such as highly controversial issues. Each group should compose three or four introductions for their list of topics to be presented by speakers designated by the group.

   The introductions for the uninteresting topics should seek to arouse interest, perhaps by presenting a novel point of view, a startling fact, or the like. However, the subject of the speech should be clear to the audience from the introduction.

   The introductions for the highly controversial topics should seek to gain a fair and open hearing for a disliked point of view, perhaps by an appeal to self-interest or to the threat of biased or limited exposure, or the like. The controversial point of view should be clear to the audience from the introduction.

   Present the introductions from each group. Discuss the strategies that were used, and suggest other possibilities. Discuss which approaches seemed to be more effective, and why.

3. Fisher and Ury, authors of *Getting to Yes*,[10] argue that getting past difficult subjects requires reconciling interests, not positions. "Interests motivate people; they are the silent movers behind the hubbub of positions" (41). Reconciling interests rather than positions works because for every interest there are usually several positions that could satisfy it and behind opposing positions lie more interests than conflicting ones. Identify a subject that creates an impasse for you and your parents, spouse, or significant other. Share these tips with them and see if together you can negotiate a truce when you discuss the subject. How difficult is it to follow this advice?

4. Locate the article "Writing About the Dead Is a Touchy Subject to Many" (*Sarasota Herald Tribune*, January 13, 2002, p. BS3) in the InfoTrac College Edition database. According to the authors, there are "strict taste rules" to guide writing on death-related subjects. Using InfoTrac College Edition, find articles on the euthanasia debate. How is the discourse on death managed in those articles? Is such discourse similar to or different from the one identified by the authors of the *Sarasota Herald* article? Why? What cultural beliefs related to death surface from these articles?

5. **Portfolio Entry 8: Subject Obstacles**
   Identify and explain the subject and purpose obstacles that plague your rhetorical acts. What, if anything, do the rhetors do to combat these obstacles? Use relevant elements of descriptive analysis to discuss their strategic choices in two pages.

NOTES

1. Bill McKibben, "A Special Moment in History," *Atlantic Monthly*, May 1998.

2. Reprinted by permission of *The New Republic*, December 18, 1985, pp. 11–12. The author was a professor of music at Brandeis University. © 1985 The New Republic, LLC.

3. See Karlyn Kohrs Campbell's works: *Man Cannot Speak for Her: A Critical Study of Early Feminist Rhetoric*, vol. 1 (New York: Praeger, 1989); "Elizabeth Cady Stanton: Woman's Rights Philosopher, Speaker, and Writer," In *Women Public Speakers in the United States: 1800–1925* (Westport, CT: Greenwood Press, 1993), pp. 76–88; Susan Schultz Huxman, "Perfecting the Rhetorical Vision of Woman's Rights: Elizabeth Cady Stanton, Anna Howard Shaw, and Carrie Chapman Catt," *Women's Studies in Communication* 23, no. 3 (Fall 2000): 307–336.

4. Blanche Glassman Hersh, *The Slavery of Sex: Feminist Abolitionists in America* (Urbana: University of Illinois Press, 1978), p. 103.

5. The text is from *The Woman's Journal,* January 23, 1892, pp. 1 and 32.

6. This is an allusion to Daniel Defoe's novel, a fictionalized version of the story of Andrew Selkirk. In the editor's introduction to *Race-ing Justice, Engendering Power,* Toni Morrison offers a powerful critique of the role of Friday in this novel, a critique that is useful in discussing the racism this allusion may reflect.

7. Lavinia, the character to whom she refers, also was raped. Act 2.4.

8. Piotr (Peter) Alekseyevich Kropotkin (1842–1921) was a Russian anarchist, imprisoned in Russia; he escaped; imprisoned later in France, then freed, he became a popular lecturer.

9. A venerated part of Greek religion that was part of the worship of Demeter (Kore-Persephone), a mother–goddess; they have remained mysteries to this day.

10. Roger Fisher and William Ury, *Getting to Yes: Negotiating Agreement Without Giving In* (New York: Viking Penguin: 1991).

chapter 10

Obstacles Arising from the Rhetor

I deas do not walk by themselves; they must be carried—expressed and voiced—by someone. As a result, we do not encounter ideas neutrally, objectively, apart from a context; we meet them as *someone's* ideas. The relationship between people and ideas is reflected in the way we talk. We speak of the Elizabethan or Victorian Ages to refer to the periods dominated by the ideas and the leadership of those reigning British monarchs. Similarly, we tend to link qualities to people; for example, particularly courageous women reformers such as abolitionist and woman's rights advocate Anna E. Dickinson and antilynching activist Ida B. Wells were each referred to as a "Joan of Arc." Early advocates of woman suffrage heightened the appeal of the woman suffrage amendment by calling it the "Susan B. Anthony Amendment," and when the equal rights amendment was first introduced in 1923, activists followed the earlier precedent by calling it the "Lucretia Mott Amendment" to link it to that intrepid Quaker activist who advocated abolition of slavery, peace, woman's rights, and separation of church and state. Even though science is popularly regarded as impersonal, we speak of Darwin's theory of evolution, Einstein's theory of relativity, Heisenberg's uncertainty principle, and curies of radioactivity (named for Nobel-Prize winning chemist Marie Sklodowska Curie). Such language reflects what we all know—that ideas are linked to individuals and that an idea as carried by one person is not the same idea when it is interpreted and defined by another.

The importance of the rhetor in the persuasive process has been recognized since people first began to think and write about the discipline of rhetoric. In the treatise on rhetoric he wrote in the fourth century B.C.E., Aristotle described three paths through which ideas were made persuasive for an audience. One of these he called *ethos,* the character of the rhetor:

> [There is persuasion] through character whenever the speech is spoken in such a way as to make the speaker worthy of credence; for we believe fair-minded people to a greater extent and more quickly [than we do others] on all subjects in general and completely so in cases where there is not exact knowledge but room for doubt. . . . character is almost, so to speak, the controlling factor in persuasion. (1.2.1356a.4)[1]

In other words, one way we are influenced is through our impressions of the rhetor—we accept the idea or believe the claim because we trust and respect the person who presents it. Moreover, says Aristotle, this is particularly true of rhetoric because it deals with social truths, what people in groups agree to believe and value, where certainty is impossible and controversy is likely. Aristotle even suggests that the character of the rhetor may be the most potent source of influence, even more powerful than the arguments and evidence or the needs and motives of the audience!

The power of the rhetor's character or ethos becomes more understandable if we comprehend the meaning of the ancient term. *Ethos* is a Greek word that is closely related to our terms *ethical* and *ethnic.* In its widest modern usage, ethos refers, not to the character or personality of an individual, but to "the disposition, character, or attitude peculiar to a specific people, culture, or group that distinguishes it from other peoples or groups."[2] When understood this way, its relationship to the word *ethnic* is obvious, for ethnic means "characteristic of a religious, racial, national, or cultural group." In other words, ethos refers to the distinctive culture of an ethnic group, and the ethos of an individual depends on how well she or he reflects the qualities valued in that culture. Put differently, your ethos does not refer to your idiosyncrasies or peculiarities as an individual but to the ways in which you mirror the characteristics idealized by your culture or group. Similarly, *ethics* is "the study of the . . . specific moral choices to be made by the individual in his [or her] relationship with others." In other words, we judge the character of another by the choices that person makes about how he or she will live with other members of the community. What is ethical is right conduct in relation to other persons in one's community or society. Ethical principles are the norms or values in a culture that describe what its members believe are the right relationships between persons. The ethos of a rhetor refers to the relationship between the rhetor and the community as reflected in rhetorical action.

When he described what contributed to the ethos of a rhetor in a rhetorical act, Aristotle wrote that it arose from demonstrated wisdom about social truths (*phronêsis*), from excellence or competence (*aretê*), and from evidence that rhetors were well-intentioned (*eunoia*) toward their communities. In other words, he believed that members of the community were influenced by evidence of good sense on practical matters of concern to the community, by indications of the rhetor's ability or expertise, and by manifestations that the rhetor had the best interests of the community, not just self-interest, in mind. In more contemporary terms, your good sense or common sense is a measure of one kind of expertise or competence on an issue, your excellence is a measure of your ability or skill (based on competence and expertise), and your goodwill is a measure of your concern for the community's interests not just how much you or your family and friends will gain.

Consider how these concepts have affected attitudes toward recent presidents. Carter, for example, is viewed as a person of high moral principle and considerable expertise as an engineer who is dedicated to the good of others. Despite his high intelligence, his wisdom on social matters came to be doubted as he fumbled efforts to influence members of Congress, and later diplomatic efforts in North Korea and Haiti in 1994 were questioned for similar reasons, a sense that he is too trusting of those whose past behavior raises doubts. Ronald Reagan was seen as someone well intentioned toward the community, but, especially in retrospect, as a man who lacked social wisdom, particularly in delegating too much to subordinates, illustrated by the problems that arose in relation to what is called the Iran-Contra affair. Bill Clinton is seen as a man of great intellectual ability and charisma but someone prone to moral lapses.

Modern research has demonstrated that Aristotle's views of ethos were remarkably apt. In contemporary studies, ethos is usually defined as the attitude a member of the audience has toward the rhetor (the source of the message) at any given moment. Experimental studies demonstrate that the source of the message has considerable effect on its impact. The earliest studies compared the effects of messages attributed to different sources, and they found that sources with high prestige for an audience had a significantly greater effect. Thus, for example, similar audiences were more favorable toward a message supporting group health care when it came from the Surgeon-General of the United States than when it was attributed to a university sophomore. Studies like these focused on *prior ethos*, or the attitude that members of the audience have toward the rhetor (the source) before the rhetorical act. Note, however, that ethos is affected by elements of the rhetorical problem. When the original surgeon-general's report on the harmful effects of smoking first appeared in 1964, for example, it had little immediate impact on behavior. The decrease in smokers in the United States from over 46 percent of the population to under 25 percent at present has occurred slowly. Moreover, no decline has occurred in the percentages of teenagers who smoke despite increasing evidence of its dangers.

PRIOR ETHOS

Attitudes toward the rhetor prior to the rhetorical act originate in five areas:

1. The rhetor's reputation or track record
2. The rhetor's appearance
3. How the rhetor is introduced to the audience
4. The context in which the rhetorical act occurs
5. The occasion of the rhetorical act

Because the attitude of the audience toward the source is so important, it is worth noting how each of these can create problems (Figure 10–1).

Reputation

Although you may not be famous, you have a reputation and a track record that can be as troublesome as that of a famous athlete, politician, or scholar. Two stories about the problems that Jesus had in his hometown of Nazareth are illustrative. On one occasion, Jesus went home and preached in his local synagogue. According to the reports in

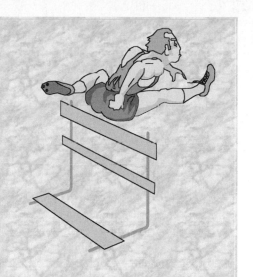

Figure 10–1
*Rhetor-Related
Rhetorical
Obstacles*

■ **Rhetor-Related
Obstacles**

- prior ethos
  - ■ reputation, appearance,
    introduction, occasion,
    context
- ethos from the
  rhetorical act
  - ■ expertise,
    trustworthiness,
    dynamism,
    identification

three gospels, he did a superb job, but those in his local community were not impressed. In effect, his neighbors asked how a local boy could know and do such things—wasn't this the carpenter's son, the son of Mary, whose brothers and sisters they knew? They were offended that an ordinary person from their community should preach and teach so. When Jesus heard what they said, he responded, "A prophet is not without honor, except in his own country, and in his own house" (Matthew 13:54–58; Mark 6:1–6; Luke 4:16–24).

It is quite likely that, as in this story, you will initiate rhetorical action in your local community or in a place in which you are personally known well. One of my students reported a difficult and embarrassing experience he had when he returned from a year of study abroad and was asked to speak at a convocation at his high school. As he walked to the podium, his friends laughed. This was little Andy Smith with whom they had grown up. What could he know about the world? The student described his struggle to gain attention and to be taken seriously, and he admitted that he never quite succeeded. As his story illustrates, you face a serious rhetorical problem when you try to establish your competence to speak to an audience in your local community, club, place of work, or neighborhood.

The second story is similar. The Gospel of John describes the process by which Jesus chose his disciples. One of them, Philip, tells another man, Nathaniel, how wonderful Jesus is. But Nathaniel responds, "Can any good thing come out of Nazareth?" And Philip answers, "Come and see" (John 1:46). Many of us come from places that, like Nazareth, are unknown and undistinguished. (One of the authors grew up on a small farm near Blomkest, Minnesota, a metropolis of some 147 residents.) Audiences may well ask, How can someone from a little town in Minnesota know anything about rhetoric or criticism or the analysis of discourse? In other words, when you are outside your local community you will have the problem of establishing your credentials and of convincing audiences that people from unusual places or small places or unknown places or places with bad reputations do have the knowledge to discuss an important subject.

Both ordinary and famous persons encounter another problem—the difficulties that arise from inconsistent behavior. We trust those whose behavior demonstrates a systematic commitment to principles, and we are wary of those who make dramatic shifts of position. For example, some doubted Manuel Noriega's conversion to Christianity because of his record of highly unethical and ruthless actions as head of the Panamanian government. Such skeptics view his conversion (a word that literally means a turnaround) as a calculated decision to appear repentant and to lessen his punishment. But if he continues to behave as a Christian would, he may confound the skeptics and convince some, at least, that this was a sincere change of heart. Your track record as a rhetor (what you have said in the past) and as a citizen (what you have done on social issues) are analogous to your driving record or credit record. Just as you will pay higher insurance premiums if you've had accidents, or have difficulties getting credit if you have not paid your bills in the past, as a rhetor you must make a greater effort if your past statements or your past actions cast doubt on your sincerity or commitment. If what you urge appears to conflict with your past record, you will encounter a serious rhetorical problem.

In rare instances, however, deviation from the past can be an asset. When a person deviates from a lifetime of commitments, his or her message is important and becomes informed criticism by an insider. Not long ago former U.S. Ambassador to the Soviet Union George Kennan said, "It is hard to understand how the Soviet system could produce a man such as Mikhail Gorbachev." As a result, Europeans and Americans found his actions opening up the Soviet Union to change and allowing divergent opinions particularly noteworthy and credible. Such action is called *reluctant testimony* because it is given reluctantly, against one's apparent interests. In such a case, inconsistency—deviation from what would be expected—can create positive ethos.

Appearance

Research that has been done on how humans form impressions of others indicates that we make initial decisions about an individual in a matter of seconds based on clothing, movement, posture, and facial expressions. Obviously, if the appearance of the rhetor (or of her or his discourse) creates negative impressions in the audience, an obstacle has been created that the rhetor must overcome to be heard, much less to influence. As a result, I believe that rhetors need to make careful choices about appearance. All of us are many different people or, if you will, we play many different roles.

Depending on the audience and occasion, rhetors try to adopt a persona that will create the least resistance in an audience. If a professor talks to students in a dormitory lounge about a film on the history of woman's rights such as *The Emerging Woman*, on a weekday evening, she would be wise to wear a favorite pair of jeans and a comfortable shirt, sit casually on the floor, and talk informally. If she speaks at a scholarship dinner at a sorority, she would be wise to wear a favorite fashionable outfit, stand straight, and speak more formally. If she moderates a debate before students, faculty, and townspeople between a local feminist and a psychiatrist on the one hand and a gay rights leader and a psychologist on the other, she would be wise to wear neat, relatively unobtrusive clothes and speak, stand, and move with an authority and formality that bespeaks a desire to be fair. Recognize that the professor is all of these people—these are not false fronts that she puts on. But if they are shifted around, problems will arise. If she is formal in the dorm lounge, students will not feel free to talk easily and ask questions. If she is casual at the sorority, its members will feel that she is not doing honor to the occasion and will be offended. If she goes casually to the debate, her dress will be taken as a visual sign of favoring one side, and she will be suspected of bias.

Appearance is less of an issue for writers, although the different looks of student papers also create impressions. A paper written in pencil suggests a first draft, not a finished product. Handwriting that is hard to decipher suggests a rather casual approach and minimal concern for the reader. Numerous spelling and typing errors suggest that the author didn't care enough to proofread; malapropisms, such as a "feudal attempt" that was not "worth wild" call your command of your subject into question; tiny margins suggest a refusal to edit down to the specified length. It is no accident that those who make presentations in person or on paper in commercial situations try hard to have them look as professional as possible—reports are in sleek covers, nicely bound, and professionally printed; visual aids are large, printed, and colorful. The impression created is of careful planning, great concern for the result, and considerable care for the comfort of the audience.

The special styles of some famous writers illustrate the impact of the visual. African American feminist bell hooks, for example, uses no capital letters in the name that she writes under, and her decision affects the way one interprets her words and imagines her persona. Some imagist poets laid out their work to make the visual form resemble the content. Most poetry is laid out in a special kind of format, which facilitates how one understands it, although it may make it harder to read well aloud. Most newspapers have shifted to a six- instead of an eight-column layout, for example, to make reading them easier, and most have now introduced color in photographs and in some areas of print and advertising.

As an alert and sensitive rhetor, you must consider the demands of the situation, the subject, and the audience. You must consider which look is most appropriate and choose from your repertoire of selves so that you will not create unnecessary obstacles that prevent your message from reaching the audience or that violate the occasion. Unless you are making a rhetorical point, as activists sometimes wish to do, you should choose a style of dress, posture, and speech that is appropriate to the occasion and the subject, and one that will not prevent the audience from approaching your speech with interest and a willingness to listen. Note that such choices should be closely related to the persona or role that you adopt in your speech.

Your Introduction

The famous French philosopher Jean-Paul Sartre commented that one of the terrifying things about human life is that when we die, our lives become the property of others to do with as they will. If you have listened to the eulogies given at funerals you will understand how frightening that can be. In a less permanent but no less fearful way, the rhetor's ethos becomes the property of the person who introduces her or him to the audience, and a potential rhetorical problem is in the making. The person who introduces you creates the climate in which you will begin to speak and can be significant in determining the initial attitude of the audience. Consider carefully what you would like to have said about yourself, and if the introducer asks you, be sure to be prepared to tell her or him. Similarly, when you introduce someone else, think about the climate you will create. A really thoughtful introducer tells the rhetor what she or he plans to say or write and asks if the rhetor would like any changes or additions. You, as a rhetor, will not be able to control all the possible problems that may arise, but you need to be aware of them.

The Context

Our initial impressions of a rhetor are influenced by context. We are likely to assume, until contrary evidence appears, that those whose articles appear on the op-ed page of the *New York Times* are knowledgeable and interesting and that those who write for *Ms.* are feminist experts in some aspect of life of particular significance for women. In such cases, and in many others, audiences will form initial impressions from the process by which you came to be speaking or writing at this time or in this place. Although you may be totally unknown, you will have positive prior ethos if you participate in the DePauw University Undergraduate Honors Conference because participants are selected competitively. If a well-liked member of a sorority invites her professor to speak at a scholarship dinner, the audience, to whom the professor is unknown, will probably assume that she is a professor who is often dynamic and interesting and who may be so on this occasion.

The context can also create a significant problem, however. Perhaps the most famous example of this involves the circumstances under which Henry Grady made a speech entitled "The New South" at a dinner of the New England society in New York City in 1886. Grady was a newspaper editor from Georgia, and he was the first Southerner to speak before this group after the Civil War. He wanted to convince his audience that there was a new South developing with which New Englanders and Northerners generally could form an economic partnership. But imagine his rhetorical problem when it turned out that the speaker who preceded him was none other than General William Tecumseh Sherman, who was famous for his ruthless march through Georgia, and who gave a speech that was most unsympathetic to the South! The introduction to Grady's speech is found below in the Materials for Analysis.

The Occasion

Still other difficulties can arise from the event of which a rhetorical act is a part. Every rhetorical act is limited by the occasion, by the kind of happening or place in which it occurs. Effective rhetorical action, which reaches the audience, must be appropriate to its context. The problem of the rhetor is to select a purpose that is consistent both with her or his beliefs and desires and with the time and place in which it occurs. Think for a moment about inappropriate rhetorical acts you have experienced, such as a commencement address on research into dread diseases that featured a large visual of a diseased tonsil, a highly partisan political speech given in a campus chapel service that was so offensive that about half the students finally walked out. Just as audiences have purposes (the needs they wish to satisfy), occasions have functions or purposes, and an effective rhetorical act must be consonant with that purpose. If the purpose of the occasion is entertainment, your rhetorical act must be entertaining—among other things, perhaps. If the purpose of the occasion is to do honor, your act must be consistent. So important is the understanding of the demands that occasions create, I treat it in more depth as a "special constraint" on rhetorical action in Chapter 14.

The rhetor is limited by the context of the occasion, and a rhetorical problem arises if the rhetor's purpose is not consistent with that of the occasion. Note that in the materials below both Henry Grady and Ida B. Wells work hard to make their discourses fit the occasion.

Rhetorical problems may arise even before the rhetor begins to produce a message. These may arise from your past, from your appearance or the role you choose to play, from the way in which you are introduced to the audience, and from a conflict between your purpose and the purpose of the occasion.

ETHOS FROM THE RHETORICAL ACT

Ethos is an attitude—the impressions or images people have of the source of a message. Like all attitudes, those about the credibility of a rhetor (or the source of the message, whether it is an individual or a medium or an institution) are general and evaluative. Unlike most other attitudes, which are unidimensional (that is, determined by only one factor), ethos is multidimensional, affected by four factors. One of these is *authoritativeness* and a second is *trustworthiness*.[3] For a rhetor to be authoritative for an audience means that he or she is perceived as informed, expert, qualified, intelligent, and reliable. This cluster of attributes is similar to those characterizing a person who, in the classical sense, showed practical wisdom and expertise on matters of social concern. For a rhetor to be trustworthy means that she or he is perceived as honest, friendly, pleasant, and more concerned with the good of the community than with personal goals. This second factor seems to combine the Aristotelian view that a rhetor must be perceived as having moral excellence and as being well intentioned toward the community. A third factor appears in some studies: *dynamism*. This means that, in some cases, the attitude toward the rhetor is affected by the degree to which he or she is emphatic, aggressive, forceful, bold, active, and energetic, but this factor functions less predictably and uniformly in diverse situations, and it is a factor that may work either positively or negatively for women speakers depending on the audience. A fourth, over-arching factor, is *identification*—the perceived similarity between the rhetor and the audience—and is a term so central to ethos formation, it receives special attention below.

The rhetor's ethos and the message do not have fixed, unchanging meanings for the audience; they interact. Once it was presumed that only the evaluation of the message was influenced by the prestige of the source from which it supposedly comes. S. E. Asch criticized this assumption and argued that authorship did not function as a source of prestige but as a context that influenced the meaning statements had for members of the audience. Such a perspective holds that meaning is in people, and when the context of a message is changed, its meaning will be interpreted differently.[4] A statement about revolution from the Declaration of Independence when attributed to Thomas Jefferson, for example, has a different meaning than if the same statement were attributed to Karl Marx. In other words, the source of an act, the rhetor or the medium in which a rhetorical act appears, are contexts that influence how the audience decides what the message means. The nature of the message itself will be influenced significantly by the source, because the source is a major part of its context. Consider how Grady and Wells interact with their texts and affect the meaning and impact of each.

Identification

The importance of the rhetor for the determination of meaning is related to two processes with special significance for persuasion: *identification* and *participation*. In Chapter 7 identification was examined as a language strategy. Here its meaning is expanded in the context of ethos. To identify means "to establish the identity of; . . . to consider as identical, equate; . . . to associate or affiliate (oneself) closely with a person or group." The word is related to identity—"the set of characteristics by which a thing is definitively recognized or known" or "the quality or condition of being exactly the same as something else."[5] If you look closely at these definitions, you will notice that they are apparently contradictory or at least ambiguous. On the one hand, these words refer to the set of characteristics that make something or someone unique, distinctive. On the other hand, these words refer to what is alike, even identical, about two or more things or persons. In other words, they are terms about the relationship between similarities and differences. Identification is possible because of similarities—we are both students and Americans interested in understanding how to use communication in order to be effective moral agents. These are possibilities for identification despite the many ways in which we may be different—based on sex, ethnicity, religious beliefs, political commitments. You can identify with me if my behavior as an author of this book consistently embodies shared goals and interests, but I can become a real person for you, rather than an impersonal author, only as you become aware of the qualities that make me different, even unique. We do not identify with generalities but with general characteristics as embodied in specific ways in an individual. Persons identify with each other, and it is as an individual that the audience will respond to you, specifically as an individual who illustrates and represents general qualities and characteristics you and they share.

Research that has been done on the development of trust helps explain this further. Trust arises out of a reciprocal pattern of interrelationships. We learn to trust by sharing, by mutual exchange, and by sensitivity to the other person. Trusting and risk-taking are two sides of the same coin, because a trusting relationship requires a willingness to engage in trusting acts of self-disclosure. Thus, within limits, others trust us to the degree that they know details about us; we are trusted as we emerge for them as unique individuals. There are limits, of course, but they are often broader than you may think.

In Rita Mae Brown's best-selling novel *Rubyfruit Jungle*,[6] for example, the protagonist, Molly Bolt is a young woman with a strong commitment to independence and a lot of artistic talent. She is an all-American girl who embodies values most Americans cherish—a sense of humor, a desire to develop her talents fully, a sense of fair play, and loyalty. She is also a lesbian. As readers, we may or may not identify with lesbians, but as the novel's sales attest, many of us can identify with the Molly Bolt who makes us laugh, who expresses our ambitions, who gets angry at unfair treatment, and who can be trusted to stick by her friends. Like Molly Bolt, rhetors need to emerge as real and distinctive individuals to audiences. The rhetorical problem is not to become a bland amalgam of the attitudes of the audience; the rhetorical problem is the risks involved in disclosing yourself as a distinctive individual to the audience.

Similarity is important in persuasion. Kenneth Burke, a contemporary rhetorical theorist, wrote: "Only those voices from without are effective which can speak in the language of a voice within."[7] At its simplest, this statement recognizes that we are most influenced by those whose voices are most like the voices we use in talking to ourselves, and the more the rhetor shares with the audience, the greater the chance he or she will have of being able to speak in ways the audience will hear and understand and feel. Empirical studies reveal that rhetors' increase their influence when they announce at the outset that their personal views (attitudes) are similar to those of the audience, that members of the audience more readily accept a rhetor's view of an issue if common ground has already been established on previous issues, and that the audience is more susceptible to influence if its members decide that the intentions of the rhetor are consistent with their own self interests.[8]

A cynical view of such findings would suggest that the rhetor should lie—tell the audience what they want to hear in order to gain the effects desired. That is good advice for only one kind of rhetorical situation: the one-shot effort at a quick payoff. The unscrupulous seller of, say, imaginary cemetery plots, who plans to hit town once, then take the money and run, may use this effectively. But most of us act as rhetors in quite different circumstances. You will be in a class for a quarter or a semester, and some of your classmates will know you in other contexts; so, even as nomadic students, it is difficult for you to wear a false face easily. It becomes even more difficult in a community in which you live and work over a period of time—the consistency of your behavior will be a test of your trustworthiness. In addition, most rhetorical acts are parts of persuasive campaigns. In such cases, you will be judged, over time, in different rhetorical actions with different audiences, and it would not only be difficult, but also most unwise to try "to fool all of the people all of the time."

The moral of the story is to find real areas of similarity that you share with the audience. Do not try to be what you are not, but make sure that they know what you share with them. If you are to be effective, you must find common grounds—yet you must also remain a unique individual who is, in fact, different from anyone else.

Social Power

Ethos is also influenced by the relationship between the rhetor and the audience. In a rhetorical context, *power* refers to the rhetor's potential for social influence—that is, influence that arises from the degree to which the audience depends on the rhetor and the rhetor depends on the audience. The classroom is a good example. As students, you depend on your instructor in significant ways; your instructor has power, and your relationship is between unequals. Your ability to graduate and your grade point average, in part, depend on your teacher, and this additional power may increase her or his ability to influence your attitudes—at least for the duration of the class. An instructor, however, also depends on the students. Any one of you can disrupt the class so it cannot continue, and the course continues period after period because you as a group permit it to do so. Because of this power, you have the ability to influence your instructor or, at least, limit her or his behavior. The rhetorical acts of students and professors are influenced and limited by their relative power. These limits are evident in any relationship involving the potential for social influence—between spouses, partners, employer and employee, homeowner and plumber, landlord and tenant, dean and department head, coach and player, sorority member and pledge, parent and child, and so on.

Obviously, such interdependent relationships are a facet of identification. As employees we may dislike the boss but recognize that our livelihood depends on the health of the business. As students we may dislike a teacher but recognize that the class must continue if we are to learn what we need and get essential credits.

Participation

The ethos of the rhetor is also related to participation by the audience in the rhetorical act. To understand this process, we must return once again to the wisdom of Aristotle. In *On Rhetoric* he described a species of argument that he called the *enthymeme*, a form of argument that he believed was peculiar to rhetoric. This form of argument is unusual because it assumes a collaborative effort by the rhetor and audience. In effect, the audience fills in details, makes connections based on their experiences, or draws conclusions based on knowledge and understandings they share with the rhetor. Sometimes they do that because of a common context, from what they know of a particular time or place. Sometimes they do it because of assumptions or values they share. Sometimes it occurs in response to a word or phrase that evokes vivid, salient associations. Sometimes it occurs in response to a visual cue, such as a smirk, a sigh, or looking at one's watch in the midst of a presidential debate, for example. The perceived character of the rhetor influences whether audience members will collaborate in creating the rhetorical act because such perceptions function as signs of shared experience, attitudes, and values, which, in turn, lead to identification, which facilitates active participation in creating and elaborating the arguments offered by the rhetor. Note how similar these concepts are to the ELM theory discussed earlier.

An enthymeme is relatively easy to describe but harder to illustrate because it relies on audience participation and requires a good bit of adaptation. The enthymeme was introduced in Chapter 5 as a general argument type. In general, an enthymeme is an argument that rests on what is already known and accepted by those addressed. Accordingly, audience members can fill in details that are omitted or only alluded to in passing or the argument evokes not just assent but elaboration because it fits their personal experiences or speaks to what they believe is likely or probable. Many jokes based on current events illustrate the process. When George Bush chose Dan Quayle for his running mate in 1988, for example, some detected an inconsistency in Quayle's statements about military service and his service in the National Guard to avoid being drafted and sent to Vietnam. One wag asked, "What's the difference between Jane Fonda and Dan Quayle? Give up? Jane Fonda went to Vietnam." The humor, if any, arises out of audience knowledge about Jane Fonda, who aroused controversy by traveling to North Vietnam and criticizing U.S. bombing of what were described as civilian targets. Without that knowledge, there is only puzzlement. Just who do you suppose might enjoy that joke particularly?

A more extended example comes from a North Carolina senatorial campaign. In his 1990 race for the Senate against African American Harvey Gantt, Jesse Helms used a commercial that showed a pair of pale male hands reading, then crushing, a letter, presumably a letter of rejection, while a voice said,

> You needed that job, and you were the best qualified. But they had to give it to a minority because of a racial quota. Is that really fair? Harvey Gantt says it is. Gantt supports Ted Kennedy's racial quota law that makes the color of your skin more important than your quali-

fications. You'll vote on this issue next Tuesday. For racial quotas: Harvey Gantt. Against racial quotas: Jesse Helms.

The responses from people in focus groups who were asked about their reactions suggest that many white North Carolina voters had ready in mind a scenario that they could link to the words of the ad, a racist scenario about unqualified minorities taking the jobs of needful blue-collar workers. The ad was powerful because it aroused that scenario in voters' minds and linked it to Gantt, which made them more likely to vote for Helms. Moreover, white males who could identify with the man in the ad were more likely to respond with that story line.[9] In addition, of course, it made those who responded well to the ad believe that Jesse Helms understood their problems and would act to ensure that they were treated fairly, thereby enhancing his ethos. Note that enthymematic argument is powerful because it is self-persuasive and because it brings to consciousness ideas or feelings based on our own experiences and knowledge. Note that part of the force of the ad based on Rodin's *The Thinker* for Jesse Ventura is based on Minnesota voters' familiarity with that sculpture and with arguments in that campaign about Ventura's competence, which allow them to participate in creating the ad's message. Tony Schwartz, an advertising genius, wrote a book arguing that powerful advertising works by prompting an enthymematic response, what he called a "responsive chord," in viewers or listeners.[10] In such cases, the rhetor produces cues that prompt members of the audience to collaborate or participate in creating the rhetoric by which they are persuaded.

The process by which the ethos of the source increases our participation is most evident in commercials made by well-known actors. Because we know little about them as individuals, we tend to believe they are like the characters they play. Bill Cosby, for instance, is best known as a comedian and for his roles as a supportive father in television sitcoms. He appears in commercials for Jell-O. Dressed casually and usually shown with a group of children, he shows us how much kids love the yummy taste of Jell-O or Jell-O pudding. The advertiser hopes that we will confuse the actor Bill Cosby with the warm, caring father that he plays on television, a move made easier by books that Cosby has written on being a father. If so, we are more likely to accept his advice on what we should feed our children.

In sum, the character of the rhetor is directly related to two important rhetorical processes: identification based on perceptions of similarity and participation based on clues provided by the rhetor's words that suggest shared experiences and knowledge. Both of these influence the ways in which audience members interpret messages and the extent to which they are willing to fill in details or draw inferences based on statements in the rhetorical act.

These, then, are the kinds of problems that may arise in rhetorical action. Some of these problems arise out of the rhetor's background, appearance, the ways she or he is introduced, and the context or occasion. More important problems arise out of the relationship between the rhetor and the message. For an act to be effective, a rhetor must be perceived by the audience as competent, practical, and trustworthy. This is particularly significant because the rhetor is a context that affects how audience members will translate and interpret a message. Specifically, ethos influences audience identification—that is, the degree to which audiences see the rhetor as an individual is closely related to trust. In addition, as the rhetor emerges as a unique person, there is an association with, an affinity for those qualities, attitudes, and characteristics that form a common ground between rhetor and audience. This process is central to ensuring that the audience will hear the message and translate it with the greatest possible fidelity. In addition, ethos influences participation, the degree to which the audience is willing to involve itself in rhetorical action, to draw conclusions, or to fill in details implied by or to embellish the suggestions made by the rhetor.

THE RHETORICAL PROBLEM: INTERRELATIONSHIPS

By this time the interrelationships among the facets of the rhetorical problem should be apparent. For example, the decisions made by an audience member about the competence of the rhetor result from decisions that the rhetor makes about the treatment of the subject and the purpose selected. The problems the rhetor has in establishing credibility arise from the characteristics of a specific audience. The rhetorical problem on a given occasion will be a function of the interaction among these three elements: audience, subject/purpose, and rhetor. Earlier chapters have explored the resources of evidence, argument, organization, and language that are available to overcome these obstacles.

MATERIAL FOR ANALYSIS I

The example of strategizing to overcome rhetorical obstacles is a speech by Henry Grady (1850–1889). Grady was born in Athens, Georgia, the son of a wealthy slave-owning aristocrat. As a teen, he witnessed the fiercest fighting of the Civil War. But though his father was killed on the battlefield while in the Confederate army, he held no grudges against the North after the war. He studied at the University of Georgia, (where there is now a school of journalism and mass communication named after him) and held a series of journalistic jobs in New York before returning to the South as a reporter-editor for the *Atlanta Constitution*. In 1880 with borrowed money, he bought a fourth interest in the paper and began a nine-year career as Georgia's most celebrated journalist.

At the age of 36, Grady became a nationally acclaimed orator. With charm and wit, and a flair for the dramatic, he preached the gospel of "the new South"—wherein he urged Southerners to support agricultural diversification, industrialization, and to welcome northern industrialists to the region. He also became an ardent cheerleader for a racially progressive Atlanta in which Blacks and Whites lived together peacefully.

Grady's prestige as an orator and journalist reached its heights when the New England Society of New York City invited him to speak at its meeting in December of 1886. Grady was the first Southerner ever to have been invited to speak to the august society composed of 300 businessmen, including such capitalists as J. P. Morgan. If the suspicious, even hostile, audience was not enough of a rhetorical problem for Grady, the arrangement of the program heightened his challenge considerably. The first speaker was a famous Presbyterian preacher, Thomas Talmadge, who delivered a powerful address describing the return of the victorious Union armies after the war. The second speaker was General William T. Sherman, famous for torching much of Grady's home state! The General concluded his speech by having the audience stand and sing the war song: "Marching Through Georgia."

Grady's stunning adaptation to this nightmarish occasion so moved his audience they were on their feet cheering before he finished. Many newspapers lavished praise on his performance and "the new South" soon became a popular slogan.[11]

The New South
by Henry Grady[12]

1   "There was a South of slavery and secession—that South is dead. There is a South of union and freedom—that South, thank God, is living, breathing, growing every hour." These words delivered from the immortal lips of Benjamin H. Hill,[13] at Tammany Hall in 1866, true then, and truer now, I shall make my text to-night.

2   Mr. President and Gentlemen: Let me express to you my appreciation of the kindness by which I am permitted to address you. I make this abrupt acknowledgment advisedly, for I feel that if, when I raise my provincial voice in this ancient and august presence, I could find courage for no more than the opening sentence, it would be well if, in that sentence, I had met in a rough sense my obligation as a guest, and had perished, so to speak, with courtesy on my lips and grace in my heart. (*Laughter*) Permitted through your kindness to catch my second wind, let me say that I appreciate the significance of being the first Southerner to speak at this board, which bears the substance, if it surpasses the semblance, of original New England hospitality (*Applause*), and honors a sentiment that in turn honors you, but in which my personality is lost, and the compliment to my people made plain. (*Laughter*)

3   I bespeak the utmost stretch of your courtesy to-night. I am not troubled about those from whom I come. You remember the man whose wife sent him to a neighbor with a pitcher of milk, and who, tripping on the top step, fell, with such casual interruptions as the landing afforded, into the basement; and while picking himself up had the pleasure of hearing his wife call out: "John, did you break the pitcher?" "No, I didn't," said John, "but I be dinged if I don't." (*Laughter*)

4   So, while those who call to me from behind may inspire me with energy if not with courage, I ask an indulgent hearing from you. I beg that you will bring your full faith in American fairness and frankness to judgment upon what I shall say. There was an old preacher once who told some boys of the Bible lesson he was going to read in the morning. The boys finding the place, glued together the connecting pages. (*Laughter*) The next morning he read on the bottom of one page: "When Noah was one hundred and twenty years old he took unto himself a wife, who was"—then turning the page—"one hundred and forty cubits long (*Laughter*), forty cubits wide, built of gopher-wood (*Laughter*), and covered with pitch inside and out." (*Loud and continued laughter*) He was naturally puzzled at this. He read it again, verified it, and then said: "My friends, this is the first time I ever met this in the Bible, but I accept it as an evidence of the assertion that we are fearfully and wonderfully made." (*Immense laughter*) If I could get you to hold such faith to-night I could proceed cheerfully to the task I otherwise approach with a sense of consecration.

5   Pardon me one word, Mr. President, spoken for the sole purpose of getting into the volumes that go out annually freighted with the rich eloquence of your speakers—the fact that the Cavalier as well as the Puritan was on the continent in its early days, and that he was "up and able to be about." (*Laughter*) I have read your books carefully and I find no mention of that fact, which seems to me an important one for preserving a sort of historical equilibrium if for nothing else.

6   Let me remind you that the Virginia Cavalier first challenged France on this continent—that Cavalier John Smith gave New England its very name, and was so pleased with the job that he has been handing his own name around ever since—and that while Miles Standish was cutting off men's ears for courting a girl without her parents' consent, and forbade men to kiss their wives on Sunday, the Cavalier was courting everything in sight, and that the Almighty had vouchsafed great increase to the Cavalier colonies, the huts in the wilderness being as full as the nests in the woods.

7   But having incorporated the Cavalier as a fact in your charming little books I shall let him work out his own salvation, as he has always done with engaging gallantry, and we will hold no controversy as to his merits. Why should we? Neither Puritan nor Cavalier long survived as such. The virtues and traditions of both happily still live for the inspiration of their sons and the saving of the old fashion. *(Applause)* But both Puritan and Cavalier were lost in the storm of the first Revolution; and the American citizen, supplanting both and stronger than either, took possession of the Republic bought by their common blood and fashioned to wisdom, and charged himself with teaching men government and establishing the voice of the people as the voice of God. *(Applause)*

8   My friend Dr. Talmadge has told you that the typical American has yet to come. Let me tell you that he has already come. *(Applause)* Great types like valuable plants are slow to flower and fruit. But from the union of these colonist Puritans and Cavaliers, from the straightening of their purposes and the crossing of their blood, slow perfecting through a century, came he who stands as the first typical American, the first who comprehended within himself all the strength and gentleness, all the majesty and grace of this Republic—Abraham Lincoln. *(Loud and continued applause)* He was the sum of Puritan and Cavalier, for in his ardent nature were fused the virtues of both, and in the depths of his great soul the faults of both were lost. *(Renewed applause)* He was greater than Puritan, greater than Cavalier, in that he was American *(Renewed applause)* and that in his homely form were first gathered the vast and thrilling forces of his ideal government—charging it with such tremendous meaning, and so elevating it above human suffering that martyrdom, though infamously aimed, came as a fitting crown to a life consecrated from the cradle to human liberty. *(Loud and prolonged cheering)* Let us, each cherishing the traditions and honoring his fathers, build with reverent hands to the type of this simple but sublime life, in which all types are honored; and in our common glory as Americans there will be plenty to spare for your forefathers and for mine. *(Renewed cheering)*

9   In speaking to the toast with which you have honored me, I accept the term, "The New South," as in no sense disparaging to the Old. Dear to me, sir, is the home of my childhood and the traditions of my people. I would not, if I could, dim the glory they won in peace and war, or by word or deed take aught from the splendor and grace of their civilization—never equaled and, perhaps, never to be equaled in its chivalric strength and grace. There is a New South, not through protest against the Old, but because of new conditions, new adjustments, and, if you please, new ideas and aspirations. It is to this that I address myself, and to the consideration of which I hasten lest it become the Old South before I get to it. Age does not endow all things with strength and virtue, nor are all new things to be despised. The shoemaker who put over his door "John Smith's shop. Founded in 1760," was more than matched by his young rival across the street who hung out this sign: "Bill Jones. Established 1886. No old stock kept in this shop."

10   Dr. Talmadge has drawn for you, with a master's hand, the picture of your returning armies. He has told you how in the pomp and circumstance of war, they came back to you, marching with proud and victorious tread, reading their glory in a nation's eyes! Will you bear with me while I tell you of another army that sought its home at the close of the late war—an army that marched home in defeat and not in victory—in pathos and not in splendor, but in glory that equaled yours, and to hearts as loving as ever welcomed heroes home. Let me picture to you the footsore Confederate soldier, as, buttoning up in his faded gray jacket the parole which was to bear testimony to his children of his fidelity and faith, he turned his face southward from Appomattox in April, 1865. Think of him as ragged, half-starved, heavy-hearted, enfeebled by want and wounds; having fought to exhaustion, he surrenders his gun, wrings the hands of his comrades in silence, and lifting his tear-stained and pallid face for the last time to the graves that dot the old Virginia hills, pulls his gray cap over his brow and begins the slow and painful journey. What does he find—let me ask you, who went to your homes eager to find in the welcome you had justly earned, full payment for four years' sacrifice—what does he find when, having followed the battle-stained cross against overwhelming odds, dreading death not half so much as surrender, he reaches the home he left so prosperous and beautiful? He finds his house in ruins, his farm devastated, his slaves free, his stock killed, his barns empty, his trade destroyed, his money worthless; his social system, feudal in its magnificence, swept away; his people without law or legal status, his comrades slain, and the burdens of others heavy on his shoulders. Crushed by defeat, his very traditions are gone; without money, credit, employment, material or training; and, besides all this, confronted with the gravest problem that ever met human intelligence—the establishing of a status for the vast body of his liberated slaves.

11   What does he do—this hero in gray with a heart of gold? Does he sit down in sullenness and despair? Not for a day. Surely God, who had stripped him of his prosperity, inspired him in his adversity. As ruin was never before so overwhelming, never was restoration swifter. The soldier stepped from the trenches into the furrow; horses that had charged Federal guns marched before the plow, and fields that ran red with human blood in April were green with the harvest in June; women reared in luxury cut up their dresses and made breeches for their husbands and, with a patience and heroism that fit women always as a garment, gave their hands to work. There was little bitterness in all this. Cheerfulness and frankness prevailed. "Bill Arp" struck the keynote when he said: "Well, I killed as many of them as they did of me, and now I am going to work." (*Laughter and applause*) Or the soldier returning home after defeat and roasting some corn on the roadside, who made the remark to his comrades: "You may leave the South if you want to, but I am going to Sandersville, kiss my wife and raise a crop, and if the Yankees fool with me any more I will whip 'em again." (*Renewed applause*) I want to say to General Sherman—who is considered an able man in our hearts, though some people think he is a kind of careless man about fire—that from the ashes he left us in 1864 we have raised a brave and beautiful city; that somehow or other we have caught the sunshine in the bricks and mortar of our homes, and have built therein not one ignoble prejudice or memory. (*Applause*)

12   But in all this what have we accomplished? What is the sum of our work? We have found out that in the general summary the free Negro counts more than he did as a slave. We have planted the schoolhouse on the hilltop and made it free to white and black. We have sowed towns and cities in the place of theories and put business above politics. (*Applause*) We have challenged your spinners in Massachusetts and your iron-makers in Pennsylvania. We have learned that the $400,000,000 annually received from our cotton crop will make us rich, when the supplies that make it are home-raised. We have reduced the commercial rate of interest from twenty-four to six per cent, and are floating four per cent bonds. We have learned that one Northern immigrant is worth fifty foreigners, and have smoothed the path to southward, wiped out the place where Mason and Dixon's line used to be, and hung our latch-string out to you and yours. (*Prolonged cheers*)

MATERIAL FOR ANALYSIS II

A second example of strategizing to overcome rhetorical obstacles is a speech by Ida B. Wells. She was born in Holly Springs, Mississippi, in 1862. Both of her parents were slaves. Yet after emancipation, it looked like Wells would have a promising, even comfortable, life. Her parents continued to work for their former master—only now for good pay. She attended a top-flight high school for freed slaves, reading all the books in the library before the age of 15. Then, tragedy struck. Both her parents died in a yellow fever epidemic within 24 hours of each other, her baby sister too. At the age of 16, Wells was left in charge of her four siblings aged 13, 11, 9, and 5.

She got a teaching job in Memphis to support her brothers and sisters by passing a rigorous examination and claiming to be 18. While teaching, Wells became a writer for the *Memphis Free Speech* newspaper. Her investigative slant began after an ugly experience with Jim Crow laws. Wells boarded a train in Memphis. Seating herself in the ladies' coach as she had always done, she began to read. She was surprised, however, when the conductor, coming by to collect tickets, refused to accept hers. Brusquely, he told her to move to the car ahead, which was reserved for smokers and blacks. Wells refused to move. Angered by her defiance, the conductor grabbed her arm to drag her out—but Wells bit him and braced herself. He called for reinforcements. It took three men to pry Wells loose and to push her out of the coach. When she tumbled down the steps, her white fellow passengers stood up and applauded. Wells did not let the incident pass. She hired a lawyer and sued the railroad for damages. She won and was awarded $500 dollars.

The Jim Crow event energized her writing career. Soon she was asked to join the staff of the *Memphis Free Speech and Headlight*, and in the summer of 1889 managed to buy a one-third interest in the paper. Shortly thereafter, tragedy struck again. One of her best friends was lynched. When no attempt was made to punish the murderer, Wells used her column to instigate an economic boycott and a mass exodus from Memphis. In two months time, several thousand black people left Memphis. Wells, with her siblings in tow, left for New York. Here, she went on a journalistic rampage to end lynchings. She documented systematically the number of lynchings in the United States, resulting in a book entitled *The Red Record*.

The speech for analysis was delivered in Lyric Hall in New York City on October 5, 1892, as part of what was said to be "[t]he greatest demonstration ever attempted by race women for one of their number,"[14] and many leading African American women were present with her on the platform. A collection taken at the end of the evening enabled the speech to be printed as a pamphlet (New York Age Print, November 1892).

As the speech indicates, Wells faced enormous obstacles. She was challenging the widespread belief, fostered by newspaper reports, that justified lynching on the grounds that it was punishment for attempted or actual rapes by black men of white women. She was an African American and a woman speaking on a topic that was sexual and violent. What follows are excerpts from her speech. Most of what is omitted is evidence and includes numerous, relatively detailed examples and extended quotations from Southern newspapers.

Her picture of the South after Reconstruction, which ended in 1877, is dramatically different from that painted by Henry Grady. Which was more likely to be treated as credible? Why?

Southern Horrors: Lynch Law in All Its Phases[15]

1   Wednesday evening May 24th, 1892, the city of Memphis was filled with excitement. Editorials in the daily papers of that date caused a meeting to be held in the Cotton Exchange Building; a committee was sent for the editors of the *Free Speech*, an Afro-American journal published in that city, and the only reason the open threats of lynching that were made were not carried out was because they could not be found. The cause of all this commotion was the following editorial published in the "Free Speech" May 21st, 1892, the Saturday previous.

> Eight Negroes lynched since last issue of the "Free Speech," one at Little Rock, Ark., last Saturday morning where the citizens broke into the penitentiary and got their man; three near Anniston, Ala., one near New Orleans; and three at Clarksville, Ga., the last three for killing a white man, and five on the same old racket—the new alarm about raping white women. The same programme of hanging, then shooting bullets into the lifeless bodies was carried out to the letter.
>
> Nobody in this section of the country believes the old thread bare lie that Negro men rape white women. If Southern white men are not careful, they will over-reach themselves and public sentiment will have a reaction; a conclusion will then be reached which will be very damaging to the moral reputation of their women.

2   "The Daily Commercial" of Wednesday following, May 25th, contained the following leader:

> Those Negroes who are attempting to make the lynching of individuals of their race a means for arousing the worst passions of their kind are playing with a dangerous sentiment. The Negroes may as well understand that there is no mercy for the Negro rapist and little patience with his defenders. A Negro organ printed in this city, in a recent issue publishes the following atrocious paragraph:
>
> "Nobody in this section of the country believes the old thread-bare lie that Negro men rape white women. If Southern white men are not careful they will over-reach themselves, and public sentiment will have a reaction; and a conclusion will be reached which will be very damaging to the moral reputation of their women."
>
> The fact that a black scoundrel is allowed to live and utter such loathsome and repulsive calumnies is a volume of evidence as to the wonderful patience of Southern whites. But we have had enough of it.
>
> There are some things that the Southern white man will not tolerate, and the obscene intimations of the foregoing have brought the writer to the very outermost limit of public patience. We hope we have said enough.

3   The "Evening Scimitar" of same date, copied the "Commercial's" editorial with these words of comment:

> Patience under such circumstances is not a virtue. If the Negroes themselves do not apply the remedy without delay it will be the duty of those whom he has attacked to tie the wretch who utters these calumnies to a stake at the intersection of Main and Madison Sts., brand him in the forehead with a hot iron and perform upon him a surgical operation with a pair of tailor's shears.

4   Acting upon this advice, the leading citizens met in the Cotton Exchange Building the same evening, and threats of lynching were freely indulged, not by the lawless element upon which the deviltry of the South is usually saddled—but by the leading business men, in their leading business centre. Mr. Fleming, the business manager and owner of a half interest in the Free Speech, had to leave town to escape the mob, and was afterwards ordered not to return; letters and telegrams sent me in New York where I was spending my vacation advised me that bodily harm awaited my return. Creditors took possession of the office and sold the outfit, and the "Free Speech" was as if it had never been.

5   The editorial in question was prompted by the many inhuman and fiendish lynchings of Afro-Americans which have recently taken place and was meant as a warning. Eight lynched in one week and five of them charged with rape! The thinking public will not easily believe freedom and education more brutalizing than slavery, and the world knows that the crime of rape was unknown during four years of civil war, when the white women of the South were at the mercy of the race which is all at once charged with being a bestial one.

6   Since my business has been destroyed and I am an exile from home because of that editorial, the issue has been forced, and as the writer of it I feel that the race and the public generally should have a statement of the facts as they exist. They will serve at the same time as a defense for the Afro-American Sampsons [sic] who suffer themselves to be betrayed by white Delilahs.

7   The whites of Montgomery, Ala., knew J. C. Duke sounded the keynote of the situation—which they would gladly hide from the world, when he said in his paper, "The Herald," five years ago: "Why is it that white women attract Negro men now more than in former days? There was a time when such a thing was unheard of. There is a secret to this thing, and we greatly suspect it is the growing appreciation of white Juliets for colored Romeos." Mr. Duke, like the "Free Speech" proprietors, was forced to leave the city for reflecting on the "honah" of white women and his paper suppressed; but the truth remains that Afro-American men do not always rape white women without their consent.

8   Mr. Duke, before leaving Montgomery, signed a card disclaiming any intention of slandering Southern white women. The editor of the "Free Speech" has no disclaimer to enter, but asserts instead that there are many white women in the South who would marry colored men if such an act would not place them at once beyond the pale of society and within the clutches of the law. The miscegenation laws of the South only operate against the legitimate union of the races; they leave the white man free to seduce all the colored girls he can, but it is death to the colored man who yields to the force and advances of a similar attraction in white women. White men lynch the offending Afro American, not because he is a despoiler of virtue, but because he succumbs to the smiles of white women.

9   The "Cleveland Gazette" of January 16, 1892, publishes a case in point. Mrs. J. S. Underwood, the wife of a minister of Elyria, Ohio, accused an Afro-American of rape. She told her husband that during his absence in 1888, stumping the State for the Prohibition Party, the man came to the kitchen door, forced his way in the house and insulted her. She tried to drive him out with a heavy poker, but he overpowered and chloroformed her, and when she revived her clothing was torn and she was in a horrible condition. She did not know the man but could identify him. She pointed out William Offett, a married man, who was arrested and, being in Ohio, was granted a trial.

10   The prisoner vehemently denied the charge of rape, but confessed he went to Mrs. Underwood's residence at her invitation and was criminally intimate with her at her request. This availed him nothing against the sworn testimony of a minister's wife, a lady of the highest respectability. He was found guilty, and entered the penitentiary, December 14, 1888, for fifteen years. Some time afterwards the woman's remorse led her to confess to her husband that the man was innocent.

11   These are her words:

"I met Offett at the Post Office. It was raining. He was polite to me, and as I had several bundles in my arms he offered to carry them home for me, which he did. He had a strange fascination for me, and I invited him to call on me. He called, bringing chestnuts and candy for the children. By this means we got them to leave us alone in the room. Then I sat on his lap. He made a proposal to me and I readily consented. Why I did so, I do not know, but that I did is true. He visited me several times after that and each time I was indiscreet. I did not care after the first time. In fact I could not have resisted, and had no desire to resist."

12   When asked by her husband why she told him she had been outraged, she said: "I had several reasons for telling you. One was the neighbors saw the fellow there; another was, I was afraid I had contracted a loathsome disease, and still another was that I feared I might give birth to a Negro baby. I hoped to save my reputation by telling you a deliberate lie." Her husband, horrified by the confession, had Offett, who had already served four years, released and secured a divorce. . . .

13   Hundreds of such cases might be cited, but enough have been given to prove the assertion that there are white women in the South who love the Afro-American's company even as there are white men notorious for their preference for Afro-American women.

14   There is hardly a town in the South which has not an instance of the kind which is well-known, and hence the assertion is reiterated that "nobody in the South believes the old thread bare lie that Negro men rape white women. . . ."

15   [T]he dark and bloody record of the South shows 728 Afro-Americans lynched during the past eight years. Not 50 of these were for political causes; the rest were for all manner of accusations from that of rape of white women, to the case of the boy Will Lewis who was hanged at Tullahoma, Tenn., last year for being drunk and "sassy" to white folks.

16   These statistics, compiled by the Chicago "Tribune" were given the first of this year (1892). Since then, not less than one hundred and fifty have been known to have met violent death at the hands of cruel, bloodthirsty mobs during the past nine months.

17   To palliate this record (which grows worse as the Afro American becomes intelligent) and excuse some of the most heinous crimes that ever stained the history of a country, the South is shielding itself behind the plausible screen of defending the honor of its women. This, too, in the face of the fact that only *one-third* of the 728 victims to mobs have been charged with rape, to say nothing of those of that one-third who were innocent of the charge. . . .

18   On March 9th, 1892, there were lynched in this same city three of the best specimens of young Afro-American manhood since the war. They were peaceful, law-abiding citizens and energetic business men.

19   They believed the problem was to be solved by eschewing politics and putting money in the purse. They owned a flourishing grocery business in a thickly populated suburb of Memphis, and a white man named Barrett had one on the opposite corner. After a personal difficulty, which Barrett sought by going into the "People's Grocery" drawing a pistol and was thrashed by Calvin McDowell, he (Barrett) threatened to "clean them out." These men were a mile beyond the city limits and police protection; hearing that Barrett's crowd was coming to attack them Saturday night, they mustered forces and prepared to defend themselves against attack.

20   When Barrett came, he led a posse of officers, twelve in number, who afterward claimed to be hunting a man for whom they had a warrant. That twelve men in citizen's clothes should think it necessary to go in the night to hunt one man who had never before been arrested, or made any record as a criminal, has never been explained. When they entered the back door, the young men thought the threatened attack was on, and fired into them. Three of the officers were wounded, and when the defending party found it was officers of the law upon whom they had fired, they ceased and got away.

21   Thirty-one men were arrested and thrown in jail as "conspirators," although they all declared more than once they did not know they were firing on officers. Excitement was at fever heat until the morning papers, two days after, announced that the wounded deputy sheriffs were out of danger. This hindered rather than helped the plans of the whites. There was no law on the statute books which would execute an Afro-American for wounding a white man, but the "unwritten law" did. Three of these men, the president, the manager, and clerk of the grocery—"the leaders of the conspiracy"—were secretly taken from jail and lynched in a shockingly brutal manner. "The Negroes are getting too independent," they say, "we must teach them a lesson."

22   What lesson? The lesson of subordination. "Kill the leaders and it will cow the Negro who dares to shoot a white man, even in self-defense."

23   Although the race was wild over the outrage, the mockery of law and justice which disarmed men and locked them up in jails where they could be easily and safely reached by the mob—the Afro-American ministers, newspapers, and leaders counseled obedience to the law which did not protect them.

24   Their counsel was heeded and not a hand was uplifted to resent the outrage; following the advice of the "Free Speech," people left the city in great numbers... .

25   Henry W. Grady in his well-remembered speeches in New England and New York pictured the Afro-American as incapable of self-government. Through him and other leading men the cry of the South to the country has been "Hands off! Leave us to solve our problem." To the Afro-American the South says, "the

white man must and will rule." There is little difference between the Ante-bellum and the New South.

26   Her white citizens are wedded to any method however revolting, any measure however extreme, for the subjugation of the young manhood of the race. They have cheated him out of his ballot, deprived him of civil rights or redress therefor in the civil courts, robbed him of the fruits of his labor, and are still murdering, burning, and lynching him.

27   The result is a growing disregard of human life. Lynch law has spread its insidious influence till men in New York State, Pennsylvania, and on the free Western plain feel they can take the law in their own hands with impunity, especially where an Afro-American is concerned. The South is brutalized to a degree not realized by its own inhabitants, and the very foundation of government, law, and order are imperiled. . . .

28   The lesson this teaches and which every Afro-American should ponder well, is that a Winchester rifle should have a place of honor in every black home, and it should be used for that protection which the law refuses to give. When the white man who is always the aggressor knows he runs as great risk of biting the dust every time his Afro-American victim does, he will have greater respect for Afro-American life. The more the Afro-American yields and cringes and begs, the more he has to do so, the more he is insulted, outraged, and lynched.

29   The assertion has been substantiated throughout that the press contains unreliable and doctored reports of lynchings, and one of the most necessary things for the race to do is to get these facts before the public. The people must know before they can act, and there is no educator to compare with the press.

30   The Afro-American papers are the only ones which will print the truth, and they lack means to employ agents and detectives to get at the facts. The race must rally a mighty host to the support of their journals, and thus enable them to do much in the way of investigation. . . .

31   Nothing is more definitely settled than [that] he must act for himself. I have shown how he may employ the boycott, emigration, and the press, and I feel that by a combination of all these agencies can be effectually stamped out lynch law, that last relic of barbarism and slavery. "The gods help those who help themselves."

Questions for Analysis

1. For both Henry Grady and Ida B. Wells, problems of prior ethos are legion. Given what you know about them and their times, identify and explain the problems they face because of their personal histories and reputations.
2. How does each use evidence to address problems of reputation?
3. How is Grady's introduction a strategic adaptation to his audience? The occasion? The situation?
4. How is Wells's use of the medium of print to teach a larger secondary audience an adaptation to ethos problems arising from appearance before an immediate audience?
5. How do different resources of language, argument, or evidence work together strategically in these speeches to assist any one of the four factors of ethos from the rhetorical act?

EXERCISES

1. Imagine you are the campaign manager for an underdog politician in your community. Identify such a candidate and create a "score card" for your candidate's ethos, both in terms of prior ethos and ethos from the rhetorical act. What can you suggest to improve your candidate's ethos appeal?

2. Discuss the impact of ethos on your judgment of your peers' in-class presentations. How do such things as appearance, punctuality, disposition, nonverbals, prior speech performances, topic selection, class attendance and participation, and so on, contribute to the formation of strong or weak credibility?

3. Corporate ethos is an important consideration for business today. Choose a local company and describe the ways in which it communicates its ethos through image advertising. Why must businesses work extra hard at humanizing themselves to their customers? Does your company use personification to create identification? If not, what other language strategies help form favorable ethos?

4. Corporate ethos is an important consideration for airlines. Listen closely to the in-flight announcements and indicate the ways in which they influence your response to the airline. Have you been on a flight when the attendants use humor to spice up the usual information? How did you react? Consult a source on voice and diction, such as *Is Your Voice Telling on You?* by Daniel Boone (Thomson Learning/Singular Publishing Group). How is ethos affected by vocal qualities?

5. In December 1997, the then 23-year-old Julia "Butterfly" Hill climbed up a 60-meter-high tree near San Francisco. She spent two years in her treehouse in an effort to protest and raise awareness about issues such as the dangers of deforestation, industrialization, and corporate power. Her efforts were met by diverse responses by members of the local community, by other environmentalist groups, by young people around the country, by the local and national forestry industry, and others. Use your InfoTrac College Edition database to locate articles about Julia Hill. Identify several responses to her protest. What can be said about Julia's ethos, judging from each of these responses? How was her appeal constrained by her age, values, appearance, behavior, reputation, style of talking? Who could and who could not identify with her or her actions? Why? How was her ethos constrained by the goals of her protest, by the topic of environmentalism itself, or by the historical, legal, social, and economic contexts in which she expressed her views? How was her ethos affected by the occasion on which she initiated her protest? How was her ethos constrained by the form of protest that she chose? What do all these considerations tell us about the challenges and possibilities of social protest? What should an activist be mindful of in designing his or her protest strategy?

6. **Portfolio Entry 9: Rhetor Obstacles**
   Identify and explain in one to two pages how rhetor-related obstacles plague your rhetorical acts. What, if anything, do the rhetors do to combat these ethos problems?

NOTES

1. *Aristotle On Rhetoric: A Theory of Civic Discourse*, trans. George A. Kennedy (New York: Oxford University Press, 1991).

2. The definitions used in this chapter are taken from the *American Heritage Dictionary of the English Language* (Boston: Houghton Mifflin, 1969).

3. Admittedly this is an oversimplification. Using factor analysis as a technique, a number of other factors have been found, but these two are the most stable and generalized across studies.

4. S. E. Asch, "The Doctrine of Suggestion, Prestige, and Imitation in Social Psychology," *Psychological Review* 55 (1948): 250–278; see Wallace Fotheringham, *Perspectives on Persuasion* (Boston: Allyn and Bacon, 1966), pp. 90–92, for a discussion of this research.

5. *American Heritage Dictionary of the English Language*, ed. William Morris (Boston/New York: American Heritage Publishing Co. and Houghton Mifflin, 1969).

6. (1973; New York: Bantam Books, 1977).

7. Kenneth Burke, *A Rhetoric of Motives* (1950; Berkeley: University of California Press, 1969), p. 39.

8. Ellen Berscheid reviews this research in "Interpersonal Attraction" in *Handbook of Social Psychology*,

3d ed. (New York: Random House, 1985), vol. 2, pp. 413–484.

9. Reports about focus group reactions to the ad are found in K. H. Jamieson, *Dirty Politics* (New York: Oxford University Press, 1992), pp. 97–100.

10. *The Responsive Chord* (New York: Doubleday, 1974).

11. See Ronald F. Reid, ed. *Three Centuries of American Rhetorical Discourse* (Prospect Heights, IL: Waveland, 1988), pp. 509–510; Also http:/www.mindspring. com/~gradyhs/grady/henrygrady.html.

12. Henry W. Grady, "The New South," in *American Public Addresses, 1740-1952*, ed. A. Craig Baird (New York: McGraw-Hill, 1956), pp. 180–188.

13. Hill, like Grady, was a Georgian. Originally he opposed secession but accepted his state's decision and sat in the Confederate Senate. After the war he supported Reconstruction policies, but championed Southern causes in the U.S. Congress.

14. Marianna Davis, ed., *Contributions of Black Women to America*, 2 vols. (Columbia, SC: Kenday, 1982), vol. 2, p. 80.

15. The question marks in parentheses in the text are Wells's insertions. "Negro" is capitalized throughout to make the usage consistent; this was a point of controversy at the time Wells spoke. The text is from Ida B. Wells, *On Lynching: Southern Horrors, A Red Record, Mob Rule in New Orleans* (New York: Arno Press, 1969), pp. 4–24.

chapter 11

Understanding Evaluation

What is the difference between people like Gene Shalitt, Jeff Greenfield, and John Madden and guests on *Movie Lounge* and *Politically Incorrect?* The first group is trained to make critical evaluations in their field of expertise: film, media, and sports, respectively; the second group is expected to "sound off" on cultural potpourri. Critical evaluations are marked by thoughtful scrutiny; sounding off displays personal opinion or gut reaction. Recalling the ELM model of persuasion, one might say that statements such as "The film was masterfully produced given its genre and budget" and "I liked it" illustrate the road to reflection versus the road to efficiency. Critics have learned to condense their informed judgments to meet the demands of a media age with rating systems like thumbs up or down, awarding stars, and 10-point scales.

We have come to rely on the judgments of trained critics or consultants because we are bombarded by rhetoric every day and know how difficult it is to make careful assessments. This chapter gives you the building blocks to form intelligent judgments of rhetorical acts. It outlines standards of evaluation necessary to complete the critical process of description, interpretation, and evaluation. Evaluation is a natural outgrowth of the two steps you have learned thus far. Your first task is one of descriptive analysis—full and detailed understanding of the rhetorical act. Your second task concerns the rhetorical problem: What obstacles did the rhetor face, and what resources were used to overcome them? Your third and final task is evaluative. The standards of evaluation introduced here should remind you of the 7 p's of rhetoric, first introduced in Chapter 1. Since rhetoric is powerful, purposive, problem-solving, poetic, pragmatic, public, and propositional, we need ways to harness and brand it.

STANDARDS FOR EVALUATION

Four standards can be used, alone or in combination, to judge rhetorical discourse. They are (1) an *artistic* standard, focused on producing an aesthetically satisfying discourse; (2) a *response* standard, focused on achieving desired effects; (3) an *accuracy* standard, focused on presenting as truthful and complete an account of the issue as is possible; and (4) a *moral* standard, focused on using ethical means and advancing ethically desirable ends for society and for rhetorical practice (Figure 11–1). Each is relevant to rhetorical action. Each has important strengths and limitations.

The Artistic Standard

The artistic standard focuses on means, on the ways in which rhetoric is poetic. The word *aesthetic* comes from the Greek word *aisthetikos*, which means "pertaining to sense perception." This original meaning is retained in the word *anaesthetic*, which refers to substances like chloroform or novocaine that cause total or partial loss of sensation. The artistic or aesthetic standard is a measure of how well a rhetorical act succeeds in altering perception, creating virtual experience, attracting and holding attention, and inducing participation and identification. It is a measure of how well an act achieves its purpose, of how creatively a rhetor responds to the obstacles faced, of how inventively a rhetor fulfills the requirements or expectations of form.

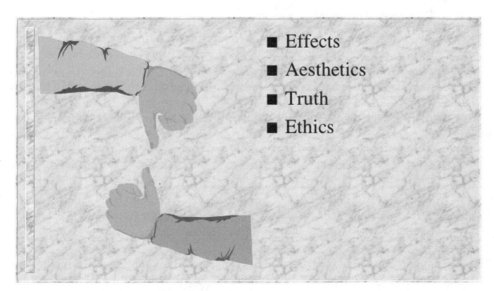

Figure 11–1
Evaluation Criteria

■ Effects
■ Aesthetics
■ Truth
■ Ethics

I rate Angelina Grimké's speech (see Chapter 8), for example, high on artistic grounds because I think she was extremely creative in responding to a difficult situation. Most rhetors would "throw in the towel" if confronted by a disruptive audience that ridiculed them and their cause, a target audience that viewed itself as powerless, and a VIP audience that was complacent or threatened by their aims and that disapproved of their gender, faith, and affiliations. In this case, the critic must recognize how many obstacles exist and anticipate limited response. Despite that obstacle-filled situation, however, one can applaud the skill with which Grimké responded to her rhetorical problem. How clever to enact the very argument you wish to advance (women can be effective public advocates) and to disarm your audience's resistance with a stunning array of argumentative and language strategies that taken together invest the cause with godliness! Moreover, the capacity of her speech to arouse our admiration attests to its enduring power, a strong indicator of aesthetic merit.

Many rhetorical acts examined in this book, such as Janine DiGiovanni's "Kosovo Diary: Madness Visible," Dr. Martin Luther King, Jr.'s, "I've Been to the Mountaintop," Abraham Lincoln's "Gettysburg Address," Helen O'Neil's "A Mercury Drop, a Deadly Lesson," and Elizabeth Cady Stanton's "The Solitude of Self" deserve high artistic ratings. Each is a gem poetically. Each is an elegantly framed rhetorical response to events difficult to understand. Each creates virtual experience and induces participation in refreshing and inventive ways. The artistic standard demands analysis of techniques, means, and strategies. These can be assessed with or without external evidence that a discourse achieved its goal. The artistic standard also reveals those works that have the capacity to endure through time as models of rhetorical action because they are deeply moving, eloquent, and original.

The limitations of the artistic standard are evident when we turn our attention to advertising and admire the skills of those who exploit the strategic resources of verbal and visual language in order to manipulate us politically or commercially. Such uses of artistry may trouble us, but the artistic standard does not provide a basis for judging the purposes or ends of rhetorical action.

The Effects Standard

The *effects standard*, the evaluation of a rhetorical act in terms of the response that it evokes, reflects the demand that rhetoric be pragmatic. Every rhetorical act must communicate, induce participation from an audience, and affect perceptions, beliefs, and attitudes. Unless some reaction occurs, the act initiated by a rhetor must be judged a failure.

But effects are difficult to isolate and verify. It is difficult to separate responses to one act from responses to other rhetoric that precedes and follows it. Most influence is the result of a campaign or of a series of experiences. Similarly, it is hard to measure just what the audience response was. Clapping may be a matter of relieved courtesy; questionnaires report only what people say occurred; the size and nature of the response may be greatly affected by the medium in which an act is presented; Web sites either don't tabulate browser visits or seldom update the number of "hits" they receive. For these reasons, it is usually difficult to determine accurately the effects of a given rhetorical act.

Examples of diverse discourses that have met with resounding success include the Harry Potter books by J. K. Rowling, which became the biggest publishing phenomenon ever, occupying an unprecedented number of weeks at the top of the *New York Times* best-seller list; *Star Wars Episode I: The Phantom Menace*—the all-time highest grossing film to that date on its opening day; ad campaigns such as "Got Milk?" "Absolut Vodka," and "Benetton," which have won coveted industry awards for impact; Billy Graham, whose inspirational sermons on tours across the globe spanning six decades have won him international acclaim; *ER* for its five-year run as the most watched show on TV, its 16 Emmys, and winner of the People's Choice Award as favorite TV dramatic series every year since it has been on the air.

The effects standard is sometimes at odds with the artistic standard. For all its box office success, *Star Wars Episode I: The Phantom Menace* received cool artistic reviews. Critics called it "juvenile," "tedious," "regressive," even "xenophobic." Former president Ronald Reagan was dubbed the "Great Communicator" and the "Teflon President" for his sustained popularity through good times and bad, yet many speech critics found that his speeches lacked presidential eloquence and enduring power.

The effects standard also raises ethical problems. Applied strictly and in isolation, it would applaud rhetoric without regard for its accuracy or social consequences. By such a measure, the finest rhetorical works would be speeches of Adolf Hitler who inspired an entire nation to believe in Aryan superiority and the elimination of all Jews! Advertising that persuades teenagers to smoke or drink despite serious health hazards also raises ethical problems. The Virginia Slims ad campaign "Find Your Voice" is a glitzy, seductive attempt to capitalize on chic feminism and encourage young women to smoke their brand. But the irony and potential harm of the ad is that the consumer might actually lose her voice to throat cancer if the ad's message is effective. Similarly, the popular and funny Budweiser ad promoting the WNBA with superstar Cynthia Cooper telling two street tough guys that they "play like a girl" makes a subtle, but disturbing, connection between sport and alcohol consumption. Clearly, the effects standard cannot be used alone; other standards need to be used with it. The starting point of much analysis, however, is an attempt to explain why and how demonstrable effects were produced.

The Truth Standard

The *truth standard* measures the similarity between the "reality" presented in a rhetorical act and "reality" as presented in other sources. In this case, the critic tests the accuracy and typicality of evidence in the discourse against other sources known to be well informed and compares the arguments selected against the pool of arguments available. Rhetoric is a part of social decision making. If we are to make good decisions, we need the best evidence available, and we need to examine all the relevant arguments. For this reason, considerations of adequacy and accuracy always are important.

But this standard also has limitations. Rhetoric is problem-solving; the truths of rhetoric are social truths, truths created and validated by people. There is no simple way to verify all rhetorical claims or to validate all rhetorical arguments. The occasions best suited to rhetorical deliberation are those in which well-intentioned, informed people disagree. A good critic has to acknowledge conflicting evidence, varying interpretations, and competing perspectives and must recognize that no simple judgment about the truth of most acts can ever be made. In addition, no discourse is ever long enough to tell the whole truth, and the constraints of space and time, which are inherent to rhetoric, complicate strict application of this standard. *AdWatch* campaigns that run during elections focus primarily on truth claims. These are important critical segments in the news, especially effective in catching and preventing outright distortions, but the reality is that all ads contain omissions, creative editing, and half-truths.

The competing rhetorical acts examined in Chapter 10 between two journalists, Henry Grady and Ida B. Wells, illustrate the importance of and the difficulties in applying a truth standard. Both rhetors used evidence convincingly to argue for entirely different assessments of Reconstruction; Grady boasts about its economic virtues, Wells decries its moral outrages. Which "truth" was more true? The media-hyped anti-tobacco Web site designed by youth for youth to warn browsers about the lies and hypocrisy of "Big Tobacco" appropriated a potent domain name: *Thetruth.com*. The Material for Analysis at the end of this chapter—an anonymously authored article on euthanasia published in the *Journal of the American Medical Association* entitled: "It's Over, Debbie"—will invite you to make difficult judgments, especially those based on truth standards.

In one respect, this standard conflicts with concerns for effects. Discourses that tell the whole truth, as far as that is possible, and adhere to strict, technical accuracy are likely to be suitable only for experts. In fact, if the truth standard were applied strictly, nearly all rhetorical acts would be judged inadequate, and the finest pieces of rhetoric would be those directed to an elite group of specialists. Given rhetoric's popular character and its role in social and public decision making, this standard alone would not be an appropriate basis for evaluating rhetorical action.

The Ethical Standard

The *ethical standard* is necessary because rhetoric is powerful, and criticism is a moral activity. It judges whether rhetoric helps or harms; whether it promotes social harmony or discord. It evaluates the social consequences of rhetorical action—both its purposes and the means by which they are achieved. It judges the long-term consequences of rhetoric for society (What happens to a political system in which voting decisions are made on the basis of 30-second television commercials?) and for future rhetorical action (How can we communicate about complex issues if norms for rhetorical action are limited to the short segments typical of commercial and cable television programming?) as well as how these are affected by new technology (How can we vote intelligently if political advertisers exploit the visual capacities of television and the unregulated congestion of cyberspace to prompt us to draw false conclusions?). Obviously, such judgments are highly controversial and, in some cases, they are directly related to the truth criterion.

Many and diverse rhetorical acts have come under heavy ethical scrutiny by politicians and advocacy groups for promoting excessive sex and violence, incivility, discrimination, and illegal activity, or for contributing generally to society's moral decline. A sample of these include the "gangsta rap" group Body Count's "Cop Killer," Eminem's "The Marshall Mathers LP," Napster's music file-sharing Web site, *Doom* video games, shock jock Howard Stern's morning show, and Louis Farrakhan's speeches on racial separatism. Ethical judgments are subjective; they require us to balance legitimate competing claims. There are limits on First Amendment freedoms, for example, but we ought to fight to see that only absolutely essential limits are set. Ethical evaluation requires that you take a close look at opposing views and at the social consequences of the ideas advocated. Then, ask yourself whether you have just defined as ethical only what is reformist or supports the status quo or what supports your point of view.

A good example for judging rhetoric using all four standards of evaluation is the classic political campaign spot for Lyndon Johnson in the 1964 presidential campaign: "The Daisy Spot." Created by media guru Tony Schwartz, the ad revolutionized political advertising in this country (Figure 11–2).

Aesthetically, the ad was an aural and visual masterpiece that responded inventively to rhetorical obstacles. The specter of the Kennedy assassination (only 11 months old) still loomed large. Politics had lost its innocence. Lyndon Johnson, the unelected president, was not a particularly likable candidate. He was a Texan, rough around the edges, whose manner was a sharp contrast to JFK's smooth, northeastern style. Schwartz, then still an obscure ad creator, convinced the Johnson campaign that he could create an ad that would solve the candidate's serious political problems and capitalize on his opponent's—Senator Barry Goldwater's—one major weakness: speaking glibly in ways that could frighten voters. Johnson bought it, and history was made. The commercial's content went like this: A little girl is sitting in a field counting petals on a daisy. In a cute way, she stumbles in her counting. As her count reaches ten, the visual motion is frozen, zooms in to the child's eye, then the viewer hears an ominous countdown. When the count reaches zero, we see a nuclear explosion and hear President Johnson say, "These are the stakes, to make a world in which all God's children can live or to go into the darkness. Either we must love each other or we must die." As the screen goes to black at the end, white lettering appears stating, "Vote for President Johnson on

Figure 11–2
"The Daisy Spot" Ad for the Johnson Presidential Campaign

VOTE FOR PRESIDENT JOHNSON
ON NOVEMBER 3.

November 3." The ad doesn't pack much power when you just read the words. But this ad gave birth to negative advertising via a clever enthymeme (it never says Goldwater will push the nuclear button, but it prompts viewers to think it); it was the first spot to use real children's voices as opposed to adults imitating children; it introduced natural sound (the actual countdown of a missile test); it used a fast-moving color and light scheme and a plethora of camera angles. Just four years earlier, the 1960 election had been marked by black and white, pre-produced jingles, cartoon images, and slow visual pacing. The Daisy Spot taught us that it is much more important for a voter to feel a candidate than to see him. In all, the Daisy Spot was in a league of its own.

The response it evoked was huge even though the ad aired only once on "Monday Night at the Movies." It created such controversy that the networks refused to run it again. A firestorm of protest erupted from Republicans who claimed that the spot accused Senator Goldwater of being trigger happy (although nowhere in the spot is Goldwater even mentioned). Goldwater's approval ratings plunged, and he never recovered. Goldwater himself credited this ad with contributing to his political defeat. The Daisy Spot is still referred to as the single most effective political ad ever produced.

Ethically, the ad was troublesome and teaches us that rhetorical ingenuity is not always synonymous with high moral standards. The sinister associations that the ad created in the minds of viewers between Goldwater and Armageddon frightened even the networks. Fearing legal retribution, they canceled future ad placements.

On truth grounds, the ad was difficult to evaluate because it was slippery. There are no facts or figures to dispute. There are no explicit claims. There are only frightening feelings and sinister associations created in the minds of viewers. Previous campaign rhetoric made the ad's enthymematic premise at least plausible. Goldwater had stated that he supported the use of tactical atomic weapons. The ad invited viewers to recall those startling admissions and contemplate the idea that he might actually use nuclear weapons in Vietnam. Special constraints weighed heavily on the ad's truth quotient.

SPECIAL CONSTRAINTS

Rhetorical evaluations must be modified in terms of the special pressures created by the context and the occasion. These special pressures or constraints (a constraint is something that limits, restricts, or regulates) include (1) *competing rhetorical action,* (2) *preceding or subsequent events,* (3) *the media of transmission,* and (4) *expectations and requirements created by the occasion.* Each of these should be examined to see if it leads us to qualify or refine our judgments about aesthetics, effects, truth, and ethics. The first two constraints will be treated here, the latter two in subsequent chapters.

Competing Rhetorical Action

Very few rhetorical acts occur in isolation, and many are part of campaigns and movements. But campaigns include competition from other persuaders—political candidates or advertisers—and movements are protests against the status quo, which will be defended by its supporters. In other words, much rhetoric occurs in a competitive environment, and it has to be judged in relation to its competition. It's nice to receive an award for excellence in advertising, for example, but it's equally important to know how well you did against competing products.

Political campaigns illustrate how competition modifies judgments. George W. Bush's performance in the 2000 presidential debates, for example, had to be assessed in comparison to that of Al Gore and in relation to each debate's format and time limits. Similarly, both Bush and Gore chose running mates that helped them refute possible claims. Dick Cheney is a highly experienced administrator with considerable foreign policy experience, a counter to Bush's limited experience in that area, and Joe Lieberman is a senator widely recognized for his integrity and probity, which helped to distance Gore from the ethical problems of the Clinton administration. In the high profile New York Senate race of 2000, Hillary Clinton's advertising campaign had to be judged against her first well-known opponent, mayor Rudy Giuliani and his abrupt withdrawal, her novice competitor and late entrant in the race, Rick Lazio, and against the protocol of her role as first lady. The powerful Daisy Spot must be assessed against its "low-tech" ad counterparts of the 1960s and against the kinds of brash rhetoric uttered by Goldwater during the campaign. A shining example of the power of competing rhetorical action on judgment was Elizabeth Hanford Dole's speech to the 1996 GOP convention on behalf of her husband, Bob. Through much of the campaign, she was compared to Hillary Rodham Clinton. Bob had been contrasted to Bill Clinton and viewed as too old, miserly, and dour. What to do to soften your own image and bolster that of your "helpmeet"? Break with tradition, move off the imposing platform, mingle with delegates, interact with audience members in an Oprahesque style, joke with Bob on the big screen, play adoring wife, and let ordinary people tell stories about how warm and likable Bob is. What a formula for success! Her unique and captivating address "stole the show" and met with rave reviews from all quarters. These cases illustrate that effective rhetoric is responsive to the specific context: It refutes precisely those charges made by the opposition; it reacts to issues of concern to this audience; it takes account of the stands of competing advocates. And what might be highly praised in one situation might be inappropriate for another.

Comparison is an integral part of assessing rhetorical acts. As you evaluate, consider the choices available and then examine the ways in which those choices were limited by opponents, by competing positions, or by events and issues. Ask yourself what was possible, given the situation. Given the opposition, what was the best strategy? Given competing persuaders, what role was possible, what purpose was reasonable? Pay special attention to attempts to respond to issues, charges, and opponents. These should help you notice one kind of constraint that limits rhetorical action.

Preceding or Subsequent Events

A rhetorical act is always one in a series of events. The meaning of a rhetorical act is not an absolute or a given; its character and meaning are always, in part, a function of the context in which it occurs. Evaluation needs to include an awareness of events that preceded and followed it because these may explain the act and modify its import.

Many examples of rhetorical acts illustrate these principles. In 1948, Margaret Chase Smith of Maine was elected to the Senate after four terms in the House of Representatives. As her career in the Senate began, Senator Joseph McCarthy, R-WI, was fanning the flames of the "Red Scare" by announcing that Communist spies had infiltrated the highest levels of the government, including the State Department. Although she was concerned about the issue, Chase Smith began cautiously to ask McCarthy for specific details, names, and numbers; McCarthy repeatedly avoided answering her questions.

After seeking the advice of journalist friends, she drafted a speech that objected to McCarthy's tactics but that never mentioned his name. She added a final statement of principles that was signed by six other Republican senators. On June 1, 1950, she addressed the Senate and delivered what came to be known as her "Declaration of Conscience" asking her Senate colleagues to "do some soul-searching . . . on the manner in which we are using or abusing our individual powers and privileges." Unless the reader knows about these prior events, the meaning of her words is not clear, and the excited reaction to her speech cannot be understood.

What has come to be called Richard Nixon's "Checkers Speech" (named for his children's dog Checkers, which was mentioned in the speech) is another example. Unless you know that Nixon had been accused of misusing funds given by wealthy supporters and was being pressured to resign as the vice-presidential candidate by the Republican National Committee, and that presidential candidate Dwight Eisenhower withheld his support even after Nixon was cleared of the charges by an audit and a legal opinion, and that his entire political future hung on whether he could generate an extraordinarily massive response from the audience, you are likely to view the speech as highly emotional and sentimental, a tearjerker. But when you know the events that preceded it, the speech takes on a slightly different hue.

What has come to be called Bill Clinton's "August 17th Speech" (likely named for its lack of a memorable image or theme) similarly showcases the importance of preceding events. Unless you remember that Clinton clung to a surprising 62 percent approval rating, even after Special Prosecutor Kenneth Starr published his 400 pages of evidence against the president, and even after the House voted to impeach him, you are likely to view his speech of self-defense (*apologia*) as too short on details, contrition, and conviction.

Earl Spencer's eulogy for his sister, Princess Diana, can only be fully appreciated if you know the troubled story of her life as a former Royal. From run-ins with the Queen, to episodes of bulimia, from the papparazzi's obsession with her, to the way in which she met her tragic death, the speech artfully "dances" between an uplifting memorial and a political statement.

As discussed earlier, the obstacle of cultural history is a long-term view of the problem of preceding events. In light of the past, a rhetor may be expected to develop a new argument, take a new perspective, develop a new role, or respond to unforeseen events. That was certainly the case for Elizabeth Cady Stanton, whose "The Solitude of Self" was crafted as a direct response to the 72-year-long intransigent resistance to woman suffrage in this country.

Subsequent events can have a variety of effects that complicate assessment. It is difficult to assess the final speech of Dr. Martin Luther King, Jr., for example, without being affected by what now seem to be his prophetic statements about his death. Similarly, in a little-known speech in 1962 in Newport, Rhode Island, President John F. Kennedy said of his family: "We are tied to the ocean. And when we go back to the sea, whether . . . it is to sail or to watch it, we are going back from whence we came." These words took on special poignancy after John F. Kennedy, Jr., lost control and crashed his single-engine plane into the sea with wife Carolyn Bessette and her sister aboard. That speech was reintroduced to millions of Americans by TV commentators, and a few of its words were splashed across a six-page full-color pullout in *Time* magazine in the wake of the accident. Subsequent events transformed those statements into memorable words that we interpret as having special significance.

Subsequent happenings can also become a truth standard against which to measure the claims of speakers. The tobacco companies now find themselves in court admitting that nicotine is addictive and that smoking causes lung cancer, emphysema, and other fatal diseases—contradicting 30 years of advertising and legal statements—in a desperate plea to reduce the enormous punitive damages awarded by jury verdicts against them. Similarly, the passage of time is the ultimate determinant of ethical judgments. Are certain rap lyrics or video games or Web sites really dangerous? Did Elvis Presley's startling new brand of rock-n-roll, complete with gyrating hips, corrupt his adoring fans? An ad campaign today for a financial service ridicules that idea, although it was taken quite seriously in the 1950s and 1960s. Furthermore, the ability of some rhetoric to withstand the test of time is clear evidence of artistic excellence. Thus, Lincoln's Gettysburg Address is no longer merely a speech made to honor those who died in the battle at Gettysburg; it remains an enduring commemoration of all those who have given their lives in battle for this nation. As time passes, you may be forced to take account of two different judgments: that of the immediate audience and that of history.

MATERIAL FOR ANALYSIS

The rhetorical act for analysis presumably is a firsthand account of a doctor performing euthanasia. It was published with the author's name withheld by request in a prestigious medical journal usually reserved for highly scientific, rigorously reviewed scholarship. The editor of the journal defended his decision to publish the piece by arguing that the story would provoke needed debate in this country over the controversial, and illegal, practice of physician-assisted suicide. Its release generated considerable controversy from all sides of the issue. Some physicians supported the author's actions and applauded his intimate portrayal of the issue; others were outraged. A grand jury in Chicago delivered a subpoena to the American Medical Association demanding the disclosure of the "murderer's" name. Still others chalked it up as a hoax, believing there were several medical inaccuracies and omissions in the story.[1]

It's Over, Debbie[2]

1   The Call came in the middle of the night. As a gynecology resident rotating through a large, private hospital, I had come to detest telephone calls, because invariably I would be up for several hours and would not feel good the next day. However, duty called, so I answered the phone. A nurse informed me that a patient was having difficulty getting rest, could I please see her. She was on 3 North. That was the gynecologic-oncology unit, not my usual duty station. As I trudged along, bumping sleepily against walls and corners and not believing I was up again, I tried to imagine what I might find at the end of my walk. Maybe an elderly woman with an anxiety reaction, or perhaps something particularly horrible.

2   I grabbed the chart from the nurses station on my way to the patient's room and the nurse gave me some hurried details: a 20-year-old girl named Debbie was dying of ovarian cancer. She was having unrelenting vomiting apparently as the result of an alcohol drip administered for sedation. Hmmm, I thought. Very sad. As I approached the room I could hear loud, labored breathing. I entered and saw an

emaciated, dark-haired woman who appeared much older than 20. She was receiving nasal oxygen, had an IV and was sitting in bed suffering from what was obviously severe air hunger. The chart noted her weight at 80 pounds. A second woman, also dark-haired but of middle age, stood at her right, holding her hand. Both looked up as I entered. The room seemed filled with the patient's desperate effort to survive. Her eyes were hollow, and she had suprasternal and intercostal retractions with her rapid inspirations. She had not eaten or slept in two days. She had not responded to chemotherapy and was being given supportive care only. It was a gallows scene, a cruel mockery of her youth and unfulfilled potential. Her only words to me were, "Let's get this over with."

3   I retreated with my thought to the nurses station. The patient was tired and needed rest. I could not give her health, but I could give her rest. I asked the nurse to draw 20 mg. of morphine sulfate into a syringe. Enough, I thought, to do the job. I took the syringe into the room and told the two women I was going to give Debbie something that would let her rest and to say good-bye. Debbie looked at the syringe, then laid her head on the pillow with her eyes open, watching what was left of the world. I injected the morphine intravenously and watched to see if my calculations on its effects would be correct. Within seconds her breathing slowed to a normal rate, her eyes closed, and her features softened as she seemed restful at last. The older woman stroked the hair of the now-sleeping patient. I waited for the inevitable next effect of depressing the respiratory drive. With clocklike certainty, within four minutes the breathing rate slowed even more, then became irregular, then ceased. The dark-haired woman stood erect and seem relieved.

4   It's over, Debbie.

Questions for Analysis

1. How would you rate this story using an aesthetic standard of evaluation? A truth standard? An ethical standard? If your judgments are uneven or difficult to make, explain. How does the class as a whole rate the story using an effects standard. In other words, does the story prompt you to view euthanasia more favorably or unfavorably?
2. How do narrative structure, descriptive language, and enthymematic arguments work together in this rhetorical act that would explain the intense and varied reactions to it?
3. What preceding or subsequent events in this country (media-hyped trials, for instance) or in your area (an exchange between political candidates or religious leaders) might affect your reaction to the story?

EXERCISES

1. As a class, arrange to attend a movie together or rent it to view at home. Be prepared to discuss it in an agreed-upon class period. Give the movie a separate evaluation using all four criteria: aesthetics, effects, truth, and ethics. Compare your results with the results of other class members in group discussions. After exchanging judgments, can you see why evaluating rhetoric is fraught with challenges? How does evaluating a film along different lines help you appreciate it better? Which standard of evaluation was the most difficult for your to apply? Why?

2. Evaluate a Web site of your choice, using the Web Site Critique template in the Appendix. The Web Site Critique is designed to help you fulfill all the critic's responsibilities when judging discourse. Recall from Chapter 2 that criticism is a process that requires first, careful description, second, recognizing aspects of the rhetorical problem, and finally, making evaluations based on four separate criteria.

3. According to the article "The Female Persuasion" (*American Demographics*, February 1, 2002, p. 24) in your InfoTrac College Edition database, women's magazines have been more successful at delivering female audiences to marketers than women-oriented TV shows. Apply the four standards outlined in Chapter 11 to the information provided in the article in order to evaluate the rhetorical performance of women's magazines. Take into consideration the immediate rhetorical purposes of the magazines as well as their larger social influence. Which standard do you consider most/least relevant, objective, common, or significant in evaluating the discourses of women's magazines?

4. **Portfolio Entry 10: Evaluation**
Evaluate your rhetorical acts according to the four criteria discussed in this chapter: aesthetics, truth, ethics, effects. Can you proclaim a single winner? In what ways were these judgments easy? Difficult? Respond in two to three pages.

NOTES

1. See Michael J. Hyde, "Medicine, Rhetoric, and Euthanasia: A Case Study in the Workings of a Postmodern Discourse," in *Readings in Rhetorical Criticism*, ed. Carl R. Burgchardt (State College, PA: Strata Publications, 1995), pp. 590–607.

2. "It's Over, Debbie," *Journal of the American Medical Association* 259 (January 1988): 272. Reprinted by permission.

chapter 12

Understanding Visual Rhetoric

Images that aim to influence us are inescapable (see Figure 12–1). Sculpture, picket and traffic signs, religious and political symbols, music videos, films, television programming, photographs, computer icons, Web sites, paintings, posters, print ads, architecture, dance, parades, corporate logos, billboards, and many other visual events enrich and clutter our symbolic landscape. This chapter examines the special characteristics and constraints of analyzing rhetorical acts that are primarily visual. In Chapter 3, you were introduced to nonverbal features of speechmaking and how to use visual aids appropriately. In public speaking, the visual aspects of rhetoric are secondary. Such nonverbals as sustained eye contact, natural gestures, and erect posture are designed to enhance, not substitute for, the verbal message. Visual aids should be used sparingly and not overshadow the rhetor's words. Visual rhetoric as examined in this chapter, however, means that the image is the entire or the dominant persuasive message. Words, if used at all, are relegated to caption status; they are handmaidens to the images. A sophisticated critique of messages that magnify the visual and minimize the verbal requires specialized knowledge of visual principles, production techniques as they relate to the elements of descriptive analysis, and the problems such rhetoric poses for evaluation.

Figure 12–1
Visual Rhetorical Images

PRINCIPLES OF VISUAL RHETORIC

Three principles or observations about visual rhetoric anchor the critical perspective advanced here. First, *visual messages are pervasive and threaten to eclipse the influence of the spoken and written word in the twenty-first century.* Children today spend seven times as much time watching television as reading. Video stores outnumber libraries three to one in most cities. A majority of adults can readily discuss the last film they saw but have some trouble recalling the last speech they heard face-to-face and unmediated, and they cannot remember when they last finished a book. Educators now refer to children as visual learners and embrace visual pedagogy (art, dance, video, and the like) to teach subjects ranging from history to health. More than 60 percent of our grocery store purchases are impulse buying, which is primarily a result of packaging—the way the product looks and its placement on the shelves. Ronald McDonald is second only to Santa Claus as a recognized icon by Americans. At sporting events, in concert halls, political rallies, even in our houses of worship, eyes turn away from the real event as soon as images begin to move on giant screens. Some critics insist that television itself has been transformed since the 1980s from a word-based rhetoric with minimal production values to a visually based mythic rhetoric that uses sophisticated production techniques to project an extreme self-consciousness of style.[1]

Visual rhetoric is pervasive, in part, because it is powerful. *Visual messages are volatile, eliciting positive and negative responses simultaneously.* The familiar expressions "Seeing is believing" and "A picture is worth a thousand words" capture their high ethos appeal. Paul Messaris, a scholar of visual literacy, writes: "Photographs come with an inherent guarantee of authenticity that is absent from words." He relates a story from the civil rights movement that captures poignantly the authority and trust we place in visual rhetoric. Dr. Martin Luther King, Jr., stood alongside a photographer watching a policeman beat a young civil rights worker. The photographer became so upset at what he was shooting that he stopped, poised to intervene. King reminded him of the importance of his work: "Unless you record the injustice, the world won't know that the child got beaten. . . . I'm not being cold blooded about it, but it is so much more important for you to take a picture of us getting beaten up than for you to be another person joining in the fray."[2] Killian Jordon, senior editor of *Life* magazine, summed up the power of a great visual by saying simply: "It tells the truth. It documents. It makes a statement: Life will never be the same."[3] And yet, other maxims remind us of the dark side of visuals. "Do not be deceived by appearances," "Do not judge a book by its cover," and from the Bible: "Cursed be the man who makes a graven or molten image." Perception and knowledge, appearance and truth, often are at odds with each other. Plato spent a lifetime telling us as much. Journalism educator Mitchell Stephens captures the negatives of visual rhetoric succinctly: "Images look real but are fake. They pretend to be what they are not. They lie. The portrait is a mute, lifeless substitute for the person; the idol, a primitive and superficial knockoff of the god. But that idol is also attractive and easy to see. It can distract from the more profound but more amorphous glories of the god."[4] The advent of digital manipulation has made the negative influences of visuals even more serious.

Despite its distracting and even dangerous implications, the enchantment and ease with which visual rhetoric is digested leads to the final premise: *Visual messages are efficient, emotional, and enthymematic in the way they persuade.* "Images," Stephens continues, "are marvelously accessible."[5] We can grasp images quickly and process the ideas

Figure 12–2
*Visual Rhetorical
Symbols*

they suggest with greater efficiency. The symbols you see in Figure 12–2 demonstrate this concise feature. For viewers young to old, crossing all educational levels, and transcending language and literacy, these symbols communicate quickly and effortlessly—especially important in a fast-paced world that demands multitasking and quick decision making.

Images also exude emotion. They "sear great events in the public memory and wring revelation from small, private moments" says *Life* magazine.[6] They are pleasing to the eye. Art historians John Walker and Sarah Chaplin observe that pleasure and pain are a central part of the experience of visual culture. These emotional states are the means by which visual culture seduces us.[7] The montage of news photos at the beginning of this chapter illustrates the pathos appeal of visual rhetoric in all its highs and lows, from the exhilaration of a sporting triumph (Barry Bonds's record-setting 73 home runs; Brandi Chastain celebrating shirtless after the USA World Cup soccer victory), to the horror and sadness of national tragedy (terrorist-directed planes crashing into the World Trade Center; an Oklahoma City fireman holding a victim of the federal building bombing; JFK, Jr., saluting the bier of his assassinated father). The "Tiny Targets" photo of children in a Los Angeles day care center being escorted by police after yet another incident of school violence so moved one New York mother that she founded the Million Mom March on Washington. Nick Ut's Pulitzer-Prize winning image of a naked, screaming Vietnamese girl in the aftermath of an U.S.-ordered napalm air strike hastened the end of the Vietnam War. Its emotional horror so tormented the U.S. army captain who ordered the air strike that he personally sought out the girl, Kim Phuc, to seek her forgiveness.[8]

Images invite viewers to draw their own persuasive conclusions; they do not argue explicitly. As such, they can create associations in ways that would be too audacious or laborious to say or write. Recall from the previous chapter the enthymematic message of the "Daisy Spot." The highly successful "Got Milk?" ad campaign encourages viewers to make all kinds of playful and health-conscious connections. Try to articulate them by looking at the picture at the beginning of the chapter. One of the first ads ever produced that capitalized on the idea that sex can sell anything was a 1965

Noxema commercial in which a beautiful Swedish blonde whispers "Men, nothing takes it off like Noxema" to striptease music. That commercial is still ranked as one of the top ten commercials of all time for suggesting what could not be verbalized.[9] The ambiguity of verbal rhetoric also means that it can produce an excess of meaning, something philosopher Umberto Eco calls "the fatal polysemy of images."[10] The Vietnam War memorial was criticized for its rich possibilities of meaning. What do the two space pictures at the beginning of this chapter ("Earthrise" and the plumes of smoke from the Challenger space shuttle) communicate, especially for those not living during these turning points in U.S. space history? The abstractness of much postmodern art has generated humor from some and protest from others for its seemingly limitless interpretations. Clearly, the enthymematic qualities of images cut both ways.

VISUAL MESSAGES AND ELEMENTS OF DESCRIPTIVE ANALYSIS

With these principles of visual rhetoric in mind, some of its special features can be introduced and analyzed (Figure 12–3). Just as we would not try to criticize a music score using only notes from the treble clef, we cannot analyze visual rhetoric using only a few perceptual cues. The rhetorical ability of any visual field is, to a great degree, a function of the artistic and production techniques utilized in its creation.[11] Two sets of specialized grammars will be introduced here: (1) *basic elements of visual communication* and (2) *technical elements of the camera.* The first set of specialized features covers a wide range of visual phenomena; the second set applies only to the mass media. Both are vital to understanding the rhetorical force of a visual's purpose, audience, tone, persona, structure, evidence, and strategies.

At least four paired elements compose the core of visual messages: (1) *figure and ground;* (2) *shapes and space;* (3) *balance and direction;* (4) *color and lighting.*[12] Visuals insist that we determine the relationship between the subject and its background if we are to understand its purpose. Scenic backdrops confer meaning on the primary object.

Figure 12–3
Visual Rhetoric and Descriptive Analysis

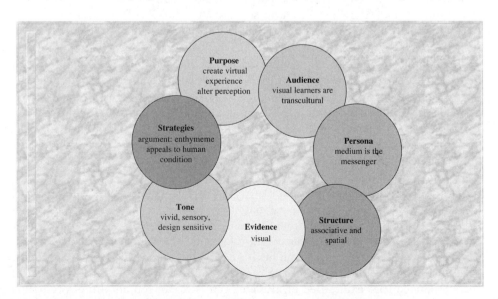

Our perception is altered greatly depending on whether a person's face is framed in a police lineup on *America's Most Wanted* or in a "Look Who's 40" lineup in the local newspaper. The three basic shapes of images—the square, triangle, and circle—conjure up distinct emotions. Typically, square-shaped objects connote straightness, honesty, and sometimes dullness. Triangular images tend to suggest conflict and action. Circular forms frequently project warmth and security. Consider the expressions: "He's a square"; "It's a love triangle"; "She has a circle of love and support." One has to remember, though, that these are not fixed associations, and breaches do not mean that the shapes lack artistic merit. The size, scale, and number of these shapes are related to how space is used. Lots of white space has often been associated with luxury, higher class, and independence; cramped space sometimes suggests the opposite. Contrast grocery ads with high-end cosmetic ads for expensive products. Examined in combination, shape and space are strategies that help us confer meaning on an image, especially in regard to such elements as purpose and tone.

Balance and direction are perceptual cues that help us organize a visual. Images present themselves as either symmetrical or asymmetrical—arranged equally or unequally on both sides of an imaginary line in the middle of a visual field. Symmetry is designed to suggest formality and is visually comforting; asymmetry tends to suggest informality and creates dissonance. Further, visuals direct our eyes to move in certain directions. Unlike the act of reading, which requires the same horizontal left-to-right eye movement, the act of perceiving has no automatic start and end point. Ads, for instance, sometimes want us to start with the copy and move to the visual or vice versa.

Color and lighting affect mood and contribute greatly to how visuals create virtual experience. Even our language reinforces this. "She has a sunny disposition"; "He's blue today"; "I see red, I'm so angry"; "He's down to earth"; "You get a gold star"; "There's a silver lining to the story"; "We're a green corporation—environmentally friendly"; "We're unsure; it's a gray area." Black-and-white photos are described as "classic"; polarized issues are depicted as "black and white"; "The Rainbow Coalition" suggests unity and even righteousness. Lighting can heighten or diminish the intensity of an image. Flat lighting (no shadows) diminishes intensity; textured lighting (varied lights and shadows) heightens intensity. Contrast the lighting in a doctor's waiting room with that in a sports bar, an educational program with a horror flick.

More specialized technical features of visual rhetoric include (1) *focus*, (2) *angle*, (3) *shot sequencing and movement*, (4) *editing*, and (5) *sound*.[13] The sharpness or fuzziness of an image helps us interpret mood and our relationship to an image. Hard focus is objective and distancing; soft focus is subjective and intimate. Pictures on identification cards are hard focus (unless they are flubbed); glamour portraits are soft focus. Angle, the position of the camera relative to its subject, projects the camera's persona and positions the viewer in relationship to the object. Media critic Joshua Meyrowitz reminds us that low-angle shots suggest power and authority; level shots connote a peer relationship with the viewer; high-angle shots are used to show that someone is small or weak.[14] Focus and angle are especially useful strategies for examining persona-audience associations.

Moreover, the type of shot (super close-up, close-up, medium close-up, medium shot, wide shot) is used strategically to alter our perceptions of an image. Close-ups project intimacy and encourage viewers to feel empathy. Television reporters are seldom shot in close-ups in order to maintain the aura of impersonal objectivity; protesters, on the other hand, sometimes try literally to get in the camera's face.[15] To move images, the camera has about as many options as a roller coaster. It can zoom, pan, tilt, roll, dolly; it can be stationary or hand-held. To sequence images in such a way as to invite enthymematic response, the camera can adopt a volatile montage structure— the juxtaposition of different images that stimulates a new meaning in the viewer's mind.[16] Music videos have demonstrated the rhetorical potency of this montage structure. Each picture looked at separately is rather benign; when edited together with fast cuts, these images take on a whole new, and often subversive, meaning. Sometimes editing is smooth and seamless (as when dissolves and fades are used); other times editing is disruptive and jarring (as when wipes and jump cuts are used). At all times, editing is vital to the pacing and rhythm of a visual. Shot selection and sequencing also act as important proofs for the visual's purpose.

Finally, sound (sound effects, natural sound, music, narration, dialogue) envelops the viewer in a pleasing virtual reality, establishes a mood, and becomes a visual poetics. The natural sound used in the "Daisy Spot" was startlingly real to viewers and heightened the ominous juxtaposition between innocence and evil that the ad was trying to convey. Charlton Heston is spokesperson for a host of corporations owing, in part, to his authoritative, soothing voice. Famous ad jingles—from Alka Seltzer's "pop, pop, fizz, fizz, oh, what a relief it is" to Budweiser's "Whaaaaas Uuuuuuup,"—use alliteration, rhythm, metaphor, personification, and a host of other poetic devices to ratchet up the emotional quotient of the visual message.

Taken together, these basic and technological features give us the tools and a vocabulary to analyze visual rhetoric in a sophisticated and meaningful way. Television critics in the industry and in academia have used these elemental and technical features of visual messages to make powerful rhetorical analyses of popular shows ranging from *Leave It to Beaver, All in the Family,* and M*A*S*H* to *Hill Street Blues* and *NYPD.* For instance, a body of research now concludes that early TV shows adopted a utilitarian approach to the relationship between the shows' narratives and their production techniques, meaning that aesthetic and technological features were camouflaged and predictable (always an establishing shot to a medium shot) and distancing (rarely were close-ups used). Contemporary shows, on the other hand, adopt a more rhetorical approach, a "more aggressive use of the camera."[17] Everything from tighter control of screen space, varied lighting, disruptive edits juxtaposed with whip pans, to hand-held cameras and wide experimentation with angles produce a chaotic visual image that overwhelms dialogue and heightens visual spectacle.[18]

PROBLEMS OF VISUAL RHETORIC

One of the things you probably noticed in the application of elements of descriptive analysis to basic and technological features of visual messages is that the terms *audience* and *persona* undergo major transformations. A viewer is different from an audience. A camera is different from a speaker or writer. Because images are made to be seen, they demand lookers, but unlike other forms of rhetoric, they do not demand an acknowledgment that a viewer exists. As Walker and Chaplin conclude: "We enjoy images voyeuristically: we can look at a scene as if we were peering into a room through a one-way mirror. Fundamental to the appeal of visual media is . . . that we can watch to our heart's content without ourselves being observed."[19] Witness the huge hit series, *Survivor,* one of the most voyeuristic shows ever produced. That voyeuristic experience is also typically a solitary one and diminishes our influence over the rhetorical act. Stephens observes that in visual culture, "we, the audience, have no influence on anything that transpires. Shows proceed entirely without us. As the pawn of such large, intractable forces, a viewer can end up feeling somewhat small."[20] And yet, the viewer is an economic entity for the visual media. Despite all the references to television viewers as "couch potatoes," they are not seen as passive voyeurs by sponsors; rather, they are conceived as active buyers and discriminating consumers.[21]

Other audience-related problems with visual rhetoric begin with misperception. The gross oversimplification of visuals leading to distortion is a byproduct of an image's wonderful efficiency and potent emotionalism. Although some of this concern has already been discussed in the section dealing with principles of visual rhetoric, other emphases need to be made here. We tend to process complicated events and issues, like war, in all-too-simplistic terms. Americans had no interest in the Kosovo conflict until pictures of ethnic Albanians herded into cattle cars, reminiscent of scenes from Nazi Germany, hit the national press and the airwaves. Outrage erupted. Ditto for the Gulf War that preceded it. Until a graphic picture of an American GI tortured and killed and dragged through the streets of Somalia found its way into our living rooms, Americans supported peace-keeping there. The abortion debate was reignited and has resulted in tougher abortion restrictions in many states because horrible pictures and videos of third-trimester abortions (labeled "partial-birth abortions") have been shown to elected officials. When domestic and international policy is made by agents of change solely or in large measure based on pictures, we have reason to be concerned. Neil Postman, an inveterate critic of visual rhetoric, once said glibly: "It is implausible to imagine that anyone like our 27th President, the multi-chinned, 300-pound William Howard Taft, could be put forward as a presidential candidate in today's world" because the shape of a man's body is just as relevant to an audience enamored by visuals as the shape of his ideas.[22]

A second audience-related problem emanating from visuals is a lack of cultural history. The lack of context, which leaves viewers guessing, is a byproduct of an image's ability to persuade enthymematically. In short, the cultural history void of visuals creates inert viewers. Lacking a way to communicate critical context, pictures lose their punch. Consider this button:

When I showed it to a class of freshman students, they interpreted it variously. All recognized the "no" circle, now common on traffic markers, that something is prohibited. But just what was prohibited was unclear. One person said, "No more hang-ups." Another said, "Don't keep me hanging." Only one person was certain. She recognized the button as one distributed by the National Abortion Rights Action League

(N.A.R.A.L.) and translated it as "No more illegal, unsafe abortions." Because the button is highly abstract, it is ambiguous. For that reason, visual rhetoric works best with viewers who are "true believers"—those who already agree. An ideal viewer for the button is a member of N.A.R.A.L. who recalls the higher rates of maternal death and sterility that resulted from illegal abortions performed under unsanitary conditions and with improper instruments, such as a coat hanger.

The persona of visual rhetoric is equally complex. Viewpoint is located in the camera, which can move from an objective or subjective role, a dominant or diminished role with the blink of an eye. The latitude of a visual persona is far-reaching. Like the Wizard of Oz, if you strip away the technological bells and whistles of the visual rhetor, you are often unimpressed by what is left. Does this mean that the rhetor's reputation is not important? (Who is the camera operator, film director, artist, or sculptor?) Can we read a visual message carefully without knowing whether a veteran or novice videographer shot it? If a right- or left-wing, male or female, Caucasian or ethnic minority, straight or gay artist sculpted it? Even written rhetoric comes with bylines and sometimes pictures of the writer. Visual rhetoric dwarfs the importance of the human rhetor. To alter a famous saying by the Canadian cultural scholar Marshall McLuhan, "The Medium Is the Messenger."

Finally, visual rhetoric is difficult to judge. How do we know, for instance, if nondiscursive rhetoric is effective, if our traditional ways of finding out require subjects to be articulate in the discursive mode? To be sure, we will always have Nielsen ratings and box office numbers, but what about the effects of other visual phenomena? Can focus group members articulate how an ad campaign, a memorial, a corporate logo works for them? Since most visual rhetoric is absorbed by solitary viewers, a sense of collective support or rejection is difficult to achieve. A corollary to the standing ovation is difficult to find when people are observing a magazine ad, whizzing by a billboard, or contemplating a piece of modern art.

How do we censure unethical images when they only suggest harm, not spell it out explicitly? Should Benetton, the hip Italian clothier, be punished for its ads on billboards and Web sites that humanize death row inmates in soft focus mug shots, show graphic violence, film an AIDS patient's last breath? It certainly is difficult to prosecute potentially harmful visual messages when the "proof" is not in the pudding but in someone's head. Still, voices of protest do work. R. J. Reynolds's hip spokes-animal "Joe Camel" was roundly criticized by educators for making kids think smoking is cool. The pressure worked, and Joe has disappeared.

How do we judge the truthfulness of a photo when digital manipulation makes it virtually impossible to detect alteration? The sinister-looking picture of O. J. Simpson at the beginning of this chapter calls attention to truth issues. In 1994, *Time* magazine placed defendant O. J. on its cover after the opening of "the trial of the century," in which he was charged with the murders of his wife and a friend. The only problem was that the picture was digitally altered. Simpson's face was purposely darkened—a retouching practice that has become increasingly common. In this case, the alteration was discovered and raised public awareness of the technique. But what about other, more covert, alterations and acts of staging? In the film, *Wag the Dog*, the use of visual deception was raised to comic proportions, but it underscores just how far technology can take us in transforming visuals into mass falsehoods.

How do we evaluate aesthetics without getting lost or mesmerized by all the fancy footwork that technology has to offer? Is *NYPD* artistically brilliant because it makes us dizzy? Because we are aware of its production values? It is challenging to balance an artistic appreciation that is sensitive to techniques but that does not lose sight of the narratives these techniques support. Meaningful aesthetic judgment requires critics who are literate in both word content and technical grammar—no small feat. These questions concerning the perils of judgment and the complex rhetor–viewer relationship further expose the volatility of visual rhetoric and underscore the importance of recognizing its special constraints if we are ever to understand how visuals influence.

MATERIAL FOR ANALYSIS

See the photo montage of key moments in U.S. culture at the beginning of this chapter. Choose one or more and address the following questions.

Questions for Analysis

1. What feelings do you have about these pictures? Must you have lived through these events for them to be meaningful to you? How do they support the three principles of visual rhetoric discussed in this chapter?
2. How does each picture create virtual experience and alter perception? How does each serve an instrumental and/or a consummatory purpose? Do some measure up better than others in achieving these purposes?
3. What is the general tone of each? How do basic elements and technical features of visual rhetoric contribute to tone?
4. Can you discern a target audience for each picture? Is it nondiscriminating? Is there a consumer interest? Do these pictures invite voyeur tendencies?
5. Which appeals are primary? Are they universal or culture specific? How do they help you form enthymematic responses?
6. Can you imagine another pictorial composite (angle, color, focus, shot sequence, balance, figure/ground, etc.) in which the reaction to the picture would be quite different?
7. Does the organization or individual credited for the photograph (persona) influence the credibility of the picture? How?
8. Do these 12 pictures, representing very different eras, events, and contexts but presented together (montage structure), influence your reaction to any one of them? How?

EXERCISES

1. Emoticons—for example, :) and :(—in e-mail are part of Internet etiquette. Why? Do you use them? Why or why not? Do they work to complement or detract from the written message?

2. Psychologists tell us that color choice is directly related to mood states. Examine several Web sites or print ads and discuss how color contributes to the tone of the site.

3. If you own a camera without a zoom lens, you know how frustrating it is to take shots of people. Find 6 to 12 photos of people you have taken that represent some of the different shots presented in this chapter. How does the type of shot affect the rhetorical value of your pictures?

4. Divide into groups. Each group is required to tape a desired music video. Discuss how montage structure

works to create certain enthymemes. Are any of these subversive? Are production values of the video pleasing? Disturbing? Explain.

5. Body piercing, tattoos, jewelry, hats, and T-shirts often function as visual rhetoric. Explain how these work as popular and concise expressions of people's beliefs. Are any of these body symbols ambiguous? Is that an oxymoron, or might that be strategic? Why?

6. Read the articles "Visual Rhetoric in Advertising: Text-Interpretive, Experimental, and Reader-Response Analyses" (*Journal of Consumer Research* 26 [June 1999]: 37) and "Images in Advertising: The Need for a Theory of Visual Rhetoric" (*Journal of Consumer Research* 21 [September 1994]: 252[22]) in the InfoTrac College Edition database. What do these articles add to your understanding of the power of visual rhetoric?

Using the InfoTrac College Edition database, go over the titles appearing in the *Petersen's Photographic* journal in the last three years. How do changes in photographic technology affect the possibilities and social roles of visual rhetoric?

7. **Portfolio Entry 11: Visuals**
Compare and contrast the ways that your three rhetorical selections use visuals to advance their purpose. Are words central to the rhetorical acts or are they reduced to caption status? Which principles of visual rhetoric are most apparent? What essential and technical aspects of visual rhetoric are important to your selections? Explain. How do they relate to Audience? Structure? Strategies? Tone? Persona? Evidence? (If visuals are not included, speculate in one to three pages how the selections could be enhanced with a visual component.)

NOTES

1. See a host of media literacy sites for studies on the prevalence of media culture, including www.medialiteracy.com; for consumer behavior and visual consumption, see Arthur Asa Berger, *Seeing Is Believing* (Mountain View, CA: Mayfield Publishing, 1998), p. 31. For a "top ten" listing of cultural icons, see A&E Network series, *The T.V. Ad*, July 2000; the argument that television programming has adopted a more self-conscious visual style is made by John Thornton Caldwell, *Televisuality: Style, Crisis, and Authority in American Television* (New Brunswick, NJ: Rutgers University Press, 1995), p. 4.

2. Paul Messaris, *Visual Persuasion* (Thousand Oaks, CA: Sage, 1997), p. 141.

3. Killian Jordan, "Editor's Note," in the "Collector's Edition, Great Pictures of the Century," *Life* (October 1999): 10.

4. Mitchell Stephens, *The Rise of the Image, the Fall of the Word* (Oxford: Oxford University Press, 1998), p. 60.

5. Stephens, p. 61.

6. *Life*, p. 16.

7. John A. Walker and Sarah Chaplin, *Visual Culture: An Introduction* (Manchester: Manchester University Press, 1997), p. 150.

8. Louise Steinman, "The Girl in the Photo," salon.com, August 3, 2000.

9. The ad was rated the sixth best ad of all time according to Arts and Entertainment network, *The TV Ad*, July 2000.

10. Umberto Eco, *The Search for the Perfect Language*, trans. James Fentress (Oxford: Oxford University Press, 1995), p. 174.

11. One of the first researchers to enunciate this clearly was David Barker, "Television Production Techniques in Communication," *Critical Studies in Mass Communication* (Sept. 1985): 234–246.

12. Many production scholars have conceptualized these components. I have taken the liberty of pairing them. For a good overview, see Berger, 53–66.

13. Berger, pp. 83, 97–99.

14. Joshua Meyerowitz, "Multiple Media Literacies," in *Television: The Critical View*, 6th ed., ed. Horace Newcomb (Oxford University Press, 2000), pp. 425–438.

15. Meyerowitz, p. 430.

16. Messaris, pp. 168–169.

17. See Barker.

18. Caldwell, p. 64.

19. Walker and Chaplin, p. 101.

20. Stephens, p. 127.

21. See Caldwell.

22. Neil Postman, *Amusing Ourselves to Death* (New York: Penguin, 1985), p. 7.

chapter 13

Understanding the Medium of Transmission

I f you were to take a basic pop culture literacy test, it would be saturated with media trivia. Many of the questions would be "no-brainers"—akin to the first several questions on *Who Wants to Be a Millionaire?* which is a popular media event in its own right. Other questions might make you think, but chances are you would not draw a blank unless you have been living in a remote corner of the globe or in a coma for much of your life. Everything from personalities, icons, slogans, acronyms, terms, even historical events would compose the test's contents. Is it any wonder that dictionaries of the mass media catalog 35,000 words in the English language related to this behemoth industry?[1] Take a moment to complete this mock quiz:

What do Rupert Murdoch, Ted Turner, and Gene Autry have in common?
In what medium do Ellen Goodman, George Will, and Maureen Doud appear?
What do Dr. Laura, the Sports Babe, and Rush Limbaugh have in common?
Which network has a peacock icon? An eye icon?
What Internet search engine's full name is Yet Another Hierarchical Officious Oracle?
What dotcom says: "Work Shouldn't Be Work!"
What do MTV, WB, BET, AP, and UPI stand for?
What do "flaming," "V-chip," "hits," "streaming," "segue," "look live," and "scoop" mean?

Can you name these products from their slogans: "Plop, plop, fizz, fizz"; "He likes it. Hey, Mikey"; "Where's the Beef?"; "You deserve a break today"?

Can you explain why the following media events have been chronicled as U.S. history: Orson Welles's broadcast of "The War of the Worlds"; FDR's fireside chats; the presidential debate between Kennedy and Nixon; the moon landing of Apollo 13; Seymour Hersh's coverage of the Vietnam War; Woodward and Bernstein's coverage of Watergate; the impact of such shows as *I Love Lucy, All in the Family, ER,* and even Super Bowl ads?

Can you identify scary moments in media history? The "Love Bug," Ted Kaczynski's "Manifesto" in the *Washington Post*? Or CNN's coverage of the Gulf War?

Check your media aptitude with the answers at the end of the chapter. This mock quiz leads to the overriding premise of the chapter: *The mass media are powerful because they pervade our culture, carry moral authority, and acquire special influence through their means of transmission.*

This chapter is a media literacy primer, which means it is designed to teach you how to engage media texts, to become discerning citizens rather than blind consumers, and even to challenge media institutions. It builds on the fundamentals, resources, and special constraints presented in earlier chapters. It takes the elements of descriptive analysis, the rhetorical problem, and standards of evaluation and asks questions such as: How do the mass media invite our assent? What are the promises and the perils of the mass media as influence peddlers? How does the medium of communication (newspaper, radio, television, and the Internet) affect the rhetorical message? How can you apply this knowledge in analyzing a news story?

THE MASS MEDIA AS RHETORICAL CONSTRUCT

The mass media are powerful because they pervade our culture. Try to imagine a day without exposure to media. One of the exercises at the end of this chapter invites you to "tune out" your favorite mass medium for one full week and record what kind of "withdrawals" you experience. If you are like most people, this will be a challenging assignment. Newspapers are delivered daily to homes; they can be found in vendors at bus stops, train depots, airports, restaurants, and hotels. Radio infiltrates doctors' and dentists' offices, malls, eateries, and elevators; it wakes us up in the morning and takes us to work. Joggers carry Walkman radios and kids bring "boom boxes" to the playgrounds. Big-screen televisions demand our attention at sporting events, political conventions, even the more intimate, religious settings at worship services, wedding receptions, and funerals. It's no surprise that the average television set is on seven hours and two minutes a day; that we listen to radio on the average of three hours a day and that we read at least one magazine or newspaper three times a week. What may come as a surprise, however, is that already by 1980, more U.S. homes had TV sets than indoor toilets, that the average adult spends more than half of his or her waking life with the media, that high school kids have clocked twice as many hours watching television as the hours spent in school, and that experts now predict that Generation Y users (ages 10–17) will spend close to one-third of their lives (23 years, 2 months) on the Internet![2]

Mass media are extraordinarily influential because they acquire intellectual and moral authority. We are loath to admit this, much preferring to engage in media bashing. The newspaper is a "rag," that prints "yellow journalism" and is only good for "lining bird cages." Television is "the boob tube," a "vast wasteland," even "chewing gum for the eyes." The internet has been called "conspiracy connection," a "congested web," even "a cyber-trap where anarchy rules." Radio personalities are referred to as "shock jocks," and as a medium radio has been accused of spewing forth more subversive discourse and propaganda than any of its media counterparts. Throughout history, we often have "killed the messenger." Since the time of the early Greeks, bad news has often resulted in scapegoating the courier. In some sense, the media have intensified that phenomenon by encouraging viewers, listeners, and subscribers to "sound off" on their "opinion lines."

Though media bashing is commonplace, the influence of the media on our lives is undeniable. For many, media are more credible and trustworthy than family, places of worship, and interpersonal relationships. Media critic Neil Postman argues that "television has become the command centre of our culture. . . . It has become an analogue to what the medieval church was in the 14th or 15th centuries. For anything to be legitimate it has to come through television."[3] Another way of documenting the media's influence is to recognize just how frequently it validates experience. Individuals who have witnessed crimes, for instance, often report that it was not until they saw, heard, or read the news of the event that the experience became real, that they believed it actually happened, and that it was important.[4] Survey results confirm media's enormous influence too. Two-thirds of all Americans depend on television as their main source of information. Sixty-three percent of Americans find television news more believable than religious institutions. When children between the ages of four and six were asked whether they liked television or their fathers better, 54 percent of those sampled chose television. Children between the ages of 11 and 17 will communicate on the Internet with persons they never have met 11 times more frequently than they will spend communicating face-to-face with their parents over the course of a lifetime.[5]

How did media personalities come to replace parents and priests as voices of authority? Why do we spend more time with a TV dinner than around a dinner table? Why are we more comfortable in a chat room with strangers than in the town square with our neighbors? Why are we more likely to be a radio caller than a speaker at city hall? Norman Rockwell's famous "Freedom of Speech" portrait is a quaint reminder of rhetoric in a relatively unmediated age. Part of the answer lies in the special rhetor–audience relationship that media creates.

The rhetorical process outlined in Chapter 1 suggests a single source and a single receiver. When the masses replace an individual receiver and a corporate rhetor takes the place of an individual source, the meaning of messages is altered significantly. Although some aspects of this unique relationship were discussed in Chapter 12 in the context of visual messages, other features need to be emphasized here. First, we must recognize that in mass-mediated communication, neither party in the rhetorical act knows who the other is. One might think that this would result in a lot of confusion and miscues in sending and receiving messages. On the contrary. As scholars John Fiske and John Hartley note, it is this inability to know the other that "imposes a discipline on the encoders which ensures that their messages are in touch with the central meaning systems of the culture and that the codes in which the message is transmitted are widely available."[6] In other words, mediated messages must be and are easy to process and thus speak to the receiver whoever he or she may be.

The persona of the mediated message is not singular but corporate. It is an *economic team*. It is identified with the image, voice, or byline of an individual, but it includes a chorus of professionals including advertisers, corporate owners, general managers, program and technical directors, gatekeepers, editors, image consultants, and Web masters. That there is no single authorial identity of the media communicator inflates the concept of "persona" and extends its influence. The image on our screen, the voice over the airwaves, the mug shot of the columnist, or the signature of the Web master operates as a "front man or woman" for the economic team. This individual media rhetor functions as a "buyer and seller"—an auctioneer of sorts—between the audience and the advertisers, but one who must command great credibility to seal the transaction. For the mass-mediated rhetorical act to develop ethos, a chorus of rhetors must continually and tirelessly exert authority, exude trustworthiness, project dynamism, and seek identification in complex ways. CBS anchorman Walter Cronkite used to end newscasts with the pronouncement, "That's the way it is." We accepted his expertise and his view of the world at face value. Ads exert authority with a nod to social science methods: "Four out of five doctors surveyed . . . " Broadcast programming exudes honesty with super close-ups of talent (anchors and reporters), and "live" unedited, unscripted coverage ("happy talk"). Print media run four-part series to exhaust all the positions on an issue. It is media's technological nature to project dynamism through captivating visuals, headlines, soundtracks, color schemes, and suspenseful, fast-moving plots. Finally, all media rhetors seek identification (the Holy Grail of their mission). We must feel comfortable with the talent, relate to the products sold, sense relevance in the stories told, embrace consumerism and free enterprise, even covet the medium of expression itself in order for the corporate persuaders to survive as an economic team.

The audience of the mediated message is *the masses*. Specifically, the immediate audience is defined in a physical sense as *receptors*. We are "viewers," "listeners," "readers," or "surfers"—terms that heighten our roles as active, sensory beings. The target audience of mass-mediated messages capitalizes on this active, sensory component. Although stereotyped as "couch potatoes" or "zombies," the audience of mass communication that is targeted by a corporate persona is imagined as anything but passive or inert. Rather, media rhetors envision their receptors as active buyers or *discriminating consumers* who fit economically desirable demographic categories. The created audience is a critical concept in mass-mediated rhetoric. Media rhetors must create a role for their large consumer base. They must convince the masses to be willing accomplices in creating consumer culture. They must invite us to become packaged and delivered to advertisers, to welcome appeals to materialism, not shun them. In so doing, media rhetors make a bargain of sorts. They do not engage in class warfare or pander to movers and shakers (hence, a VIP audience is irrelevant), and they give us some (illusion of) control over the message. With the remote control in hand, or with the click of a mouse, or the turn of a dial or page, the audience-as-willing-consumer—"calls the shots." Mass audiences are impatient for "the hook" that prompts them to stick around and absorb the message. Media rhetors know this and try to track our changing tastes with countless surveys and ratings instruments (e.g., Arbitron, Nielsen, and Gallup). Audience members are also more likely to assume this created role because they are anonymous; and because they are anonymous, they can surrender to their *voyeuristic tendencies*. There is a certain luxury in knowing that the rhetor is not watching you personally and that "tuning out" a message will not hurt anyone's feelings, just as tuning in a message will not require you to explain to anyone your media consumption habits, one reason that pornography sites on the Internet are visited by millions of people.

The instrumental purpose of the mass-mediated message is to make money for its rhetors— the media team of investors. As Kathleen Hall Jamieson and I have noted, the primary purpose of mediated messages is "to attract and hold a large audience for advertisers."[7] In essence, the audience is the product that is "sold" to the advertiser via the program. The mass media earn about $134 billion a year. Most of that income is collected from advertisers who have wooed their target audience in mass numbers to purchase their service or product or invest in their cause. Much of that profit is then used to reinvest in more consumers. A typical full-page ad in the *Wall Street Journal* costs $105,000; a 30-second television commercial in prime time costs $120,000.[8] Although some media forms are intended to explain (e.g., the documentary), and others to alter perception (e.g., the news) and still others to formulate belief (e.g., talk shows), the primary purpose of all media programming (messages) and hosts (rhetors) must be to initiate action (buy the program's products). *The consummatory purpose of the mass media is to entertain, to create virtual experience in captivating ways.* The two work in tandem. Buying a company's product is not tantalizing unless the product is surrounded by pleasing messages. We'll tolerate a merciless barrage of ads (more than one out of every four minutes of viewing time) if a program is highly entertaining, and we're even more tolerant if the ads themselves are amusing.

THE MEDIUM IS THE MESSAGE

One of the "p's" of rhetoric maintains that "rhetoric is powerful" because it can help or harm. The mass media show that this can be a double-edged sword. *The mass media create many paradoxes for us.* They give us enormous amounts of information more quickly than ever, but now we have an "information glut" and don't know how to process it all. The mass media make us less provincial, more a "global village" in sharing news from all over the world, yet media consumption is one of our most solitary and lonely activities. They give us convenient, nonstop coverage of the lives of VIPs, yet usurp their right to privacy. The mass media bring a nation together (coverage of celebrations and tragedies), yet they also divide us (coverage of wars, conflict, and crime). They educate us on a range of topics in such a way that we can take charge of everything from our health to our wealth. But they also have been implicated in everything from an increase in violence and aggressive behavior in youth, hate-crimes in adults, a "mean-world syndrome" that can lead to depression in the elderly, attention-deficit disorder in toddlers, incivility in our elected officials, and a debasing of our values that lead many to immoral and unhealthy behavioral choices (smoking, drug abuse, teenage sex, truancy, suicide, divorce, bigotry, domestic violence).

The promises and the perils of the mass media can be better understood by looking closely at how a channel uniquely filters a message. *Because the medium (the channel) is such an important, but taken-for-granted, rhetorical dimension of the message, it invites our assent in seductive ways.* As aspiring media critics, it is important for you to know that the individual medium of expression has benefits and limitations. This requires recognition that the medium itself is a constraint. Chapter 12 suggested that the medium is really part of the messenger. In terms of the rhetorical problem, there are many

Figure 13-1
Medium of
Transmission

	Television	Newspaper **Fatal fire**	Radio	Internet
Primary Strength	Uses visual storytelling	Has permanence	Reaches most segmented audience	Empowers users (audience)
Primary Weakness	Lacks depth	Requires literacy	Has no visuals	Uses unreliable sources

rhetor-related obstacles in mass communication. Each transmission source has a prior ethos. It has a specific reputation for helping and for hindering an audience in its entertaining, profit-seeking mission (Figure 13–1).

The print media (especially newspapers) still cling to an authoritative reputation for their (1) *linearity*, (2) *permanence*, and (3) *in-depth coverage*. Our talk demonstrates how much we value that kind of discursive expression. Children are told to "toe the line," "walk the straight and narrow," and to follow a "clean line of thought." On the other hand, we are told, "avoid circular reasoning," and "don't make waves."[9] A "reader" often chooses to consume the news via this sense receptor because he or she can glance back over the page, pause, reflect, read again, and save and retrieve the article for another time. This is a huge advantage over the other ephemeral and mostly disposable media. The print media also are especially suited to fulfill the rhetorical purpose of explaining the who, what, where, when, and in particular, the how and why of an event. By contrast, a 30-minute local newscast does not even begin to cover the amount of information that is presented on the front page of a newspaper. In its glory days (1800–1920s), before the competition moved in, print journalism enjoyed preeminent status as the single media source of daily information.

The print media have many limitations. Newspapers (1) *are dated*, (2) *require literacy*, (3) *cost the consumer directly*, and (4) *take time to digest*. If you rely on a newspaper for weather, you know how frustrating dated information can be. If you want to know who won an election, a game, or the lottery, you don't turn to the newspaper first. Increasingly, reading literacy is a problem in maintaining healthy newspaper subscriptions as more and more people become visual learners. Even among those who say they like to read, many complain they do not have time to read a paper every day. And then there is the irritant of the cost factor—unlike radio or TV, the medium bills you directly for its message.

Radio has a colorful and checkered history in mass-media lore. *Its primary strength is that it can achieve intimacy with a more sharply delineated demographic profile of listeners who remain loyal.* It is also the most portable medium. President Franklin Roosevelt was the first to realize the value of connecting with the citizenry via radio. He reached millions of Americans instantly in his "fireside chats." The medium allowed him to "chat" with Americans as citizens, peers, and members of a common national family united in their efforts to combat the perils of the Great Depression. Listeners could hear his confidence, steadiness, and optimism. They could feel the warmth of his delivery. His New England accent became recognizable and comforting. Roosevelt's detractors, such as Senator Huey Long of Louisiana and Father Charles Coughlin of Detroit, developed their own radio shows and wooed millions of disadvantaged Americans to be fearful of his policies. The fame of these two radio hosts marked the beginning of a colorful relationship between subversive discourse, charismatic personalities, and the airwaves. Intimacy between rhetor and audience can still be achieved today, as is evident in the popularity of "talk radio"—the second most popular format behind country music. "Callers" and listeners alike become fiercely loyal to their show's host (a real boon for advertisers). Rush Limbaugh listeners, for instance, call themselves "dittoheads." Although in its infancy radios were not portable, they are today. With transistor, car, and clock radios, the medium can accompany us throughout our daily lives. Of all the media, students often find this one the hardest to "tune-out" in fulfilling the first assignment at the end of this chapter.

Radio's deficiencies did not become evident until the advent of television. Suddenly, *its non-visual character was a disadvantage*. Why merely listen to someone if we could see and listen? Television also stole the immediacy that radio once claimed over print. Radio has maintained a loyal base, but at a price. Today, radio is blamed for much of the coarseness in our discourse (shock radio) and the vulgarity of our music (the explosion of alternative music stations). Radio also holds the dubious distinction of being the medium most heavily regulated by the federal government.

Television is currently the preeminent medium. *It captures the largest audience faster than any other medium. The visual nature of its message invites our assent in especially satisfying ways.* As detailed in Chapter 12, visuals are captivating because they are efficient, emotional, and enthymematic. Television can entertain us better than any other medium because the use of moving pictures makes creating virtual experience effortless. With the advent of 24-hour news stations and advanced remote technology, TV takes us "up close and personal" anywhere on the globe at any time. As media consumers gain more and more familiarity with visual symbols, words and sounds alone will influence us less and less. Even in 1960, when TV viewership was relatively new, the influence of moving visuals was dramatic in the first televised presidential debate between John F. Kennedy and Richard M. Nixon. Both candidates were seasoned debaters and well versed on the issues, but in terms of a style compatible with television, Kennedy was better prepared. Nixon looked pale and ill (in fact, he had recently been hospitalized); he wore heavy makeup and was visibly sweating. He was not as clean-shaven as Kennedy. He glanced nervously at a clock in the studio. Kennedy, on the other hand, appeared to enjoy the setting. Smiling and relaxed, his tanned youthfulness was now perceived as a strength, not a weakness. Not surprisingly, viewers believed Kennedy won the debate by a wide margin. Interestingly, some research suggests that Americans who listened to the debate on the radio thought Nixon had won.

The limitations of television have been widely documented. Three are worth examining here: (1) *Television lacks depth and perspective*, (2) *it converses in sensationalism*, and (3) *it is not child-proof*. Because the screen is two-dimensional, reporters look as large as the burning buildings by which they stand. Because the screen in most homes is usually small (12–25 in.), it cannot reflect the actual scope or magnitude of a scene. Over time, this compact view blunts our reaction to triumphs and tragedies. Content concerns create other distorted perspectives. The average "sound-bite" has gone from 18 seconds in 1982 to 5 seconds in 2000. It's difficult to speak intelligibly in that amount of time, let alone explain something clearly. Even the 60-second ad is a rarity, giving way to 30-second and even 15-second varieties. Because television dramatizes what it covers, it is prone to sensationalism. Ads tell us that you can lose your friends if you eat the wrong potato chips. Sitcoms show us that family conflict can be resolved in 22 minutes. The news tells us, "If it bleeds, it leads." Sports coverage captures "the thrill of victory and the agony of defeat," but not the tedium of training, studying one's opponent, and the mind games or strategies between points, downs, or innings. Educators and parents have long voiced concern that television is an "open-admission technology."[10] Television provides the same information to adults as children. The screen has a mesmerizing effect on even small children. Print, on the other hand, shelters the child. A parent can read about a grizzly murder in the morning paper and not have to worry about any one else being exposed to the message. If the TV is on, parents may find themselves fumbling for answers to "Who is he shooting?"

The Internet is the heir apparent to media dominance in the twenty-first century. The technical makeup of the computer allows it to capture newspaper, radio, and TV in its "web of influence" and project each in a new, user-friendly form. Its primary strengths, then, are (1) *its convergence capabilities* and (2) *the ways in which it can empower media audiences*. Though still in its infancy, the Internet is developing "streaming" capacities for radio signals and TV images. On-line newspapers have been around for several years. Now, with a click of a mouse, the media consumer can engage in "one-stop shopping." She can read her morning paper on-line while eating breakfast, listen to her favorite radio station while paying bills or purchasing products on-line, and watch only those features of the six o'clock newscast that interest her when she comes home from work at 7:00 P.M. with her children in tow! The Internet is a media supermarket, and like a discriminating shopper, you can "fill your cart" with those products (stories) that you want. Not surprisingly, these strengths make the Internet "hot property." More and more Americans are using the Internet as a gateway to broadcast information. Listening to radio stations online has tripled in two years, up from 6 percent in 1998 to 20 percent in summer 2000. Fifteen percent of all Americans have viewed on-line video. "Web-casting is rapidly approaching critical mass."[11] High-definition TV is on the horizon. Soon we will be able to access the Internet via the television screen. Of course, the most distinctive and empowering feature of the Internet is the way in which its multiple search engines allow us to find Web sites about any topic under the sun. It is a glorified *Encyclopedia Britannica* and *National Inquirer* wrapped into one.

This leads to the Internet's limitations: *Because there is no official gatekeeper, anarchy rules the Internet*. We are flooded with information that is true and false, helpful and dangerous, dated and current, simplified and complicated, crude and sophisticated. In short, getting information from the Internet is like taking a sip of water from a fire hose. You may drown in a sea of information and never slake your thirst. Adding insult to injury, you may have jeopardized your privacy if you gave out personal information on a nonsecure site. Some tips for navigating in this treacherous environment were presented in Chapter 3, especially in relation to how to judge a Web site's credibility. The Web site critique exercise in Chapter 11 tests your media literacy in challenging ways by inviting you to conduct a descriptive analysis, assess the rhetorical problem, and evaluate a Web site of your choosing. You may wish to revisit that assignment after reading this chapter.

Rhetors from all four media recognize that they have rhetorical problems in terms of their reputations. Internet services are producing more sophisticated search engines, virus checks, and privacy alerts; they are even encouraging legal sanctions against some Web site content. Television executives have bowed to pressure to rate family entertainment, they have experimented with family-sensitive news formats, and they actively encourage viewers to check out their Web sites for more in-depth coverage. Radio stations have become partners of television stations, especially in weather-casting, and have welcomed Web-casting as a way to shore up a dwindling audience base and to reemphasize their portability. Newspapers now hire graphic artists as journalists to cater to the visual consumer, encourage readers to go on-line to capture up-to-date information, and post mug shots of their columnists to invite a more intimate bonding with readers.

MASS MEDIA AND THE SEVEN ELEMENTS OF DESCRIPTIVE ANALYSIS APPLIED

The various instrumental and consummatory purposes in the following news story, chosen for its permanence, "evergreen" quality, and entertainment value, will be unpacked (Figure 13–2). Your task, in the questions that follow, will be to apply other key elements of descriptive analysis, determine relevant rhetorical obstacles, and judge the news story based on the four standards of evaluation. Completing exercises like this one will help you join the growing ranks of media critics that our nation's educators are grooming from kindergarten through postsecondary schools.

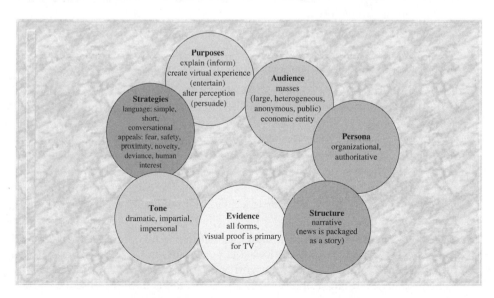

Figure 13-2
News Rhetoric and Descriptive Analysis

Terror on School Bus Ends with Hijacker's Death

by Gail Epstein, Frances Robles, and Martin Merzer[12]

Knight-Ridder News Service

1   Miami—A waiter fond of poet Ralph Waldo Emerson attends morning prayers at his church, then steps across the street and hijacks a school bus. Owing $15,639.39 in back taxes, wielding what he says is a bomb, Catalino Sang shields himself with disabled children.

2   Follow my orders, he says, or I will kill the kids. "No problem, I will," said driver Alicia Chapman, 48, crafty and calm. "But please don't hurt the children."

3   The saga of Dade County school bus No. CX-17 begins.

4   Soon, a phalanx of squad cars trails and flanks a busload of innocents. Two desperate parents jump into their own cars and join the pursuit. Also in the caravan is School Superintendent Octavio Visiedo in his black Buick Park Avenue. Someone has abducted 13 of his students.

5   Now, traveling at 20 mph, a trooper pulls within six inches of the bus, tossing in his personal cell phone. "I was scared to death," says officer John Koch. "But I had to do what I had to do. I've got a little girl. She's 3. She's my life."

6   Word spreads. The workday is halted, a region temporarily frozen with dread. Motorists gaze in astonishment; office workers gather at windows to watch the 15-mile, slow-speed chase. Somehow, the odyssey of O. J. Simpson has blended into the movie "Speed," and it is unfolding Thursday—live and real—in South Florida and on national TV.

7   Finally, it ends outside Joe's Stone Crab, a landmark known around the world. It ends with gunfire from a police marksman and shattered glass and officers diving into danger to rescue young hostages. It ends with a deranged man dead, one student slightly injured.

8   It ends with cops wearing bulletproof vests hugging kids carrying Lion King schoolbags.

9   It ends about as well as it can. The kids are safe.

10   Most are in Joe's, drinking Coke and ginger ale, eating french fries and vanilla ice cream. They can have a balanced meal some other time. Now, they need comfort. Some already are reliving the experience.

11   "A bad man on a bus made us drive a long way," says Brian Morales, 7, subjected to an unexpected lesson about life in the 1990s.

12   As Brian says this, Sang's body is sprawled under a yellow tarpaulin, surrounded by officers still tingling with adrenaline. Sang was 42, an immigrant from the Dominican Republic. Married. Two children, one of them a high school honors student.

13   He owned two Chinese restaurants, but they were consuming his re-sources. So he waited on tables at Joe's and was known to recite Emerson's verse as he dished up the stone crabs and mustard sauce. His favorite poem was "Success": "The profoundest thought or passion sleeps as in a mine, until it is discovered by an equal mind and heart."

14 Sang quit in a huff Wednesday night. Co-workers said he was talking to himself, seemed weighted with stress.

15 But that is only part of the story.

16 Another part belongs to Chapman, the bus driver, on the job only 17 months. Largely because of her, 13 children are alive today.

17 "She followed the most important rule: You protect the lives of the children," said Henry Fraind, spokesman for the Dade school system. "We are taught to protect the children at all costs."

18 "We would classify the driver as a modern-day hero. The driver could not have done any better."

19 And another part belongs to the police—men and women who train for these situations hoping never to employ that training, men and women suddenly confronted by the most intense challenge imaginable, men and women who stormed that bus and saved those kids.

20 "Had we known he was not armed, we would not have shot him," said Metro-Dade police Director Fred Taylor. "But we did believe that he was armed. He (the police marksman) did exactly what he was trained to do."

21 Based on witness accounts, this is what happend: Eight-thirty A.M., Thursday, November 2, 1995. Another school day. The kids were being picked up for Blue Lakes Elementary, a school with 618 students, about one-third of them in special education programs.

22 Chapman was on her usual run. She was widely regarded as an excellent driver, one with real concern for the kids.

23 She stopped the bus just across the street from the Alpha & Omega Church, which serves an Evangelical congregation. Two children normally were picked up here.

24 Chapman had no way of knowing that Sang was distraught and had just left the church. "He was yelling," Taylor said. "He was not rational at the time. When he left his home this morning, he told one of his daughters to pray for him."

25 Sang was under considerable pressure. The income from his job at Joe's was being used to subsidize his two restaurants. But no one knows precisely what set him off Thursday morning as bus CX-17 began its run.

26 One of the children waiting at the bus stop was Daniel Castellanos. His mother, Nubla, was with him.

27 A few minutes later, a neighbor pounded on the Castellanos' front door. It was opened by Maurice Castellanos, Daniel's father.

28 "She said, 'Don't panic, but some man pushed Nubla onto the bus,'" Castellanos said. "I reacted in a way that was more like puzzled. A bus? A car?"

29 Later, his wife filled him in.

30 "This guy crosses Miller (Road) and motions to her that he has something on his side. He told her, 'Get inside!'"

31 "My wife sat down, and he told the bus driver to close the door and proceed. He told them it was a kidnapping and he was in trouble with the IRS. He went to the back of the bus, and my wife noticed he was placing things under the seats."

32 "She thought it was a bomb. She was hysterical (within) but managed to stay collected."

33   As the bus worked its way toward the Palmetto Expressway, the hijacker ordered Chapman to call authorities over her two-way radio, which proved unreliable. He demanded a cell phone from the police.

34   Nubla Castellanos began speaking with Sang.

35   "She pleaded with him not to hurt anybody," said Maurice Castellanos, who hurried to the bus stop. "He said he had children, too, and wouldn't hurt anyone."

36   "He told her to get off the bus with my son and another child who was crying a lot and realized what was going on. I feel like she was able to save that child."

37   That other child was Brian Morales, the 7-year-old who spoke about the "bad man" on the bus.

38   State trooper John Koch, a nine-year veteran, was on patrol nearby when his radio crackled with the news. With the bus now on the expressway, Koch joined the caravan of squad cars. At times, he ran interference for the bus, keeping cars and trucks away. Hearing on his scanner that Sang needed a cellular phone and was going to start hurting the children if he didn't get one, Koch pulled up next to the bus and pitched his own phone to the driver.

39   Using the cell phone, Sang told police he wanted to exit at 82nd Avenue and stop at an Internal Revenue office. They told him he already was beyond that exit. OK, he said, we'll go to Joe's Stone Crab.

40   Now, the bus had turned the corner of Biscayne and Washington, coasting toward Joe's entrance. One of the students jumped out.

41   A member of the Metro-Dade Special Response Team, a SWAT unit, saw a movement from Sang that gave the impression that he was about to detonate a bomb.

42   Officer Joe Derringer, crouched beside the bus, fired a single shot through a window, striking Sang.

43   Sang died in the alley. Later, police said he was unarmed. The bomb he claimed to carry was a student's portable oxygen canister.

The instrumental purpose: to explain, to alter perception, to initiate action
The consummatory purpose: to create virtual experience

How does the story explain?
It informs the reader of a timely event that happened early yesterday morning, and it treats important issues of ongoing concern in our culture: rampant crime, terrorism, and the safety of our children. Specifically, it tackles the appropriate who, what, where, when, and why questions that a good journalist should cover. Note, however, how unadorned, "just the facts" are.

What: A man hijacks a school bus of children claiming he has a bomb.
Who: A waiter by the name of Sang, a 42-year-old immigrant from the Dominican Republic, married, with two children, owned two restaurants.
Where/When: 8:30 A.M., Thursday, November 2, 1995, in Miami, Florida, in the Blue Lakes school district at the Alpha and Omega Church.
How: Sang boarded a school bus and demanded that the driver follow his orders or he would kill the kids. The bus driver complied. Soon police followed the school bus,

and a few parents followed in their own cars. After Sang demanded a cell phone, the police tossed a cellular phone to him. Near Joe's Crab House, a police marksman shot Sang with a single bullet. He died. The children and bus driver were safe. Later, police discovered that he was unarmed.

Why: Sang was pressed for money. He owed $15,000 in back taxes. He waited tables at Joe's to make ends meet. He quit the night before, seemingly distressed over something.

How does the story create virtual experience?

It entertains the reader. This story attracts and holds a large audience for advertisers because it is compelling and invites our participation. It "dresses up" the facts with a pleasing story line.

Word choice—dramatic: "saga," "phalanx," "frozen with dread," "odyssey of O. J. Simpson chase," like "the movie *Speed*," "tingling with adrenaline," "the radio crackled with the news," "the driver is a modern-day hero."

Language devices—repetition: "It ends. . . It ends. . . It ends. . . ."

Suspenseful narrative structure: We don't know until the last line that "he was unarmed. The bomb he claimed to carry was a student's portable oxygen canister."

Memorable evidence (quotes): "I was scared to death. But I had to do what I had to do. I've got a little girl. She's 3. She's my life."

How does the story alter our perception?

It persuades the reader subtly. This news coverage shapes events. It alters the perception of a reader through reordering (editing) and a writing style that is highly descriptive. This approach to the story gives the event added significance, scope, and human interest.

Editing: Cutting and pasting allow the story to unfold in a memorable, dramatic way that fuels tension, conflict, and fear (basic appeals). The story has a slow-motion, surreal feel in reinforcing a gnawing theme that even kids on a school bus are not safe from crime.

Narrative-dramatic structure: Beholden to the formula of good drama, the article must have a "good guy" (the police) and a "bad guy" (the hijacker). The article is sympathetic to the police point of view. "It ends with cops wearing bullet-proof vests hugging kids carrying Lion King schoolbags. It ends about as well as it can. The kids are safe." Imagine your response had the piece begun with the last two paragraphs of the story.

How does the story initiate action?

It persuades the reader less subtly. Although the story does not say, "Please see the ads our wonderful sponsors have prepared for you at the bottom of this page," it insists that the reader be exposed to these sales pitches with creative layout and design features.

Layout and design: This is a front-page story, complete with a large, dramatic headline and a 4 × 6 accompanying photo of the incident's aftermath. The dramatic language and suspenseful narrative plot demand that the reader actually follow the rhetor's instructions: "see HIJACKER, page 8A." One's eye is attracted to the directive by its strategic placement in the photo's byline. Once on page 8A, the reader enters the commercial zone. She must weave through a barrage of ads to finish the story.

Questions for Analysis

1. Who are the multiple *rhetors* of this news story? How does each contribute to one of the rhetorical purposes enunciated above? What is the specific *persona* of the reporters? How does their role contribute to the moral authority of the mass media?

2. How does the story invite us to play the *created audience* role so vital to the mass media industry? How does the story deal with the *audience obstacle* of lack of motivation? What "hooks" does it provide to keep us attentive?

3. How is *ethos* (authority, trustworthiness, dynamism, and identification) created in the story? Is one dimension more evident than others? Explain.

4. How does this piece demonstrate that "*the medium is the message*"? Discuss the specific strengths and weaknesses of print media in this regard. What *rhetor-related obstacle* do you think is primary?

5. How would you rate this news story on aesthetics? truth? ethics? effects? Consider the following:

   Aesthetics: Does the news story conform to the requirements of a good story? What was the angle of the story? Did it maintain attention? What was particularly memorable about the way the story was reported? How dramatic was it? Did it have a catchy lead? Headline? Photo? Overall, did the story contribute in satisfying ways to creating virtual experience?

   Truth: Do the rhetors report impartially? Is their treatment fair? What of importance is not reported? Why? Was the reporter actually at the scene of the event reported? If so, is that fact established in the story? If so, how? If not, is that fact evident in the report? What is the reporter's source of firsthand information? Are the remarks of "sources" ever corroborated? How much of the report was based on press reports provided by other agencies? Overall, did the story capture enough factual material to explain the event well?

   Ethics: Is the mass audience better served by the news? Who, if anyone, benefited from the coverage? Who, if anyone, was damaged by the coverage? How? Overall, did the story cross any ethical line in altering our perception of the event?

   Effects: Do you have evidence to suggest that this kind of piece is critical for winning large ratings? Increasing circulation? Is there evidence that the story ran in many newspapers owned by the chain? How might you find out what kind of impact this story had on a readership? Overall, do you think the story works to support the commercial purpose of the media—to initiate consumer action on the sponsor's products?

EXERCISES

1. Elizabeth Dole's speech to the 1996 GOP convention on behalf of her husband and GOP nominee Bob Dole is a strong example of how the medium of transmission can alter our reaction to it. One-half of the class should read the text of Elizabeth Dole's speech (the *New York Times* ran a full transcript). The other half should watch it on video (GOP archives). Discuss how the strengths and limitations of the two media (print and television) are evident in this case. Drawing on your knowledge of visual messages outlined in Chapter 12, discuss how the basic elements and technical features of visual messages are at work in the video presentation.

2. Choose any media form (radio, TV, Internet, newspaper) and try to live without using it for a full week. Discuss your experience in class. How difficult was this to do? How did it alter your daily habits? How dependent are you on this technology?

3. Examine how a current event is treated by your local newspaper versus a local TV or radio station. Use key elements of descriptive analysis to track the difference in coverage.

4. Mass media require that we examine a *collective rhetor* that is generally camouflaged. Think how peculiar it would be for us to say: "I'm going to call the president of Media General, the news and technical directors, the assignment editor, the anchor, the photographer, the reporter, the satellite truck driver, and the video editor to complain about or compliment the message I just heard." Since we cannot identify the single persona of mass-mediated messages, what ethical challenges arise for newsmakers and news consumers?

5. Arrange to visit a radio station, a television station, or a newspaper. Examine how the news of the day is "manufactured." How are decisions made to give events news space? How is the news business demystified by this tour?

6. As a class, select a sitcom for viewing. What aspects of the show can be described as sensational? What aspects distort perspective? Count the number of laugh tracks that you hear. What purpose do they serve?

How does the show exemplify some of the paradoxes of the mass media?

7. The entertainment industry uses multiple channels to reach consumers. The Walt Disney Corporation, for instance, combines Web tools, retail outlets, TV and cable channels, publishing houses, recording studios, and other media in marketing its products. It is a true multinational corporate empire with incredible influence over the imagination of children all over the world. Locate articles related to the Disney Corporation in your InfoTrac College Edition database. Based on your research, what is the distinction or connection between the corporation's creative and commercial missions? Try to find out why Disney has been picketed and boycotted in recent years. What have the issues been about? What medium of transmission has been the most frequent target of concern? Why?

8. **Portfolio Entry 12: Constraints of the Medium** Evaluate your rhetorical acts in terms of the strengths and weaknesses of their respective media of transmission. In two or three pages, discuss how influential the medium is in your evaluation of the acts in terms of aesthetics, truth, ethics, and effects.

NOTES

1. See Richard Weiner, *Webster's New World Dictionary of Media and Communications*, 2nd ed. (New York: Wiley, 1996).

2. See Shirley Biagi, *Media Impact*, 2nd ed. (Pacific Grove, CA: Wadsworth, 1992); Neil Postman and Steve Powers, *How to Watch TV News* (New York: Penguin, 1992); Kathleen Jamieson and Karlyn Kohrs Campbell, *Interplay of Influence* (Belmont, CA: Wadsworth, 2001); *Media & Values Newsletters* (Los Angeles: Center for Media and Values, 1993); TV ALERT: A Wake-Up Guide for Television Literacy (Media Literacy Workshop Kit)(Los Angeles: Center for Media and Values, 1993); AP News Industry News, Press Release, August 28, 2000.

3. Canadian Broadcasting Corporation interview with Neil Postman, July 2, 2000, posted at http://www.myna.com, p. 1.

4. Ibid, p. 1.

5. Peggy Chassen and Carol Itulsizer, *The TV Smart Book for Kids* (East Rutherford, NJ: Dutton Press Penguin/Putnam, 1983); William Fore, *The Electronic Golden Calf: Images, Religion, and the Making of Meaning* (Cambridge, MA: Cowley Publications, 1990); Michael Fortino, *There Is an Internet E-mergency* (New York: The Fortino Group, 2001); George Gerbner and Larry Gross, "Living with Television: The Violence Profile," *Journal of Communication* 26 (1976): 172–199; Tipper Gore, *Raising PG Kids in an X-Rated Society* (Nashville, TN: Abingdon Press, 1987); Gary Gumpert and Robert Cathcart, eds., *Inter Media: Interpersonal Communication in a Media World*, 3rd ed. (New York: Oxford University Press, 1986); *Media & Values*, published quarterly by the Center for Media and Values, an educational, not-for-profit organization (Los Angeles: National Sisters Communication Service, 1993–on); Joshua Meyrowitz, *No Sense of Place: The Impact of Electronic Media on Social Behavior* (New York: Oxford University Press, 1989); Neil Postman and Steve Powers, *How to Watch TV News* (New York: Penguin Books, 1992).

6. John Fiske and John Hartley, *Reading Television* (London: Routledge, 1989), p. 81.

7. Campbell and Jamieson, p. 4.

8. Biagi, p. 15.

9. Tony Schwartz, *The Responsive Chord* (New York: Anchor, 1973), p. 7.

10. Postman and Powers p. 148.

11. Arbitron Internet Information Service (AP News Service, September 5, 2000).

12. Reprinted with permission of Knight Ridder/Tribune Information Services.

ANSWERS TO MOCK QUIZ

What do Rupert Murdoch, Ted Turner, and Gene Autry have in common?
All three people (Murdock, Turner, and Autry) owned or still own major media outlets. Which outlets are those?

In what medium do Ellen Goodman, George Will, and Maureen Doud appear?
All three (Goodman, Will, and Doud) have syndicated columns in newspapers. What is the importance of syndication?

What do Dr. Laura, the Sports Babe, and Rush Limbaugh have in common?
All three (Dr. Laura, the Sports Babe, and Rush Limbaugh) are or have been controversial figures on radio and television. What makes such controversial figures successful in mass media? What kinds of problems can arise because of the controversy they generate?

Which network has a peacock icon? An eye icon?
Networks use icons for quick identification. The peacock identifies NBC; CBS uses an eye. What does ABC use?

What Internet search engine's full name is Yet Another Hierarchical Officious Oracle?
Obviously, this is Yahoo!

What dotcom says: "Work Shouldn't Be Work!"
Monster.com uses the slogan "Work Shouldn't Be Work!"

What do MTV, WB, BET, AP, and UPI stand for?
MTV is Music Television; WB is Warner Brothers; BET is Black Entertainment Television; AP is Associated Press; UPI is United Press International. How and why do such acronyms become separated from their original meanings? Do you see this pattern among corporate logos?

What do "flaming," "V-chip," "hits," "streaming," "segue," "look live," and "scoop" mean?
"Flaming" refers to highly emotional messages, usually in all-capital letters, on Internet sites. The V-chip enables parents to censor the TV watching of their children.

"Hits" are the number of visitors to a Web site. "Streaming," briefly, is Internet broadcasting using broadband capacity (this could be the basis of a good project to explore new developments in media). "Segue" is a media term for a transition. "Look live" is a reporter recorded on videotape on location; during playback the reporters appears to be live. "Scoop" is a journalistic term for getting a story before competitors do.

Can you name these products from their slogans: "Plop, plop, fizz, fizz"; "He likes it. Hey, Mikey"; "Where's the Beef?"; "You deserve a break today"?
"Plop, plop, fizz, fizz" refers to Alka-Seltzer. "Mikey" liked Life cereal. "Where's the beef?" was a Wendy's slogan (appropriated by Walter "Fritz" Mondale in a presidential debate in 1984). McDonald's ads sang about deserving a break today.

Can you explain why the following media events have been chronicled as U.S. history: Orson Welles's broadcast of "The War of the Worlds"; FDR's fireside chats; the presidential debate between Kennedy and Nixon; the moon landing of Apollo 13; Seymour Hersh's coverage of the Vietnam War; Woodward and Bernstein's coverage of Watergate; the impact of such shows as I Love Lucy, All in the Family, ER, and even Super Bowl ads?
Each of these events demonstrated the kind of impact mass media can have on public reactions, citizen participation, political events, the possibilities inherent in the sitcom, and the impact of a single exposure to an ad. Pick one or more to explore.

Can you identify scary moments in media history? The "Love Bug," Ted Kaczynski's "Manifesto" in the Washington Post? *Or CNN's coverage of the Gulf War?*
These are a series of scary moments chronicled in media history. What others should be added? Where was the Murrah Federal Building and what happened to it? Why is the date 9/11 etched in U.S. history?

chapter 14

Understanding Occasion

A popular TV game show, *Name That Tune*, tested contestants' musical knowledge. The object was to be first at naming the song after hearing only its first few notes. A rhetorical counterpart to that game might be called *Name That Occasion*. Let's see what kind of contestant you are in naming these "old chestnuts" from only the first few words:

1. "Dearly beloved, we are gathered here . . ."
2. "Your Honor, we request that Exhibit A . . ."
3. "Mr. Speaker, with all due respect to my colleague from the state of . . ."

Pretty easy game, huh? Even without hints such as who the speaker or audience is, or what the title of the speech is, or even when it was delivered, you can probably provide the answers easily. The first is from a solemn religious ceremony, maybe a wedding or even a eulogy; the second is from a courtroom setting, probably from the middle part of a trial when evidence is being presented; the third is from a political or legislative occasion, such as a heated debate on a bill in Congress.

It is important for critics to understand occasions that trigger such well-defined rhetorical expectations. For practical reasons, as discussed in Chapter 11, we can better evaluate the effectiveness and artistry of a given piece of discourse if we can compare it to others like it (preceding rhetorical action). For philosophic reasons, we discover that as symbol users we are creatures of convention. In other words, we are comforted by the "ghosts" of Rhetoric Past. Even for sociological reasons, we can learn that well-defined rhetorical occasions tell us something about a culture's values. For instance, the rise of some kinds of discourse (e.g., corporate damage-control rhetoric) or the decline of others (e.g., Fourth of July orations) is a clue to the communal needs of a society at any given time.

This chapter documents our reliance on rhetorical precedents, introduces the classical origins of *rhetorical genres*, and examines instances when rhetoric does not neatly conform to the implicit "rules" of a given occasion. Applications will be made to the three-part conceptual core of this book: elements of descriptive analysis, the rhetorical problem, and standards of evaluation. In sum, this chapter gives you the knowledge and tools to function as a discerning analyst when confronted with the special constraints of rhetorical occasions.

OUR GROUPING IMPULSE AND ARISTOTLE'S RHETORICAL GENRES

Human beings have a need to categorize, pigeonhole, label, form clusters, set parameters, typecast, discriminate. The naming function of language (as discussed in Chapter 7) demands it. Our grouping impulse starts early. From a scientific perspective (recall from Chapter 1 that even a "perspective" is a discriminating function), we want children to learn that dogs are different from cats, mammals from amphibians, vegetables from fruits. From a sociological perspective, we learn to categorize young people as "nerds" or "jocks," "teacher's pet" or "class clown." Politically, we learn to distinguish among Republicans and Democrats and Greens and to be aware of voting blocs like "wired workers" and "soccer moms." From a religious perspective, we learn the difference between Christians and Jews, Hindus and Buddhists. Every time you fill out a survey that asks demographic questions (age, sex, occupation, economic bracket, ethnicity, and religious, political, or professional affiliations) you are validating the impulse to categorize.

Our need to categorize extends to rhetoric too. The labeling and explanation of rhetorical forms that endure has an ancient and venerable heritage. Long before media literacy practitioners began to encourage consumers to understand the differences between the "formulas" of the sitcom and the docudrama, between the image ad and the issue ad, and to lobby the entertainment industry to adopt rating systems to assist us in our discriminating media tastes, Aristotle said to his students: "The kinds of rhetoric are three in number, corresponding to the three kinds of hearers."[1]

Specifically, Aristotle described three types or genres of rhetoric: (1) *deliberative* rhetoric dealing with future policy, which emerged in legislatures and dealt with expediency/inexpediency or practicality/impracticality issues; (2) *forensic* rhetoric dealing with criminal charges and punishment of past behavior, which emerged in the law courts and dealt with justice/injustice; and (3) *ceremonial* or *epideictic* (from *epideixis*, to show forth or display) rhetoric dealing with a person, place, or idea in the present moment, which emerged on special occasions and dealt with praise/blame.[2] Everywhere he looked in Athenian society, Aristotle saw these types of speech on a regular basis. Some became classics: Demosthenes' political oratory, "On The Crown"; Socrates' trial

Figure 14–1
Aristotelian Genres

	Forensic (judicial)	**Deliberative (political)**	**Epideictic (ceremonial)**
Aim	Justice/injustice	Expediency or inexpediency	Praise or blame
Time	Past	Future	Present
Issue	Questions of fact	Questions of policy	Questions of value
Audience	Jurors	Voters	Observers

on the charge of corrupting the youth recorded in Plato's *Apology*; and Pericles' funeral oration (*epitaphios*) for the Athenian soldiers who fell in the Peloponnesian War. It is a remarkable testament to the endurance of these types of speeches that they are still commonplace as we enter the twenty-first century! To be sure, our speech genres are more complex and varied than in Aristotle's day, but these three groupings are still standard bearers in our culture (Figure 14–1).

Epideictic or ceremonial rhetoric, tied to specific occasions, demands special kinds of evaluation because of the requirements and expectations created by these occasions. Typical examples of epideictic rhetoric are inaugural addresses, Fourth of July speeches, commencement addresses, awards ceremony rhetoric, and eulogies. Such speeches appear on occasions that recur at regular intervals, and our experience with such rhetoric and the traditions that have developed around them create special constraints on rhetorical action. For each kind of occasional address, distinct expectations exist.

In general, however, epideictic rhetoric is closer to the *nondiscursive* than to the discursive end of the continua of rhetorical action. Its very name suggests its *consummatory purpose*; that is, we are to celebrate or commemorate the occasion, and speakers are expected to display their artistic skills and be judged on their performance. The language of such rhetoric tends to be formal, poetic, and figurative. Structurally, it is likely to explore various aspects of a feeling or attitude. The occasions themselves suggest that supporting materials are likely to emphasize what is psychologically appealing and what reflects cultural values. Finally, such addresses are more likely to develop ritualistically, another indicator of their close ties to occasions, than to provide logical arguments.

The eulogy (*eu* = well, *logos* = to speak; in short, to praise) is one kind of epideictic rhetoric. It appears on the occasion of a burial or memorial service as a result of a death. The death of any person, especially one we love and admire, forces us to confront our own mortality, and such deaths, especially violent deaths and those of children, disrupt the human community of which the deceased were a part. The eulogy meets certain very basic human needs. These can be specified in terms of the elements of descriptive analysis. Its purpose is fourfold: (1) *It acknowledges death early in the*

Figure 14-2
*Eulogistic Rhetoric
and Descriptive
Analysis*

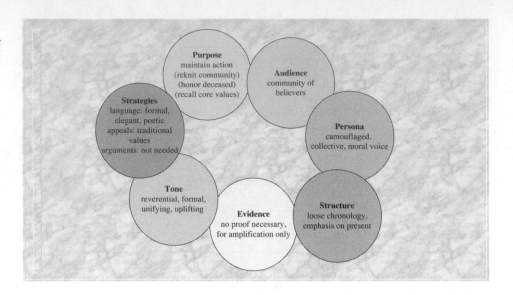

discourse. (2) *It keeps the deceased at the center of the discourse.* (3) *It reunites the sundered community.* (4) *It immortalizes the deceased.* It shifts the relationship between the living and the deceased to suggest that although dead in the flesh, the deceased lives on in spirit—in children, good deeds, or in principles—reassuring the living that a kind of immortality exists for all of us. The tone of the eulogy is personal (death is an intimate matter) and somber, and it frequently uses language strategies, such as metaphors of re-birth, to express the idea of immortality. The persona of the eulogist is camouflaged. Support material for "proof" is not necessary because the audience is already a community; what would ordinarily be evidence is used here to illustrate and amplify. Because of its consummatory purpose, the structure of a eulogy must emphasize the present, glo-rify the past, and hold out hope for the future. If a eulogy is to satisfy and comfort the audience, it must perform these functions in some way (Figure 14–2).

Eulogies disappoint us when they do not meet our expectations. In terms of the rhe-torical problem, the subject obstacle of *cultural history* looms large. All too often, eulo-gies fail to conform to cultural norms, to be reassuring in their familiarity, to be part of a long-standing rhetorical tradition. A popular self-help book today reminds people to avoid this major pitfall. Author Roger Rosenblatt, sternly warns: "It's not about you. If you're giving a eulogy, try to focus on the deceased!"[3] Another related cultural history pitfall is that eulogies sometimes wander into controversial territory. This is a big "no-no" because arousing controversy prevents the reunification of the community. A clas-sic example of this violation occurred when Senator Charles Percy bluntly advocated gun control and an end to the war in Vietnam in a eulogy for Senator Robert F. Kennedy, who died of gunshot wounds in 1968. He shocked the audience and violated audience expectations and failed to perform the eulogistic function of unification. In other words, the characteristics of the eulogy become bases for evaluating this particu-lar kind of occasional rhetoric.

The presidential inaugural address is another example of epideictic rhetoric, al-though the requirements for such a speech are less rigid and specific. Still, we expect the president to speak on this occasion (the Constitution does not require it) and to perform these rhetorical functions: (1) *Reunify the nation.* Because the inauguration follows a long and divisive political campaign, we expect the newly elected president to reunify the nation. (2) *Rehearse traditional values.* Because this is an occasion tied to fundamental national values (the speech is now given after the presidential oath of office has been administered), we expect the president to rehearse those values for us and make them come alive for us again. (3) *Enact the presidency.* Because we fear the power of the executive, we expect presidents to be humble, to admit limitations, and to ask for the help of Congress, the people, and God in their efforts to govern. And yet we expect presidents to show vigor and vision—to welcome the challenges of executive power. Enacting the presidency is a *rhetorical tightrope* of sorts. Finally, (4) *set forth guiding principles.* Because this is the beginning of a new administration, we expect presidents to indicate the philosophy and tone of their administrations, to suggest in broad terms the foreign and domestic policies that are of primary importance. Presidential inaugural addresses vary greatly, but these expectations are criteria that can be used to evaluate how well a president meets audience expectations.[4]

These rules of the eulogy and inaugural are also bases for distinguishing competent from outstanding efforts. In terms of standards of evaluation, we can judge effectiveness by the degree to which a given inaugural or eulogy pays homage to its identifying rhetorical markers. Use these criteria, for example, to compare a contemporary inaugural (Bush, Clinton) to that of John Kennedy. In the analysis section, you will be asked to evaluate a eulogy (Reagan's Challenger eulogy) based on its implicit rules. In each case, go further and ask if the speech not only met audience expectations but met them in ways that were deeply moving, adapted to the occasion, and highly original; in short, is it aesthetically pleasing? *We can judge artistry by the way in which the discourse weaves conventional rhetorical choices with inventional or innovative ones.* This is tricky business. Think back to the opening *"Name that Occasion"* excerpts. They are dull. An artistic eulogy must meet the expectations for its form (conform to the demands of cultural history) but do so in fresh, not predictable ways (show an individual stamp of authenticity). On the other hand, we have considerable practice in doing this. We expect regular television programming to be predictable; sitcoms, for example, are supposed to be funny, with each episode complete in itself, but when a particular show becomes too predictable, we stop watching it. Long-running sitcoms illustrate the combination of the predictable and innovative. M*A*S*H* and *Seinfeld* are good examples, and it's fun to watch them even now in reruns.

GENRE VIOLATIONS AND RHETORICAL HYBRIDS

What happens when the "rules" of a genre are purposely violated? We may laugh at the brazenness of twisted form. James Thurber's satiric adaptation of *Little Red Riding Hood* (see Chapter 6) and James Finn Garner's *Politically Correct Bedtime Stories* are good examples. We may smile wryly at the irony in bumper stickers like *Practice Senseless Beauty and Random Acts of Kindness.* We may wince at the bumbling effort to fulfill an epideictic address. In the film *Four Weddings and a Funeral,* Hugh Grant makes a fool of himself in trying to offer a toast to the groom. We may even frown, groan, and stick out our tongues and blow—which is what young children do when I have read aloud to them *The Paper Bag Princess* by Robert Munsch.[5] And yet all of these rhetorical acts are alike in their aim to entertain by turning convention on its head.

Some rhetorical acts, however, violate audience expectations in order to agitate more powerfully for a cause, jolt audiences out of their complacency, and receive media attention (if it's deviant, it's news). Elizabeth Cady Stanton's "The Solitude of Self" (1892), examined for the many obstacles arising from the subject in Chapter 9, can be appreciated on another level for its ability to disarm legislators precisely because it violated standard norms of deliberative address. Expecting to hear another argumentative treatise on the merits of woman suffrage, Stanton's audience was in for a real surprise. The speech contained no proper introduction, no resolution to argue, no evidence to substantiate a policy, no plea that legislators act like agents of change, and no logical form. And yet its nondiscursive purpose (a dramatic expression that women are unique, alone, and self-sovereign), haunting tone, narrative structure, artistic language, and appeals to the universal experiences of the human condition gave the speech such empathic force that her audience of male legislators reacted with stunned, contemplative silence. The speech created such a stir that Stanton was asked to give it on two other occasions. This major rhetorical violation worked because of an intractable cultural history problem. Leaders of the woman's rights movement had already spent 50 years delivering countless deliberative speeches explaining why women should have the right to vote. Sadly, they had gained little and still faced much resistance. Further, Stanton herself was in the twilight of her career at age 76 and had the stature to create a speech that completely defied categorization, ruled out refutation, and perfected persuasion. Stanton had learned from bitter experience that chivalry was a comforting worldview for many people at the time and could not be refuted in logical ways. (How do you formulate an argumentative treatise to make men feel less superior and women less inferior?) Engaging in some rhetorical deviance was her way to jolt agents of change out of their complacency and agitate more powerfully "on another plane" for woman's rights.

Forty years earlier, Frederick Douglass, a freed slave from Maryland, took the same rhetorical tack in agitating for the antislavery cause. His Fourth of July Address delivered in Rochester, New York, on July 5, 1852, is a model of elegance (see Chapter 7), but it is also a classic in terms of the ways that the epideictic genre can be subverted in the name of protest, in part by tactics that initially appear to meet expectations before shifting gears. Rather than praise and honor Americans, he shamed and scolded them; rather than idealize a glorious past, he held up the Constitution for ridicule; rather than look optimistically to the future, he saw gloom and doom. Although Douglass risked bodily harm in delivering such a sacrilegious speech, its vitriolic content attracted media attention and helped make him a leader in the antislavery cause.

These two speeches on behalf of woman's rights and civil rights are not isolated examples of generic surprises. In fact, minority rhetors who champion unpopular causes are much more likely to use a *rhetoric of subversion*. In order to combat huge audience obstacles when facing powerful elites who are committed to maintaining the status quo, disenfranchised rhetors must sometimes ruffle feathers rhetorically and resort to shock tactics.[6] In 1968, at the Mexican City Olympics, two U.S. track stars in the 200 meter run, Tommie Smith and John Carlos (gold and bronze medalists, respectively) shocked the nation and the world at the victory ceremony by standing barefoot with heads bowed and a single black-gloved fist raised during the national anthem. The athletes described the gesture as a tribute to their ethnic heritage and a protest over race relations and police brutality against African Americans in this country. Both athletes were banned from the Olympic Village and sent home by the IOC and the U.S. Olympic Committee. Vanessa Redgrave shocked the Academy awards in her acceptance speech as Best Supporting Actress for her role in *Julia* with a broadside aimed at the Jewish Defense League, which she called "a small group of Zionist hoodlums." Even as Redgrave was speaking, the audience began to boo and hiss.[7] In the early 1990s, a group of female artists called "The Guerrilla Girls" drew attention to the long-standing privileging of male artists and male-owned art galleries in this country by showing up at black-tie art show openings across the country in gorilla costumes!

Most rhetors who step outside the security of a standard rhetorical form do so more timidly than Douglass or Stanton and only under special circumstance. We call these rhetorical acts *hybrids*. Like a hybrid crop such as turkey red wheat, which combines two strains of grain for a heartier yield, rhetorical attempts to combine genres can endure. Conversely, like a hybrid animal such as a platypus, which combines the features of a duck and a beaver, rhetorical hybrids can look and sound quirky. The key to a rhetorical act that wants to fold deliberative rhetoric into a eulogy and look more like a bumper crop than an odd-looking aquatic mammal is to consider the following: (1) *Does the occasion, such as the manner of death, invite a deliberative subform?* If a young person has died senselessly at the hands of a drunk driver, for example, expressing a desire to support the efforts of M.A.D.D. or S.A.D.D. is understandable. (2) *Were the deceased and the eulogist in agreement on the policy issue?* If you had a friend who died as a result of being shot with a handgun but who was an avid member of the NRA, you would be ill-advised to promote tougher gun control, even if you as the eulogist supported that cause. (3) *Is the policy promoted as a tribute to the deceased?* If you suggest that people of good faith should show compassion to persons with AIDS at a funeral for an AIDS victim, it must be phrased as a tribute to that individual. (4) Finally, and most critical, *is the deliberative theme introduced in such a way that the epideictic features of the address clearly predominate?* Is it seven-eighths ceremonial in nature? Is there ever a moment in reading, listening, or viewing a tribute when you wonder: What happened to the deceased? You will have a chance to examine a eulogistic hybrid along these lines in the "Material for Analysis" later in the chapter.

THE APOLOGETIC GENRE AND THE MEDIA AGE

Some genres are so complex and "high stakes" that they require the kind of rhetorical maneuvering found in politicized tributes. One such animal is what Aristotle called an *apologia*—or what we label today as the rhetoric of self-defense, image-repair, or crisis management. Even Aristotle was puzzled about how to categorize the speech of self-defense. He never dignified the rhetorical form by giving it separate "species" status, but he noted that an apologia shares features from all three classical genres. As *forensic discourse*, apologists must ask for revised judgments of their past actions. They must redefine the reality portrayed by their accusers and deal in *questions of fact*—Was an act (misdeed, crime) committed? But apologists are not performing in a courtroom in front of jurors and a judge and so do not seek justice. As *deliberative discourse*, apologists must wrest argumentative control over the alleged misdeed from the hands of their accusers if they wish to survive and recover politically or economically. But apologists are not appealing to voters per se, nor do they aim to present *questions of policy* in problem-solution form to make an expedient case. As *epideictic discourse*, apologists engage in image repair, seeking to restore their honor by treating *questions of value* in front of

Figure 14–3
Apologetic Rhetoric and Descriptive Analysis

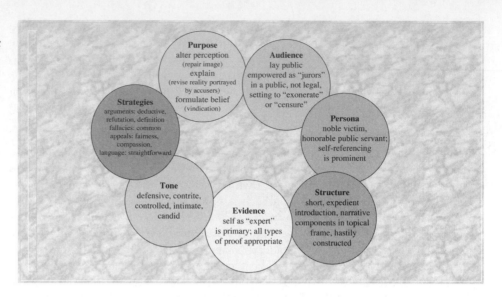

observers who exercise their voyeuristic tendencies in what can best be described as a spectacle of rhetorical grace or awkwardness under fire. But apologists are consumed with the past, not the present, and the ceremonial expectations of voicing noncontroversial themes to an audience of a community of believers does not describe the apologia either. It is indebted to all three genres, but its allegiance to none makes the apologia challenging to create and critique.

In terms of elements of descriptive analysis, the purpose of an apologia reflects its multifaceted heritage (Figure 14–3). As epideictic discourse, it aims to alter perception (repair an image). As forensic rhetoric, it aims to explain (revise the reality portrayed by the accusers), and as deliberative speech, it aims to formulate belief (seek vindication). The audience is the lay public, but we fondly, and with the assistance of media, cast ourselves in the role of "moral guardians" in a public, not legal, trial either to exonerate or censure the beleaguered rhetor. The apologist's persona must exude morality and trustworthiness. Rhetors often project a kind of "noble victim" self-defense. The tone is contrite, intimate, and candid, but it can often be defensive, serious, and counteraccusatory too. Structurally, apologias are seldom gems of cohesiveness or intricacy. Serious accusations demand timely responses. The poetic features of rhetoric are often exchanged for the pragmatic. But lots of evidence, especially in terms of personal testimony, and strategies especially arguments and appeals are well suited to the form. Specifically, scholars have identified the following recurring arguments in apologias: (1) *bolstering* character ("We are a good and noble company"; "I am an honest and trustworthy person; consider my whole record."); (2) *denial* ("The charge is completely false"); (3) *differentiating* this act/actor from others ("Yes, certain incidents did occur, but consider the circumstances"); (4) *transcending* the immediate occasion or issue/attack ("Let's take a fresh approach. The real thing we should be discussing is . . ."); (5) *attack the accuser or shift the blame* ("Consider the source!" "It's a smear tactic by my opponent!" "The press is overstepping its boundaries"); (6) *corrective action* ("We will repair the damage"); and (7) *confession* ("I'm sorry.")[8]

Apologetic rhetoric abounds in political, religious, sports, and corporate arenas. An avalanche of high-profile crises have flourished in this country. Richard Nixon's

"Checker's Speech" and his multiple Watergate defenses, Ted Kennedy's "Chappaquiddick Address," Ronald Reagan's "Iran-Contra apologia," and Bill Clinton's damage control in the "Lewinsky scandal" suggest that politicians have been most vulnerable to crisis response rhetoric. But televangelists charged with extortion, Catholic priests charged with sexual abuse of young boys, and Scientologists charged with unethical, cult-like recruitment tactics remind us that even in the most moral of arenas, image-repair discourse has flourished. Our fascination with and near worship of sports has brought with it uncompromising scrutiny as well. In "America's game," we have Pete Rose of the Cincinnati Reds banished from the Hall of Fame for his betting on the game and John Rocker of the Atlanta Braves chastised publicly from all quarters, even his own club, for his hateful rhetoric toward minorities. In each case, their well-publicized speeches of self-defense failed. In the Olympic games, we have world class athletes called to explain why they failed drug tests and the IOC itself called to explain its bidding practices in selecting host cities. In the college ranks, we have Division I football and basketball programs forced to defend their recruitment tactics to the NCAA, individual coaches (Bobby Knight, Woody Hayes) forced to explain their abusive behavior toward players, and players forced to explain their academic fraud or "point shaving" scams. Indeed, sports apologia has become a sport in itself. Corporate rhetors in both the profit and non-profit sector have seen the sharp rise of this rhetorical genre and know they are not immune. Many corporate cultures rehearse plans for responding to crisis. Crisis plans, damage control teams, and consultants with specific skills in how to repair a corporation's image in the wake of damaging accusations are now regularly part of public affairs and communication divisions. They have many models of success (Tylenol and the cyanide poisonings; Chrysler and the federal bailout; the United Way and CEO fraud; Pepsi and the syringe scare, to name but a few). They have even more models of failure (the *Exxon Valdez* oil spill; Dow Chemical and the manufacturing of napalm; Dow Corning and silicone breast implants; Sears and auto repair fraud; TWA and the crash of flight 800, Union Carbide and the Bhopal disaster, and the nuclear scare at Three Mile Island). The "jury" is still out on the Firestone Tire recall and the "roll-over factor" of the Ford Explorer sports utility vehicle as well as the Enron bankruptcy and Arthur Andersen accounting scandal.

This litany of rhetors from diverse arenas all forced to "air their dirty rhetorical laundry" in public invites questions. Why is it that you are more likely to read, watch, or hear an apologia in the next month than a eulogy, a debate, or a trial? Part of the answer lies in the rise of the mass media (recall Chapter 13). Media have blurred distinctions between public and private lives in their need to play journalistic watchdog (a role consumers praised media for performing in uncovering illegal activities in the Watergate affair), fulfill commercial obligations (the more dirt you can dig, the higher the ratings), and satisfy our desire for entertainment (vilifying scapegoats is cathartic). Another part of the answer lies in the evolution of our concept of citizenship. No longer passive, faceless masses, today individuals identify with an activist N.I.M.B.Y. (not in my back yard) outlook. If you suspect foul play at your workplace, you can seek protections and become a whistle blower. If you suspect a product defect, you can alert the Consumer Protection Agency. If you wonder why your local, state, or federal representative never returns your phone calls, you can tip off your local media to do an investigative piece.

The genre of apologia should remain a keen interest of rhetorical critics no matter its ebb and flow. It is a genre that is unlikely to decay. In civilized society, people must fight with words, not clubs. The genre is keenly connected to the double-edged sword of democracy. Only in a democracy can people demand public accountability of prominent figures and only in a democracy must public figures engage in a sometimes painful, embarrassing form of discourse that reveals to the whole world their human foibles. The genre's symbolic power and historical persistence are tied to its rhetorical complexity. The litmus test for success is this: Who tells the better story, the accuser or the apologist? It is a high-stakes rhetorical battle that apologists cannot afford to lose. It is the ultimate symbolic test of grace under pressure for a public figure. The genre is a public purging of sins and a reaffirmation of the ethical norms of a society often presented in theatrical proportions to bring pleasure to spectators; it is the most intimate form of secular discourse. The purging of sins in public can be ennobling and cathartic. The visual media are especially equipped to provide the excess and exaggeration that this type of theater demands. The psychological appeal of the genre is best summed up by communication scholar Edward Corbett: "What perversity is there in the human psyche that makes us enjoy the spectacle of human beings desperately trying to answer the charges leveled against them? Maybe secretly, as we read or listen [or watch] [or log on], we say to ourselves, 'Ah, there but for the grace of God go I.' "[9]

MATERIAL FOR ANALYSIS

I. President Bill Clinton's Apologia on the Lewinsky Matter, August 17, 1998

On October 8, 1998, Congress voted to begin impeachment hearings of President William Jefferson Clinton. It was only the third time in 222 years that Congress had done so, with Andrew Johnson and Richard Nixon also sharing that unpleasant distinction. The hearings concerned one of the most sensational scandals in U.S. history—a sexual relationship between the president and a White House intern named Monica Lewinsky. The matter set precedents on legal grounds and the ethics of media coverage. Clinton became the first sitting president to face a lawsuit—the Paula Jones case, in which Lewinsky's name first surfaced (before the Supreme Court's ruling, presidents had been immune from lawsuits until they left office); Clinton agreed under pressure to testify before a grand jury; the courts ruled that Clinton's lawyers were not covered by attorney–client privilege and had to testify if subpoenaed and that the Secret Service agents also did not have special protective status and could be compelled to testify. Clinton's grand jury testimony was televised, special prosecutor Kenneth Starr's 400-plus-page sexually explicit report to Congress was released on the Internet, and special late-night shows sprang up like weeds, creating a phenomenon dubbed "Clinton fatigue."[10]

The case generated important debate on two key questions: Can presidents have private lives that are protected from media scrutiny? (Are some presidential crises personal and others public?) What is an impeachable offense? (Is a sexual affair a "high crime and misdemeanor"? Does lying about it to a grand jury under oath constitute such a crime?) Although Americans overwhelmingly condemned the president for his actions, the public gave Clinton high job performance ratings (62%–65%), and Starr high negative ratings for his overly zealous and wildly expensive fishing expeditions.

After refusing to speak openly about the charges for almost a year, Clinton finally went on national television after completing a four-hour deposition for the grand jury. His appearance, demeanor, and the setting were unremarkable—perhaps strategically so. The speech took place in the "map room"—a room with little color and no sign of presidential decorum. Clinton was composed but impersonal in presentation. He wore a bland gray suit. The speech was surprisingly short (four minutes), especially for Clinton who had a reputation for lengthy public address. Reaction to the speech was evenly split, with many registering disappointment that the president did not explain himself more clearly and did not express sufficient remorse. The house voted to impeach, but the Senate did not vote to convict him. Clinton's approval ratings held steady while Republicans in the House lost several seats in the 1998 elections, prompting a surprise move by the influential House Speaker, Newt Gingrich, to resign. Though exonerated legally, the scandal cost Clinton respect on the Hill, tarnished the presidency, and became a crusading issue for Republicans in the 2000 presidential elections.

1   Good evening.

2   This afternoon in this room from this chair I testified before the office of Independent Council and the Grand Jury. I answered their questions truthfully, including questions about my private life; questions no American citizen would ever want to answer. Still, I must take complete responsibility for all my actions both public and private. And that is why I am speaking to you tonight.

3   As you know, in a deposition in January, I was asked questions about my relationship with Monica Lewinsky. While my answers were legally accurate, I did not volunteer information. Indeed, I did have a relationship with Ms. Lewinsky that was not appropriate. In fact, it was wrong. It constituted a critical lapse of judgment and a personal failure on my part for which I am solely and completely responsible. But I told the Grand Jury today and I say to you now that at no time did I ask anyone to lie, to hide or destroy evidence, or to take any unlawful action. I know that my public comments and my silence on this matter gave a false impression. I misled people including even my wife. I deeply regret that.

4   I can only tell you that I was motivated by many factors. First, my desire to protect myself from the embarrassment of my own conduct. I was also very concerned about protecting my own family. The fact that these questions were being asked in a politically inspired lawsuit which has since been dismissed was a consideration too. In addition, I had real and serious concerns about an independent council investigation that began with private business dealings twenty years ago. Dealings I might add about which an independent federal agency found no evidence of any wrongdoing by me or my wife over two years ago. The independent council investigation moved on to my staff and friends, then into my private life, and now the investigation itself is under investigation.

5   This has gone on too long, cost too much, and hurt too many innocent people. Now this matter is between me, the two people I love most, my wife and our daughter, and our God. I must put it right. And I am prepared to do whatever it takes to do so. Nothing is more important to me personally. But it is private and I intend to reclaim my family life for my family. It's nobody's business but ours. Even presidents have private lives.

6   It is time to stop the pursuit of personal destruction and the prying into private lives and get on with our national life. Our country has been distracted by

this matter for too long. And I take my responsibility for my part in all of this. That is all I can do. Now it is time. In fact, it is past time to move on. We have important work to do. Real opportunities to seize. Real problems to solve. Real security matters to face.

7   And so tonight, I ask you to turn away from the spectacle of the past seven months. To repair the fabric of our national discourse. And to return our attention to all the challenges and to all the promise of the next American century.

8   Thank you for watching and good night.

Questions for Analysis

1. How is President Bill Clinton's apologia indebted to all three of the classical genres: forensic, deliberative, and epideictic? Specifically, how does his apologia alter perception: "I am an honorable person and wish to restore integrity to the office" (epideictic aim); explain: "These are the pertinent facts in the case" (forensic aim); and formulate belief: "These charges are politically motivated" (deliberative aim)? Where does the speech use the past, present, and future time frames? Deal with issues of fact, value, and policy? Treat the audience as jurors, observers, and voters? Is there a balance in the borrowing from these genres? Is one genre more prominent than the others? Does the intermingling of genres help or hinder the organization of the speech? Does it assist you in recognizing why apologetic messages are difficult to create and win approval?

2. How well does the speech conform to the seven elements of descriptive analysis for apologetic rhetoric (see Figure 14–3)? How does this "expectation guide" help you issue an evaluation based on the artistic standard? Is your aesthetic evaluation consistent or inconsistent with the effects evaluation offered in the set-up section to Clinton's speech?

3. How would you rate this speech on ethical grounds? Is it forthcoming enough? Should it be? Larger ethical issues loom in this case such as these: Was the Lewinsky matter really a "high crime" and thus an impeachable offense or an illicit affair and thus a moral wrong? Is the real wrong having an affair or lying about it under oath? Are some presidential crises personal and others public? Do presidents have private lives? Should the moral problems of the president be legislated in the halls of Congress? Should they be prosecuted by a grand jury? Forgiven by the church? Even discussed by the public? Were we better served by an independent prosecutor and the resulting Starr report or the impeachment proceedings? Begin a discussion of ethics by asking yourself: Are you embarrassed or encouraged by the fact that a textbook would reprint this rhetorical low point in the Clinton presidency? Is your answer related to your political party affiliation? Explain. Is it possible for you to have an ethical evaluation and an aesthetic evaluation of this speech that are opposed to one another?

4. What apologetic arguments do you see in the speech? Choose from denial, bolstering, transcendence, differentiation, confession, corrective action, and attack the accuser. Do they complement one another or do they clash? Explain. Which of these arguments is especially suited for the forensic genre? The epideictic genre? The deliberative genre?

5. It is difficult to analyze this speech without taking into account the dizzying array of media images that surrounded it, including the following: Clinton's finger wagging,

the Clinton–Lewinsky embrace in the crowd scene played in slow motion ad nauseam, Clinton's lower lip biting and folded prayer-like hands, Kenneth Starr's coy smile and "no comment," the boxes full of the Starr report being sent to the Judiciary committee; the sequestering of Monica and her mother by FBI agents; the photo spread of Monica in Marilyn Monroe–style poses in *Vanity Fair*; the carefully orchestrated presidential outings with Bill, Hillary, and Chelsea holding hands; the elaborate visual aids of the House Republicans; the flamboyant lawyer Ginsburg, the grim-faced Linda Tripp, and many others. Literally, a parade of memorable characters marched before us on our TV screens. How do these images shape our emotional response to the speech? Do you have a different reaction to the speech now several years later when you are distanced from this barrage of media images?

6. How does Clinton's apologia reveal the "double-edged sword of democracy" discussed in this chapter? How does it reinforce the promise and perils of the mass media? And how does it underscore the commercial/entertainment dimensions of news? (Recall Chapter 13.) What does this speech tell us about U.S. culture at the end of the twentieth century?

II. President Ronald Reagan's Challenger Tribute, January 29, 1986

On January 28, 1986, with swirling media attention and NASA optimism, the space shuttle Challenger was launched with seven crew members, including the first non-astronaut, a school teacher, Christa McAuliffe. With the world and many children watching, the Challenger exploded a little over one minute into the flight. What the Kennedy assassination was to the baby boomers, the Challenger tragedy became to generation X'ers. People remember where they were when they saw or heard the news of the crash. That millions of school children were watching the launch in their classrooms only added to the anguish of this national loss. Americans were simply unprepared for a space tragedy of this magnitude.

NASA had experienced problems in the past. In the first Apollo launch, three astronauts were killed in a fire on the launching pad, but the program was in its infancy. When Apollo 11 landed on the moon, we forgot about the risks, and faith in NASA grew. Three astronauts were almost lost on Apollo 13, but their mission ended successfully. From 1967 until the Challenger disaster, NASA had never lost an astronaut.

Reasons for the disaster began to circulate almost immediately, although the official report of the explosion would not be released for four months by a presidential commission investigating the incident. Finger-pointing at NASA was swift and harsh. Technical problems in the design of the O-ring seals, which caused the crash, had been known for almost a decade. A general lack of communication at NASA prevented the concerns from being taken seriously. Further, NASA was charged with being overly concerned with commercializing its program—whipping up public support and public funds—by initiating the teacher-in-space idea. The campaign to make the launch entertaining and educational deemphasized the calculated risks of manned space exploration. NASA's foray into public relations turned into a nightmare.

President Ronald Reagan, an enthusiastic supporter of space exploration, was faced with the task of confronting a national tragedy, dealing with the accusations of technical incompetence, bureaucratic oversight, and a kind of zealotry that led to the death of a civilian, all on very short notice. Reagan was scheduled to give the State of the

Union Address that same evening. He scrapped those plans and instead gave a tribute that merged subtle deliberative themes into the epideictic genre.

1 Ladies and gentlemen. I planned to speak to you tonight to report on the State of the Union. But the events of earlier today have led me to change those plans. Today is a day for mourning and remembering. Nancy and I are pained to the core by the tragedy of the shuttle Challenger. We know we share this pain with all of the people of our country. This is truly a national loss.

2 Nineteen years ago, almost to the day, we lost three astronauts in a terrible accident on the ground. But we've never lost an astronaut in flight; we've never had a tragedy like this. And perhaps we've forgotten the courage it took for the crew of the shuttle but they, the Challenger seven, were aware of the dangers and overcame them and did their jobs brilliantly.

3 We mourn seven heroes: Michael Smith, Dick Scobee, Judith Resnik, Ronald McNair, Ellison Onizuka, Gregory Jarvis, and Christa McAuliffe. We mourn their loss as a nation together.

4 The families of the seven—we cannot bear, as you do, the full impact of this tragedy but we feel the loss and we're thinking about you so very much. Your loved ones were daring and brave and they had that special grace, that special spirit that says, "Give me a challenge and I'll meet it with joy." They had a hunger to explore the universe and discover its truths. They wished to serve and they did—they served all of us.

5 We've grown used to wonders in this century; it's hard to dazzle us. For 25 years the United States space program has been doing just that. We've grown used to the idea of space, and perhaps we forget that we've only just begun. We're still pioneers. They, the members of the Challenger crew, were pioneers.

6 And I want to say something to the schoolchildren of America who were watching the live coverage of the shuttle's takeoff. I know it's hard to understand that sometimes painful things like this happen. It's all part of the process of exploration and discovery; it's all part of taking a chance and expanding man's horizons. The future doesn't belong to the fainthearted. It belongs to the brave. The Challenger crew was pulling us into the future and we'll continue to follow them.

7 I've always had great faith in and respect for our space program, and what happened today does nothing to diminish it. We don't hide our space program, we don't keep secrets and cover things up. We do it all up front and in public. That's the way freedom is and we wouldn't change it for a minute. We'll continue our quest in space. There will be more shuttle flights and more shuttle crews and, yes, more volunteers, more civilians, more teachers in space. Nothing ends here. Our hopes and our journeys continue.

8 I want to add that I wish I could talk to every man and woman who works for NASA, or who worked on this mission, and tell them: "Your dedication and professionalism have moved and impressed us for decades, and we know of your anguish. We share it."

9 There's a coincidence today. On this day 390 years ago, the great explorer Sir Francis Drake died aboard ship off the coast of Panama. In his lifetime the great frontiers were the oceans, and a historian later said, "He lived by the sea, died on it, and was buried in it." Well, today we can say of the Challenger crew, their dedica-tion was, like Drake's, complete. The crew of the space shuttle Challenger honored

us by the manner in which they lived their lives. We will never forget them nor the last time we saw them this morning as they prepared for their journey and waved goodbye and "slipped the surly bonds of earth to touch the face of God."

10 Thank you.

Questions for Analysis

1. How does this speech conform to the general requirements of epideictic speaking when the seven elements of descriptive analysis in this chapter are applied to it? Does this speech demonstrate the four recurring eulogistic themes? How well? What do you think are some of the distinctive qualities that Ronald Reagan brings to the conventional demands that a eulogy makes?

2. What language strategies do you see in this eulogy? (See Figure 7–1.) Which are primary? Do they work to complement key eulogistic themes? How? What questions of value emerge in the address about U.S. character and innovation? Are they time-bound or timeless? Explain.

3. Locate a videotape or clips of the address (your library, interlibrary loan, Internet sites). How do Ronald Reagan's pitch, rate, volume, vocal variety, enunciation, posture, eye contact, and facial expression enhance the eulogy? Can you see from this aspect of the address alone why Ronald Reagan was sometimes called "The Great Communicator"? Why might nonverbal and visual aspects of rhetoric be more important for the epideictic genre than other genres?

4. Given what you know about some of the controversial issues that emerged in the media almost immediately after the crash, how does Reagan incorporate deliberative themes in the tribute? What specific paragraphs do this? Are the various positions that Reagan takes enthymematic? Explain. How well do you think this speech adheres to the guidelines proposed in this chapter for how to merge deliberative elements in epideictic rhetoric tastefully?

5. The president of the United States has many roles to play. In the event of a national loss, the president must play the role of moral leader, a fitting epideictic persona. And yet the president is still the leader of the free world, and any major media address by him or her is scrutinized for political implications. Since NASA is closely tied to what Aristotle called "matters of the state," is President Reagan obligated to introduce political themes in this eulogy in ways that nonpresidents are not?

6. In science museums, I-MAX theaters, Web site albums, and the like, the Challenger crew has been memorialized. How do the principles of visual rhetoric discussed in Chapter 12 enhance the features of the epideictic genre? Locate one visual tribute from the crash and discuss the ways that the basic and/or technical features of visual rhetoric work in that piece to create the appropriate mood of epideictic discourse. What rhetorical problems can visual tributes create? What are the power and the limitation of the familiar picture showing cascading plumes of smoke (see Figure 12–1) in terms of fulfilling the purpose of epideictic rhetoric?

EXERCISES

1. Here is a passage from Earl Spencer's tribute to his sister Princess Diana at her funeral in Westminster Abbey in September 1997. Identify the key eulogistic themes. How does it capitalize on one of the many controversial points surrounding Diana's life and death—that she was stripped of her royal title after

divorcing Prince Charles—and show signs of being a rhetorical hybrid (merging deliberative elements)? Is this tasteful?

> Diana was the very essence of compassion, of duty, of style, of beauty. All over the world she was a symbol of selfless humanity, a standard-bearer for the rights of the truly downtrodden, a truly British girl who transcended nationality, someone with a natural nobility who was classless, who proved in the last year that she needed no royal title to continue to generate her particular brand of magic.

2. Here are two passages from presidential inaugural addresses. The first is from John Kennedy's inaugural; the second from Bill Clinton's first inaugural. Compare and contrast them in terms of the four themes of presidential inaugurals. Is one the "ghost" of the other? Explain.

> In your hands, my fellow citizens, more than in mine, will rest the final success or failure of our course. Since this country was founded, each generation of Americans has been summoned to give testimony to its national loyalty. The graves of young American who answered the call to service are found around the globe. Now the trumpet summons us again—not as a call to bear arms, though arms we need; not as a call to battle, though embattled we are; but a call to bear the burden of a long twilight struggle, year in, and year out, "rejoicing in hope, patient in tribulation"—a struggle against the common enemies of man: tyranny, poverty, disease, and war itself. Can we forge against these enemies a grand and global alliance, north and south, east and west, that can assure a more fruitful life for all mankind? Will you join in that historic effort? In the long history of the world, only a few generations have been granted the role of defending freedom in its hour of maximum danger. I do not shrink from this responsibility; I welcome it. I do not believe that any of us would exchange places with any other people or any other generation. The energy, the faith, the devotion which we bring to this endeavor will light our country and all who serve it—and the glow from that fire can truly light the world. And so, my fellow Americans, ask not what your country can do for you; ask what you can do for your country. (JFK's inaugural address)

> My fellow Americans, you, too, must play your part in our renewal. I challenge a new generation of young Americans to a season of service—to act on your idealism by helping troubled children, keeping company with those in need, reconnecting our torn communities. There is so much to be done— enough, indeed, for millions of others who are still young in spirit to give of themselves in service, too. In serving, we recognize a simple but powerful truth: We need each other. And we must care for one another. Today, we do more than celebrate America; we rededicate ourselves to the very idea of America. An idea born in revolution and renewed through two centuries of challenge. An idea tempered by the knowledge that, but for fate, we—the fortunate and the unfortunate—might have been each other. An idea ennobled by the faith that our nation can summon from its myriad diversities the deepest measure of unity. An idea infused with the conviction that America's long heroic journey must go forever upward. And so my fellow Americans, as we stand at the edge of the 21st century, let us begin with energy and hope, with faith and discipline, and let us work until our work is done. The Scripture says, "And let us not be weary in well-doing, for in due season we shall reap, if we faint not." From this joyful mountain top of celebration, we hear a call to service in the valley. We have heard the trumpets. We have changed the guard. And now—each in our own way, and with God's help—we must answer the call. (Clinton's first inaugural address)

3. Attend a commencement. Rate the commencement address in terms of the basic epideictic elements. Interview three to five people afterward. Did they like it or not? Why? Do their responses echo some of the audience expectations of the genre that you have learned?

4. As a class watch the ceremonies for the Academy Awards, the Grammys, the Tonys, or the Emmys. Rate the acceptance speeches in terms of conformity to epideictic themes. Did you see any rhetorical hybrids (deliberative themes merged in epideictic address)? Did the merger work? As a class, vote on a winner.

5. Video tributes sometimes accompany or even take the place of speech tributes. What are their special rhetorical strengths and weaknesses at fulfilling the requirements of epideictic form (recall Chapter 12)?

6. The following are excerpts from corporate apologia. Identify the apologetic argument type (bolstering, denial, differentiation, transcendence, attack the accuser, corrective action, confession) that you see in each:

   a. "The completely ridiculous and false story that the President of the *Procter & Gamble* company appeared on a talk show to discuss the company's connection to Satanism has been resurfacing in your area. It is a variation of the lie that was spread in 1990. None of this is true." (*Procter & Gamble*, press kit)

b. "We're part of your community and thousands of others all over the country. We have a shared interest in safety. For us, just like you, it's always safety first." (*Domino's Pizza*, flyer)

c. "There is a difference between United Way of America and United Way of the Plains." (Open letter, local *United Way*)

d. "Finally, and most importantly, I want to tell you how sorry I am that this accident took place. We at Exxon are especially sympathetic to the residents of Valdez and the people of the state of Alaska." (Open letter, *New York Times*, *Exxon*)

e. "If you see any careless driving by Domino's Pizza drivers, contact the store or call this toll-free number: 1-800-DOMINOS." (*Domino's Pizza*, flyer)

7. The following accusatory scenarios invite you to respond by crafting "mock" apologies. Form groups of four. Together construct a fitting response to the charge leveled against you. A primary argument strategy is suggested for each scenario. Choose a group spokesperson to give a one-minute speech of self-defense to the class. Vote for a winner. How did nonverbal features (posture, eye contact, facial expression, gestures, body movement, and so on) factor into your assessment of whether to exonerate or censure?

a. Situation 1: You have been accused of cheating on an exam in this class. Two witnesses have testified to the accuracy of the charge, claiming specifically that you brought crib notes and had a detailed test code written on the bottom of your shoe. (Tip: Frame your response around transcendence)

b. Situation 2: You have been charged with reckless driving by some of your peers who believe that you may also have been driving while under the influence of alcohol—though the charges have not been empirically verified by anyone. (Tip: Frame your response around differentiation)

c. Situation 3: Rumor has it that you have failed to observe the visitation hours in the women's/men's dorms on several occasions this semester. (Tip: Frame your response around denial)

d. Situation 4: You were seen by two campus security persons shouting obscenities out of your dorm window at 2:00 A.M. last Friday. (Tip: Frame your response around bolstering)

8. Check with your university. Do you have a "crisis plan"? If so, ask to see it. What are its public relations components? Do they support the genre of apologia as applied to the elements of descriptive analysis?

9. Bring an apologia to class (sports, religious, political, corporate). It may be in the form of an advertisement, a speech, a video news release, newsletter or Web site segment, flyer, or the like. You have two to three minutes to give an oral critique to show its indebtedness to the classical genres. How is it like forensic discourse? Deliberative discourse? Epideictic discourse? Which genre is it most like? Does it resemble expectations for a typical apologetic message as judged by the seven elements of descriptive analysis? What special problems are posed in critiquing written apologetic discourse, especially in terms of evaluating persona?

10. Read Ross K. Baker's article "Lincoln on a Computer" (*American Demographics* 9 [June 1987]: 72[1]) from the InfoTrac College Edition database. Compare Baker's text to Lincoln's original text (see Chapter 2). What aspects of the speech seem permanent and what aspects seem doomed to change? What does this tell you about the balance between timeliness and timelessness in rhetorical appeals? How would you define Lincoln's speech? Is it a deliberative, epideictic, forensic, or hybrid piece of discourse? Why?

Using the InfoTrac College Edition database, locate the article "They Laughed When I Stood Up to Give the State of the Union Address" (*Time*, February 7, 1994, p. 16[1]). The article provides quotations from the State of the Union speeches of former presidents. Despite the historical and political differences between their presidencies, the quotations seem startlingly similar. What does this tell you about the generic constraints imposed by the rhetorical occasion? How should we approach this kind of speech? What kinds of questions could aid us in uncovering the political significance of a State of the Union address? What kinds of questions could aid us in unpacking the strategic ambiguity of epideictic discourse?

NOTES

1. Aristotle, *On Rhetoric*, trans. Lane Cooper (Englewood Cliffs, NJ: Prentice-Hall, 1932), p. 16.

2. Aristotle, *On Rhetoric*.

3. Roger Rosenblatt, *Rules for Aging* (San Diego: Harcourt, 2000).

4. For extended discussion of inaugurals, see K. K.

Campbell and K. H. Jamieson, *Deeds Done in Words: The Genres of Presidential Governance* (University of Chicago Press, 1990), pp. 14–51.

5. This story pokes fun at the classic mold of the prince coming to save the princess from a horrible dragon. The princess in Munsch's book must save the prince by outsmarting a dragon. She succeeds, but once rescued the prince demands that she leave him to fetch more appropriate princess attire (the dragon had destroyed her home and clothes and she is only wearing a paper bag). The princess tells him that he is arrogant and runs off by herself to live happily ever after.

6. This thesis is developed in Karlyn Kohrs Campbell, "Inventing Women: From Amaterasu to Virgina Woolf," *Women's Studies in Communication* 21, no. 2 (1998): 111–116.

7. See Stephen E. Lucas, *The Art of Public Speaking,* 4th ed. (New York: McGraw-Hill, 1992), p. 82.

8. See especially Wil A. Linkugel and B. L. Ware, "They Spoke in Defense of Themselves: On the Generic Criticism of Apologia," *The Quarterly Journal of Speech* 59 (1973): 273–283; W. L. Benoit, *Accounts, Excuses, and Apologies: A Theory of Image Restoration Strategies* (Albany: University of New York, 1995).

9. E. Corbett, Foreword, in Halford Ross Ryan (ed.), *Oratorical Encounters: Selected Studies and Discourses of Twentieth-Century Political Accusations and Apologies* (New York: Greenwood, 1988), p. xi.

10. See Steffen W. Schmidt, "The Clinton-Lewinsky Scandal and American Politics," http://www.wadsworth.com/politics.

appendix

Presentation Guidelines
Presentation Templates

- *Speech to Create Virtual Experience*
  Storytelling Rhetorical Act
- *Speech to Alter Perception*
  Definitional Rhetorical Act
- *Speech to Explain*
  Instructional Rhetorical Act
- *Speech to Formulate Belief*
  Public Service Rhetorical Act
- *Speech to Initiate Action*
  Policy Rhetorical Act
- *Speech to Maintain Action*
  Ceremonial Rhetorical Act

Web Site Critique Template

Materials in the appendix may be duplicated..

PRESENTATION GUIDELINES

The primary purpose of the storytelling presentation is to create virtual experience. You learn how to tell a rhetorical narrative that is coherent, authentic, and highly descriptive. Your narrative must contain the elements of a good story. Your aim is to show your audience that you are a gifted narrator by telling them a captivating story that makes a timely point in a novel, memorable way. You will need to understand the instrumental and consummatory purposes of a rhetorical act.

The primary purpose of the definitional presentation is to alter perception. You learn how to define a concept unfamiliar and/or often misinterpreted in familiar, clear terms. Your aim is to shape audience knowledge by defining a term clearly, accurately, and imaginatively. You will need to understand the fundamentals of rhetorical action, especially "Your Rhetorical Act" tips and the ten definitional strategies outlined in "The Resources of Evidence" in order to give depth and precision to your chosen term for this rhetorical act. (See Figure 4–3.)

The primary purpose of the instructional presentation is to explain. You learn how to define, explain, and analyze the who, what, where, when, why, and how of a subject in an unbiased way. Your aim is to give the audience new, comprehensive information in order to expand their awareness and understanding of your subject. You will need to understand how evidence, argument, and organization work to help you meet the objectives of this rhetorical act.

The primary purpose of the public service presentation is to formulate belief. You learn how to move your audience to accept a point of view and support the idea of a program or initiative. Your aim is to shape audience belief around a "question of value" by developing a convincing promotion similar to a public service announcement. You will need to understand all the resources for rhetorical action, and problems of rhetorical action, especially audience-related obstacles, in order to be successful with this rhetorical act.

The primary purpose of the policy presentation is to initiate action. You learn how to create dissonance by presenting a pressing social problem and then provide consonance by proposing a workable solution. Your aim is to construct a case around a controversial "question of policy." You will need to understand cognitive dissonance, problem-solution structure, the motivated sequence, and all the problems of rhetorical action, audience, subject, and rhetor obstacles in order to achieve results with this rhetorical act.

The primary purpose of the ceremonial presentation is to maintain action. You learn how to offer an inspirational tribute to an idea, person, institution, or an event. Your aim is to "rally" your audience to reflect, admire, and honor their commitment to your subject. You will need to understand the special constraints of rhetorical action, especially "Understanding Occasion" and the demands of epideictic address in order to fulfill the expectations of this rhetorical act.

For each of these presentations, *your instructor will make specific assignments* regarding topic clearance, time, types of sources and research expectations, outlines, strategy reports, note cards, visual aids, types and amount of resources for rhetorical action, attention to problems of rhetorical action, and other special grading criteria.

Speech to Create Virtual Experience
Storytelling Rhetorical Act
Evaluation Form

Speaker _____

Time +/–
Notecards +/–
Subject +/–

Introduction

Sets the Scene

Establishes a Mood

Introduces Characters

Explains Inception of Plot

Coherence of Story

Authenticity of Story

Audience Adaptation

Middle

Rising Action Develops

Thesis Begins to Unfold

Characters Experience Conflict

Plot Climaxes

Descriptive Language

Meaningful Thesis

End

Resolution of Conflict

Reinforcement of Thesis

Verbal Delivery

Rate

Volume

Pitch

Vocal Variety

Pause

Enunciation

Nonverbal Delivery

Eye Contact

Facial Expression

Poise

Gesture

Movement

Other Assignment Specifics

Final Comments on Back

Speech to Alter Perception
Definitional Rhetorical Act
Evaluation Form

Speaker _____

Time +/–
Notecards +/–
Subject +/–

Definitional Strategy #1

Clarity

Appropriateness

Development

Other Definitional Strategies

Definitional Strategy #2

Clarity

Appropriateness

Development

Eye Contact

Definitional Strategy #3

Clarity

Appropriateness

Development

Familiarity

Other Assignment Specifics

Final Comments on Back

Speech to Explain
Instructional Rhetorical Act
Evaluation Form

Speaker _____

Time +/–
Notecards +/–
Subject +/–

Introduction

Attention

Clear Thesis and Relevance

Preview

Balance

Organization

Pattern

Clarity

Appropriateness

Balance

Transitions

Smooth

Diversified

Evidence

Amount

Variety

Correctly Cited

Balance

Appropriateness

Conclusion

Foreshadowed Clearly

Appropriate Closing Technique

Balance

Nonverbal Delivery

Verbal Delivery

Visual Aid

Choice of Visual

Interaction with Visual

Knowledge of Topic

Adaptation to Audience

Ethical Responsibility

Other Assignment Specifics

Final Comments on Back

Speech to Formulate Belief
Public Service Rhetorical Act
Evaluation Form

Speaker _____

Time +/–
Notecards +/–
Subject +/–

Introduction

Attention
Clear Thesis and Relevance
Preview
Balance

Organization

Pattern
Clarity
Appropriateness
Balance

Transitions

Smooth
Diversified

Evidence

Amount
Variety
Correctly Cited
Appropriateness
Balance

Topic Knowledge (competence)

Audience Adaptation (identification)

Other Assignment Specifics

Visual Aid/Poise

Posture
Confidence
Choice of Visual
Interaction with Visual

Language

Accuracy
Appropriateness
Vividness

1st Value Appeal

2nd Value Appeal

3rd Value Appeal

Eye Contact

Delivery Enhancement

Volume
Rate
Vocal Variety
Pronunciation
Articulation
Dynamism
Dramatic Pause
Pitch

Conclusion

Foreshadowed Clearly
Appropriate Closing Technique
Balance

Ethical Responsibility

Final Comments on Back

Speech to Initiate Action
Policy Rhetorical Act
Evaluation Form

Speaker _____

Time +/–
Notecards +/–
Subject +/–

Attention Step

    Gets Attention

    Creates High Dissonance

Need Step

    Statement of Purpose

    Preview of Problem Area

    Selection, Organization of Arguments

Satisfaction Step

Visualization Step

Action Step

Ethos

    Competence
    Trustworthiness
    Identification

Evidence/Argument

    Amount
    Variety/Placement
    Citation

Language

    Accuracy
    Appropriateness
    Vividness

Verbal Delivery Factors (Dynamism)

    Rate
    Volume
    Enunciation
    Vocal Variety
    Dramatic Pause
    Pitch

Nonverbal Delivery Factors (Dynamism)

    Eye Contact
    Facial Expression
    Poise
    Movement
    Gestures

Other Assignment Specifics

Final Comments on Back

Speech to Maintain Action
Ceremonial Rhetorical Act
Evaluation Form

Speaker _____

Time +/–
Notecards +/–
Subject +/–

Introduction

    Attention

    Clear Thesis and Relevance

    Preview

    Balance

Organization

    Pattern

    Clarity

    Appropriateness

    Balance

Transitions

    Smooth

    Varied

Ethos

    Knowledge

    Trustworthiness

    Dynamism

    Identification

Other Assignment Specifics

Language

    Accuracy

    Appropriateness

    Vividness

    Specific Language Strategies

Appeals

    Unity

    Traditional Values

    Continuity

Mood

    Inspiration

    Celebration

    Honor

        reverence

        humor

Visual Aid

    Choice of Visual

    Interaction with Visual

Verbal Delivery

Nonverbal Delivery

Conclusion

    Foreshadowed Clearly

    Appropriate Closing Technique

    Balance

Final Comments on Back

Web Site Critique Template
Topic Approval

Critic _____

Proposed Web Site Subject Matter _____

Search Engine Used _____

URL Address _____

List Placement/Prominence _____

I chose this site because _____

I think the site has rhetorical significance because _____

──────────────── To Be Completed by Instructor ────────────────

Rhetorical Significance

    Does site promote/advocate a cause, idea, issue? +/–

    Is it sufficiently complex? (multiple pages, visuals, links) +/–

    Does it avoid using explicitly offensive materials? +/–

Instructor's Approval   Yes/No

Additional Comments:

Format Suggestions:

1. single space
2. 10–11 pt. type
3. complete sentences
4. "C+P+A" seamless movement

Web Site Critique Template

Critic _____

Identifying Information. What is the subject matter? What search engine did you use? Why? What is the URL address of your Web site? Where does it appear on the list of Web sites related to this subject?

Purpose. What is the primary rhetorical purpose of the Web site (creating virtual experience, altering perception, explaining, formulating belief, initiating action, maintaining action)? What is the controlling idea, thesis, or response desired? Where are these purposes most clearly realized? Why is this purpose significant? (How does it explain other rhetorical choices represented by another element of descriptive analysis?)

Audience: Who is the target audience for this Web site? Where can this be verified? Why is this audience targeted?

Persona: What role does the creator of this Web site play? Is it easily discernible or not? Do you know who created the Web site? Is it singularly or corporately authored? What specific credentials, if any, are provided to enhance the ethos of the site's creator? Is the Web site well maintained (nothing is "under construction") and is it sufficiently sophisticated (visuals, links, etc.) to enhance the prestige of the rhetor's persona? Where are these features most clearly identifiable? Why is this persona adopted?

Tone: What is the prevailing attitude projected by the site? How do visuals, word choice, punctuation, layout and design (basic and technical features of visual rhetoric) contribute to the "feel" of the site? Where is that most prevalent? Why is this attitudinal quality important?

Evidence: What evidence (VASES) does the site use to substantiate its claims? Does the site use lots of evidence? little evidence? sufficient evidence for its subject matter and its target audience? How are the strengths and weaknesses of the types of evidence demonstrated? In regard to visuals, how are the three principles of visual rhetoric supported or challenged? Where are good excerpts to document these types of evidence? Can you account for the type and amount of evidence used in the site?

Structure: What is the prevailing organizational structure (sequence, topical, logical)? How does the organizational structure support or challenge the prevailing value identified for it? Does the site have links? Are they easy to navigate or do they take you places without any way of getting back? Does the site have organizational coherence? Why do you suppose the site is designed in this manner?

Strategies: Choose ONE dimension of strategy (language, argument, or appeals) to critique. If language, what language strategies are evident? Where? Why? If argument, what argument types (general and specific) are evident? Where? Why? If appeals, what values underscore the rhetoric? Where? Why?

Evaluation: How do you rate this Web site on aesthetic grounds? Why? How do you assess this Web site on truth grounds? Can you? How do you judge this Web site on ethical grounds? Why? How do you evaluate this Web site based on effects? Do you know how many persons visited the site? Do you know what publicity it has received from being listed as links on other sites? Is this a site you will visit again?

Index

Dickens, C., 8
  Oliver Twist, 8, 19
Dickinson, A. E., 224
DiGiovanni, J., 15, 66, 99, 177
  Madness Visible: Kosovo Diary (excerpt),
    15–18, 20, 99
DiMaggio, J., 75, 81
Discursive rhetoric, 69, 106, 121
Dole, E., 284
Dole, R., 175, 284
Douglass, F., 174–175, 178, 181, 183, 215,
    292
  "What to the Slave Is the Fourth of July?"
    (excerpt), 178–181
  "Fourth of July Address," 292
Drescher, S., 205
  "Public Opinion and British Colonial
    Slavery," 205
Dukakis, M., 100–102
Dynamism, 231, 274, 284

Eco, U., 264, 270
Eftekhari, S., 63
  *The Unfair Treatment of Arabs in U.S.
    Media*, 63–66
Eisenhower, D. D., 106, 256
Elaboration Likelihood Model (ELM), 97–99,
    100, 193–194, 234, 248
Enactment, 107, 170, 291
Enthymeme, 99, 100–102, 104, 119, 162
  as form of argument, 234–235
  as self-persuasion, 235
Enumeration, 107–109, 119
Epideictic (or ceremonial) rhetoric, 288–293,
    301
  defined, 288
  eulogy, 289–290
  presidential inaugural, 290–291
  evaluation of, 291
Epstein, G., 280
  "Terror on School Bus Ends with
    Hijacker's Death," 280
Ethos, 66, 69, 86, 225–236, 246 (*See also*
    Source, credibility of)
  defined, 69
  from the rhetorical act, 231–236, 246,
    274, 284
  from the rhetor, 225, 236
  prior ethos, 226–231, 245, 246, 275–279
Eulogy, 289–290
  rhetorical purpose of, 289–290
  rhetorical problem of, 290
Euthanasia, 257, 258
Evaluation of style, 163–164, 318
Evidence, 23, 31–32, 68–85, 102, 106, 146–
    147, 165, 316 (*See also* Supporting
    materials; VASES)
  authority (expertise), 42, 69, 81–84, 118
  factual, 103, 106
  psychological, 103, 106
  types of, 69
Example, 69–72
Expertise, 42–43, 81–84, 92, 107, 161

Fable, 67, 129
Fallacies, 119, 120, 121
False analogy, 120
False dilemma, 120
Faulty cause and effect, 120
Feedback, 14–15, 21
Feminism, 85, 98, 112, 128, 132, 204
Ferraro, G., 170
Festinger, L., 139, 154, 204
Figurative analogy, 79–81, 160
Figurative language, 105–106, 162 (*See also*
    Metaphor)
Fisher, R., 222, 223
Fiske, J, 273
Fonda, J., 234
Forensic rhetoric, 288
Fotheringham, W., 246
Four Weddings and a Funeral, 291
Freedman, J. L., 204
Freeman, J., 108, 154

Gallup, G., 74, 274
Gantt, H., 234–235
Ginsburg, R. B., 170
Glittering generality, 120
Goffman, E., 183
Goldwater, B., 99, 171
Gonzales, E., 120
Goodman, E., 177, 271
Gorbachev, M., 228
Gordon, D., 65, 66
Gore, A., 93, 103
Gore, T., 285
Gould, S. J., 2, 19, 75, 87
Grady, H., 230, 236, 241, 244, 245, 247
  "The New South," 230, 237–240
    (excerpt), 247
Grimké, A., 107, 170, 181, 198, 199, 202
  address at Pennsylvania Hall (excerpt),
    199–202
  "Appeal to the Christian Women of the
    South," 198
Guerrilla Girls, 293
Guilt or glory by association, 120
Gun control, 18, 192

Hammerback, J. C., 182
Hartley, J., 273
Hasdorf, A., 204
  "They Saw a Game: A Case Study," 204
Hasty generalization, 120
Hayne, R. Y., 168–170
Haywood, C. R., 9, 12, 19
Health care reform, 171, 189
Hellman, L., 105–106, 121
  "Commencement Address at Bernard
    College" (excerpt), 106, 121
Helms, J., 234–235
Hersh, S., 272
Heston, C., 266
Hill, A., 128, 187–188
  at Hill-Thomas hearings, 128, 187–188
Hill, B. H., 237, 247

Horton, W., 101–102
Hovland, C. I., 204
Hrbek, K., 192, 204
Huxman, S. S., 86, 120, 222
Hyde, M. J., 259

Ibsen, H., 105–106
  A Doll's House, 105
Identification, 141, 159, 172, 175–177,
    232–234
  as ethos formation, 232–233
  in mass communication, 274, 284
  as rhetorical obstacle, 232–233
Inductive structure, 99, 119, 146
Inertia, 188, 197–198
Inferential leap, 90–91
Inherency, 93, 144
Interact or transact, 100
Introduction, 49, 63, 66, 165
  adaptation to the audience, 140–142, 245
  as element of prior ethos, 226, 229–230
Invention, 96–100, 164
Issues, 92–96
  dramatization of, 167, 278
  of fact, 92, 97, 293, 298
  of policy, 93–96, 139, 293, 298
  of value, 92–93, 97, 293, 298

Jackson, J. L., 171, 181
Jamieson, K. H., 121, 247, 275, 285, 304
Jefferson, T., 23, 231
Jesus, 226–228
Joan of Arc, 145
Johnson, L. B., 253
Jordan, B., 170
Jordan, K., 262, 270
Justification, 89, 91–92, 118, 127 (*See also*
    Reason)

Katz, W. L., 11, 20
Kennedy, E. M., 295
  "Chappaquiddick Address," 295
Kennedy, J. F., 23, 42, 131, 170, 171, 177,
    181, 234, 253, 256, 272, 277, 291, 302
  Inaugural Address (excerpt), 302
Kennedy, J. F., Jr., 256, 263
Kennedy, R. F., 290
Kilbourne, J., 183
King, M. L., Jr., 7, 23, 27, 29–33, 99, 105,
    147, 171, 173, 177, 202, 250, 256, 262
  "Black Power," 154
  "I Have a Dream," 105, 173
  "I've Been to the Mountain Top" (excerpt
    of conclusion), 28–29, 250
Kropotkin, P. A., 218, 223

Labeling, 108–109, 119, 156–159, 172, 177
  (*See also* Naming)
Language, 32, 102, 105–106, 155–177 (*See
    also* Metaphor)
  connotation, 156–158, 164
  denotation, 156, 157
  dimensions of, 155–160